PERFECT WORLD

7 Rie Aruga

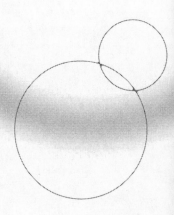

Research Help /
Kazuo Abe (Abe Kensetsu Inc.)

contents

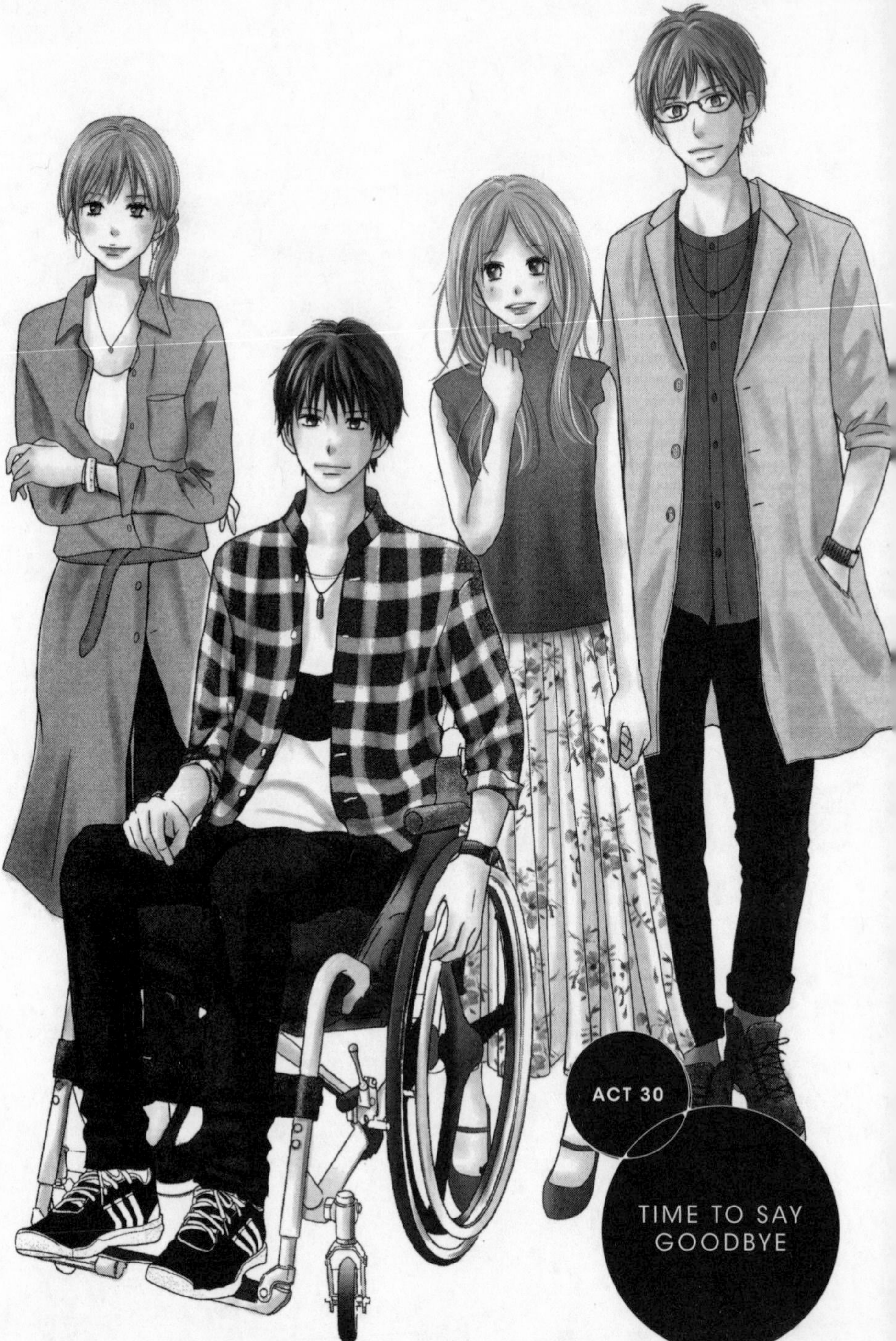
ACT 30
TIME TO SAY GOODBYE

PERFECT WORLD

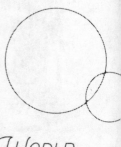

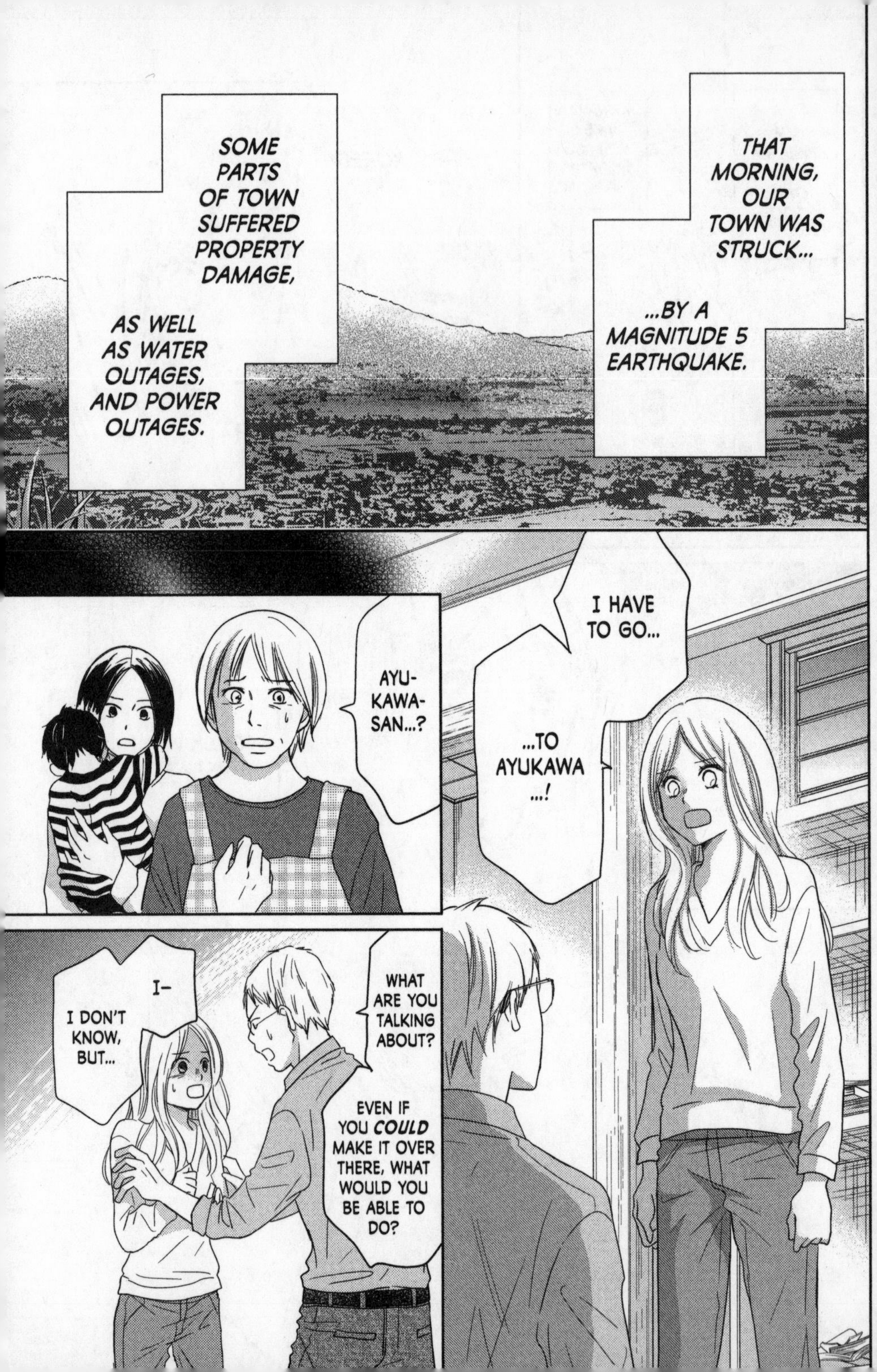
THAT MORNING, OUR TOWN WAS STRUCK...
...BY A MAGNITUDE 5 EARTHQUAKE.
SOME PARTS OF TOWN SUFFERED PROPERTY DAMAGE,
AS WELL AS WATER OUTAGES, AND POWER OUTAGES.
I HAVE TO GO...
...TO AYUKAWA ...!
AYU-KAWA-SAN...?
WHAT ARE YOU TALKING ABOUT?
EVEN IF YOU *COULD* MAKE IT OVER THERE, WHAT WOULD YOU BE ABLE TO DO?
I–
I DON'T KNOW, BUT...

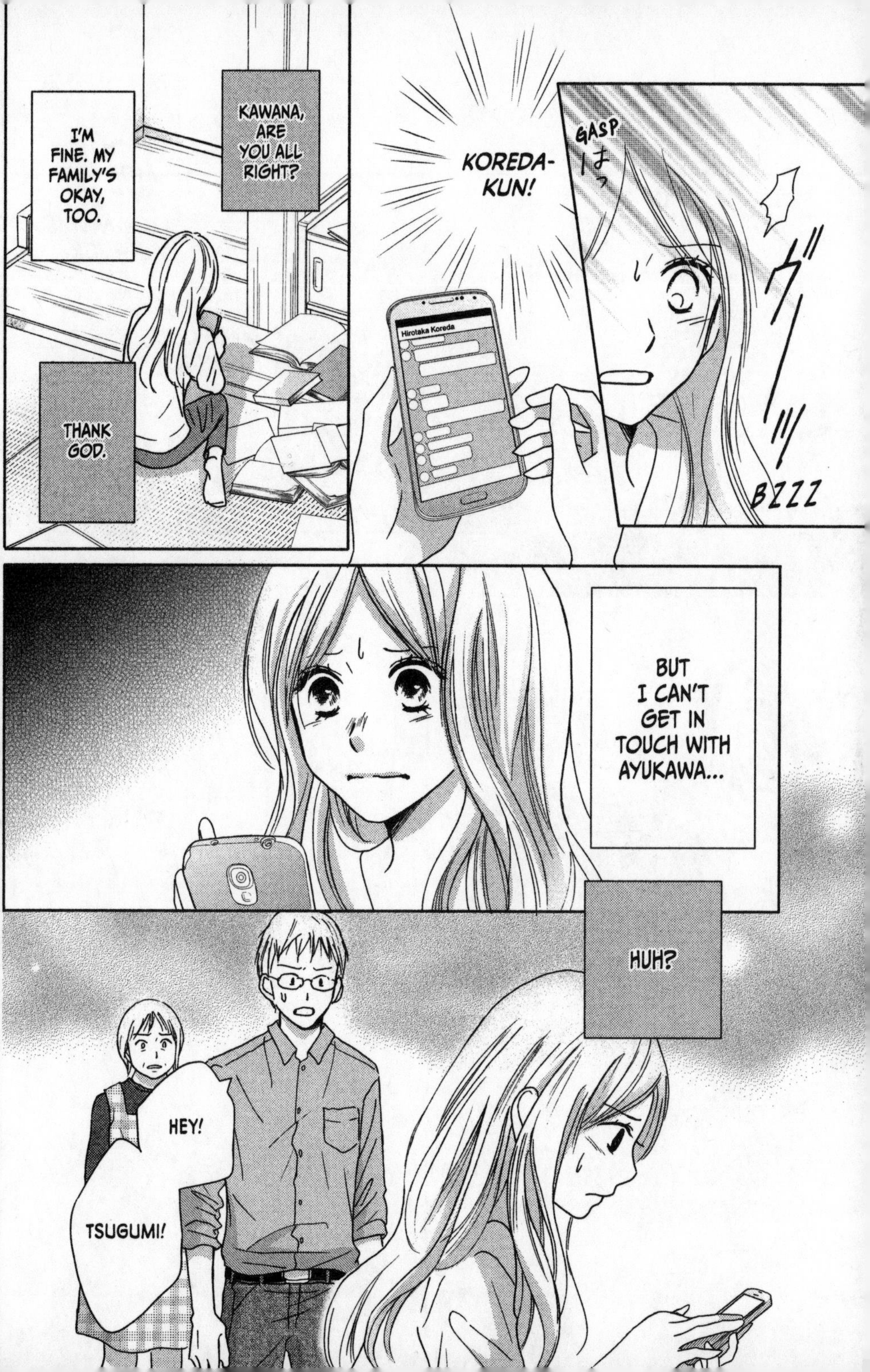
GASP
はっ
BZZZ
KOREDA-KUN!
Hirotaka Koreda
KAWANA, ARE YOU ALL RIGHT?
I'M FINE. MY FAMILY'S OKAY, TOO.
THANK GOD.
BUT I CAN'T GET IN TOUCH WITH AYUKAWA...
HUH?
HEY!
TSUGUMI!

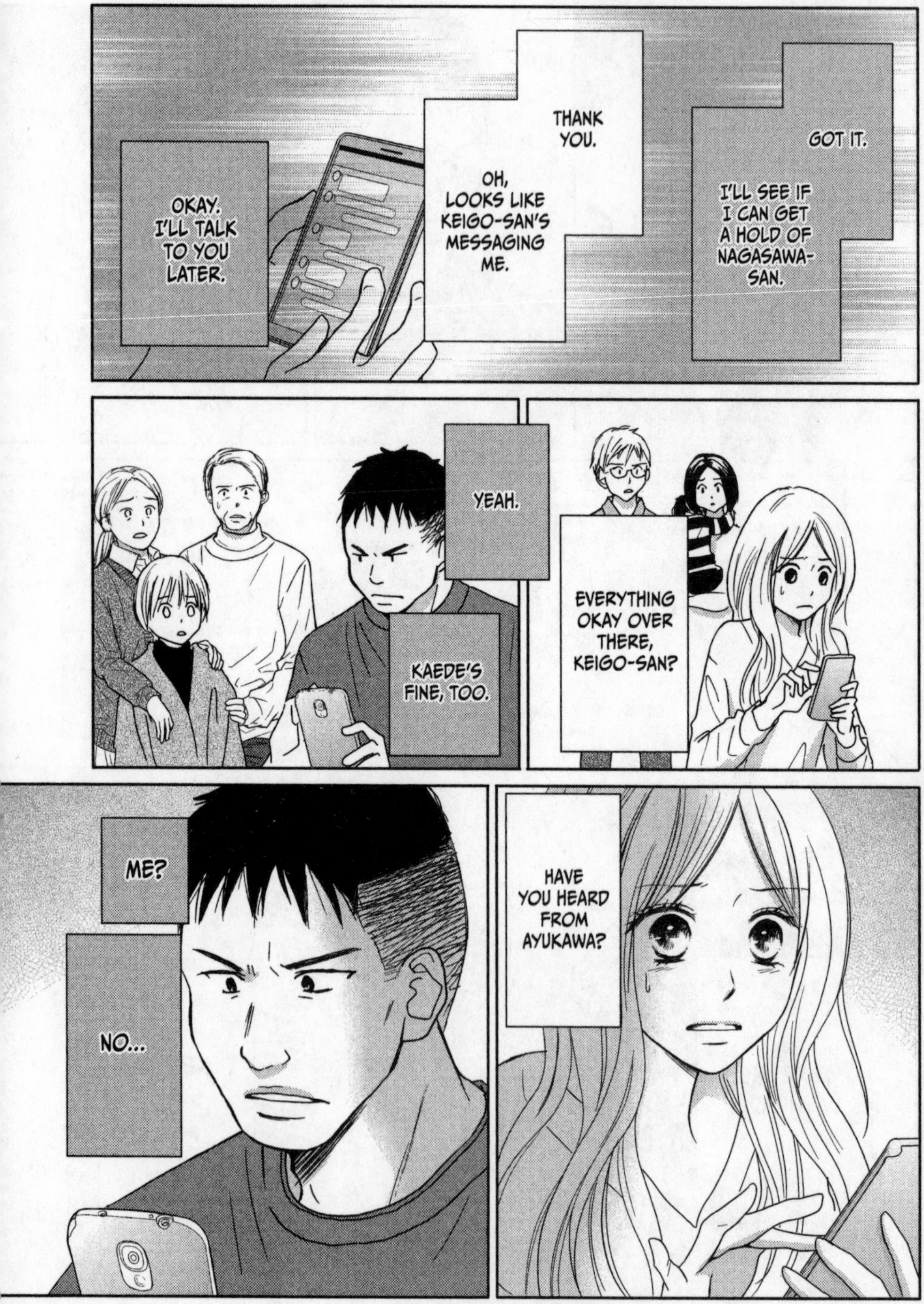
GOT IT.
I'LL SEE IF I CAN GET A HOLD OF NAGASAWA-SAN.
THANK YOU.
OH, LOOKS LIKE KEIGO-SAN'S MESSAGING ME.
OKAY. I'LL TALK TO YOU LATER.
EVERYTHING OKAY OVER THERE, KEIGO-SAN?
YEAH.
KAEDE'S FINE, TOO.
HAVE YOU HEARD FROM AYUKAWA?
ME?
NO...

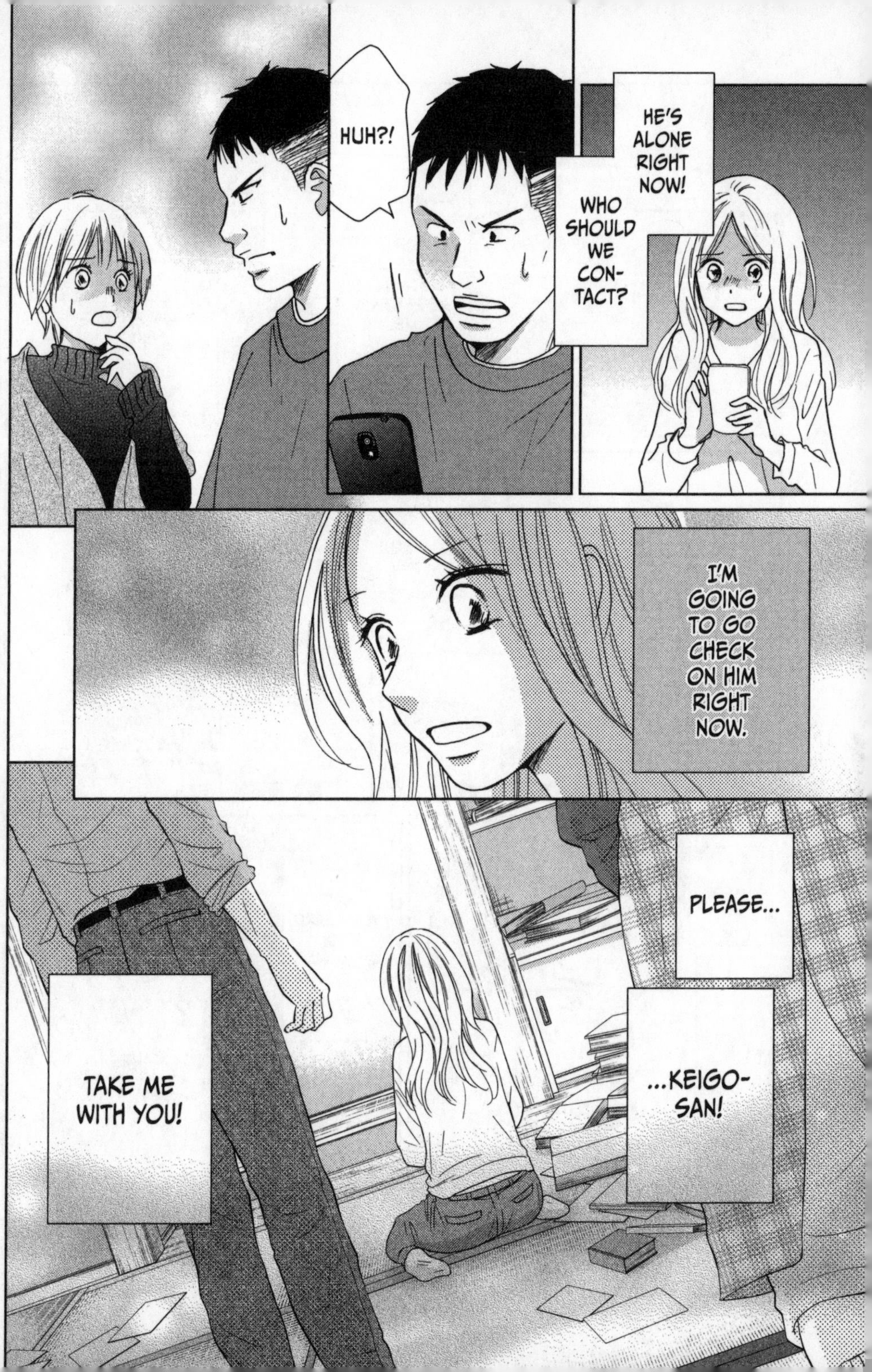
HE'S ALONE RIGHT NOW!
WHO SHOULD WE CON-TACT?
HUH?!
I'M GOING TO GO CHECK ON HIM RIGHT NOW.
PLEASE...
...KEIGO-SAN!
TAKE ME WITH YOU!

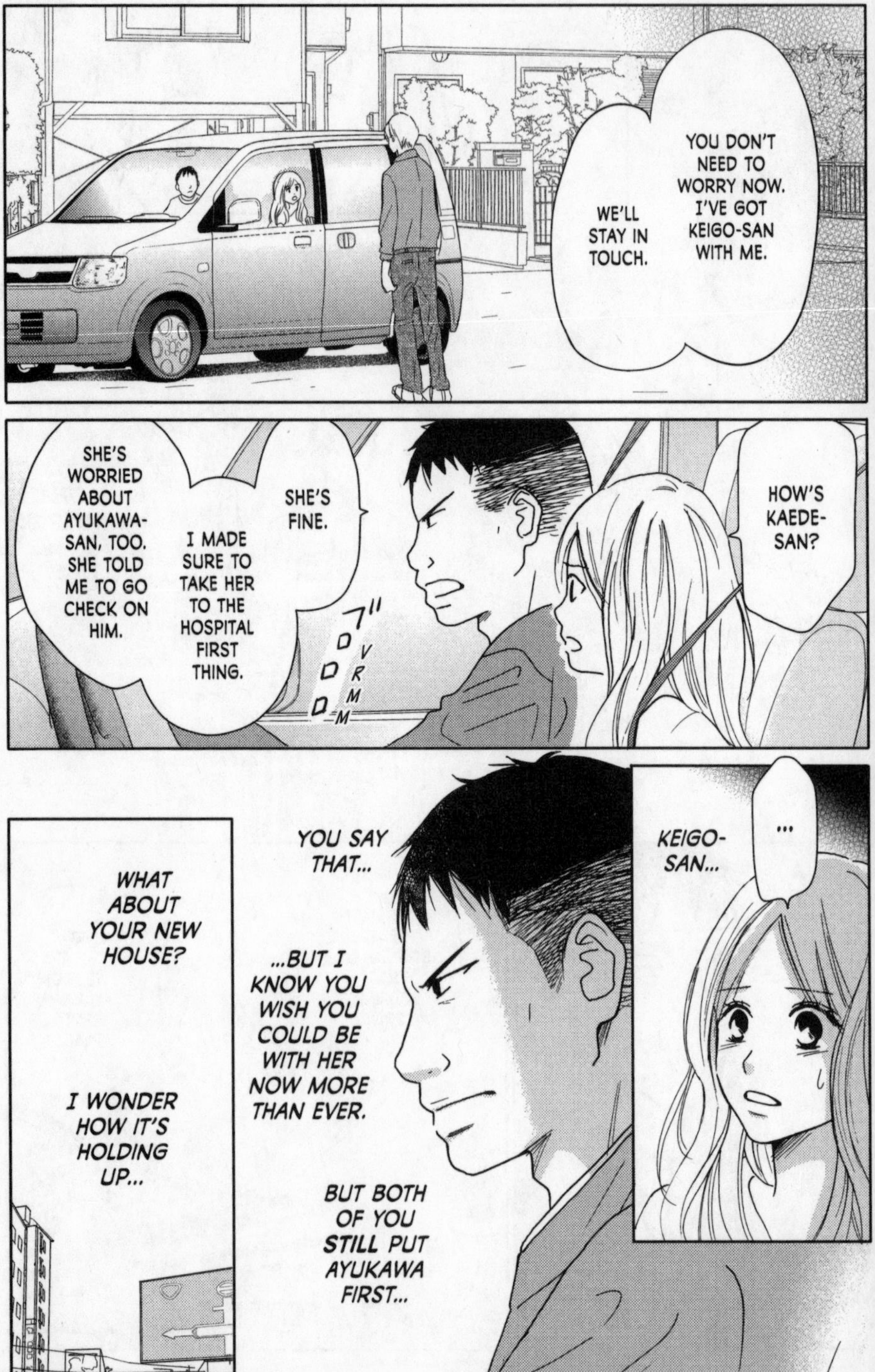
YOU DON'T NEED TO WORRY NOW. I'VE GOT KEIGO-SAN WITH ME.
WE'LL STAY IN TOUCH.
HOW'S KAEDE-SAN?
SHE'S FINE.
I MADE SURE TO TAKE HER TO THE HOSPITAL FIRST THING.
SHE'S WORRIED ABOUT AYUKAWA-SAN, TOO. SHE TOLD ME TO GO CHECK ON HIM.
VRMM
DDD
...
KEIGO-SAN...
YOU SAY THAT...
...BUT I KNOW YOU WISH YOU COULD BE WITH HER NOW MORE THAN EVER.
BUT BOTH OF YOU **STILL** PUT AYUKAWA FIRST...
WHAT ABOUT YOUR NEW HOUSE?
I WONDER HOW IT'S HOLDING UP...

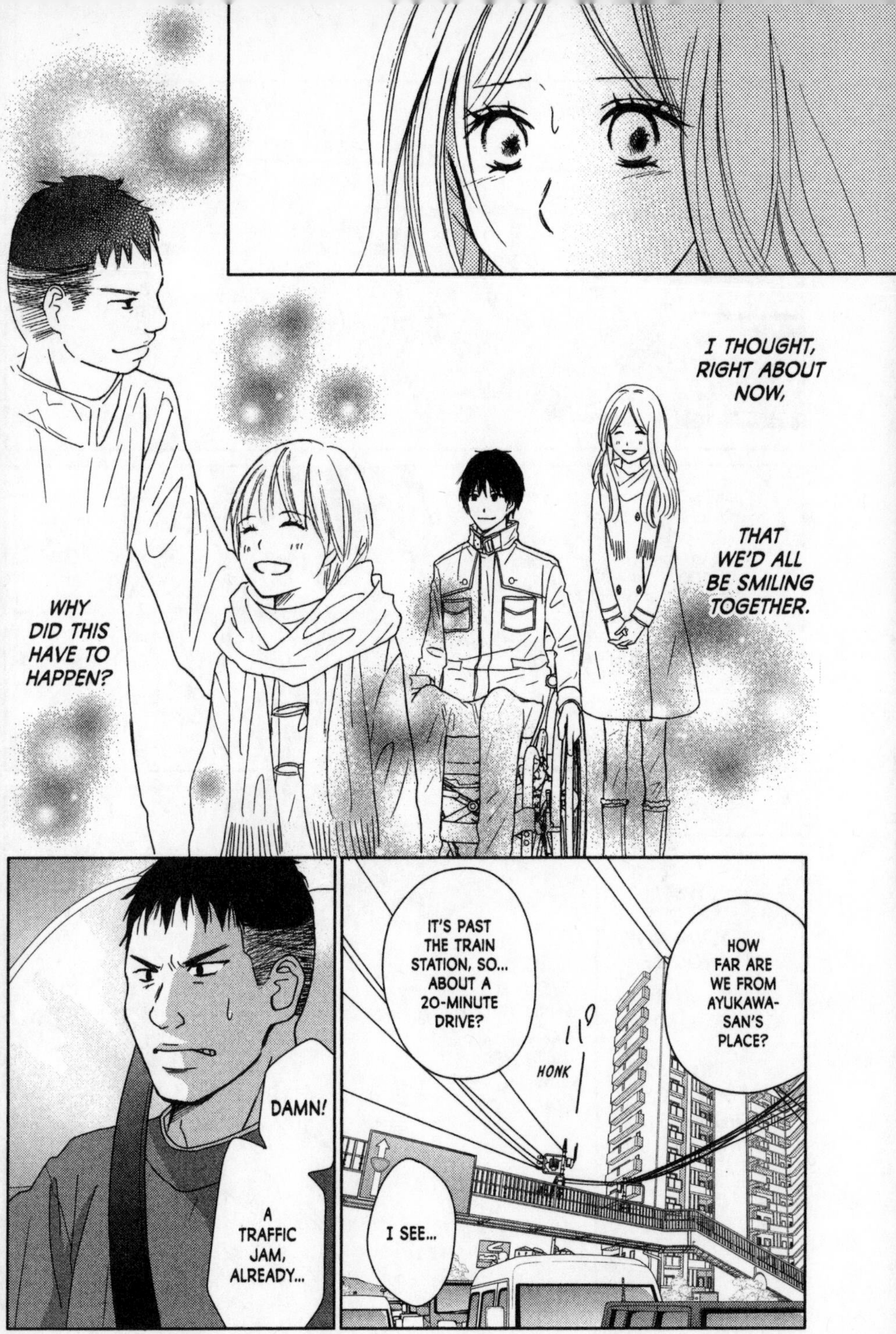
I THOUGHT, RIGHT ABOUT NOW,
THAT WE'D ALL BE SMILING TOGETHER.
WHY DID THIS HAVE TO HAPPEN?
HOW FAR ARE WE FROM AYUKAWA-SAN'S PLACE?
IT'S PAST THE TRAIN STATION, SO... ABOUT A 20-MINUTE DRIVE?
HONK
I SEE...
DAMN!
A TRAFFIC JAM, ALREADY...

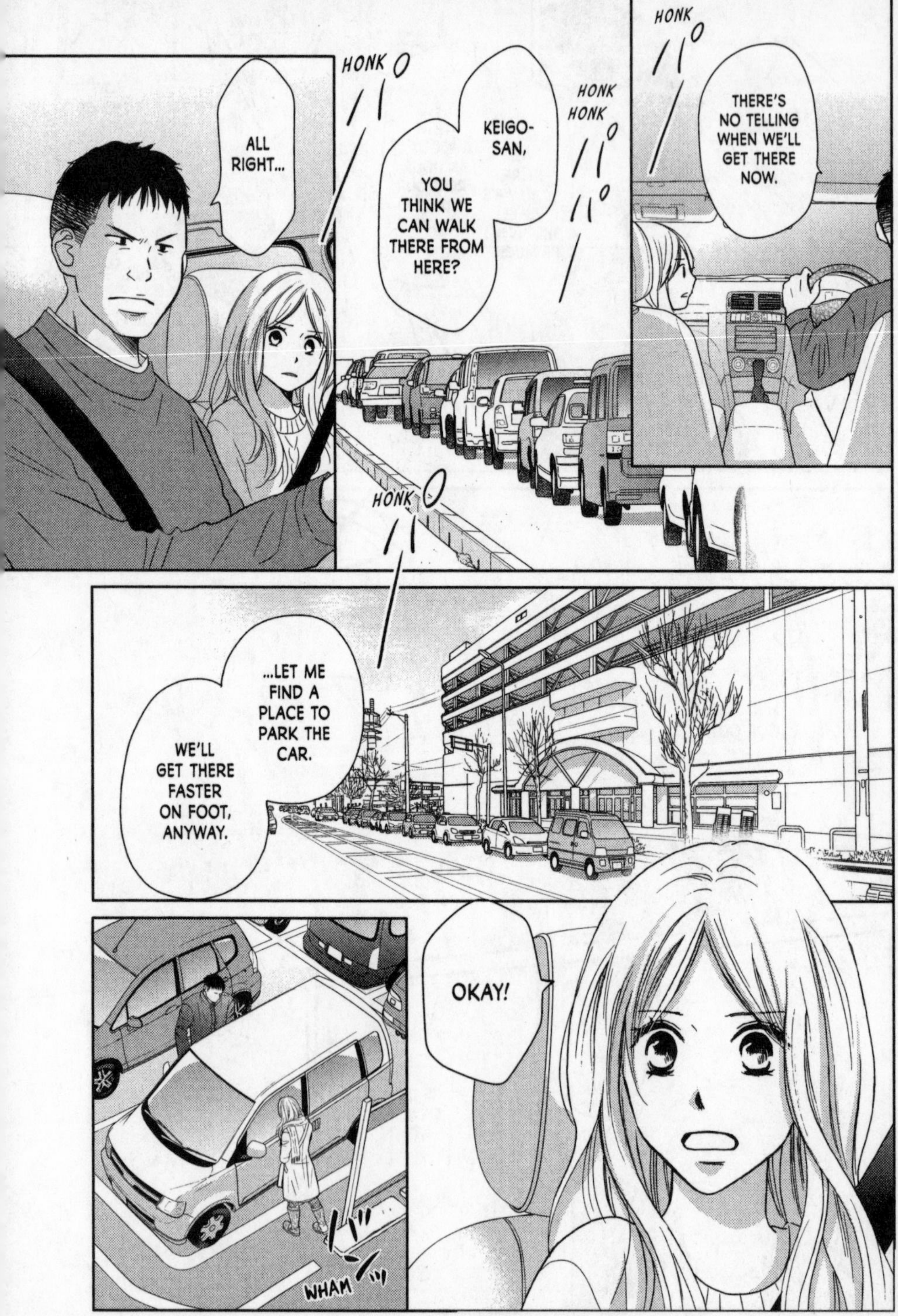
HONK
THERE'S NO TELLING WHEN WE'LL GET THERE NOW.
HONK HONK
KEIGO-SAN,
YOU THINK WE CAN WALK THERE FROM HERE?
HONK
HONK
ALL RIGHT...
...LET ME FIND A PLACE TO PARK THE CAR.
WE'LL GET THERE FASTER ON FOOT, ANYWAY.
OKAY!
WHAM

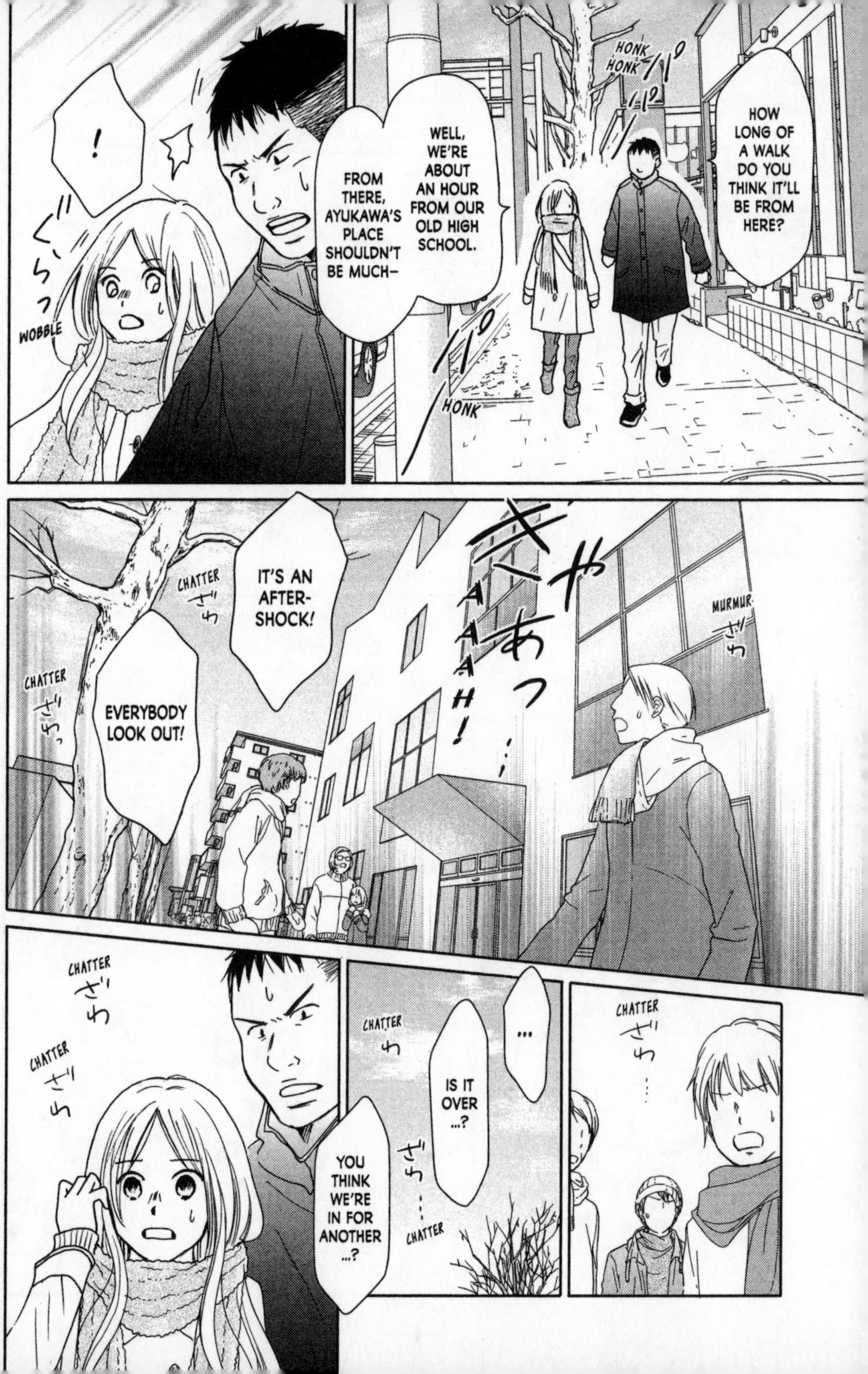
HONK
HONK
HOW LONG OF A WALK DO YOU THINK IT'LL BE FROM HERE?
WELL, WE'RE ABOUT AN HOUR FROM OUR OLD HIGH SCHOOL.
FROM THERE, AYUKAWA'S PLACE SHOULDN'T BE MUCH—
HONK
!
ぐらっ
WOBBLE
きゃあっ
AAAAH!
MURMUR
ざわ
IT'S AN AFTER-SHOCK!
CHATTER
ざわ
EVERYBODY LOOK OUT!
CHATTER
ざわっ
CHATTER
ざわ
...
IS IT OVER ...?
CHATTER
わ
ざわ
CHATTER
YOU THINK WE'RE IN FOR ANOTHER ...?
CHATTER
ざわ
CHATTER
ざわ

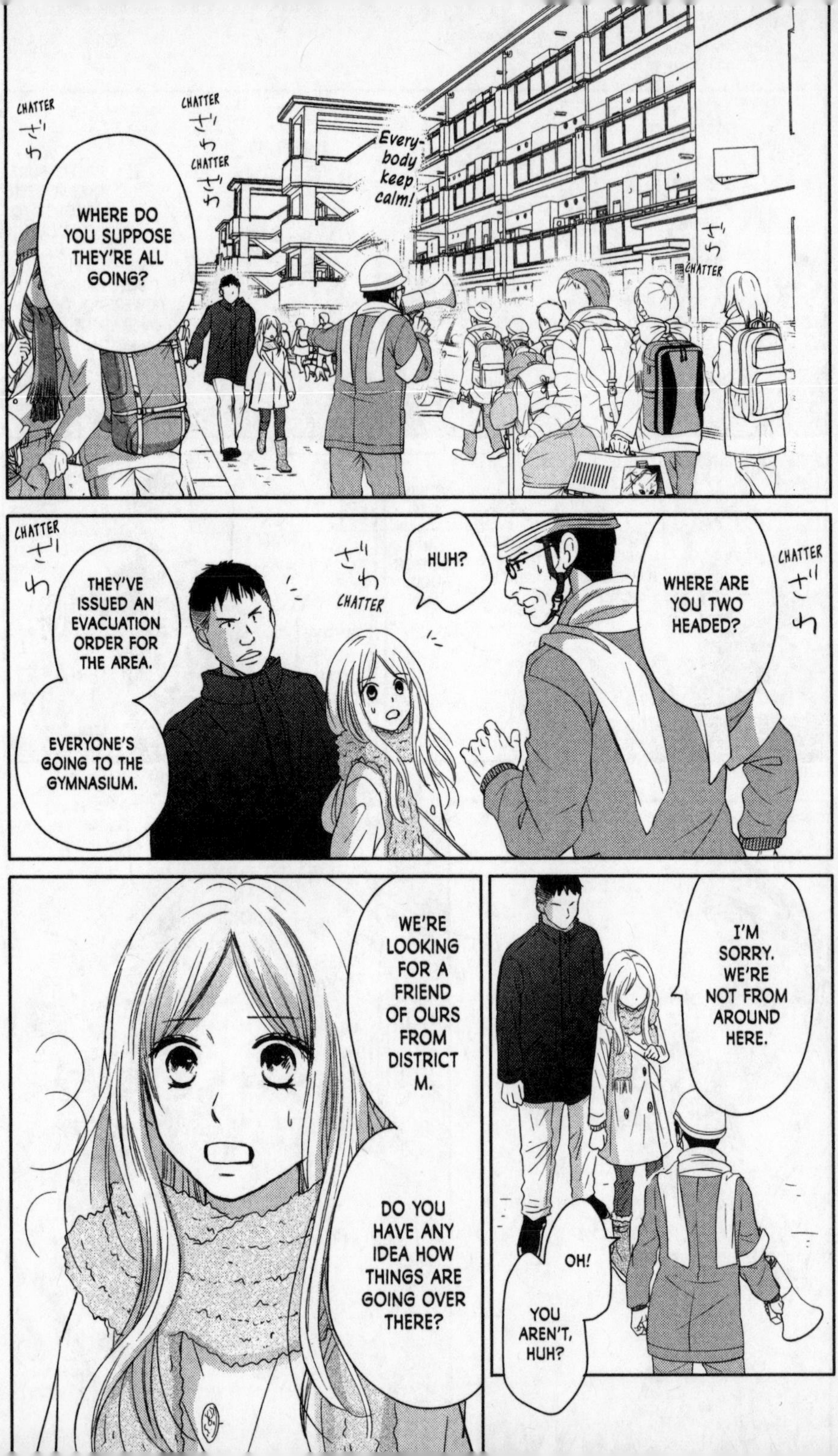
CHATTER
ざわ
Every-body keep calm!
CHATTER
ざわ
CHATTER
CHATTER
ざわ
WHERE DO YOU SUPPOSE THEY'RE ALL GOING?
CHATTER
ざわ
WHERE ARE YOU TWO HEADED?
HUH?
ざわ
CHATTER
CHATTER
ざわ
THEY'VE ISSUED AN EVACUATION ORDER FOR THE AREA.
EVERYONE'S GOING TO THE GYMNASIUM.
I'M SORRY. WE'RE NOT FROM AROUND HERE.
OH!
YOU AREN'T, HUH?
WE'RE LOOKING FOR A FRIEND OF OURS FROM DISTRICT M.
DO YOU HAVE ANY IDEA HOW THINGS ARE GOING OVER THERE?

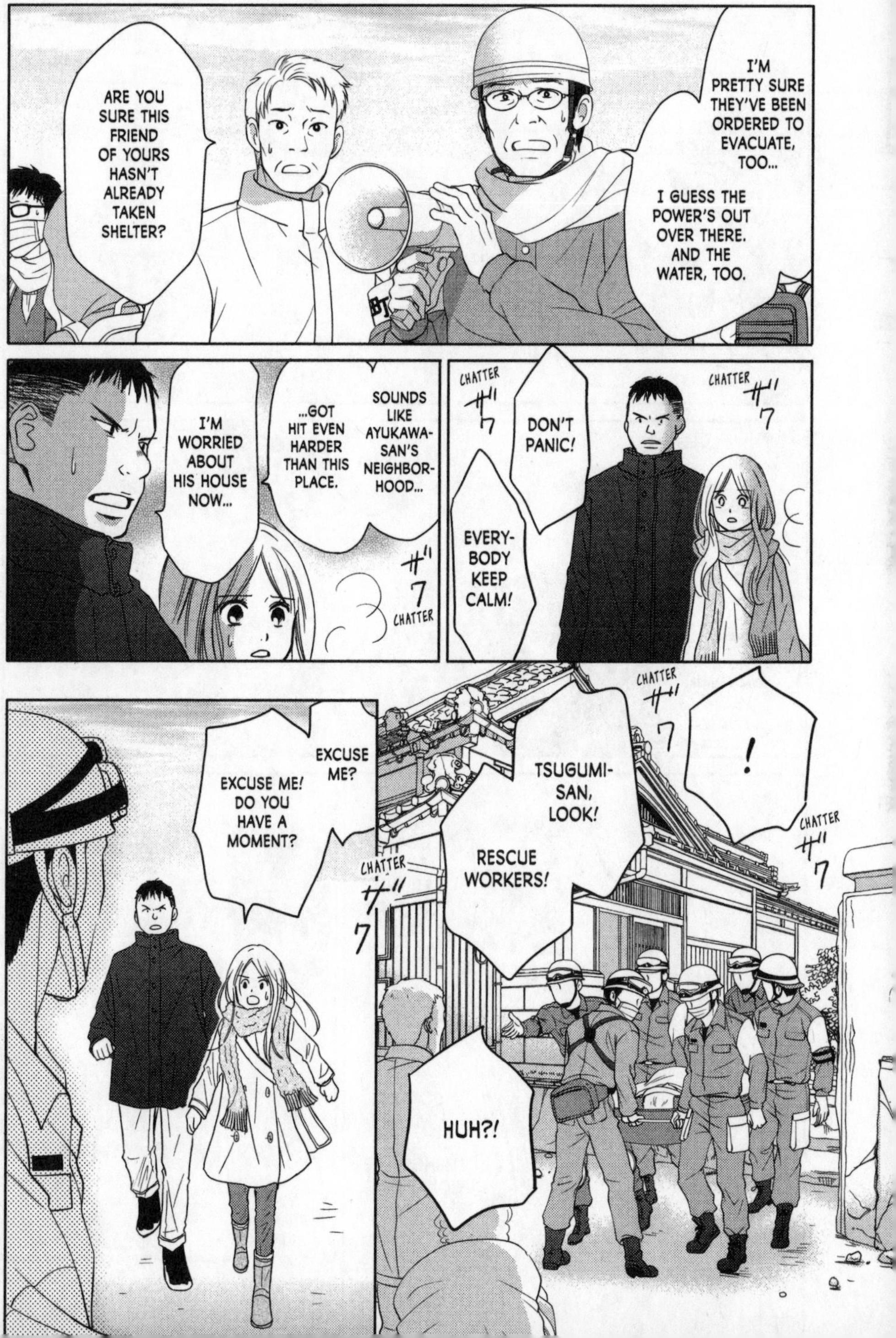
I'M PRETTY SURE THEY'VE BEEN ORDERED TO EVACUATE, TOO...
I GUESS THE POWER'S OUT OVER THERE. AND THE WATER, TOO.
ARE YOU SURE THIS FRIEND OF YOURS HASN'T ALREADY TAKEN SHELTER?
CHATTER
CHATTER
DON'T PANIC!
EVERYBODY KEEP CALM!
SOUNDS LIKE AYUKAWA-SAN'S NEIGHBORHOOD...
...GOT HIT EVEN HARDER THAN THIS PLACE.
I'M WORRIED ABOUT HIS HOUSE NOW...
CHATTER
!
CHATTER
TSUGUMI-SAN, LOOK!
RESCUE WORKERS!
CHATTER
HUH?!
EXCUSE ME?
EXCUSE ME! DO YOU HAVE A MOMENT?
CHATTER

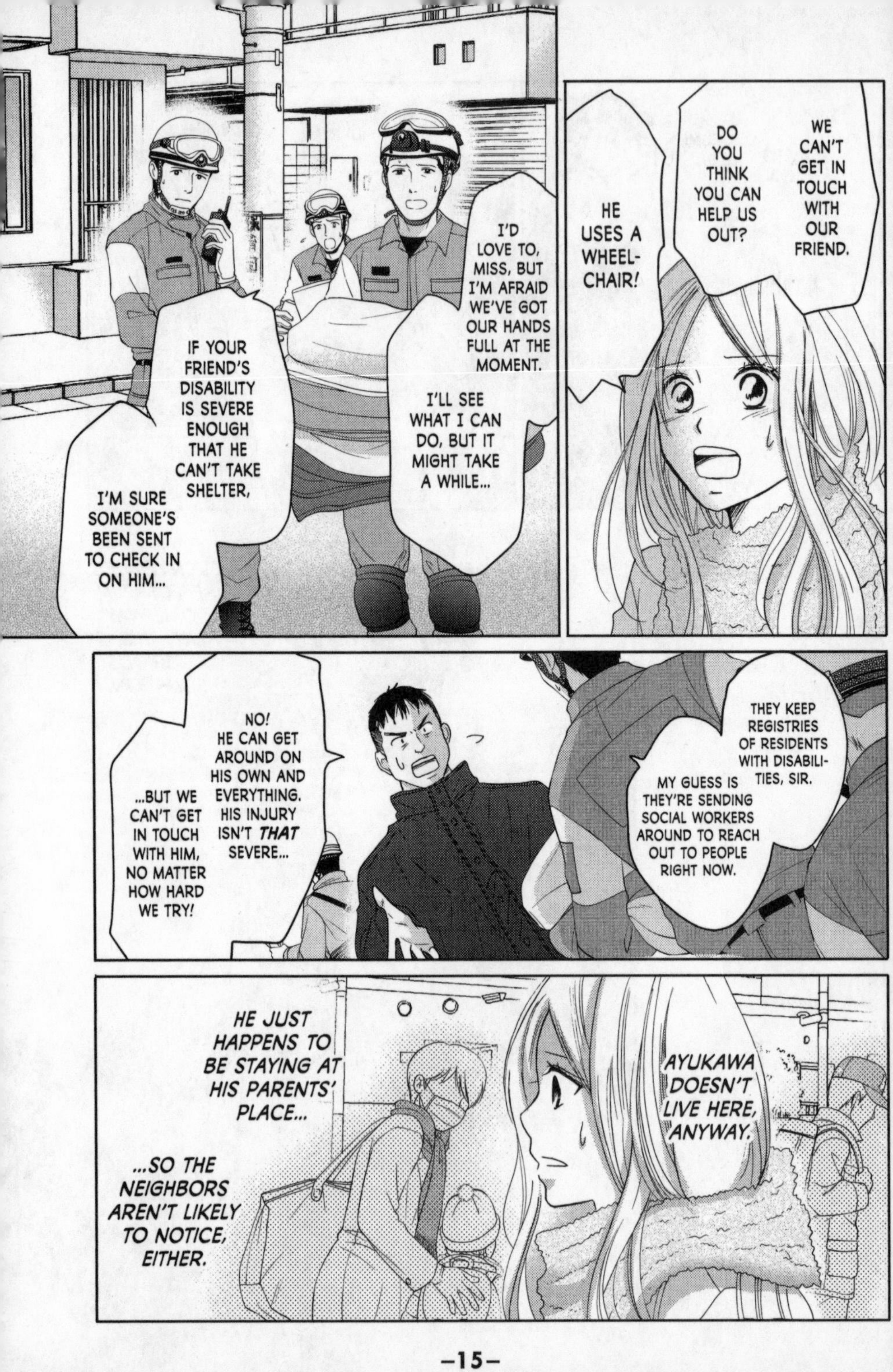
WE CAN'T GET IN TOUCH WITH OUR FRIEND.
DO YOU THINK YOU CAN HELP US OUT?
HE USES A WHEEL-CHAIR!
I'D LOVE TO, MISS, BUT I'M AFRAID WE'VE GOT OUR HANDS FULL AT THE MOMENT.
I'LL SEE WHAT I CAN DO, BUT IT MIGHT TAKE A WHILE...
IF YOUR FRIEND'S DISABILITY IS SEVERE ENOUGH THAT HE CAN'T TAKE SHELTER,
I'M SURE SOMEONE'S BEEN SENT TO CHECK IN ON HIM...
THEY KEEP REGISTRIES OF RESIDENTS WITH DISABILI-TIES, SIR.
MY GUESS IS THEY'RE SENDING SOCIAL WORKERS AROUND TO REACH OUT TO PEOPLE RIGHT NOW.
NO! HE CAN GET AROUND ON HIS OWN AND EVERYTHING. HIS INJURY ISN'T *THAT* SEVERE...
...BUT WE CAN'T GET IN TOUCH WITH HIM, NO MATTER HOW HARD WE TRY!
AYUKAWA DOESN'T LIVE HERE, ANYWAY.
HE JUST HAPPENS TO BE STAYING AT HIS PARENTS' PLACE...
...SO THE NEIGHBORS AREN'T LIKELY TO NOTICE, EITHER.

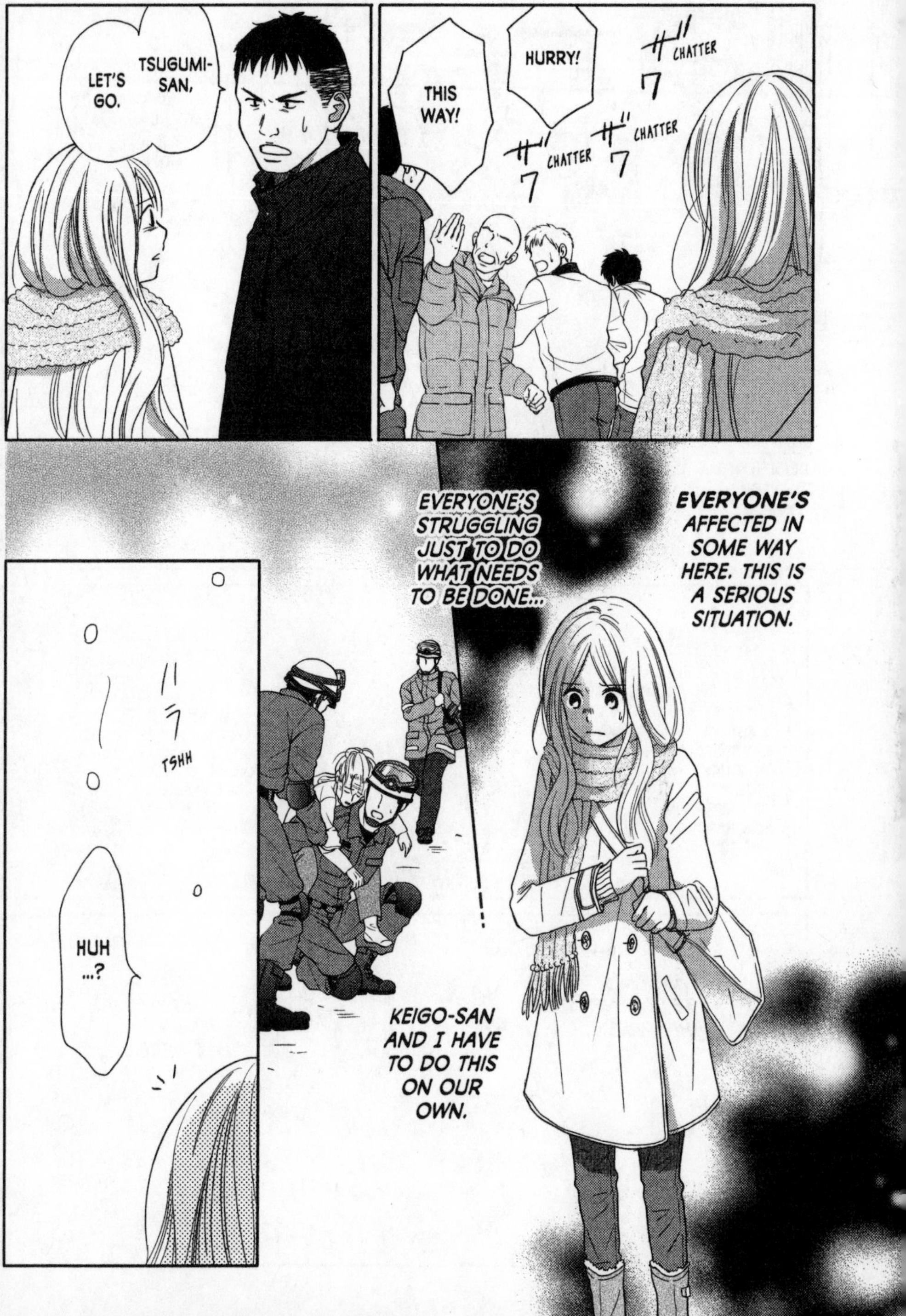
CHATTER
HURRY!
CHATTER
THIS WAY!
CHATTER
TSUGUMI-SAN, LET'S GO.
EVERYONE'S AFFECTED IN SOME WAY HERE. THIS IS A SERIOUS SITUATION.
EVERYONE'S STRUGGLING JUST TO DO WHAT NEEDS TO BE DONE...
KEIGO-SAN AND I HAVE TO DO THIS ON OUR OWN.
TSHH
HUH ...?

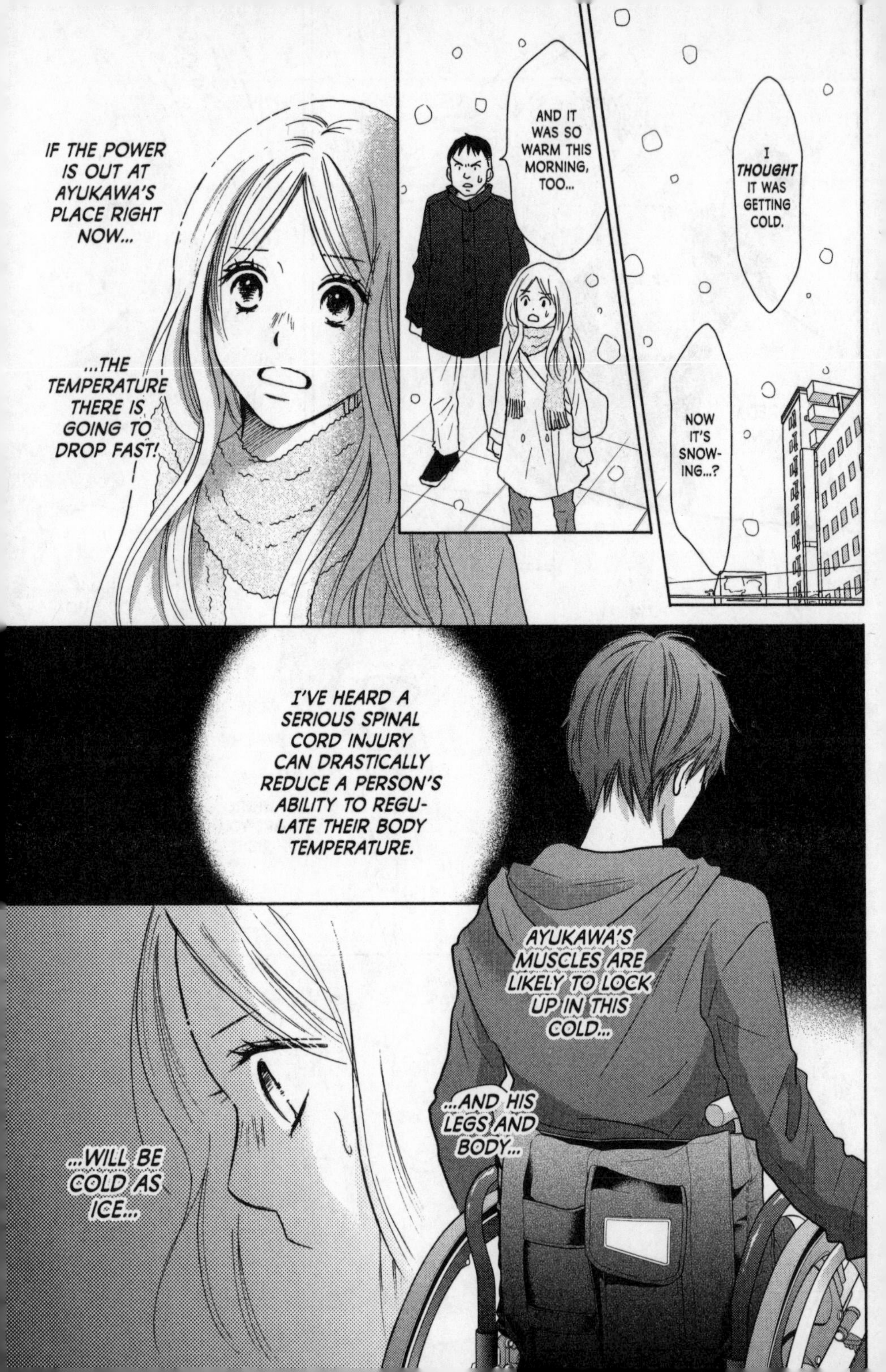
I *THOUGHT* IT WAS GETTING COLD.
NOW IT'S SNOWING...?
AND IT WAS SO WARM THIS MORNING, TOO...
IF THE POWER IS OUT AT AYUKAWA'S PLACE RIGHT NOW...
...THE TEMPERATURE THERE IS GOING TO DROP FAST!
I'VE HEARD A SERIOUS SPINAL CORD INJURY CAN DRASTICALLY REDUCE A PERSON'S ABILITY TO REGU- LATE THEIR BODY TEMPERATURE.
AYUKAWA'S MUSCLES ARE LIKELY TO LOCK UP IN THIS COLD...
...AND HIS LEGS AND BODY...
...WILL BE COLD AS ICE...

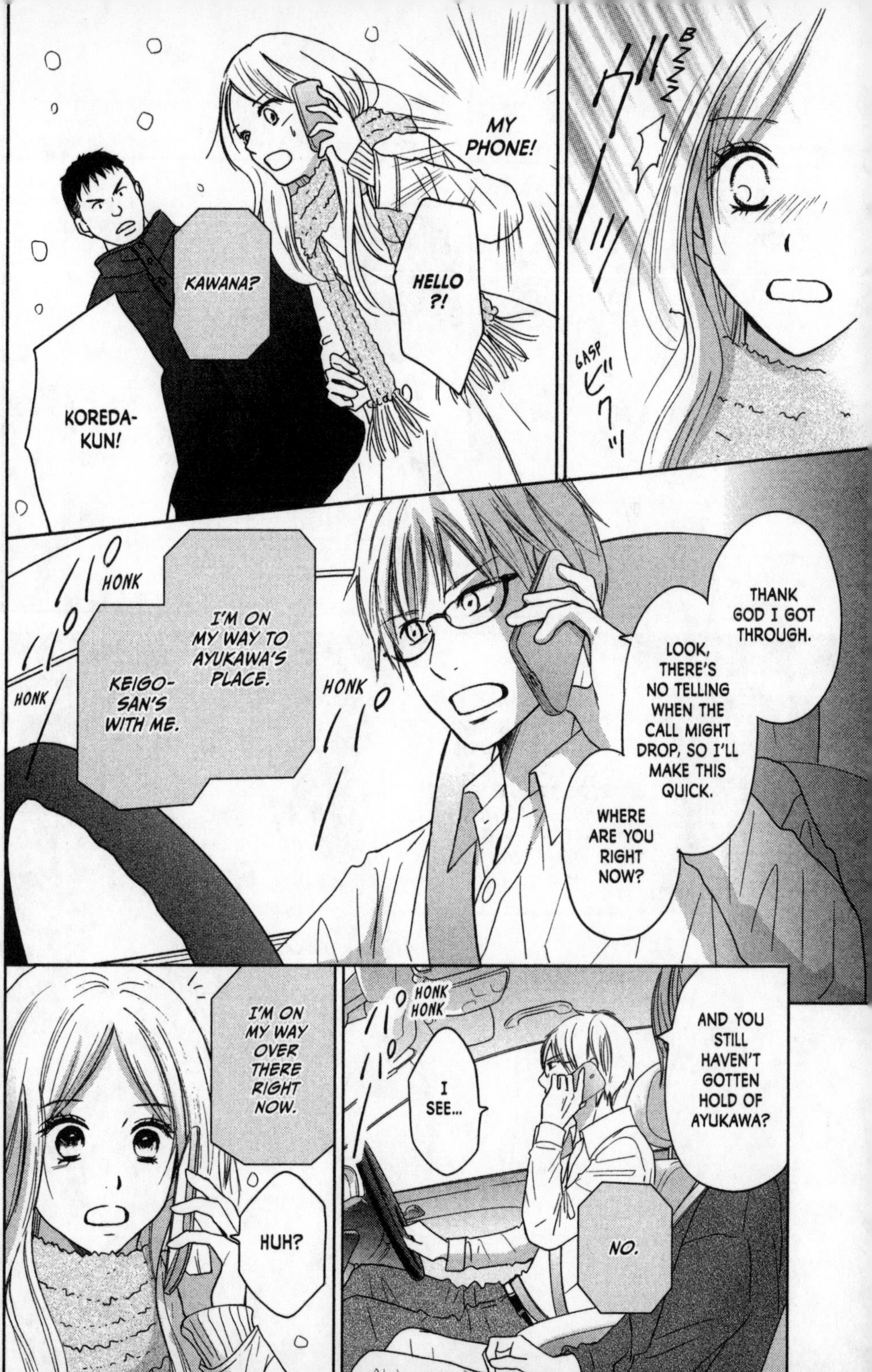
BZZZ
GASP
MY PHONE!
HELLO?!
KAWANA?
KOREDA-KUN!
THANK GOD I GOT THROUGH.
LOOK, THERE'S NO TELLING WHEN THE CALL MIGHT DROP, SO I'LL MAKE THIS QUICK.
WHERE ARE YOU RIGHT NOW?
HONK
I'M ON MY WAY TO AYUKAWA'S PLACE.
KEIGO-SAN'S WITH ME.
HONK
HONK
AND YOU STILL HAVEN'T GOTTEN HOLD OF AYUKAWA?
HONK HONK
I SEE...
NO.
I'M ON MY WAY OVER THERE RIGHT NOW.
HUH?

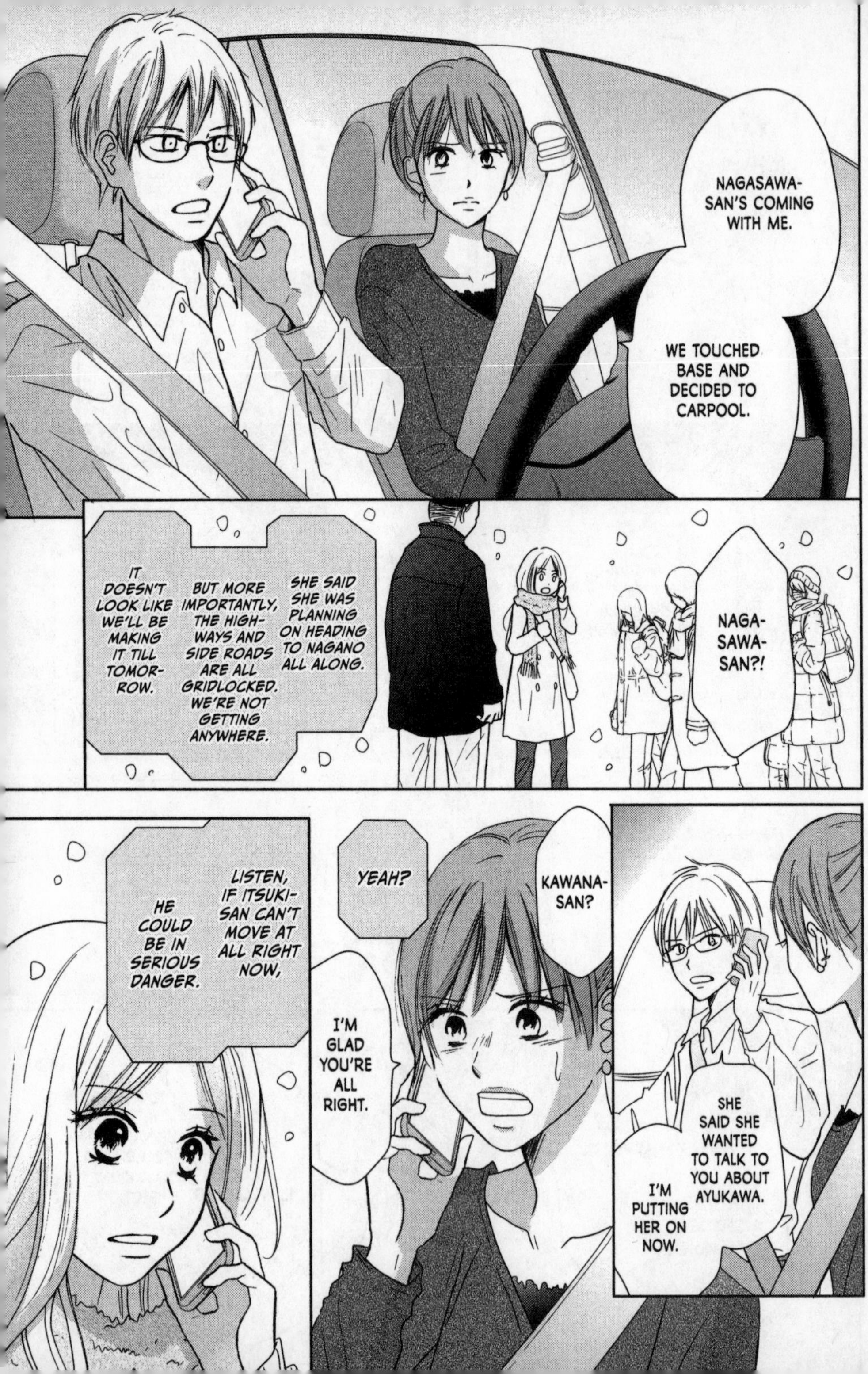
NAGASAWA-SAN'S COMING WITH ME.
WE TOUCHED BASE AND DECIDED TO CARPOOL.
NAGA-SAWA-SAN?!
SHE SAID SHE WAS PLANNING ON HEADING TO NAGANO ALL ALONG.
BUT MORE IMPORTANTLY, THE HIGH-WAYS AND SIDE ROADS ARE ALL GRIDLOCKED. WE'RE NOT GETTING ANYWHERE.
IT DOESN'T LOOK LIKE WE'LL BE MAKING IT TILL TOMOR-ROW.
SHE SAID SHE WANTED TO TALK TO YOU ABOUT AYUKAWA.
I'M PUTTING HER ON NOW.
KAWANA-SAN?
YEAH?
I'M GLAD YOU'RE ALL RIGHT.
LISTEN, IF ITSUKI-SAN CAN'T MOVE AT ALL RIGHT NOW,
HE COULD BE IN SERIOUS DANGER.

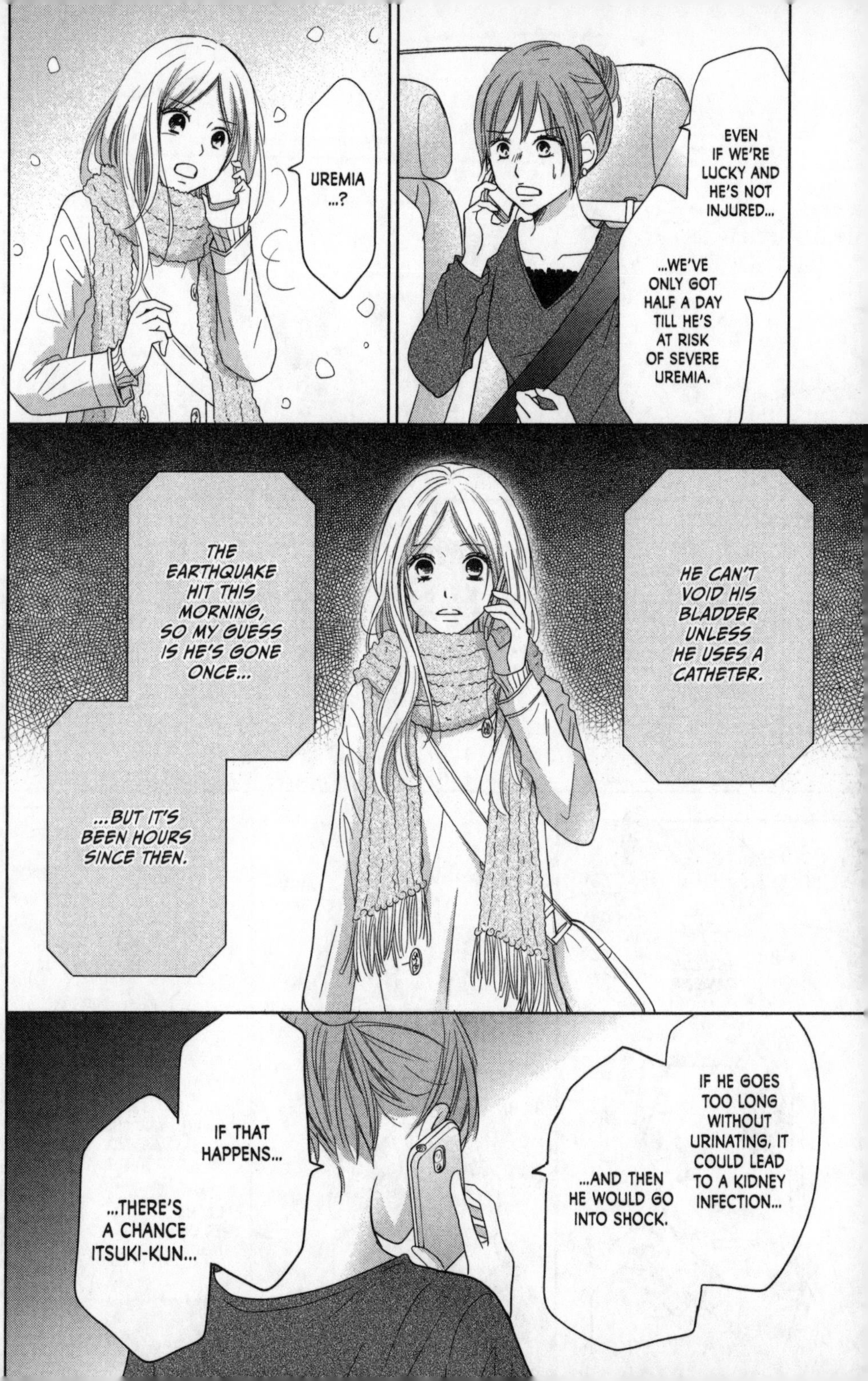
EVEN IF WE'RE LUCKY AND HE'S NOT INJURED...
...WE'VE ONLY GOT HALF A DAY TILL HE'S AT RISK OF SEVERE UREMIA.
UREMIA ...?
HE CAN'T VOID HIS BLADDER UNLESS HE USES A CATHETER.
THE EARTHQUAKE HIT THIS MORNING, SO MY GUESS IS HE'S GONE ONCE...
...BUT IT'S BEEN HOURS SINCE THEN.
IF HE GOES TOO LONG WITHOUT URINATING, IT COULD LEAD TO A KIDNEY INFECTION...
...AND THEN HE WOULD GO INTO SHOCK.
IF THAT HAPPENS...
...THERE'S A CHANCE ITSUKI-KUN...

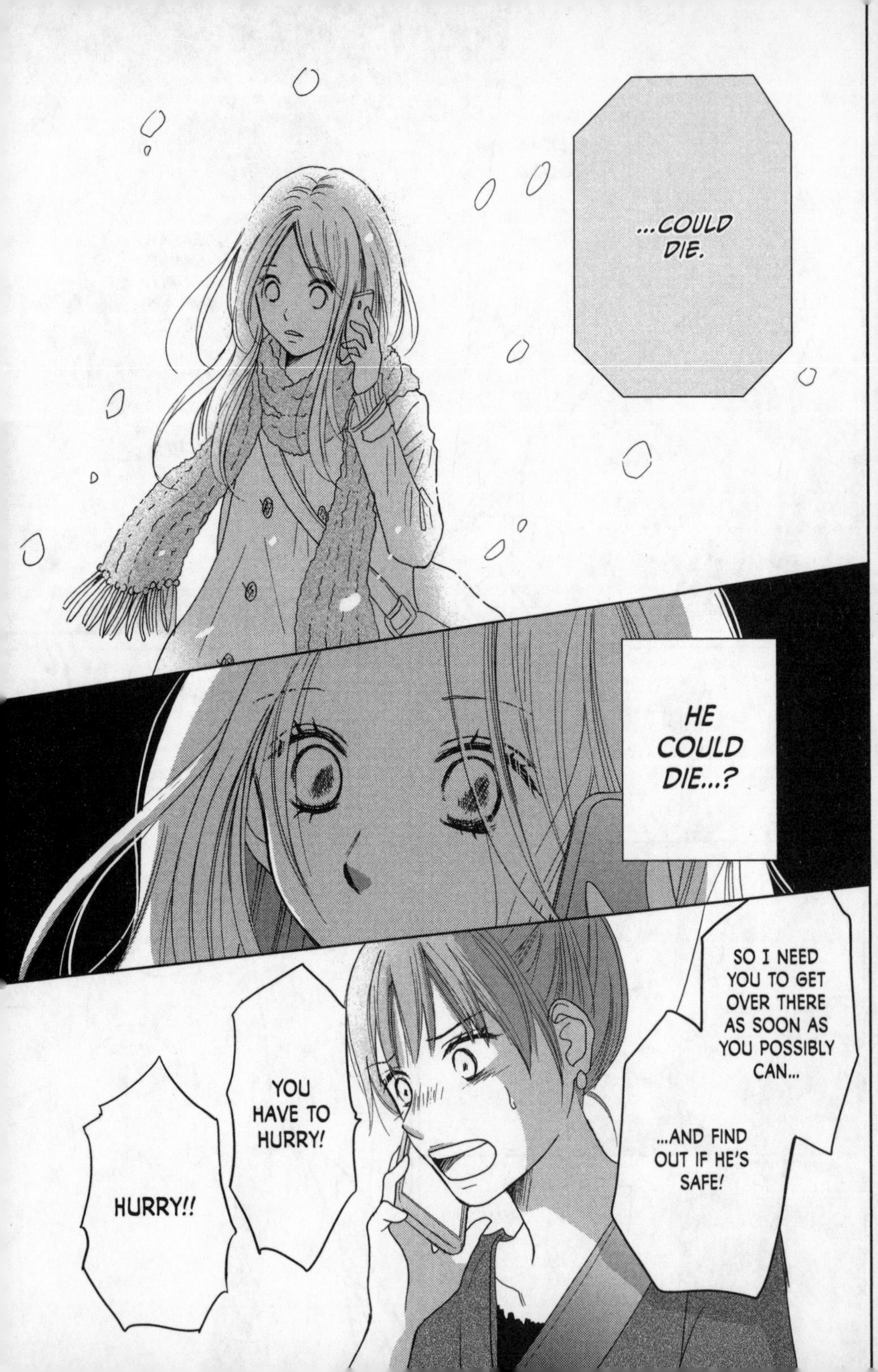
...COULD DIE.
HE COULD DIE...?
SO I NEED YOU TO GET OVER THERE AS SOON AS YOU POSSIBLY CAN...
...AND FIND OUT IF HE'S SAFE!
YOU HAVE TO HURRY!
HURRY!!

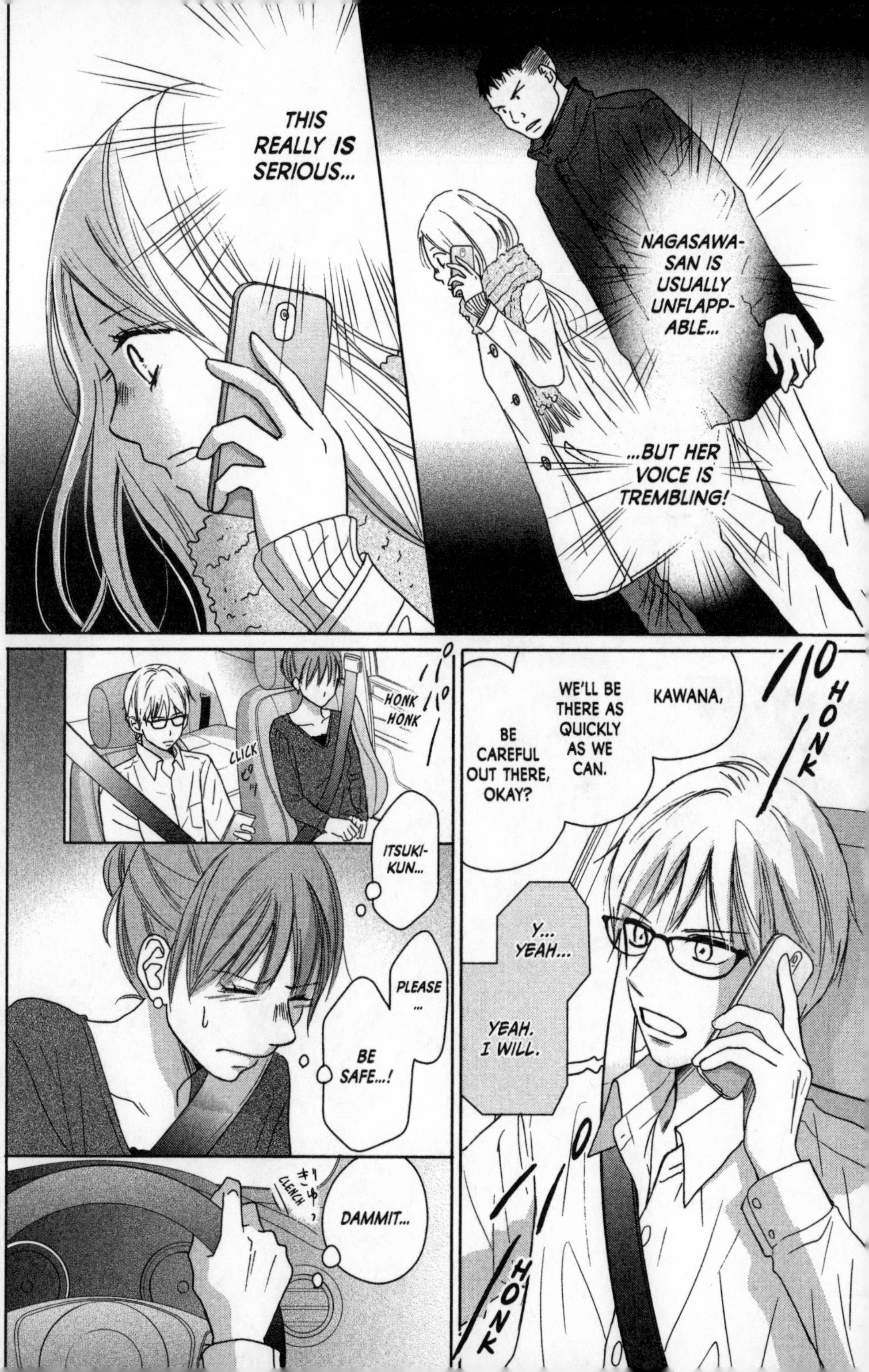
NAGASAWA-SAN IS USUALLY UNFLAPPABLE...
...BUT HER VOICE IS TREMBLING!
THIS REALLY IS SERIOUS...
HONK
KAWANA,
WE'LL BE THERE AS QUICKLY AS WE CAN.
BE CAREFUL OUT THERE, OKAY?
Y... YEAH...
YEAH. I WILL.
HONK
HONK HONK
CLICK
ITSUKI-KUN...
PLEASE...
BE SAFE...!
CLENCH
DAMMIT...

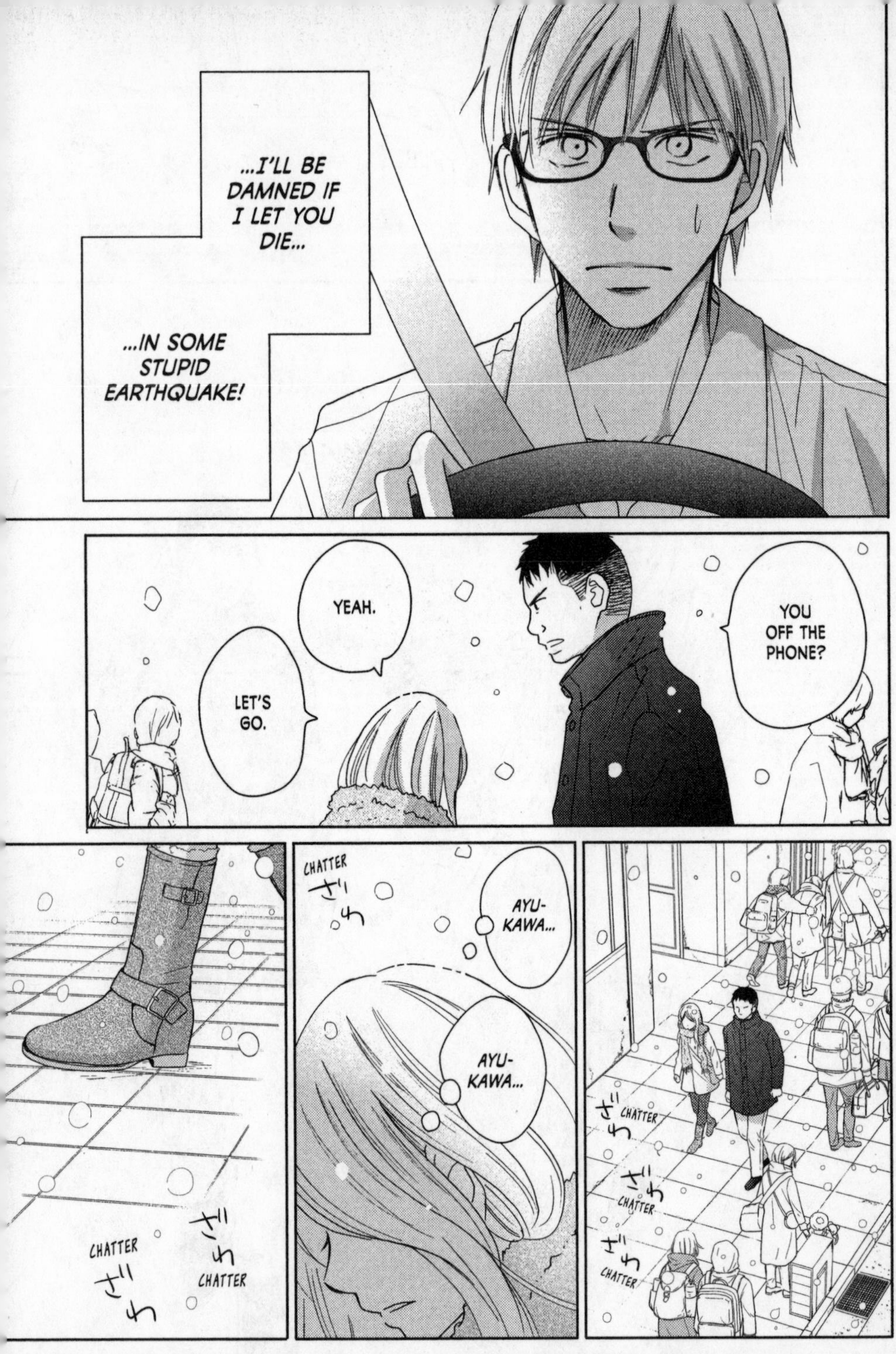
...I'LL BE DAMNED IF I LET YOU DIE...
...IN SOME STUPID EARTHQUAKE!
YOU OFF THE PHONE?
YEAH.
LET'S GO.
ざわ
CHATTER
ざわ
CHATTER
ざわ
CHATTER
ざわ
CHATTER
AYU-KAWA...
AYU-KAWA...
ざわ
CHATTER
ざわ
CHATTER

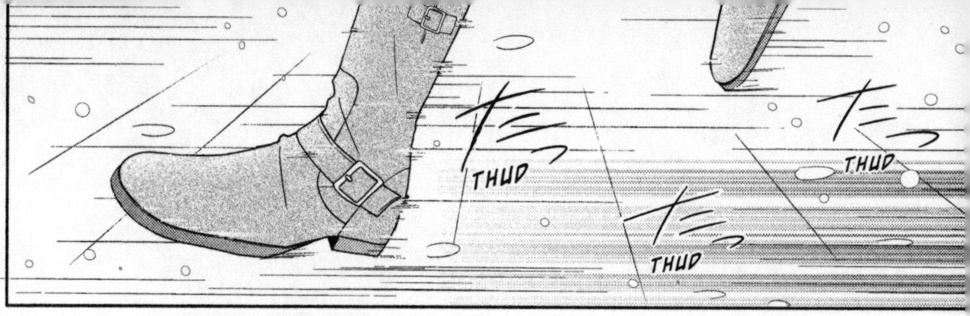
THUD
THUD
THUD

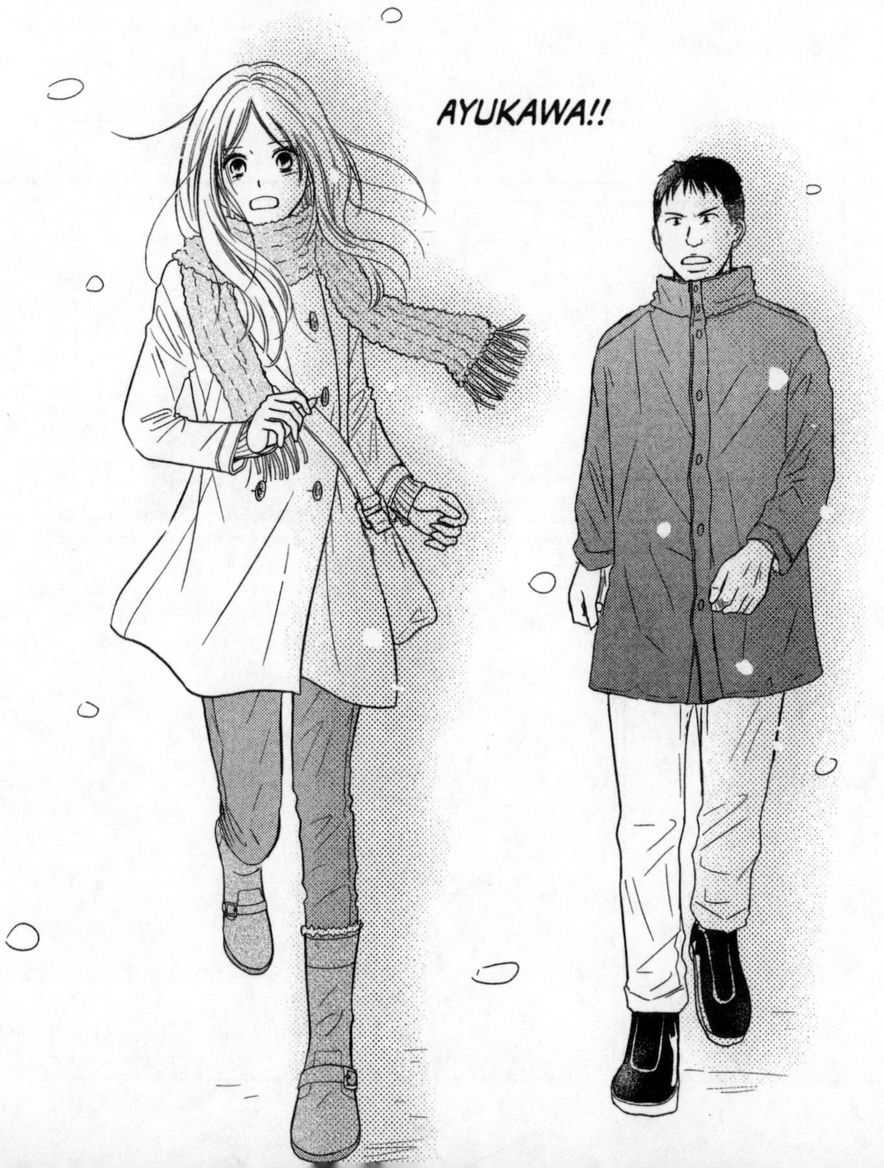
AYUKAWA!!

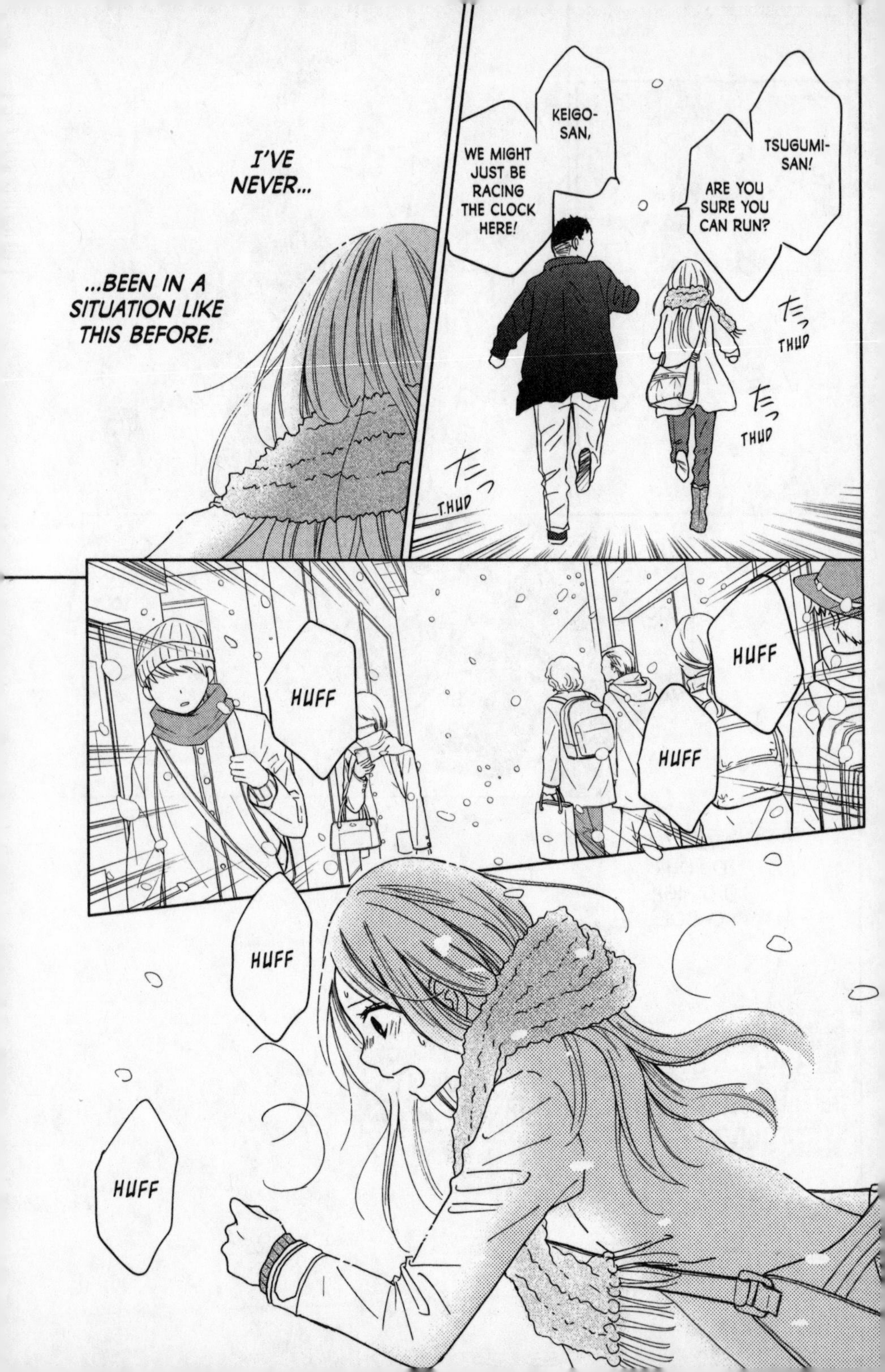
TSUGUMI-SAN!
ARE YOU SURE YOU CAN RUN?
KEIGO-SAN,
WE MIGHT JUST BE RACING THE CLOCK HERE!
たっ
THUD
たっ
THUD
たっ
T.HUD
I'VE NEVER...
...BEEN IN A SITUATION LIKE THIS BEFORE.
HUFF
HUFF
HUFF
HUFF
HUFF

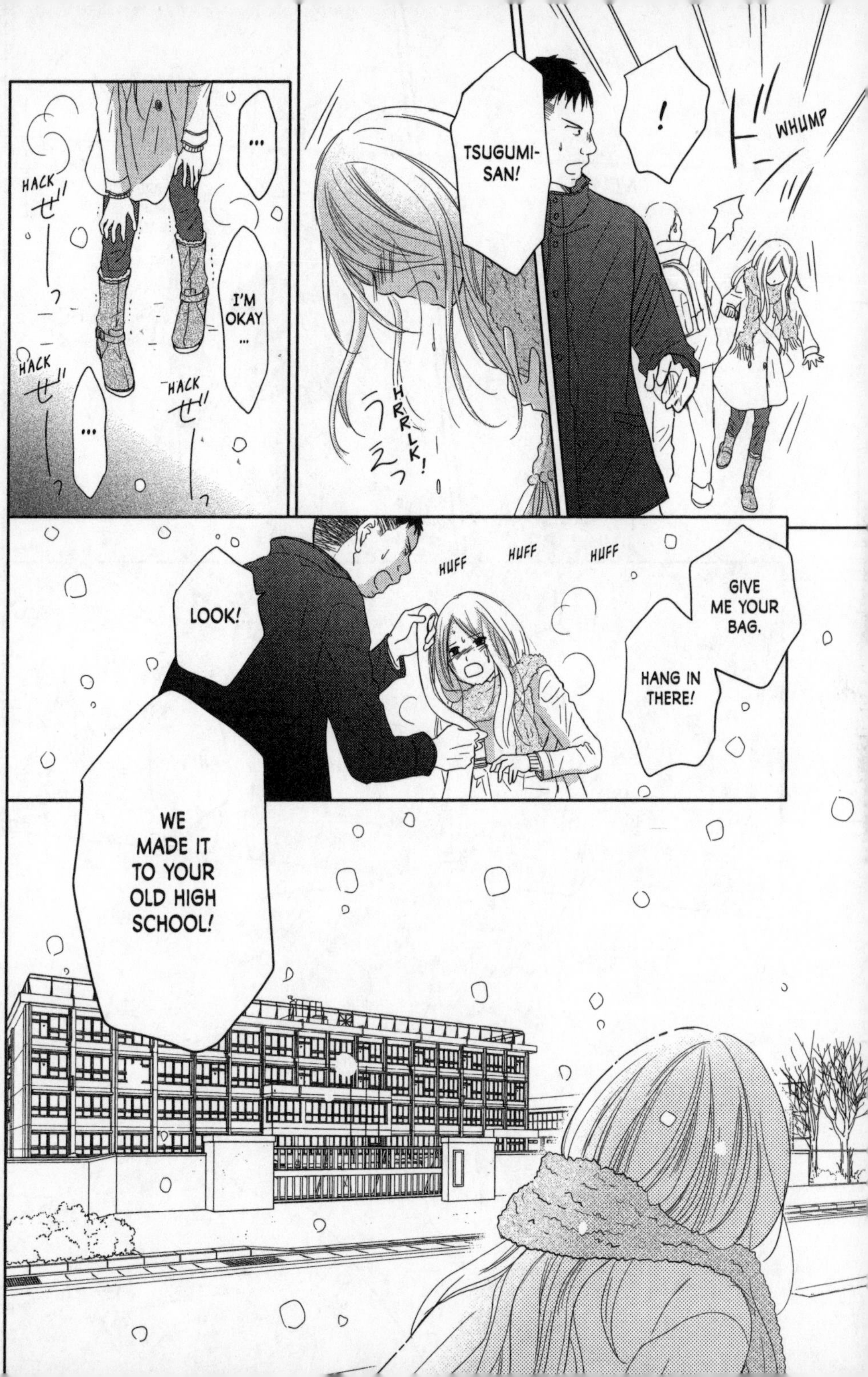
!
WHUMP
TSUGUMI-SAN!
HRRLK!
...
I'M OKAY ...
HACK
HACK
HACK
...
GIVE ME YOUR BAG.
HANG IN THERE!
HUFF
HUFF
HUFF
LOOK!
WE MADE IT TO YOUR OLD HIGH SCHOOL!

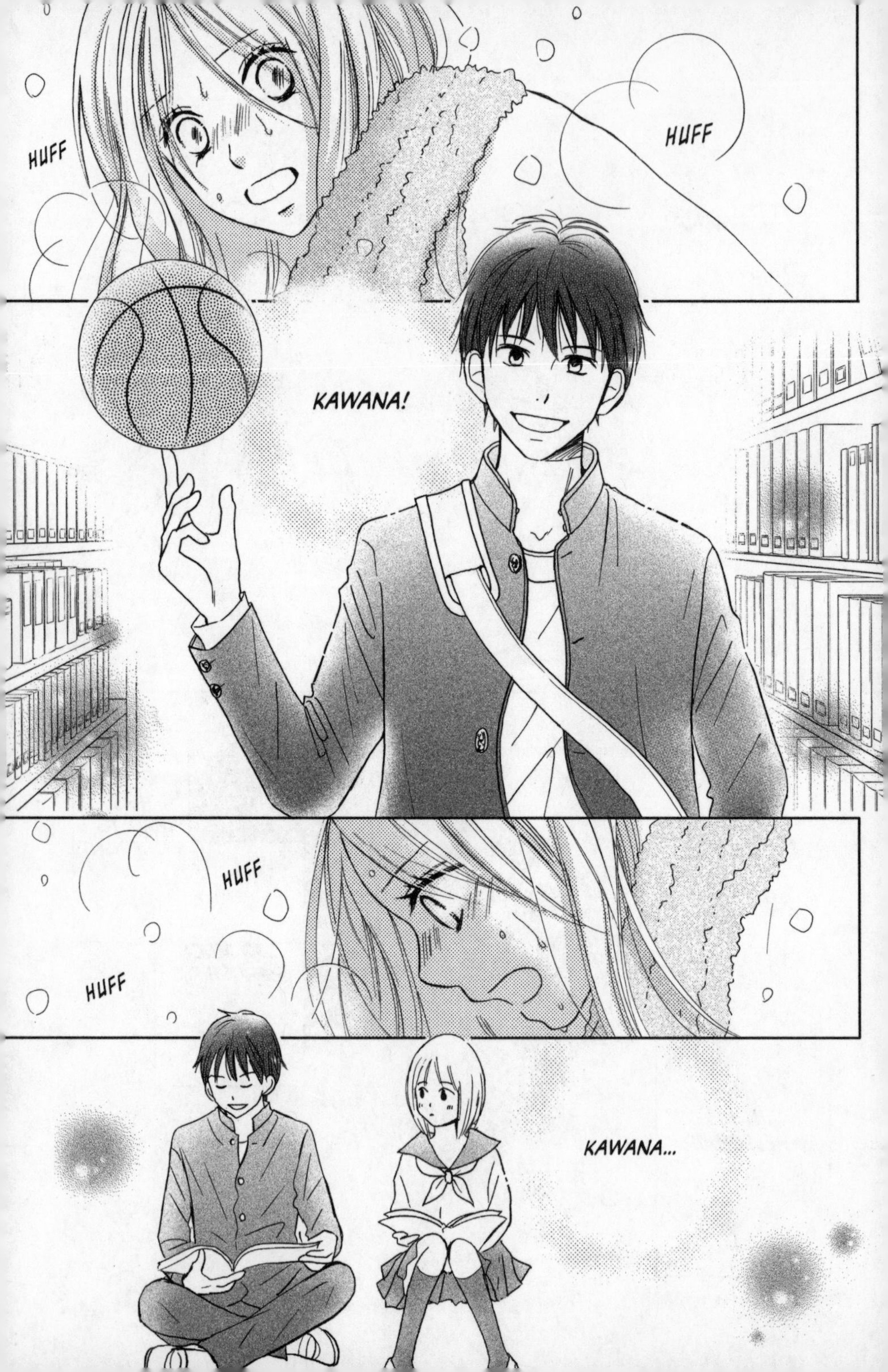
HUFF
HUFF
KAWANA!
HUFF
HUFF
KAWANA...

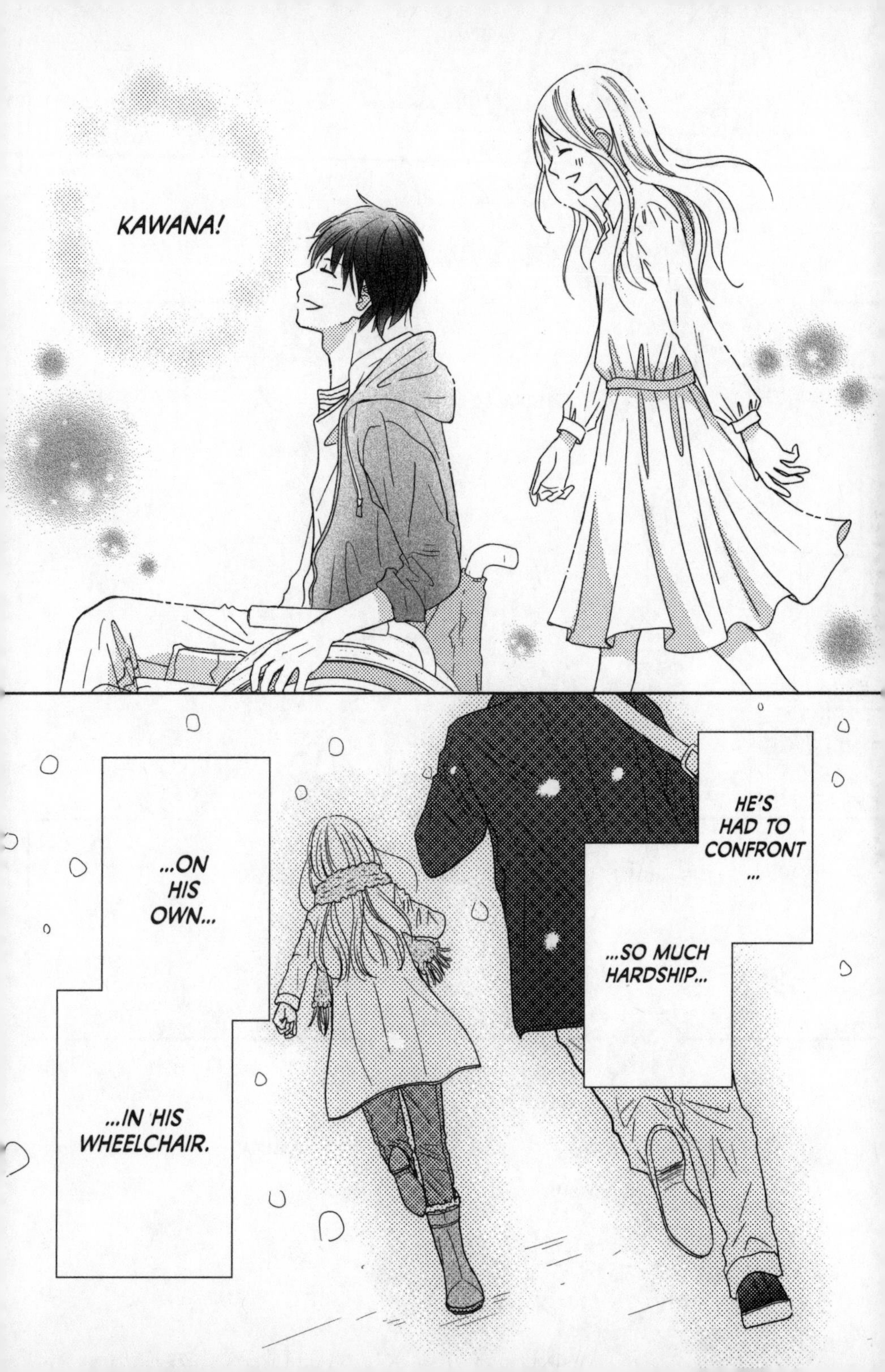
KAWANA!
HE'S HAD TO CONFRONT ...
...SO MUCH HARDSHIP...
...ON HIS OWN...
...IN HIS WHEELCHAIR.

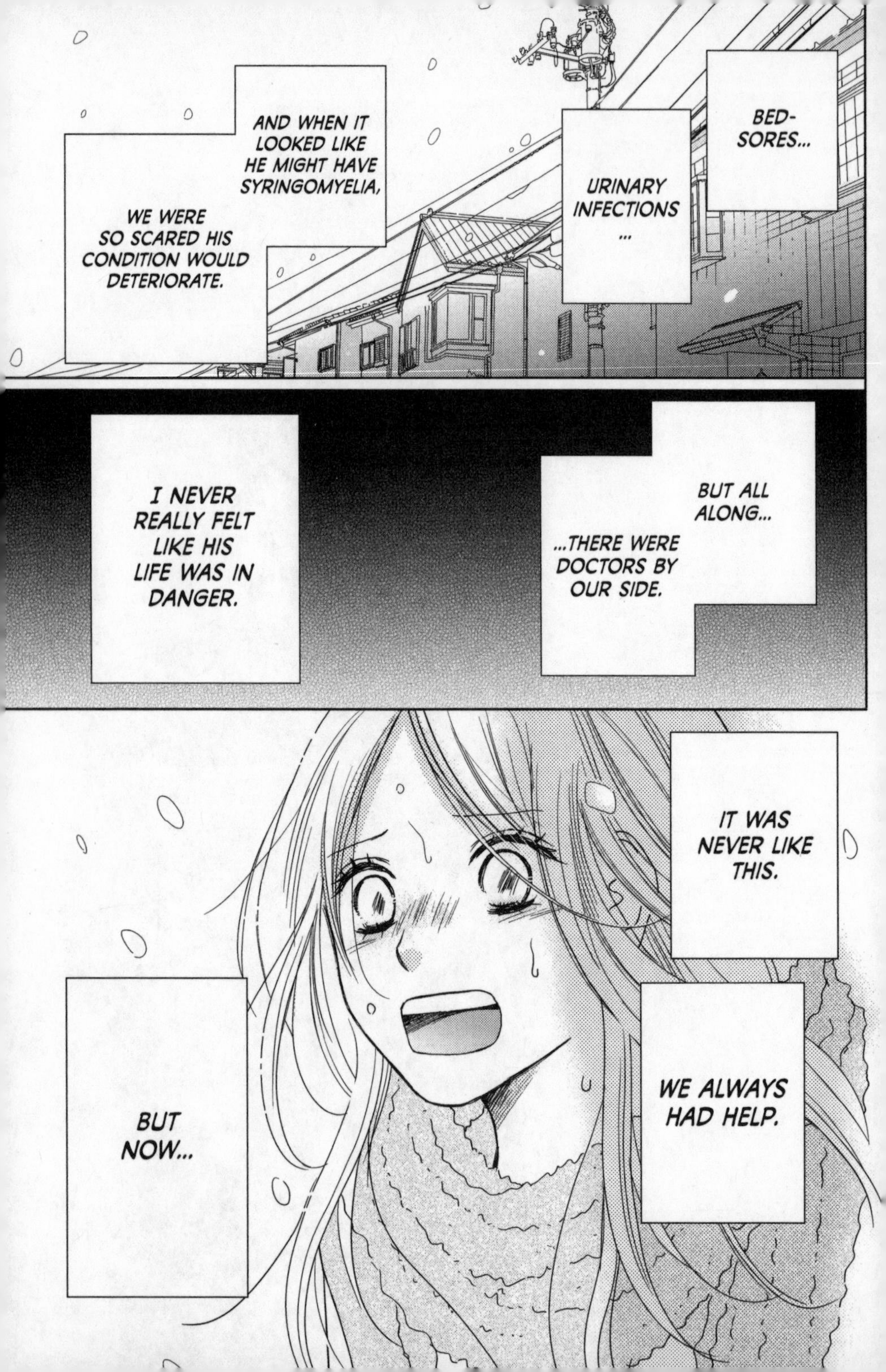
BED-SORES...
URINARY INFECTIONS ...
AND WHEN IT LOOKED LIKE HE MIGHT HAVE SYRINGOMYELIA,
WE WERE SO SCARED HIS CONDITION WOULD DETERIORATE.
BUT ALL ALONG...
...THERE WERE DOCTORS BY OUR SIDE.
I NEVER REALLY FELT LIKE HIS LIFE WAS IN DANGER.
IT WAS NEVER LIKE THIS.
WE ALWAYS HAD HELP.
BUT NOW...

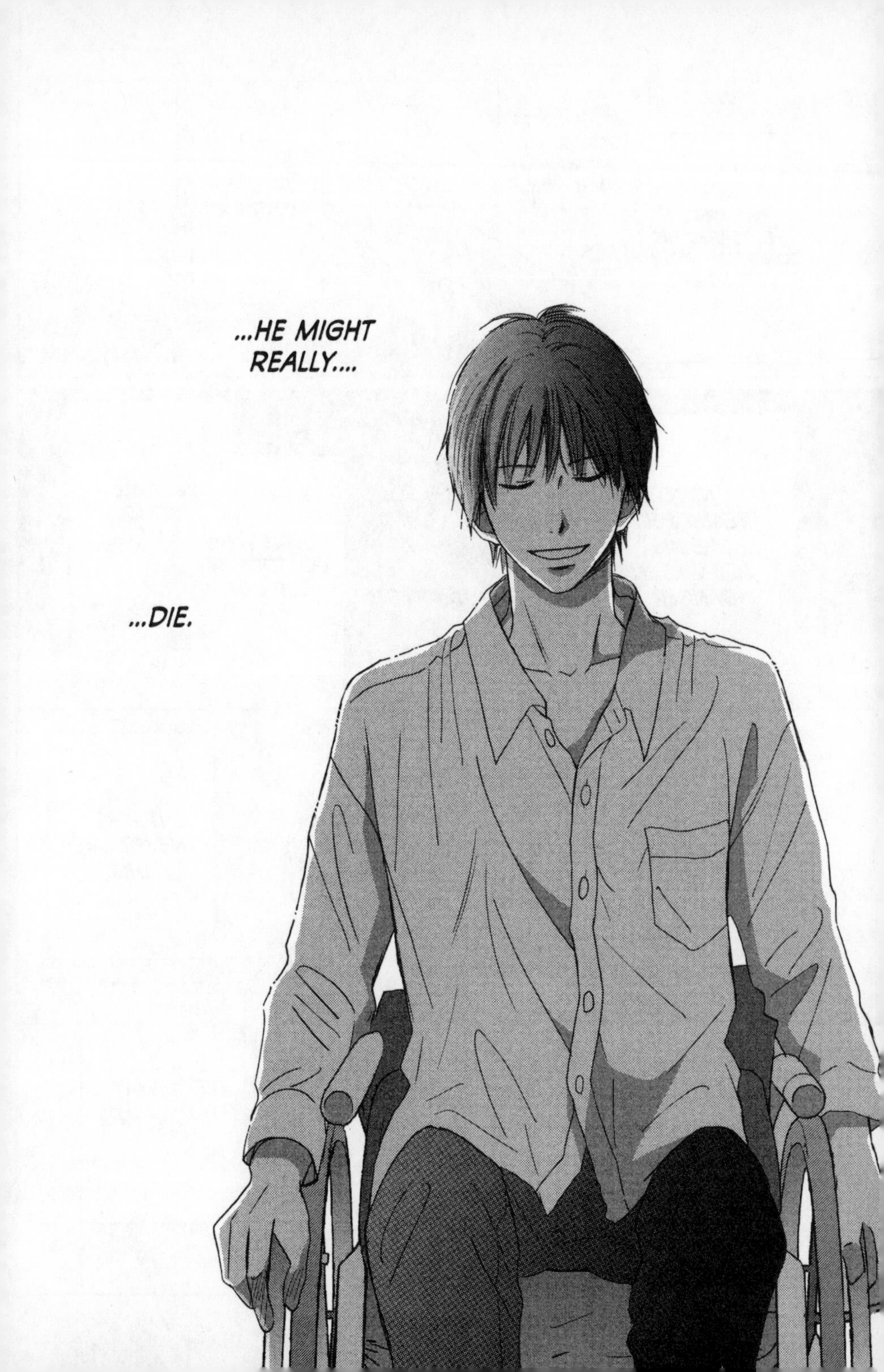
...HE MIGHT REALLY....
...DIE.

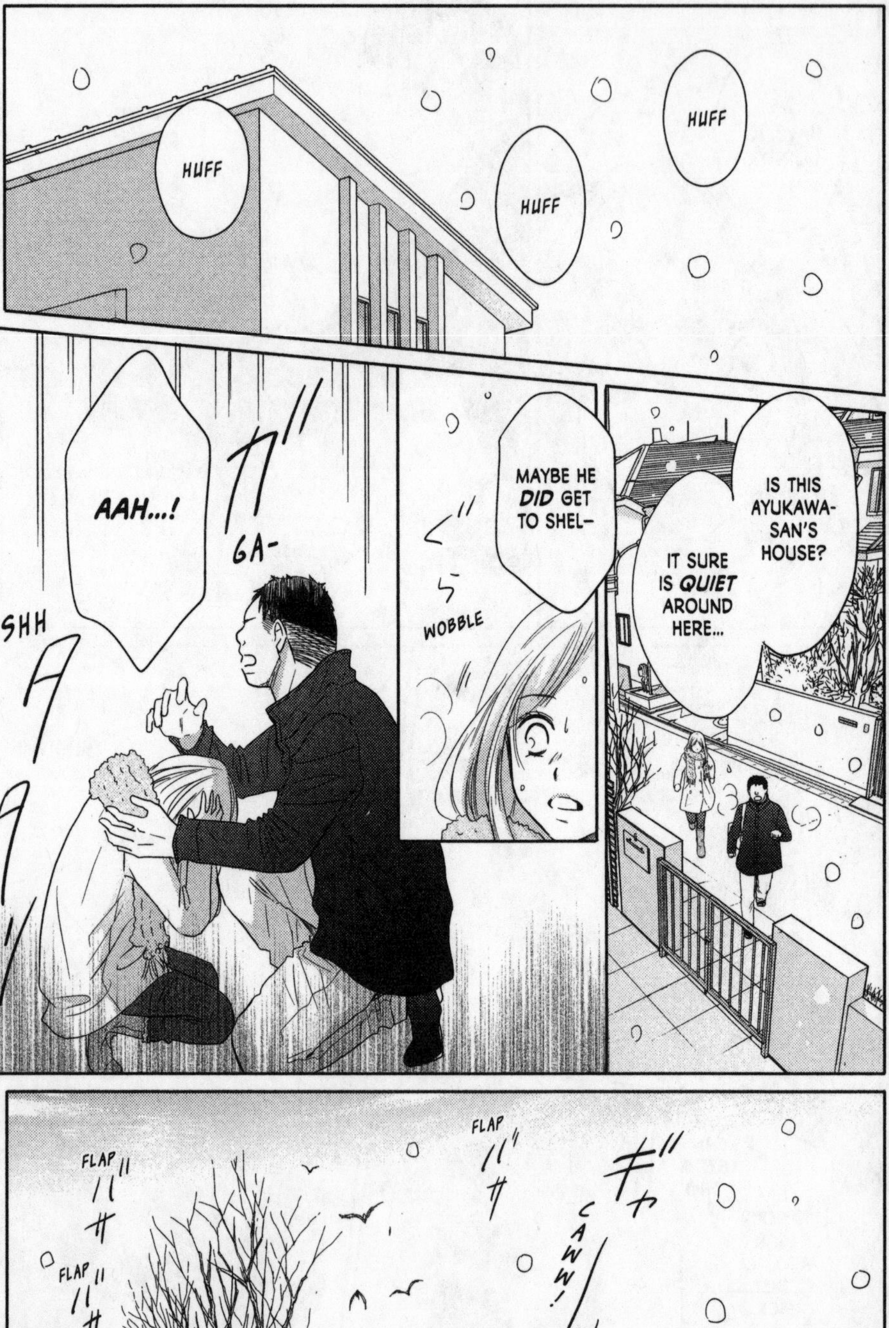
HUFF
HUFF
HUFF
IS THIS AYUKAWA-SAN'S HOUSE?
IT SURE IS *QUIET* AROUND HERE...
MAYBE HE *DID* GET TO SHEL–
WOBBLE
AAH...!
GA-
GSHH
CAWW!
FLAP
FLAP
FLAP

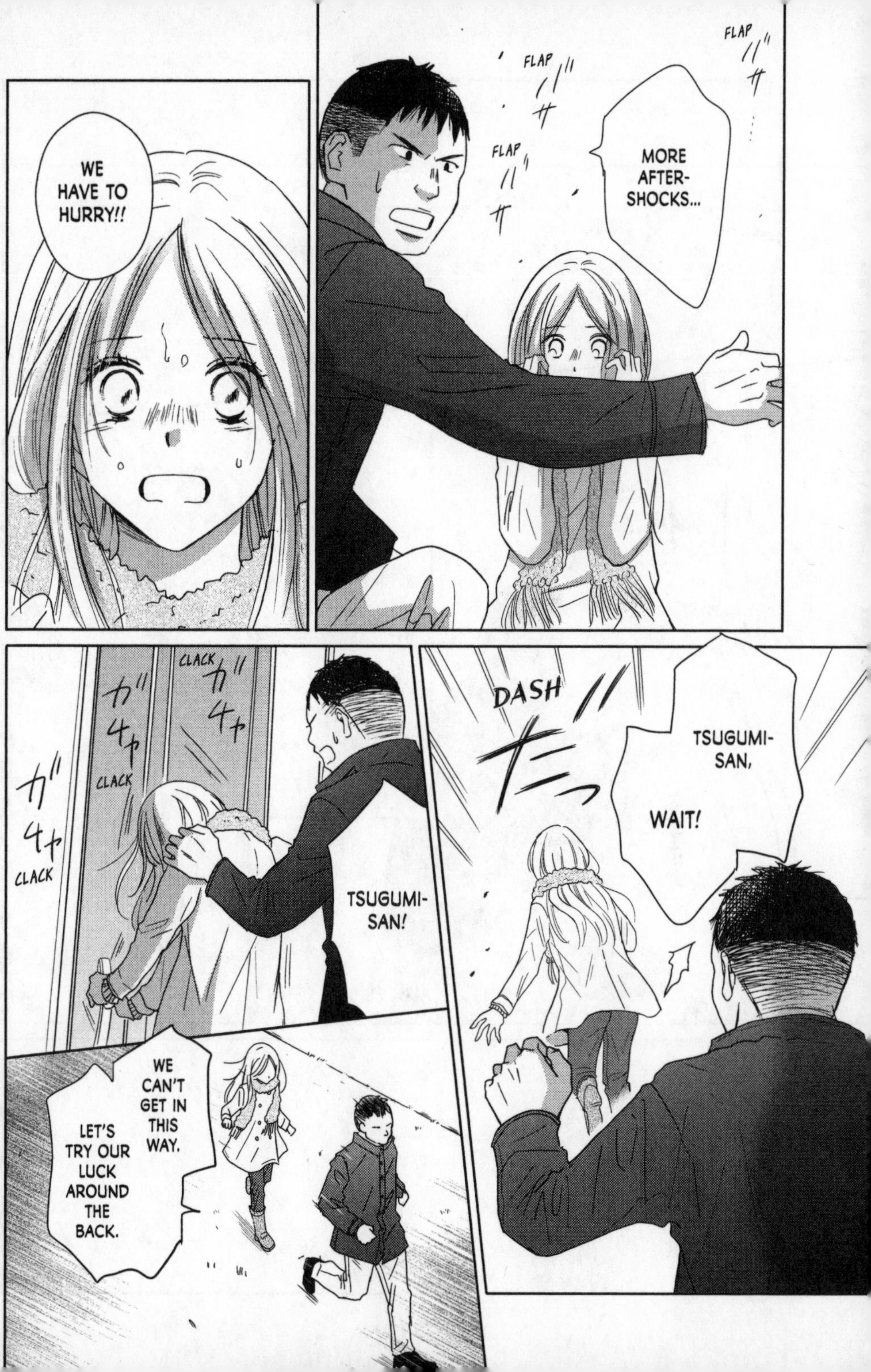
FLAP
FLAP
FLAP
MORE AFTER-SHOCKS...
WE HAVE TO HURRY!!
DASH
TSUGUMI-SAN,
WAIT!
CLACK
CLACK
CLACK
TSUGUMI-SAN!
WE CAN'T GET IN THIS WAY.
LET'S TRY OUR LUCK AROUND THE BACK.

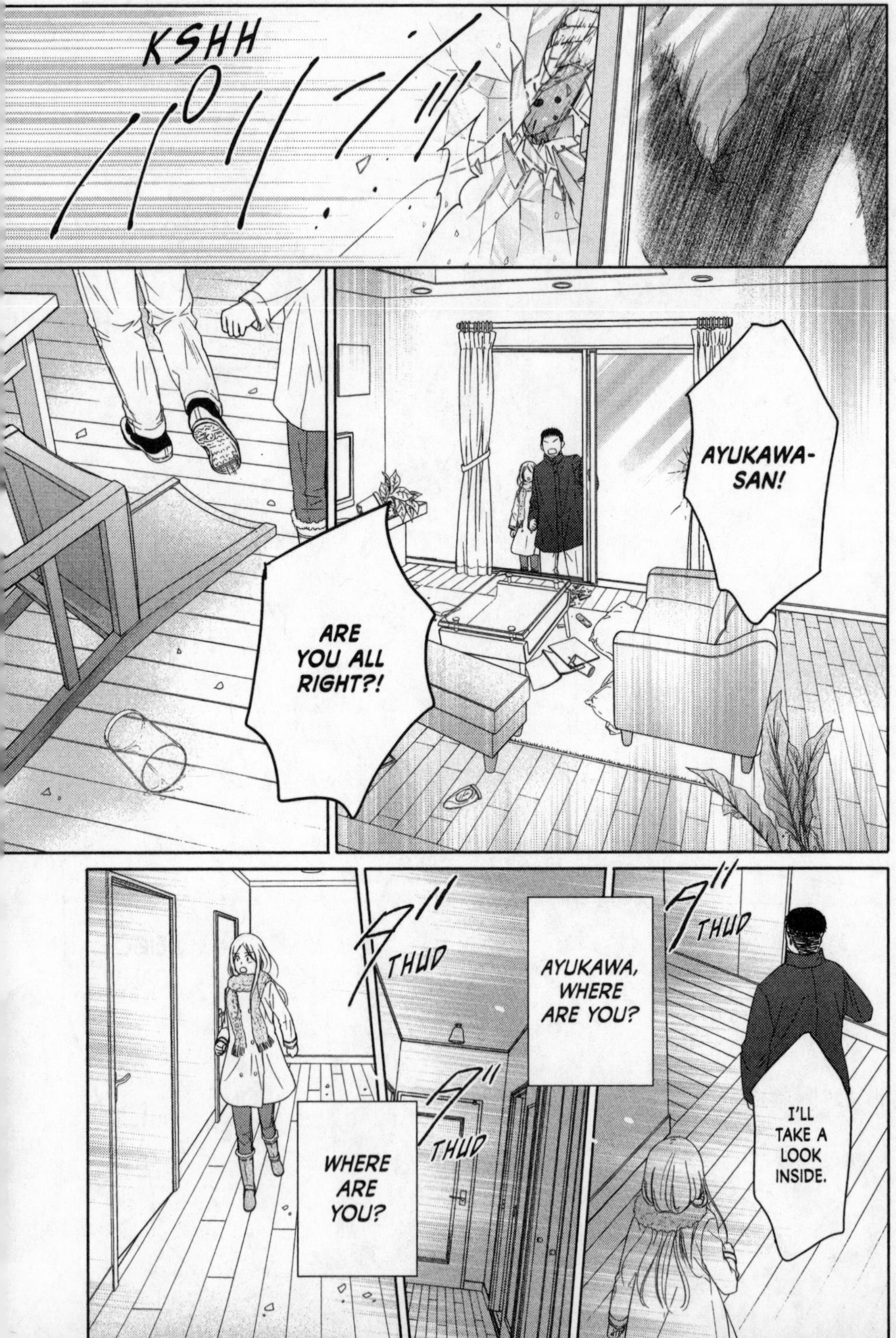
KSHH
AYUKAWA-SAN!
ARE YOU ALL RIGHT?!
THUD
I'LL TAKE A LOOK INSIDE.
AYUKAWA, WHERE ARE YOU?
THUD
WHERE ARE YOU?
THUD

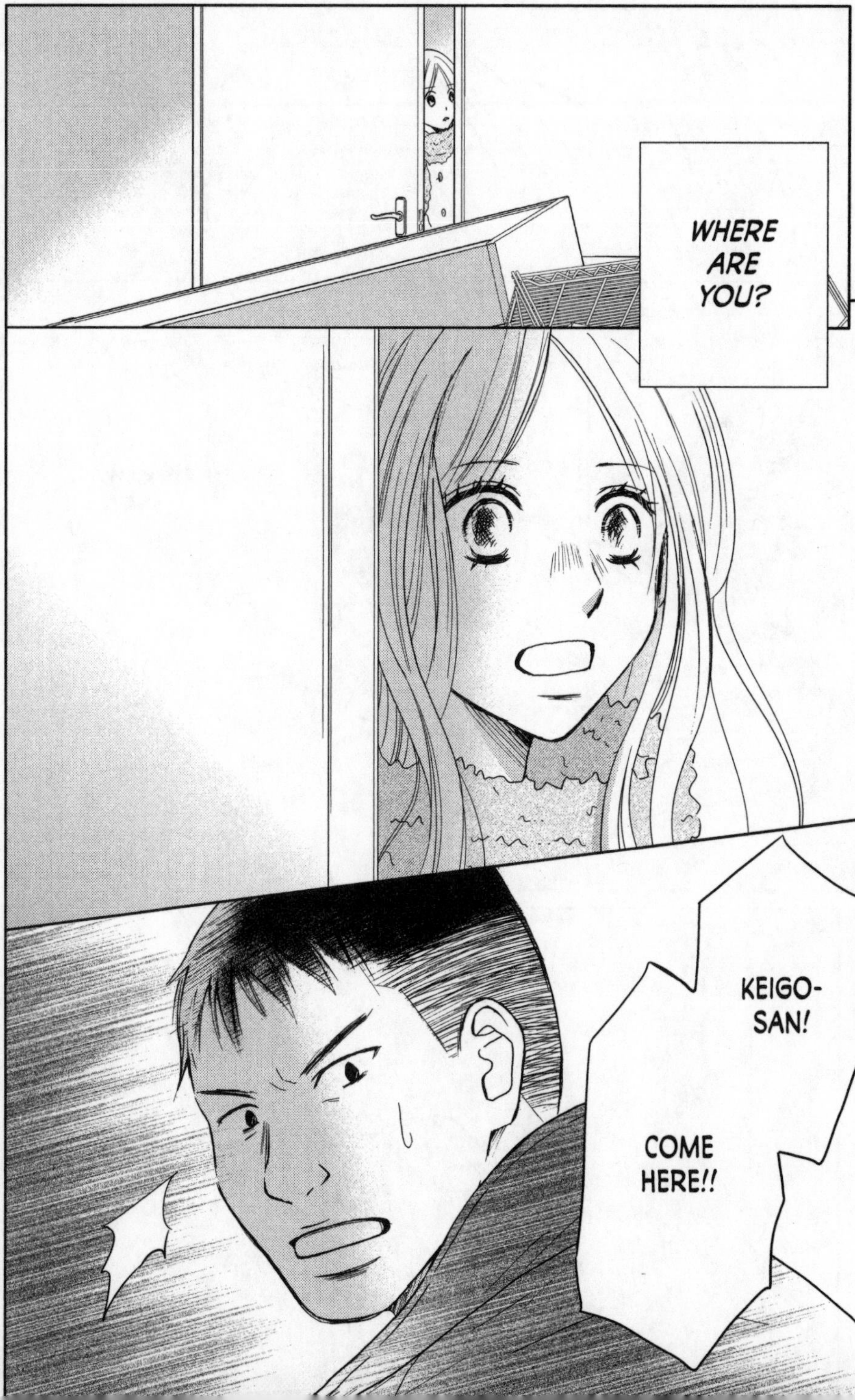
WHERE ARE YOU?
KEIGO-SAN!
COME HERE!!

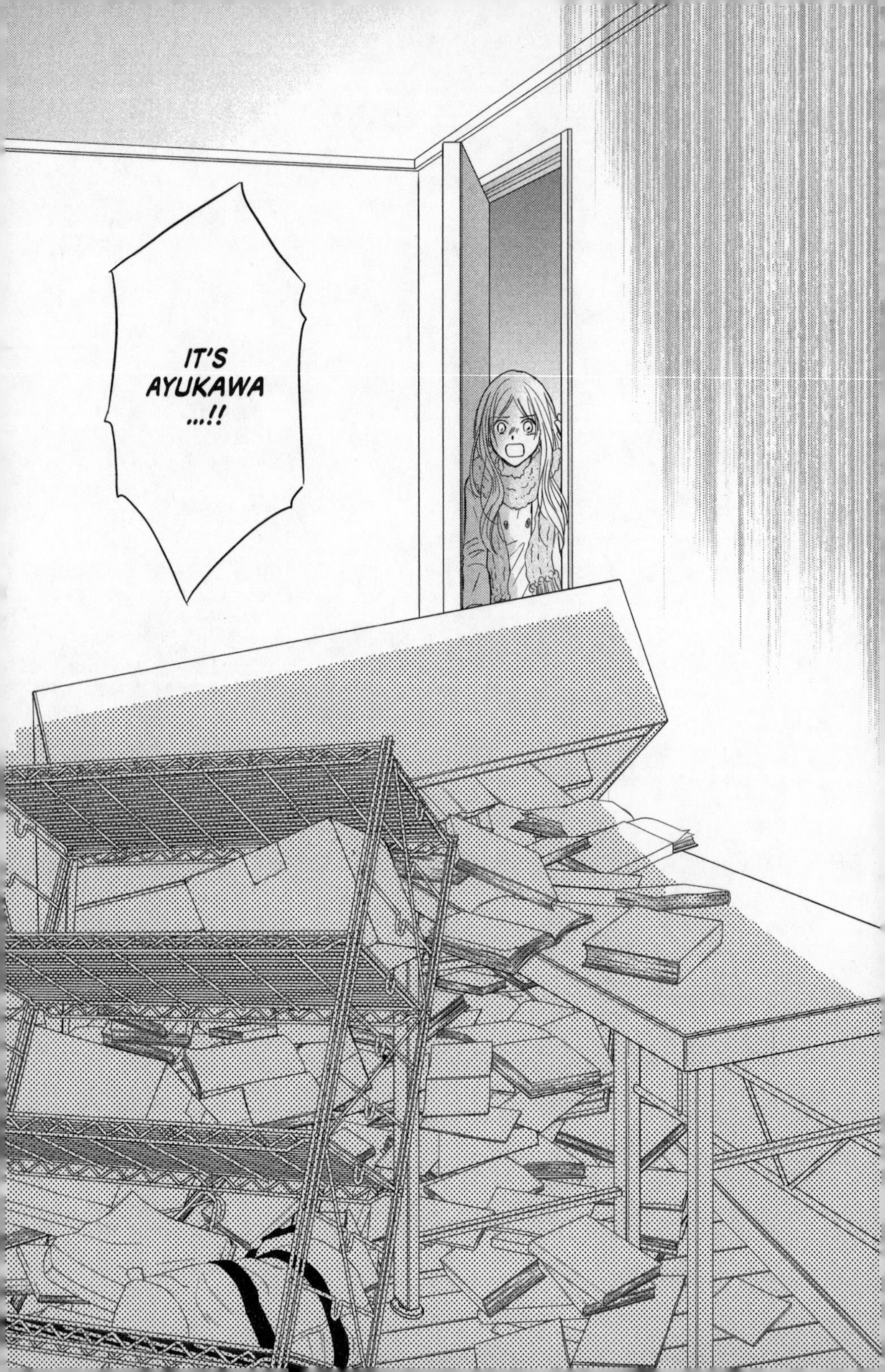
IT'S AYUKAWA ...!!

PERFECT WORLD

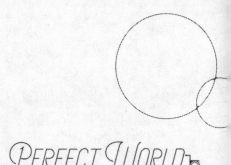

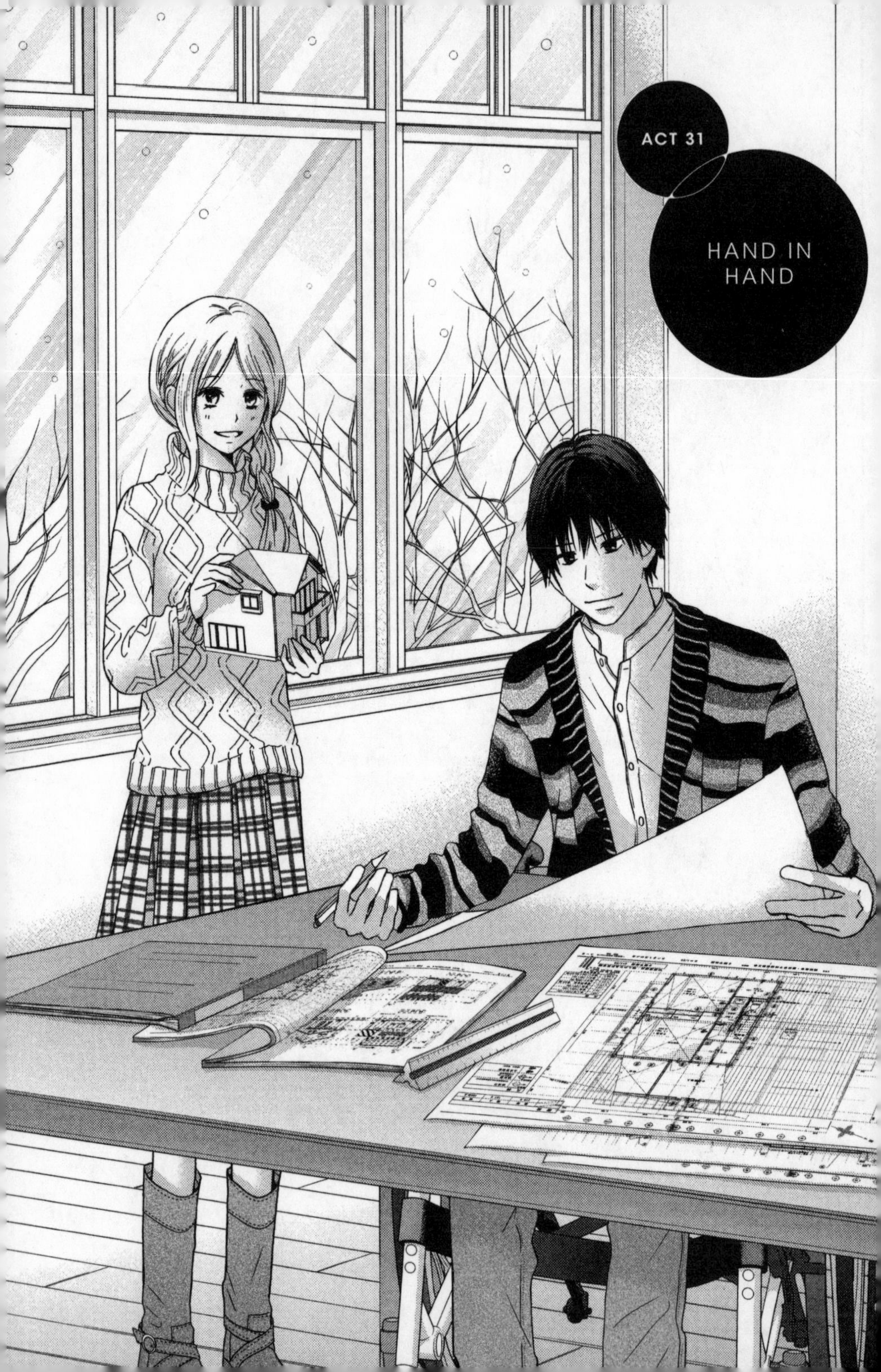
ACT 31
HAND IN HAND

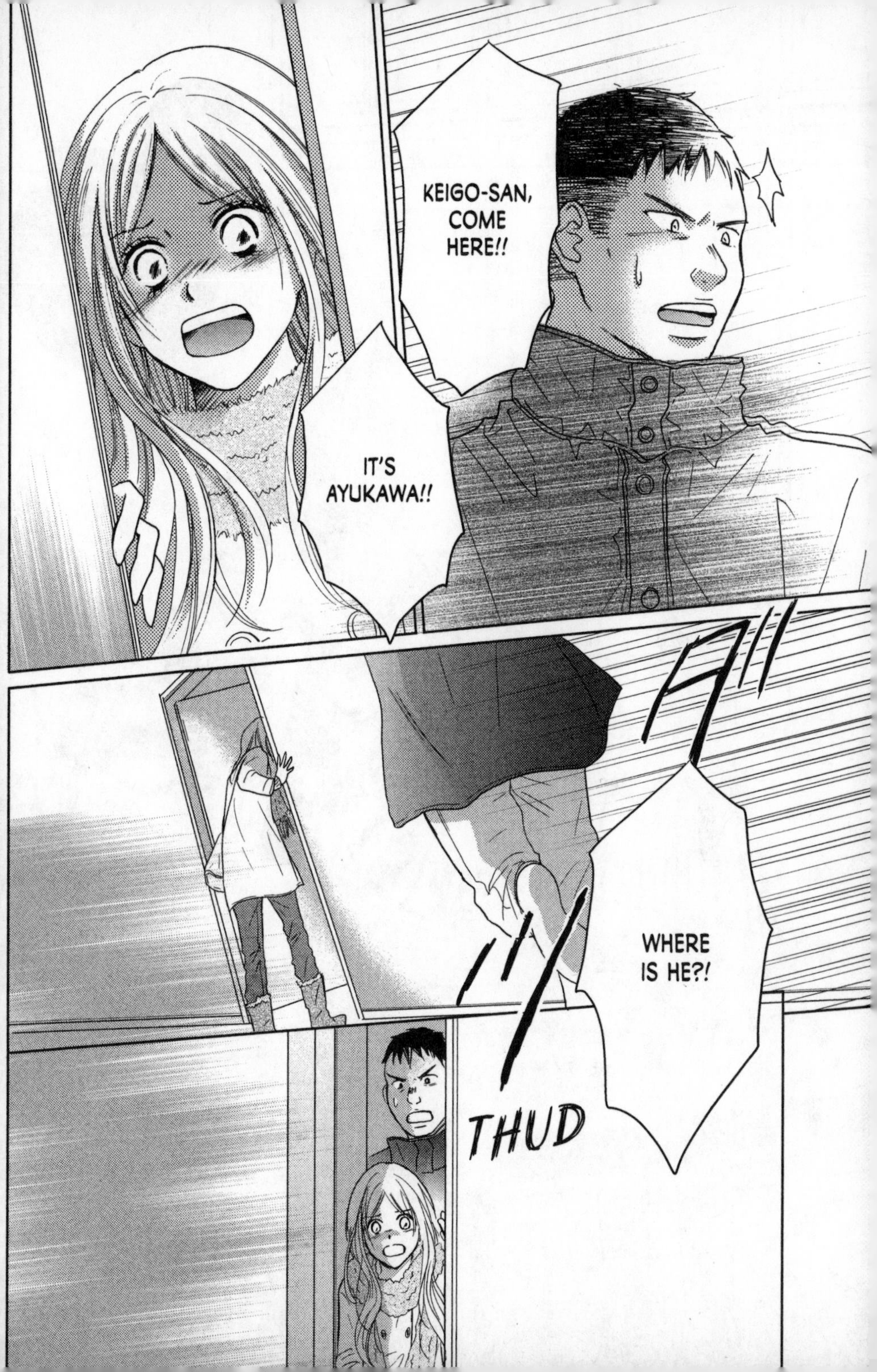
KEIGO-SAN, COME HERE!!
IT'S AYUKAWA!!
WHERE IS HE?!
THUD

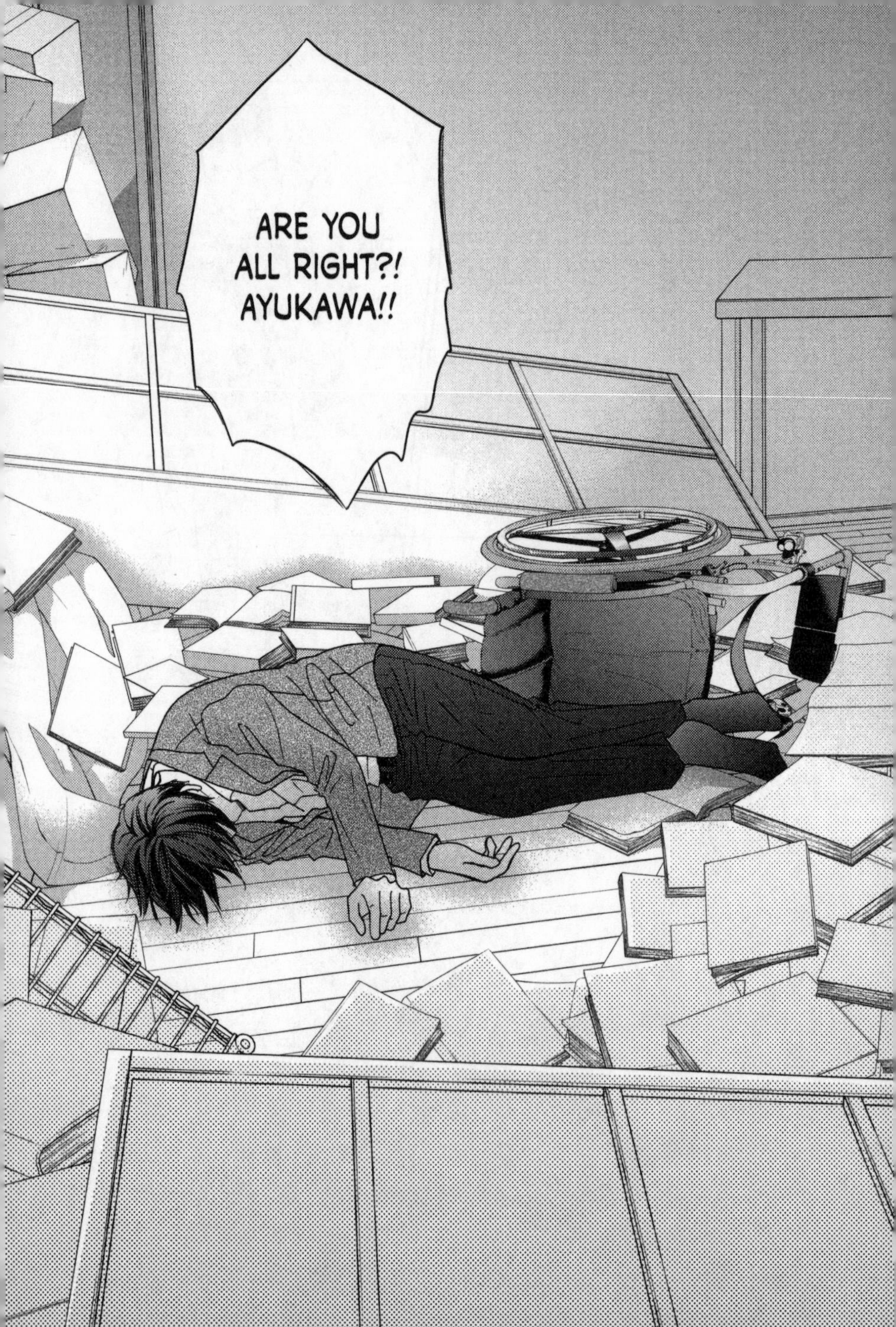
ARE YOU ALL RIGHT?! AYUKAWA!!

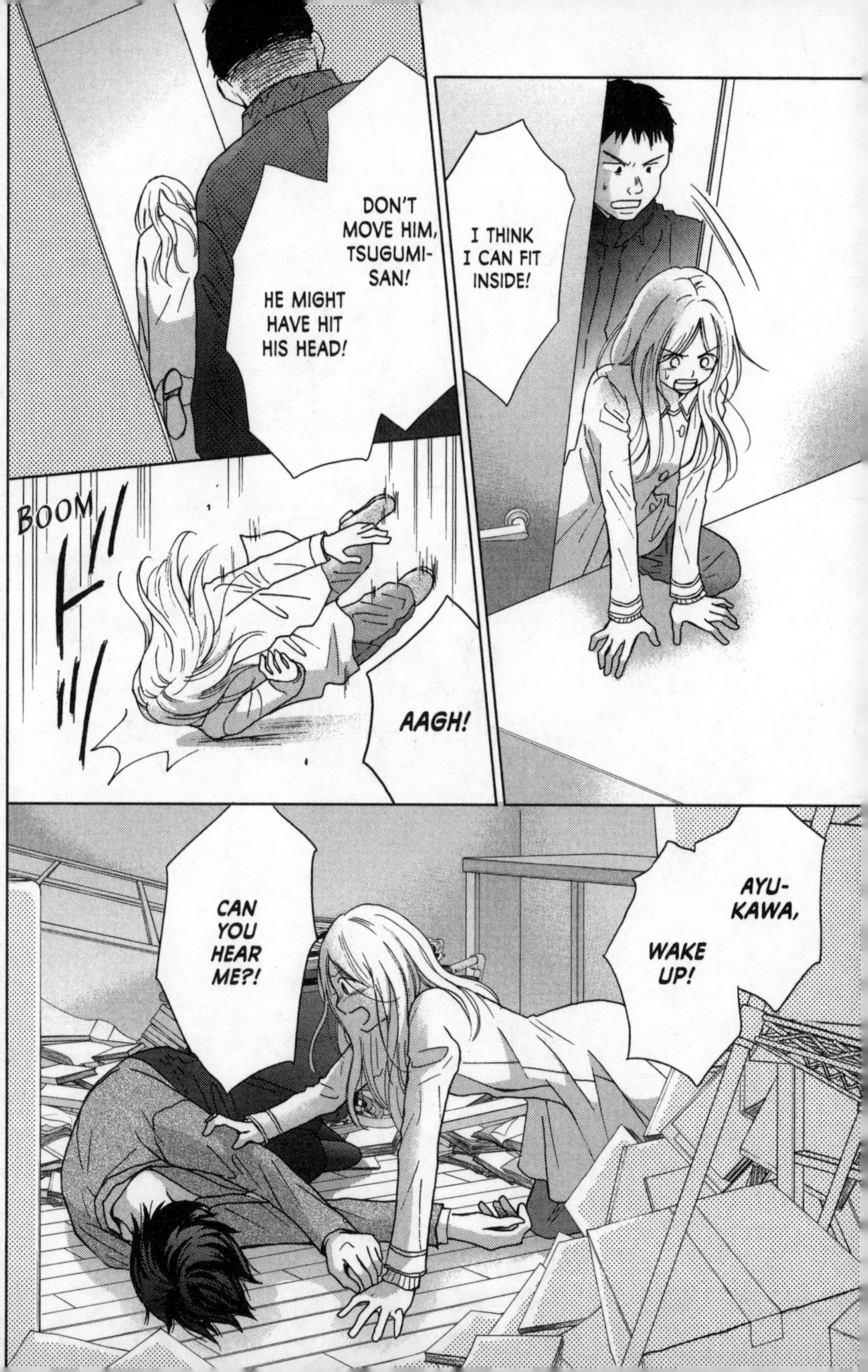
I THINK I CAN FIT INSIDE!
DON'T MOVE HIM, TSUGUMI-SAN!
HE MIGHT HAVE HIT HIS HEAD!
BOOM
AAGH!
AYU-KAWA,
WAKE UP!
CAN YOU HEAR ME?!

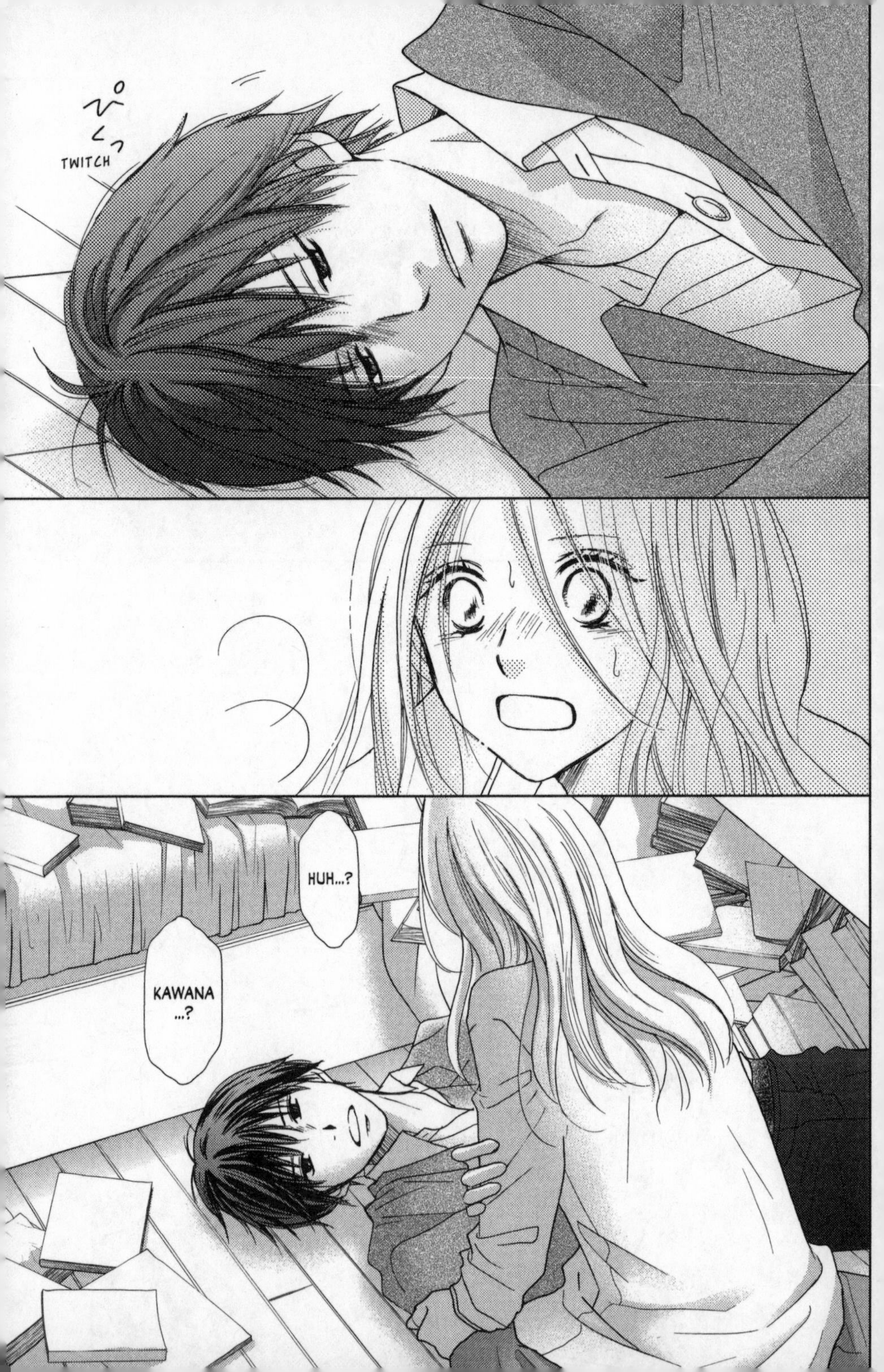
ぴくっ
TWITCH
HUH...?
KAWANA ...?

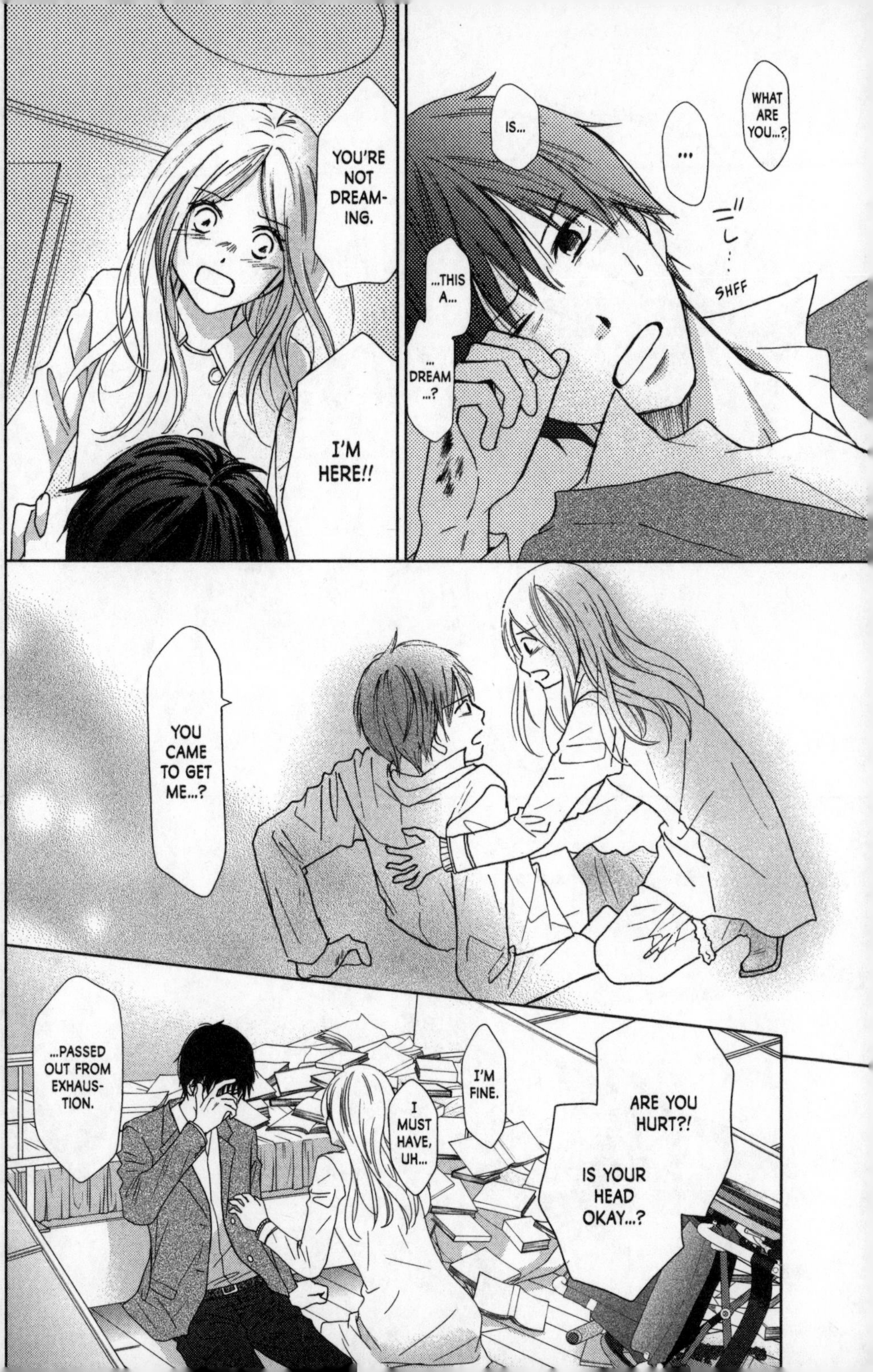
WHAT ARE YOU...?
...
IS...
...THIS A...
...DREAM...?
SHFF
YOU'RE NOT DREAM-ING.
I'M HERE!!
YOU CAME TO GET ME...?
ARE YOU HURT?!
IS YOUR HEAD OKAY...?
I'M FINE.
I MUST HAVE, UH...
...PASSED OUT FROM EXHAUS-TION.

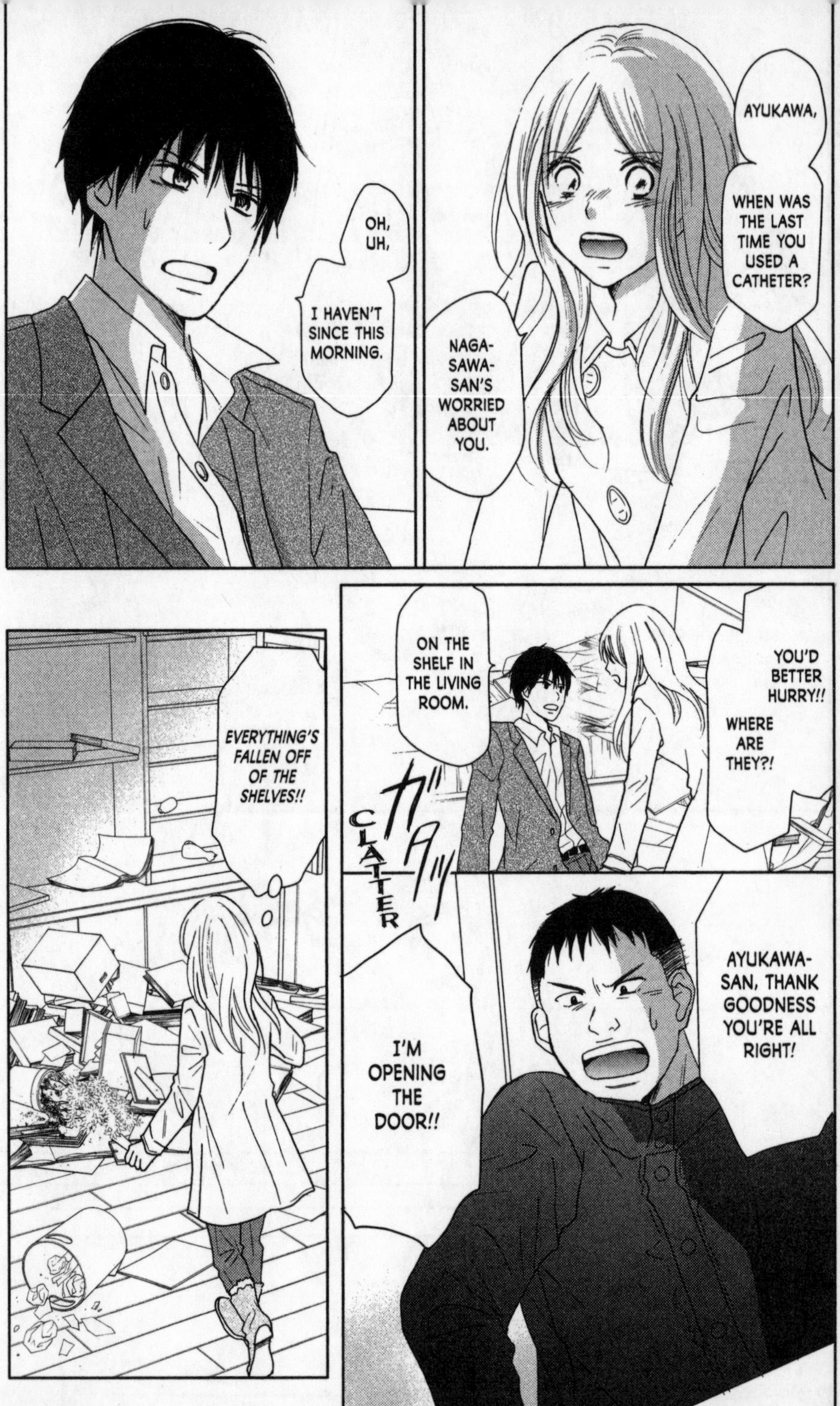
AYUKAWA,
WHEN WAS THE LAST TIME YOU USED A CATHETER?
NAGA-SAWA-SAN'S WORRIED ABOUT YOU.
OH, UH,
I HAVEN'T SINCE THIS MORNING.
YOU'D BETTER HURRY!!
WHERE ARE THEY?!
ON THE SHELF IN THE LIVING ROOM.
CLATTER
AYUKAWA-SAN, THANK GOODNESS YOU'RE ALL RIGHT!
I'M OPENING THE DOOR!!
EVERYTHING'S FALLEN OFF OF THE SHELVES!!

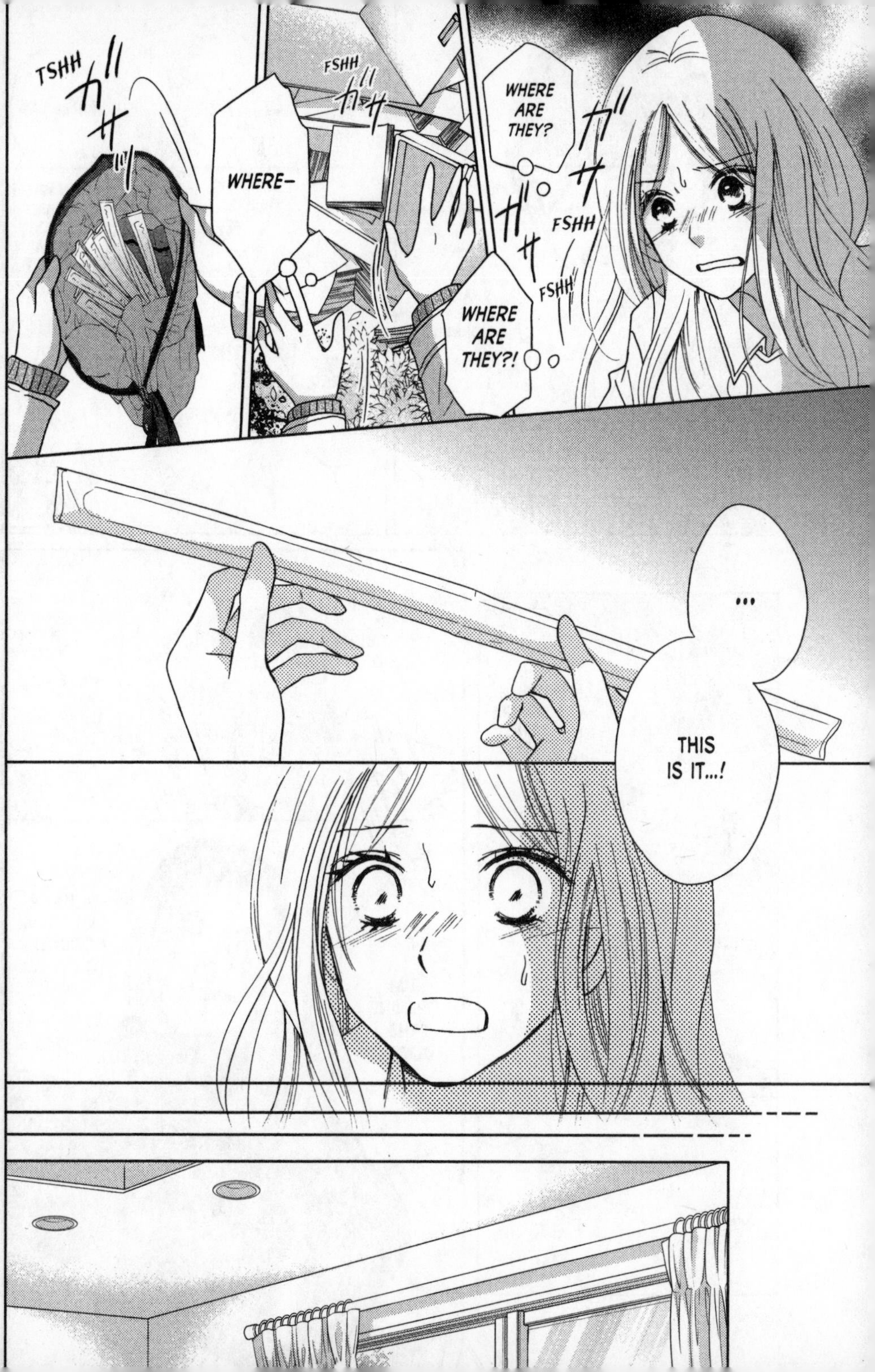
WHERE ARE THEY?
FSHH
FSHH
WHERE ARE THEY?!
WHERE–
FSHH
TSHH
...
THIS IS IT...!

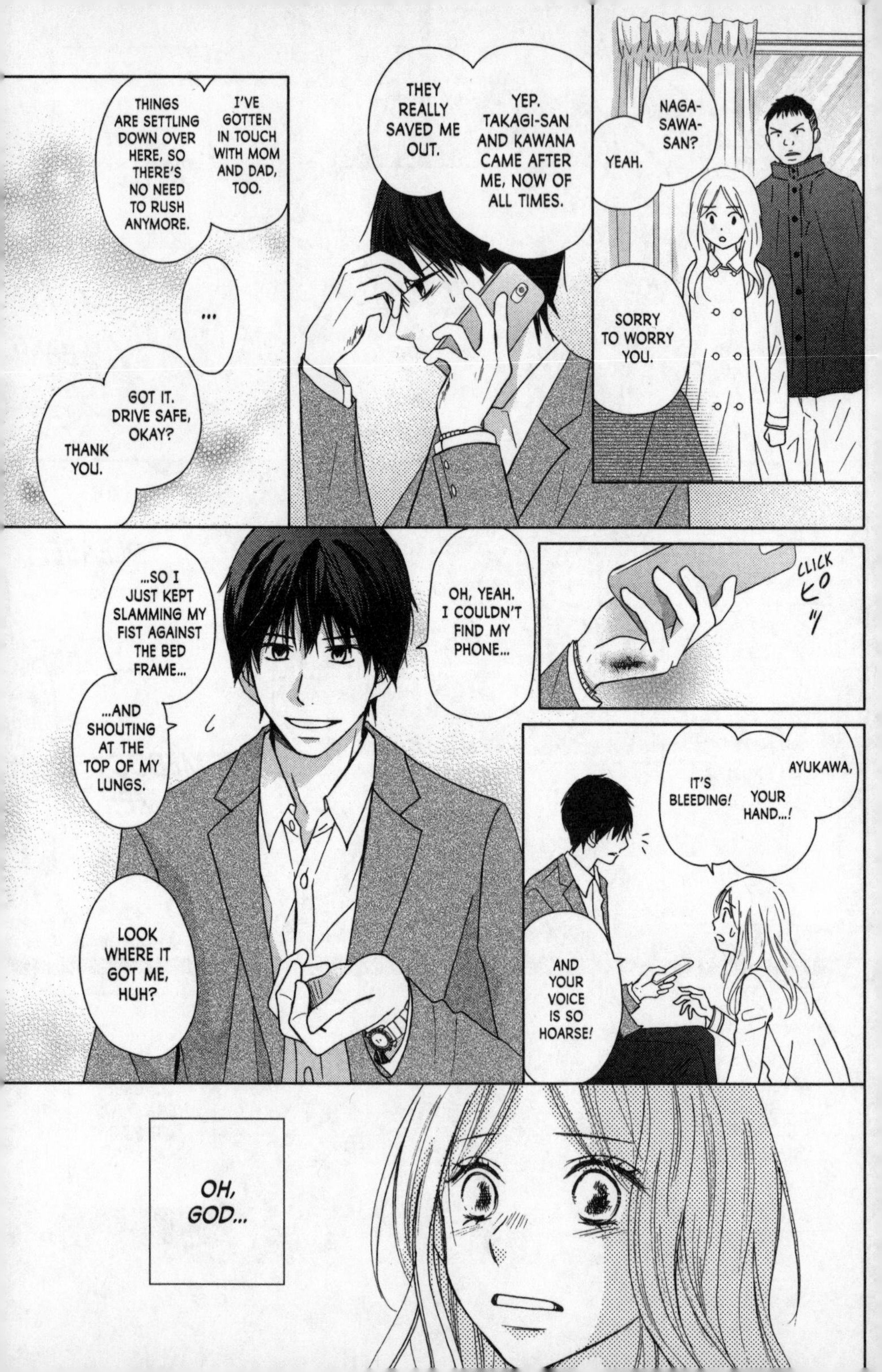
NAGA-SAWA-SAN?
YEAH.
SORRY TO WORRY YOU.
YEP. TAKAGI-SAN AND KAWANA CAME AFTER ME, NOW OF ALL TIMES.
THEY REALLY SAVED ME OUT.
I'VE GOTTEN IN TOUCH WITH MOM AND DAD, TOO.
THINGS ARE SETTLING DOWN OVER HERE, SO THERE'S NO NEED TO RUSH ANYMORE.
...
GOT IT. DRIVE SAFE, OKAY?
THANK YOU.
CLICK
ピッ
AYUKAWA, YOUR HAND...!
IT'S BLEEDING!
AND YOUR VOICE IS SO HOARSE!
OH, YEAH. I COULDN'T FIND MY PHONE...
...SO I JUST KEPT SLAMMING MY FIST AGAINST THE BED FRAME...
...AND SHOUTING AT THE TOP OF MY LUNGS.
LOOK WHERE IT GOT ME, HUH?
OH, GOD...

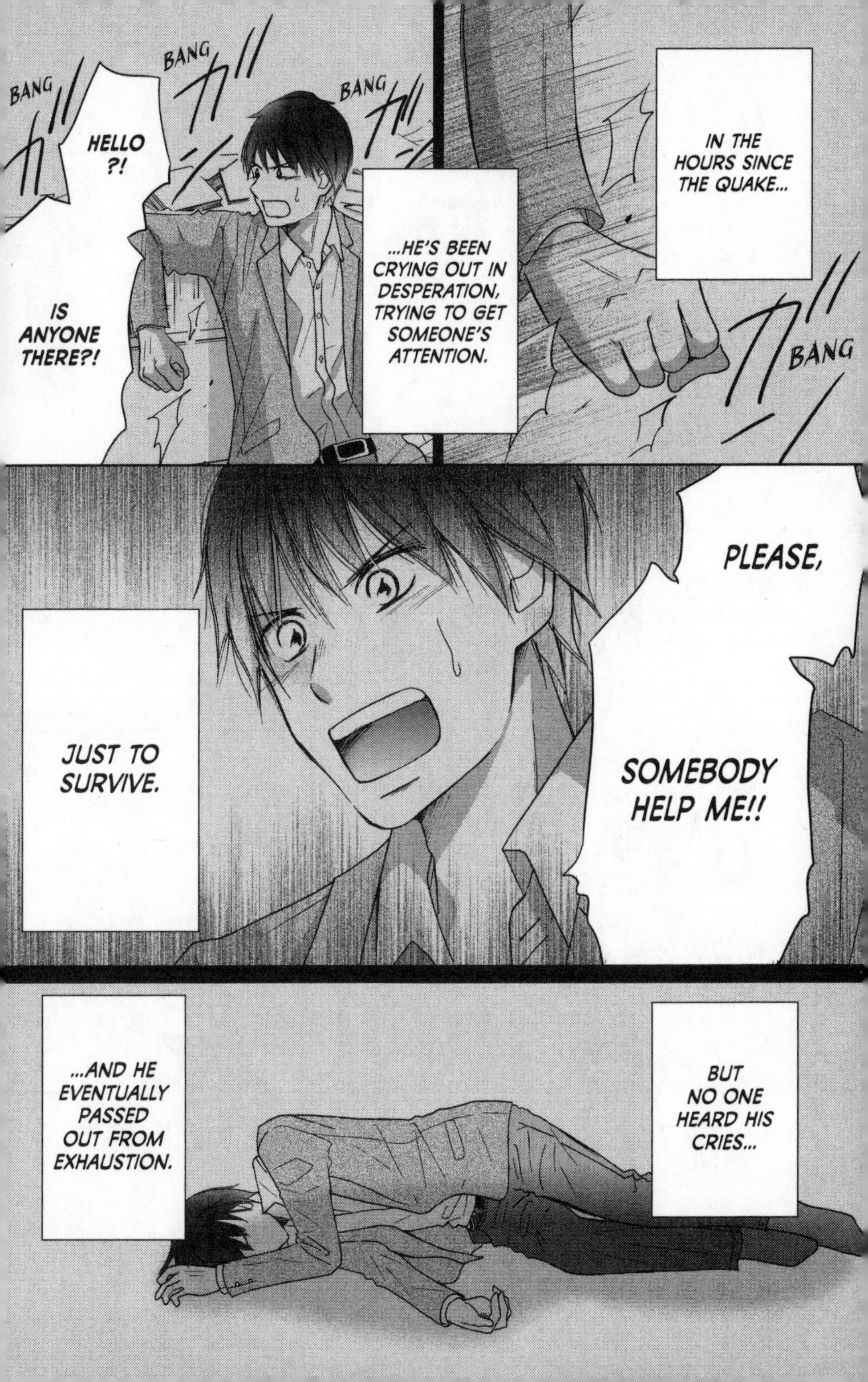
IN THE HOURS SINCE THE QUAKE...
ガ BANG
...HE'S BEEN CRYING OUT IN DESPERATION, TRYING TO GET SOMEONE'S ATTENTION.
ガ BANG
ガ BANG
ガ BANG
HELLO ?!
IS ANYONE THERE?!
PLEASE,
SOMEBODY HELP ME!!
JUST TO SURVIVE.
BUT NO ONE HEARD HIS CRIES...
...AND HE EVENTUALLY PASSED OUT FROM EXHAUSTION.

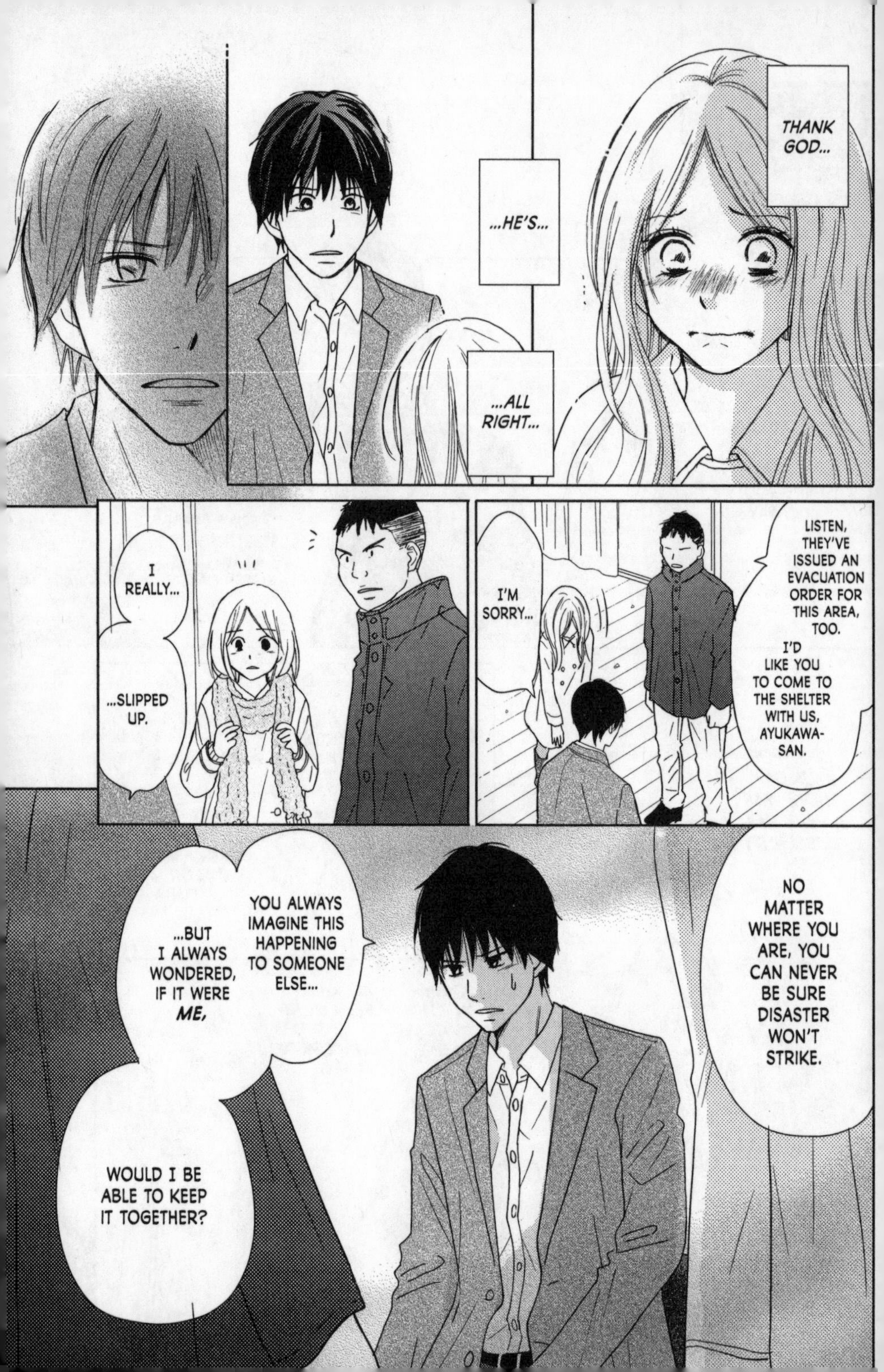
THANK GOD...
...HE'S...
...ALL RIGHT...
LISTEN, THEY'VE ISSUED AN EVACUATION ORDER FOR THIS AREA, TOO.
I'D LIKE YOU TO COME TO THE SHELTER WITH US, AYUKAWA-SAN.
I'M SORRY...
I REALLY...
...SLIPPED UP.
NO MATTER WHERE YOU ARE, YOU CAN NEVER BE SURE DISASTER WON'T STRIKE.
YOU ALWAYS IMAGINE THIS HAPPENING TO SOMEONE ELSE...
...BUT I ALWAYS WONDERED, IF IT WERE *ME,*
WOULD I BE ABLE TO KEEP IT TOGETHER?

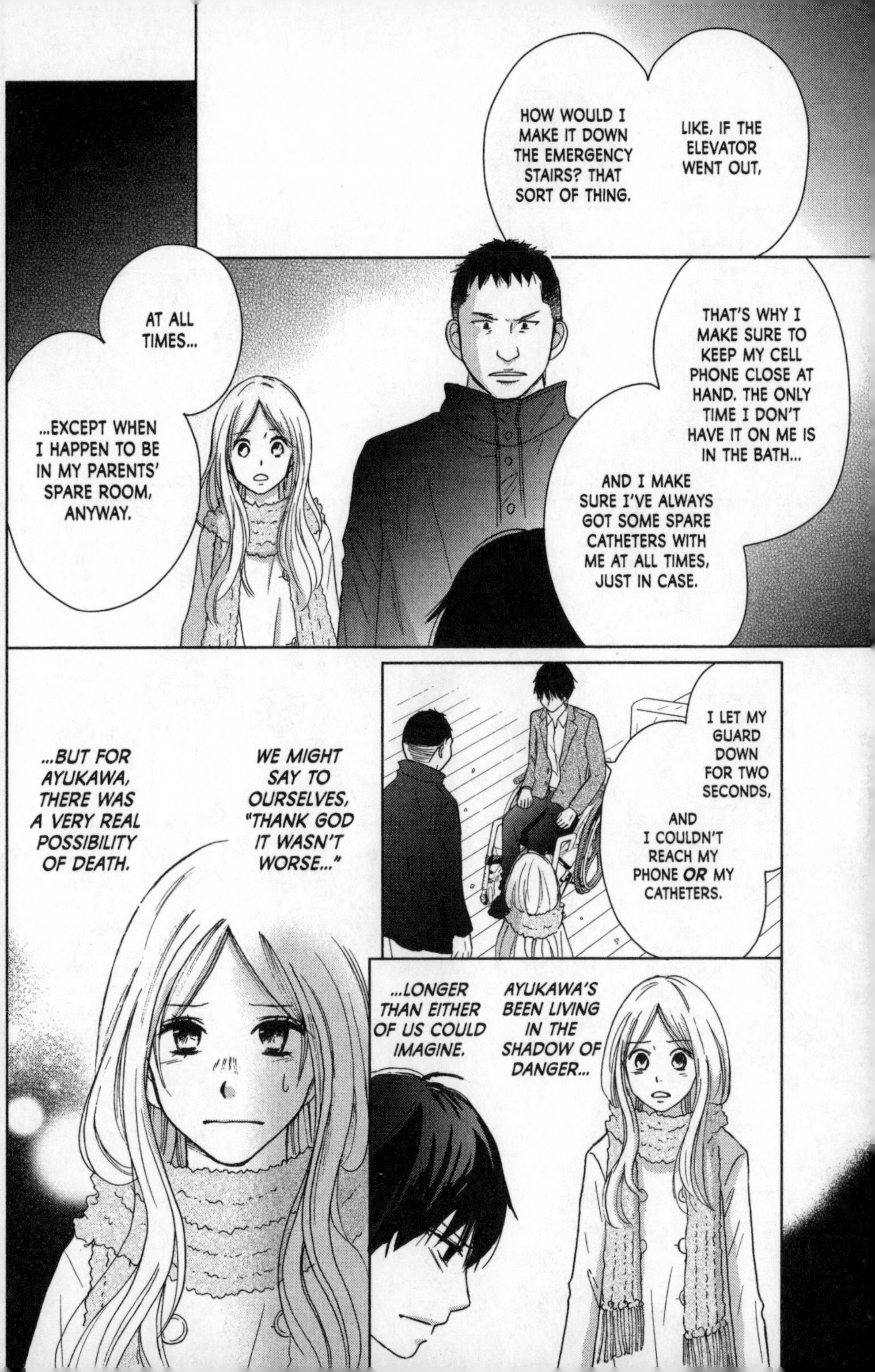
LIKE, IF THE ELEVATOR WENT OUT,
HOW WOULD I MAKE IT DOWN THE EMERGENCY STAIRS? THAT SORT OF THING.
THAT'S WHY I MAKE SURE TO KEEP MY CELL PHONE CLOSE AT HAND. THE ONLY TIME I DON'T HAVE IT ON ME IS IN THE BATH...
AND I MAKE SURE I'VE ALWAYS GOT SOME SPARE CATHETERS WITH ME AT ALL TIMES, JUST IN CASE.
AT ALL TIMES...
...EXCEPT WHEN I HAPPEN TO BE IN MY PARENTS' SPARE ROOM, ANYWAY.
I LET MY GUARD DOWN FOR TWO SECONDS,
AND I COULDN'T REACH MY PHONE *OR* MY CATHETERS.
AYUKAWA'S BEEN LIVING IN THE SHADOW OF DANGER...
...LONGER THAN EITHER OF US COULD IMAGINE.
WE MIGHT SAY TO OURSELVES, "THANK GOD IT WASN'T WORSE..."
...BUT FOR AYUKAWA, THERE WAS A VERY REAL POSSIBILITY OF DEATH.

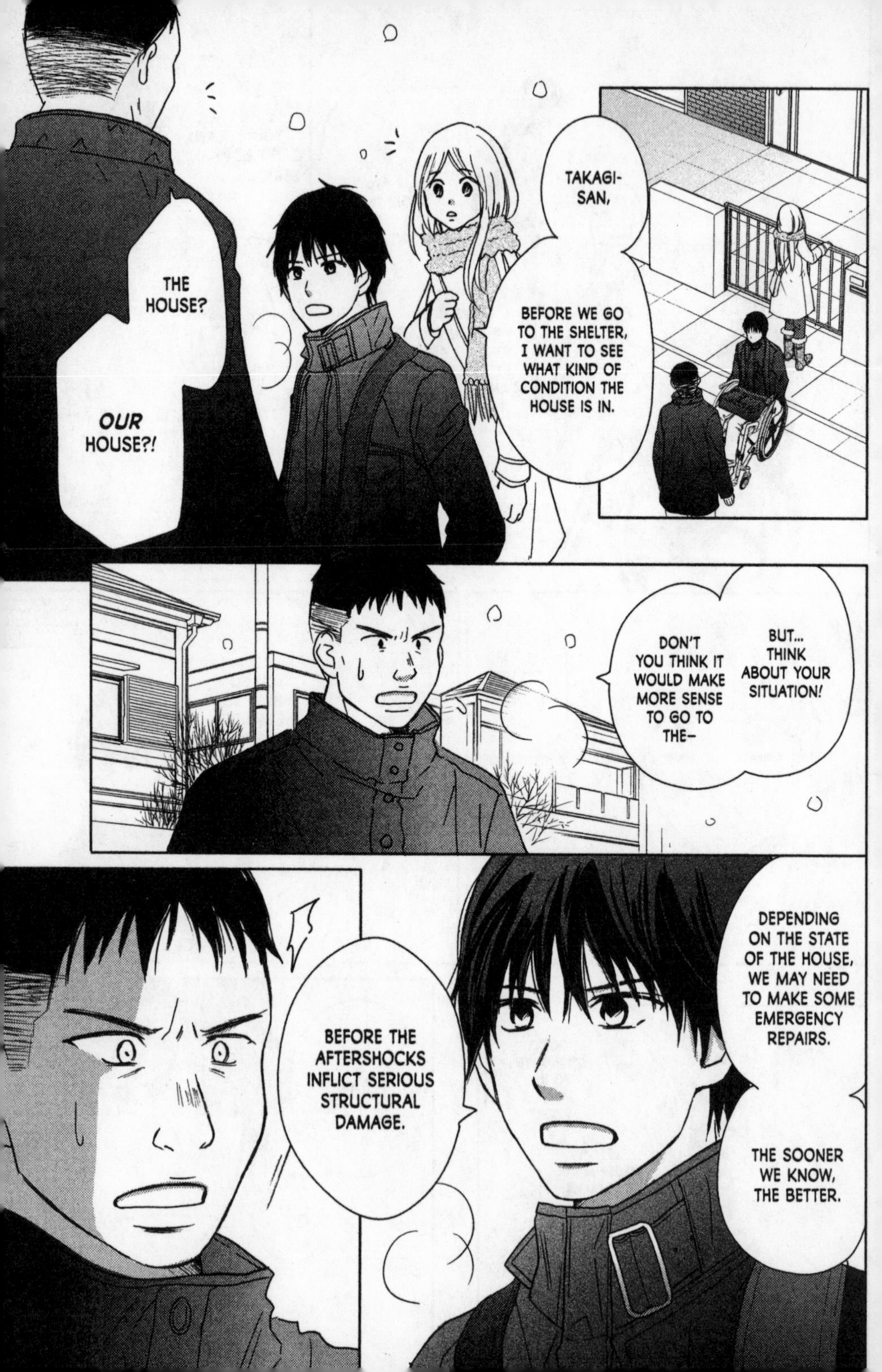
TAKAGI-SAN,
BEFORE WE GO TO THE SHELTER, I WANT TO SEE WHAT KIND OF CONDITION THE HOUSE IS IN.
THE HOUSE?
OUR HOUSE?!
BUT... THINK ABOUT YOUR SITUATION!
DON'T YOU THINK IT WOULD MAKE MORE SENSE TO GO TO THE–
DEPENDING ON THE STATE OF THE HOUSE, WE MAY NEED TO MAKE SOME EMERGENCY REPAIRS.
THE SOONER WE KNOW, THE BETTER.
BEFORE THE AFTERSHOCKS INFLICT SERIOUS STRUCTURAL DAMAGE.

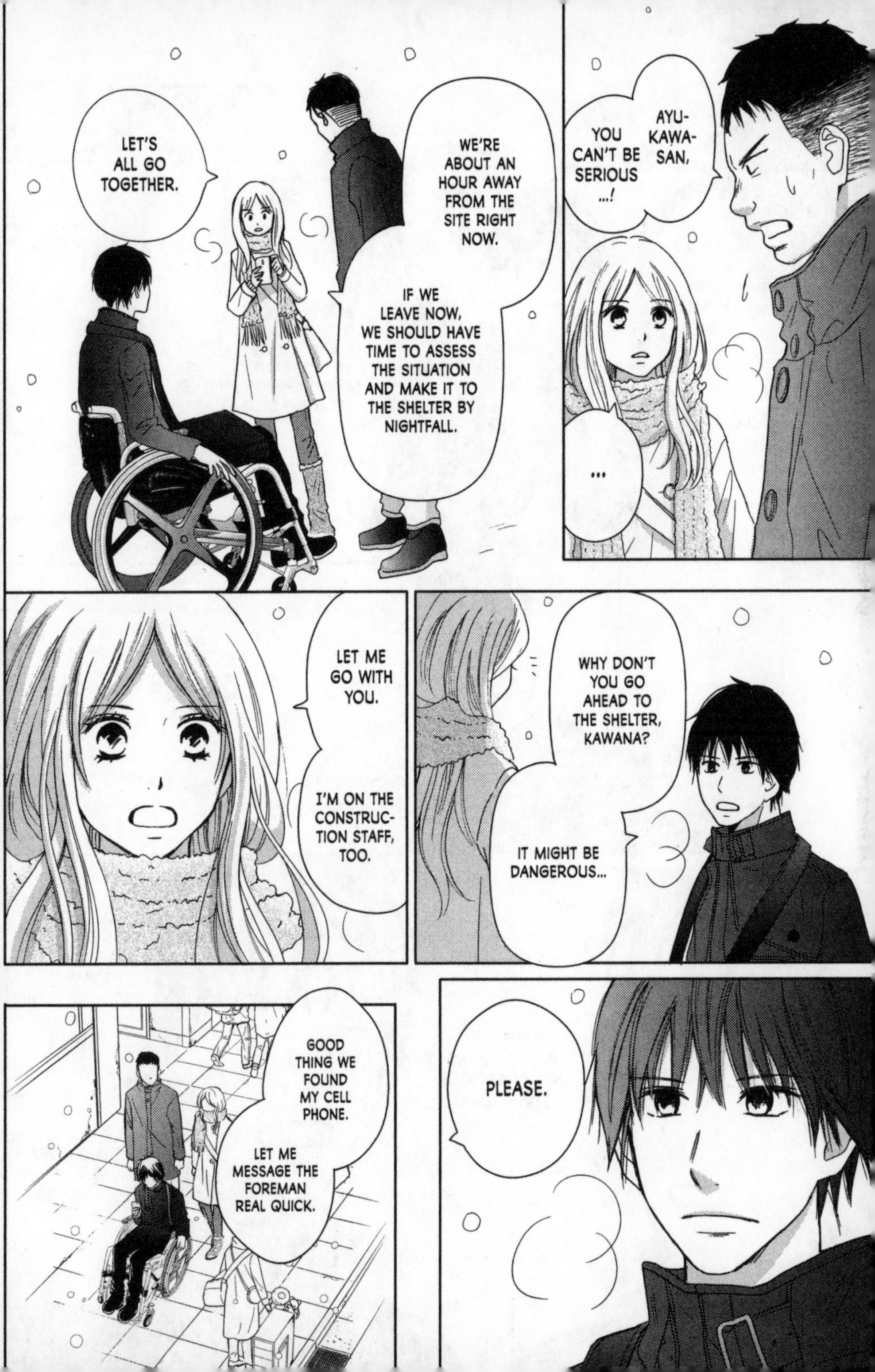
AYU-KAWA-SAN, YOU CAN'T BE SERIOUS ...!
...
WE'RE ABOUT AN HOUR AWAY FROM THE SITE RIGHT NOW.
IF WE LEAVE NOW, WE SHOULD HAVE TIME TO ASSESS THE SITUATION AND MAKE IT TO THE SHELTER BY NIGHTFALL.
LET'S ALL GO TOGETHER.
WHY DON'T YOU GO AHEAD TO THE SHELTER, KAWANA?
IT MIGHT BE DANGEROUS...
LET ME GO WITH YOU.
I'M ON THE CONSTRUC-TION STAFF, TOO.
PLEASE.
GOOD THING WE FOUND MY CELL PHONE.
LET ME MESSAGE THE FOREMAN REAL QUICK.

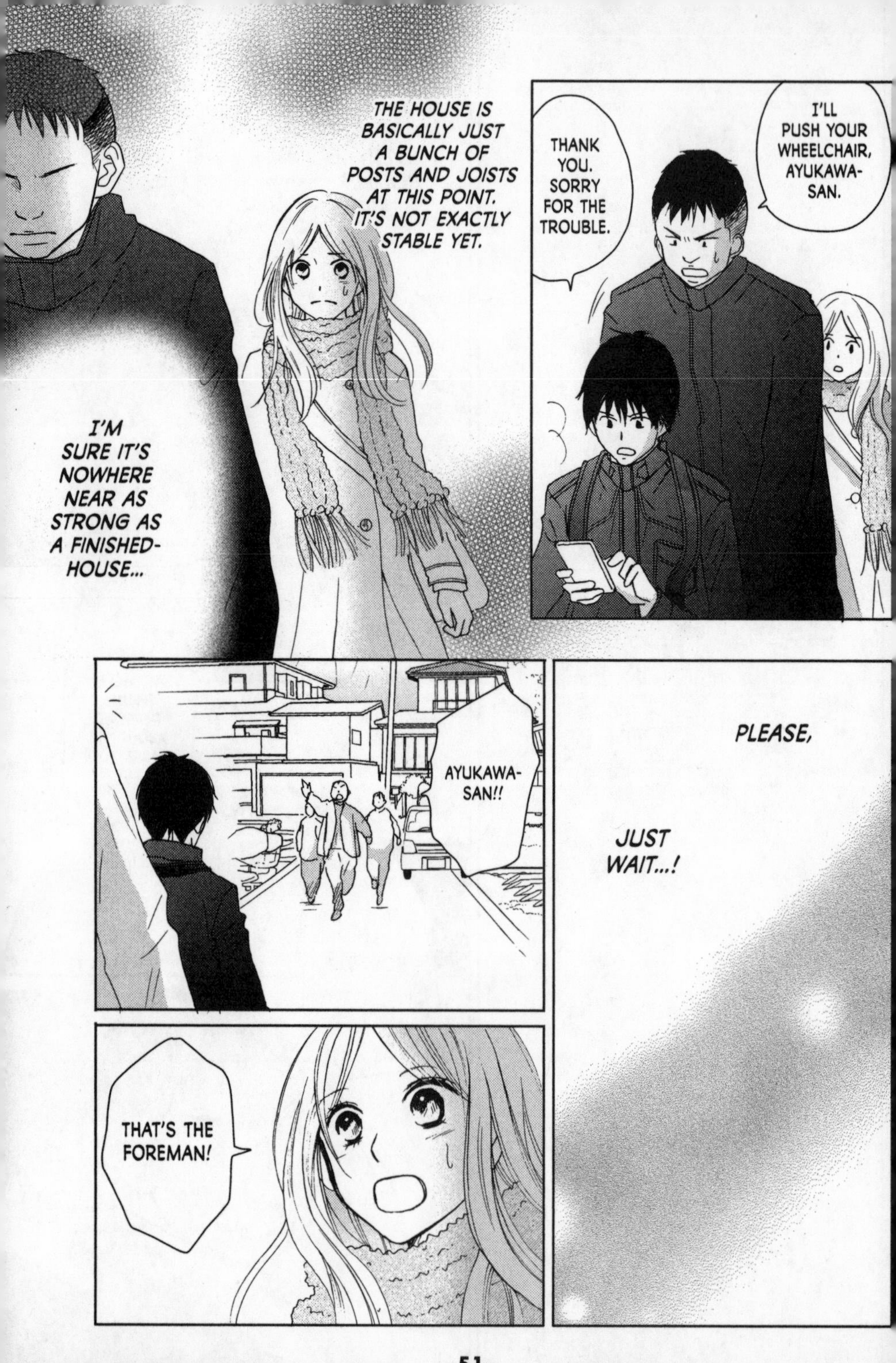
I'LL PUSH YOUR WHEELCHAIR, AYUKAWA-SAN.
THANK YOU. SORRY FOR THE TROUBLE.
THE HOUSE IS BASICALLY JUST A BUNCH OF POSTS AND JOISTS AT THIS POINT. IT'S NOT EXACTLY STABLE YET.
I'M SURE IT'S NOWHERE NEAR AS STRONG AS A FINISHED-HOUSE...
PLEASE,
JUST WAIT...!
AYUKAWA-SAN!!
THAT'S THE FOREMAN!

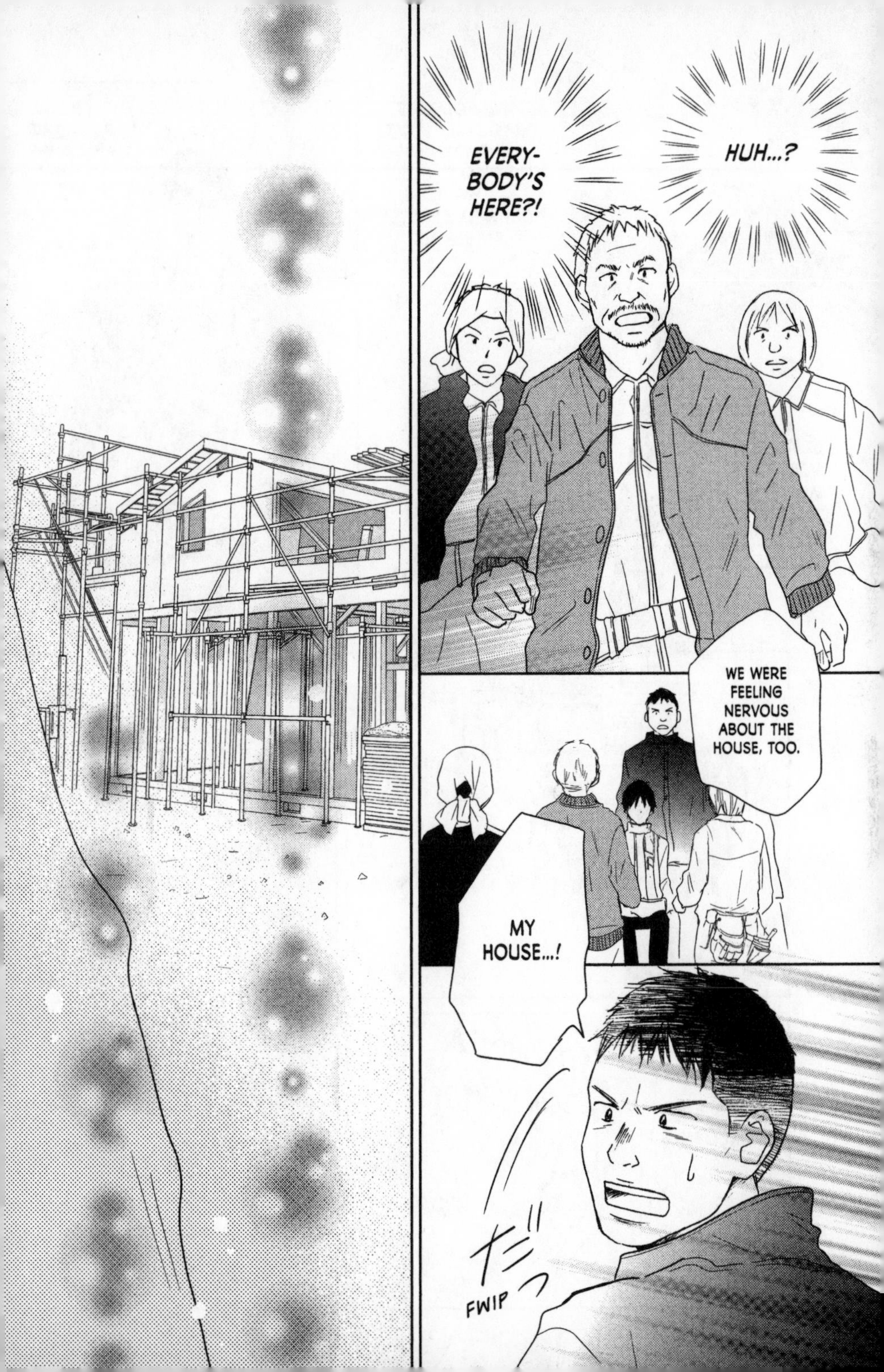
HUH...?
EVERY-BODY'S HERE?!
WE WERE FEELING NERVOUS ABOUT THE HOUSE, TOO.
MY HOUSE...!
FWIP

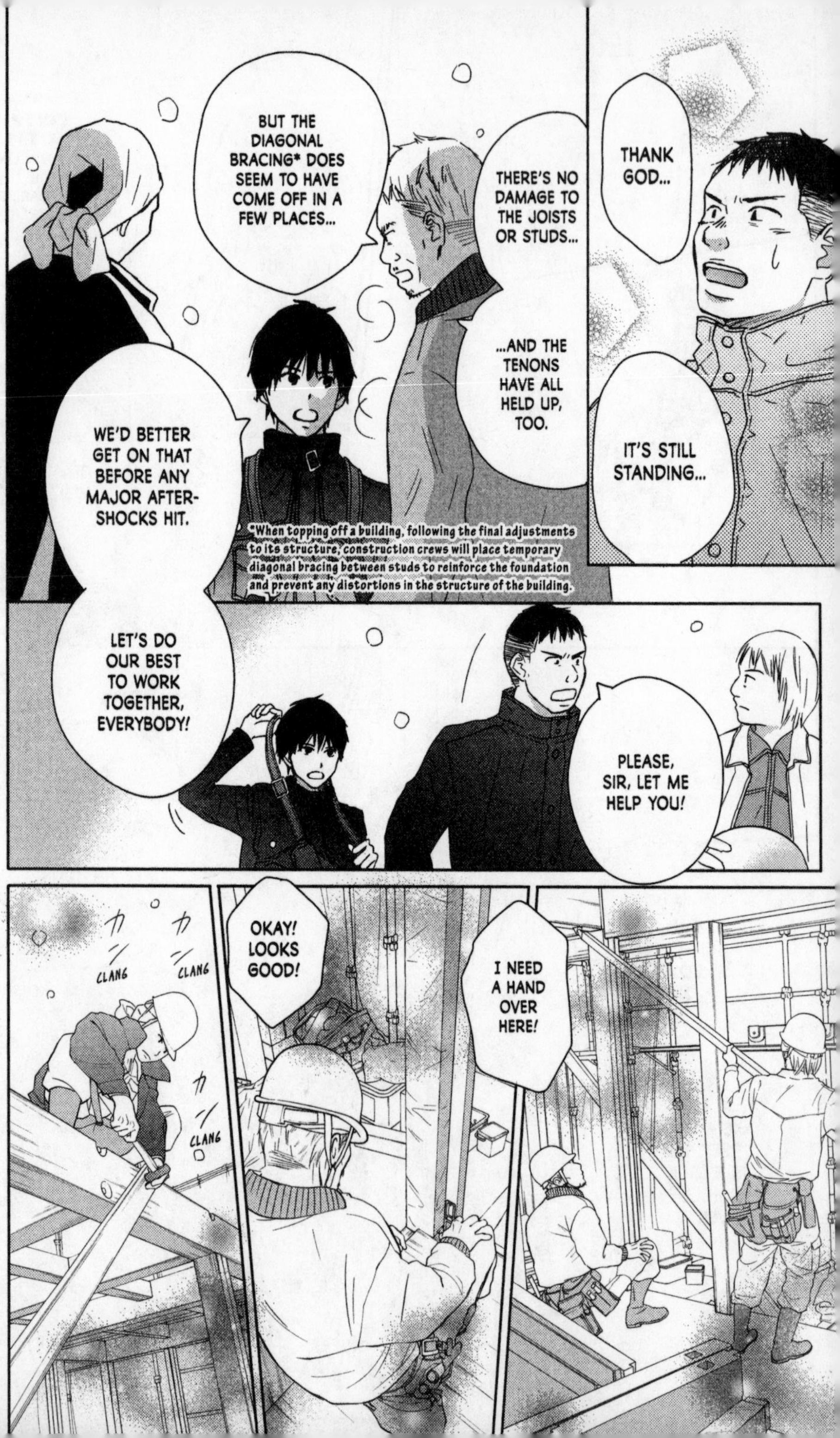
THANK GOD...
IT'S STILL STANDING...
THERE'S NO DAMAGE TO THE JOISTS OR STUDS...
BUT THE DIAGONAL BRACING* DOES SEEM TO HAVE COME OFF IN A FEW PLACES...
...AND THE TENONS HAVE ALL HELD UP, TOO.
WE'D BETTER GET ON THAT BEFORE ANY MAJOR AFTER-SHOCKS HIT.
*When topping off a building, following the final adjustments to its structure, construction crews will place temporary diagonal bracing between studs to reinforce the foundation and prevent any distortions in the structure of the building.
PLEASE, SIR, LET ME HELP YOU!
LET'S DO OUR BEST TO WORK TOGETHER, EVERYBODY!
I NEED A HAND OVER HERE!
OKAY! LOOKS GOOD!
カン CLANG
カン CLANG
カン CLANG

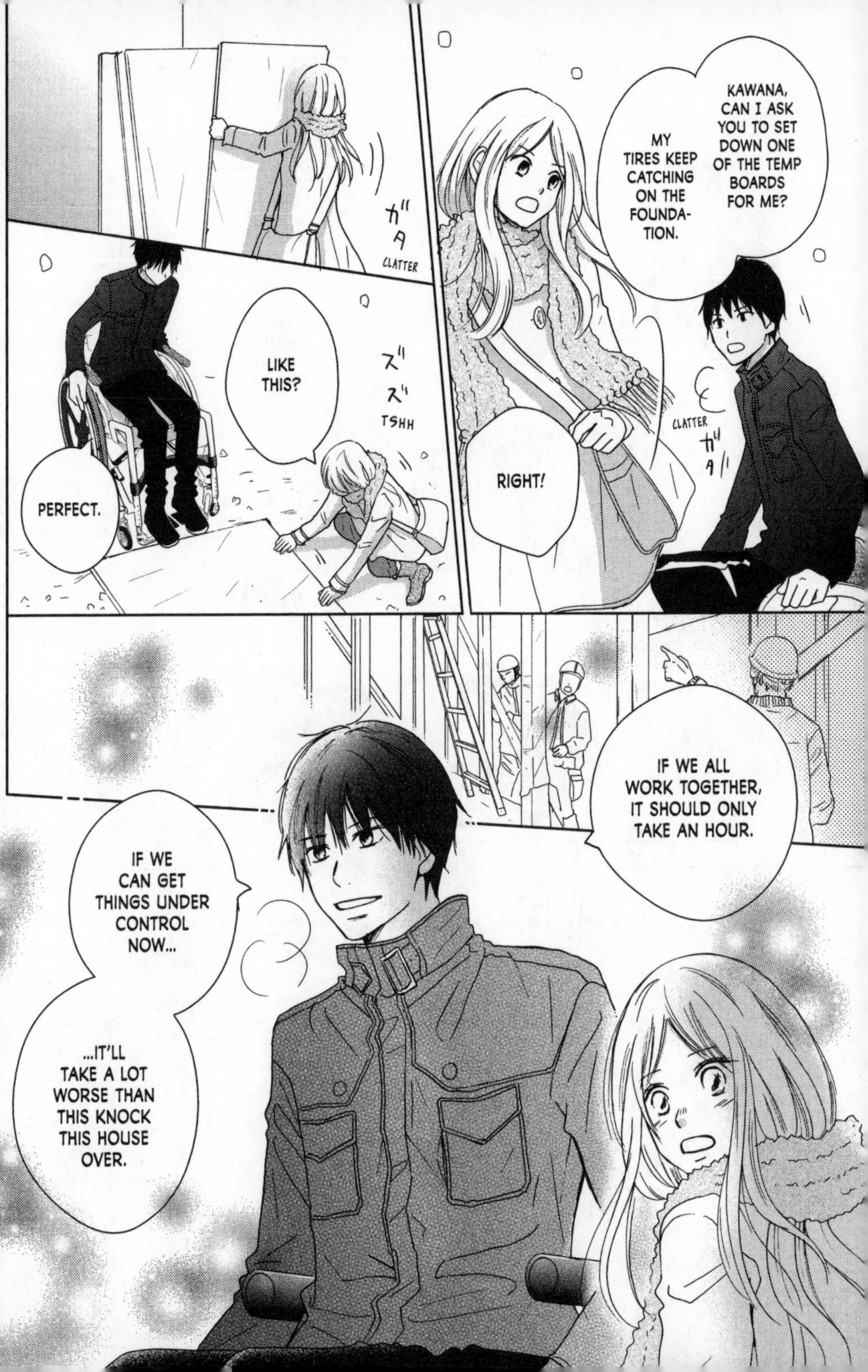
KAWANA, CAN I ASK YOU TO SET DOWN ONE OF THE TEMP BOARDS FOR ME?
MY TIRES KEEP CATCHING ON THE FOUNDATION.
ガタ
CLATTER
RIGHT!
ガタ
CLATTER
LIKE THIS?
ズズ
TSHH
PERFECT.
IF WE ALL WORK TOGETHER, IT SHOULD ONLY TAKE AN HOUR.
IF WE CAN GET THINGS UNDER CONTROL NOW...
...IT'LL TAKE A LOT WORSE THAN THIS KNOCK THIS HOUSE OVER.

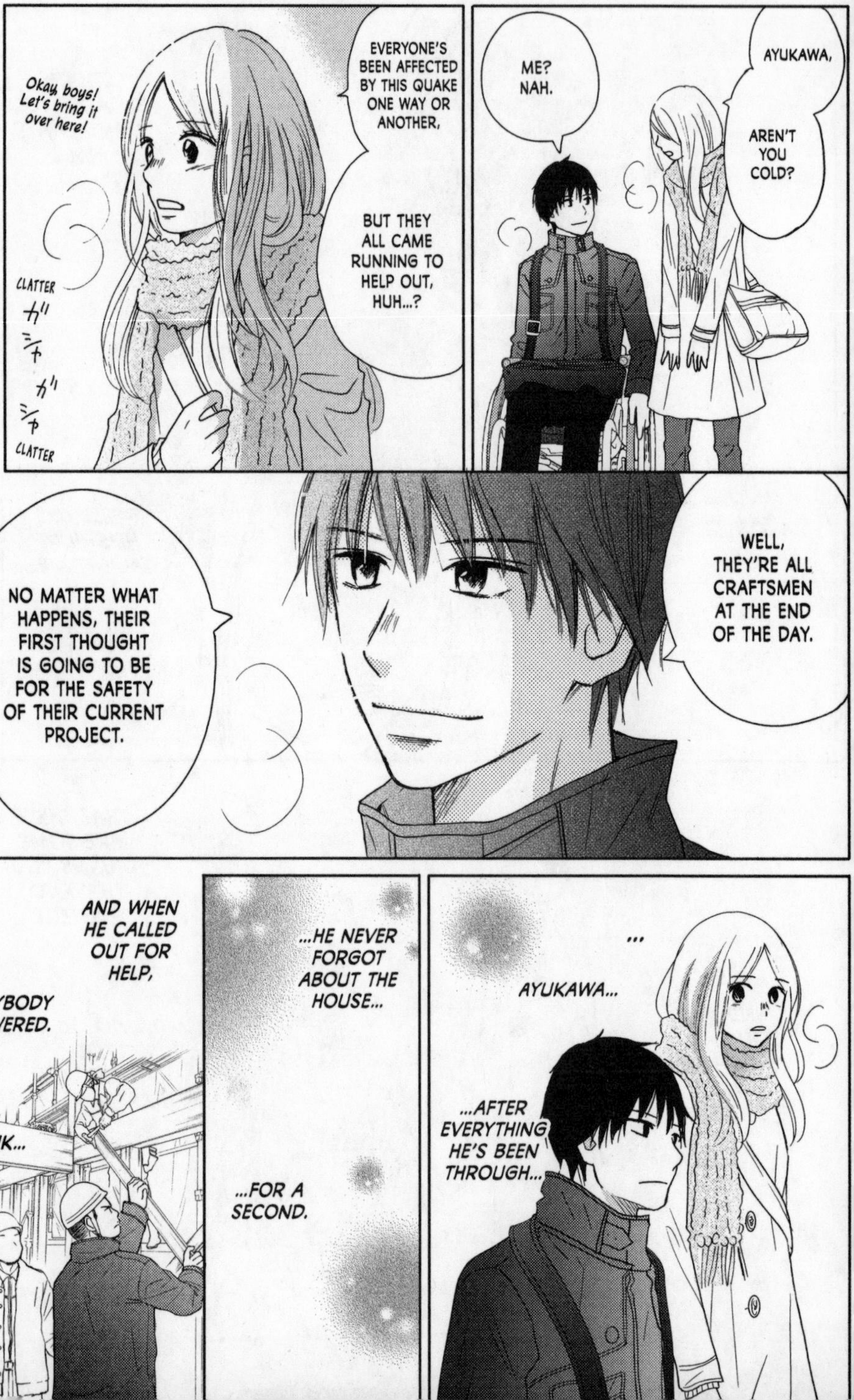
AYUKAWA, AREN'T YOU COLD?
ME? NAH.
EVERYONE'S BEEN AFFECTED BY THIS QUAKE ONE WAY OR ANOTHER,
BUT THEY ALL CAME RUNNING TO HELP OUT, HUH...?
Okay, boys! Let's bring it over here!
CLATTER
ガシャ
ガシャ
CLATTER
WELL, THEY'RE ALL CRAFTSMEN AT THE END OF THE DAY.
NO MATTER WHAT HAPPENS, THEIR FIRST THOUGHT IS GOING TO BE FOR THE SAFETY OF THEIR CURRENT PROJECT.
...
AYUKAWA...
...AFTER EVERYTHING HE'S BEEN THROUGH...
...HE NEVER FORGOT ABOUT THE HOUSE...
...FOR A SECOND.
AND WHEN HE CALLED OUT FOR HELP,
EVERYBODY ANSWERED.
I THINK...

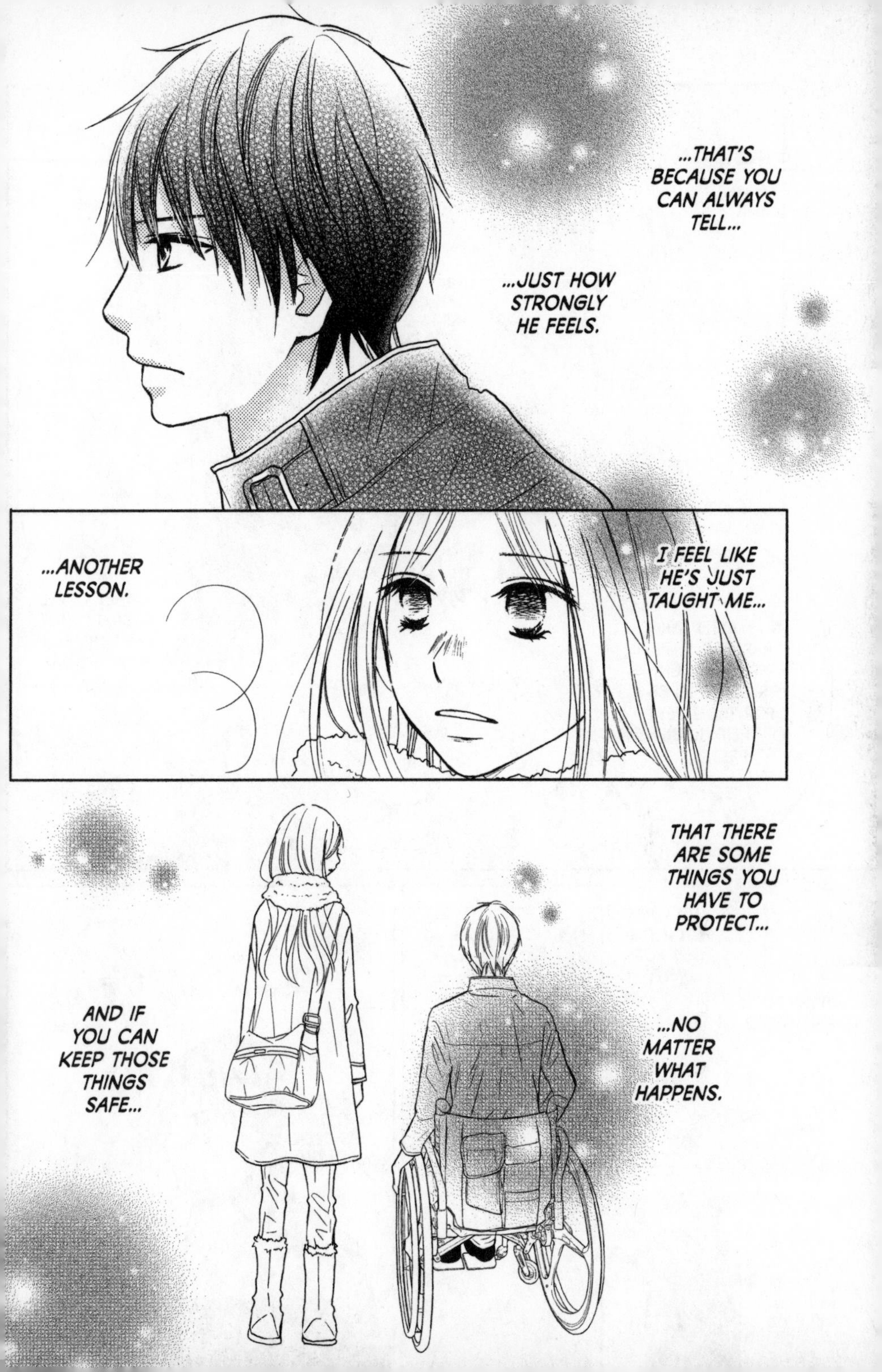
...THAT'S BECAUSE YOU CAN ALWAYS TELL...
...JUST HOW STRONGLY HE FEELS.
I FEEL LIKE HE'S JUST TAUGHT ME...
...ANOTHER LESSON.
THAT THERE ARE SOME THINGS YOU HAVE TO PROTECT...
...NO MATTER WHAT HAPPENS.
AND IF YOU CAN KEEP THOSE THINGS SAFE...

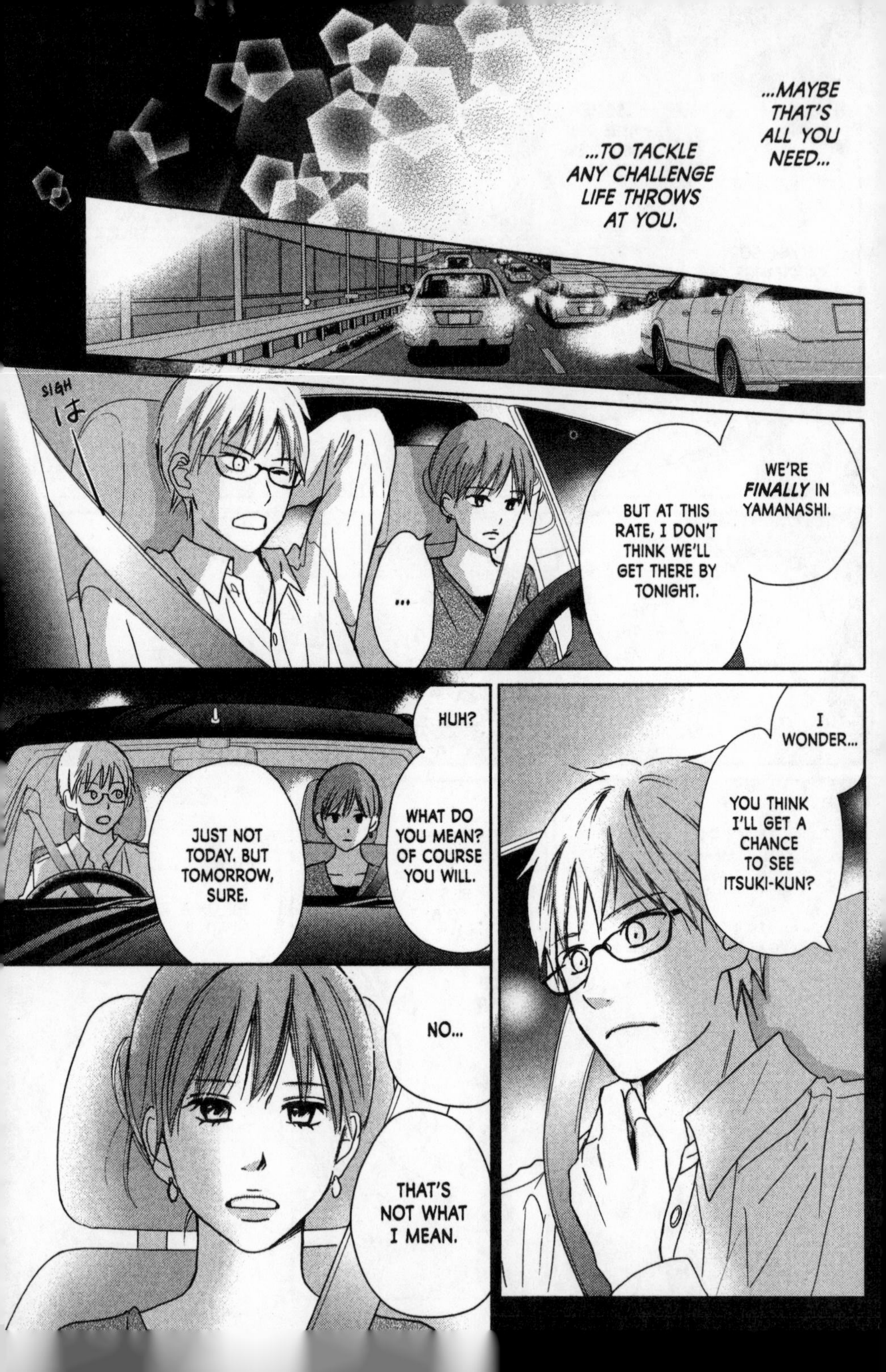
...MAYBE THAT'S ALL YOU NEED...
...TO TACKLE ANY CHALLENGE LIFE THROWS AT YOU.
WE'RE *FINALLY* IN YAMANASHI.
BUT AT THIS RATE, I DON'T THINK WE'LL GET THERE BY TONIGHT.
...
SIGH
は
I WONDER...
YOU THINK I'LL GET A CHANCE TO SEE ITSUKI-KUN?
HUH?
WHAT DO YOU MEAN? OF COURSE YOU WILL.
JUST NOT TODAY. BUT TOMORROW, SURE.
NO...
THAT'S NOT WHAT I MEAN.

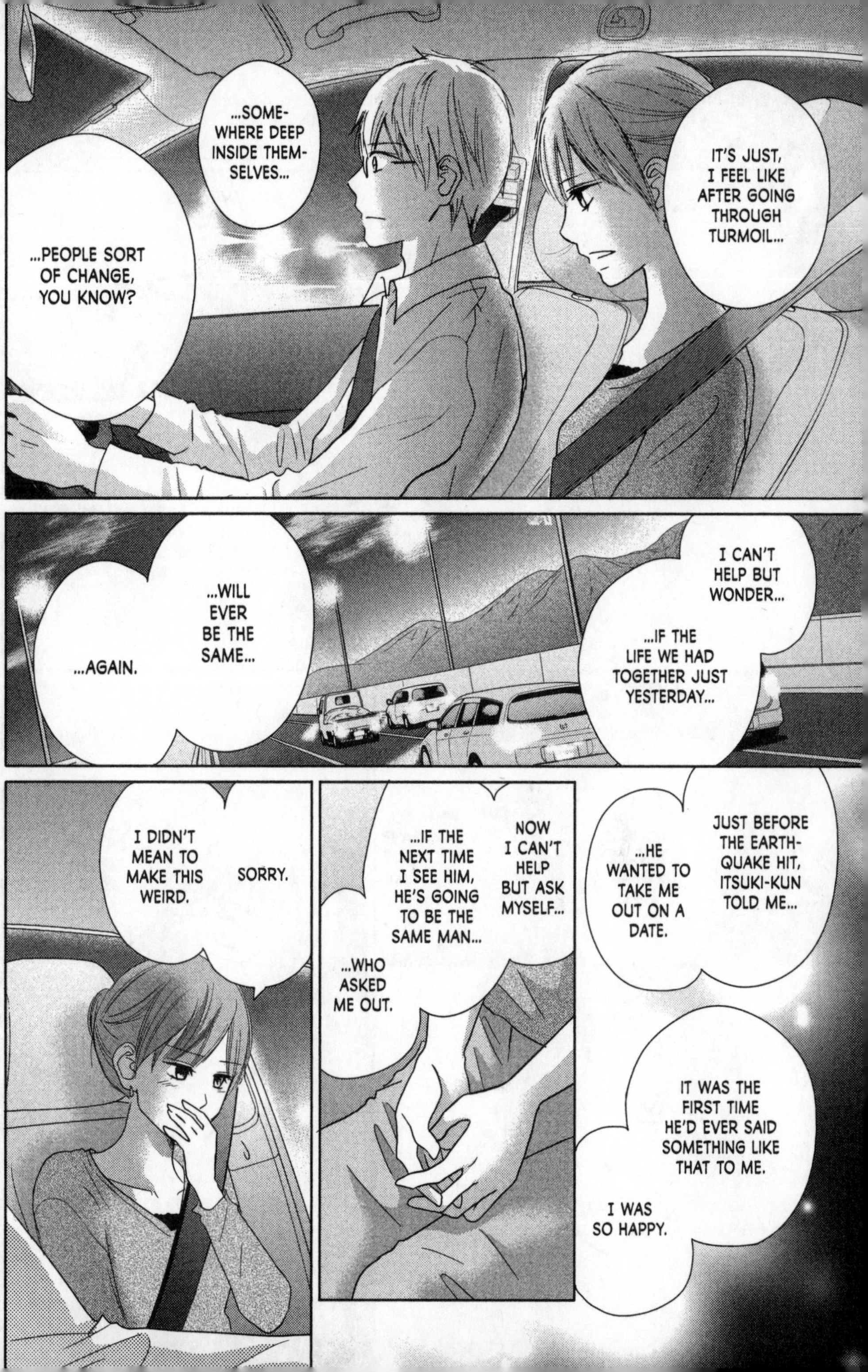
IT'S JUST, I FEEL LIKE AFTER GOING THROUGH TURMOIL...
...SOME-WHERE DEEP INSIDE THEM-SELVES...
...PEOPLE SORT OF CHANGE, YOU KNOW?
I CAN'T HELP BUT WONDER...
...IF THE LIFE WE HAD TOGETHER JUST YESTERDAY...
...WILL EVER BE THE SAME...
...AGAIN.
JUST BEFORE THE EARTH-QUAKE HIT, ITSUKI-KUN TOLD ME...
...HE WANTED TO TAKE ME OUT ON A DATE.
IT WAS THE FIRST TIME HE'D EVER SAID SOMETHING LIKE THAT TO ME.
I WAS SO HAPPY.
NOW I CAN'T HELP BUT ASK MYSELF...
...IF THE NEXT TIME I SEE HIM, HE'S GOING TO BE THE SAME MAN...
...WHO ASKED ME OUT.
SORRY.
I DIDN'T MEAN TO MAKE THIS WEIRD.

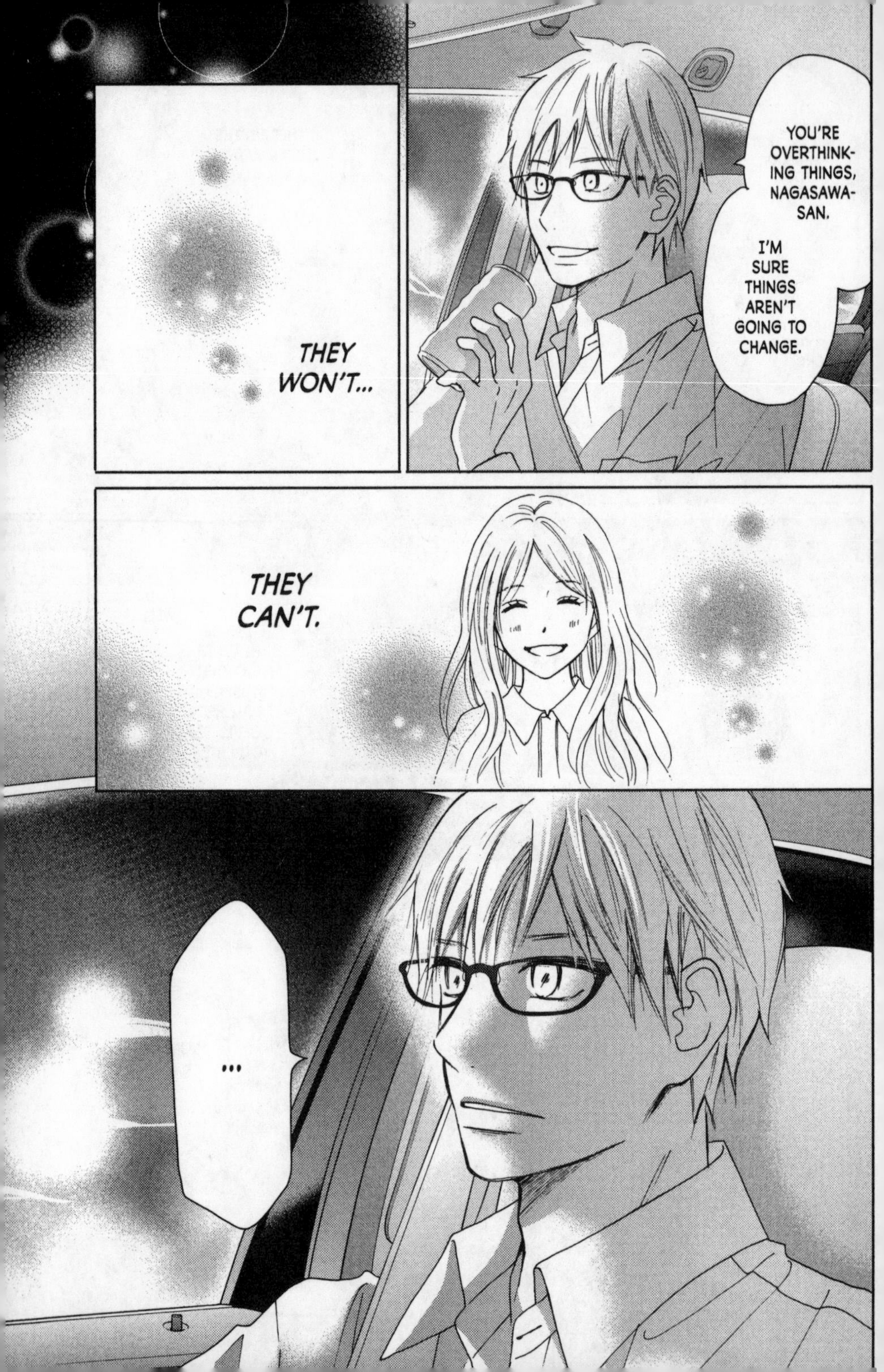
YOU'RE OVERTHINKING THINGS, NAGASAWA-SAN.
I'M SURE THINGS AREN'T GOING TO CHANGE.
THEY WON'T...
THEY CAN'T.
...

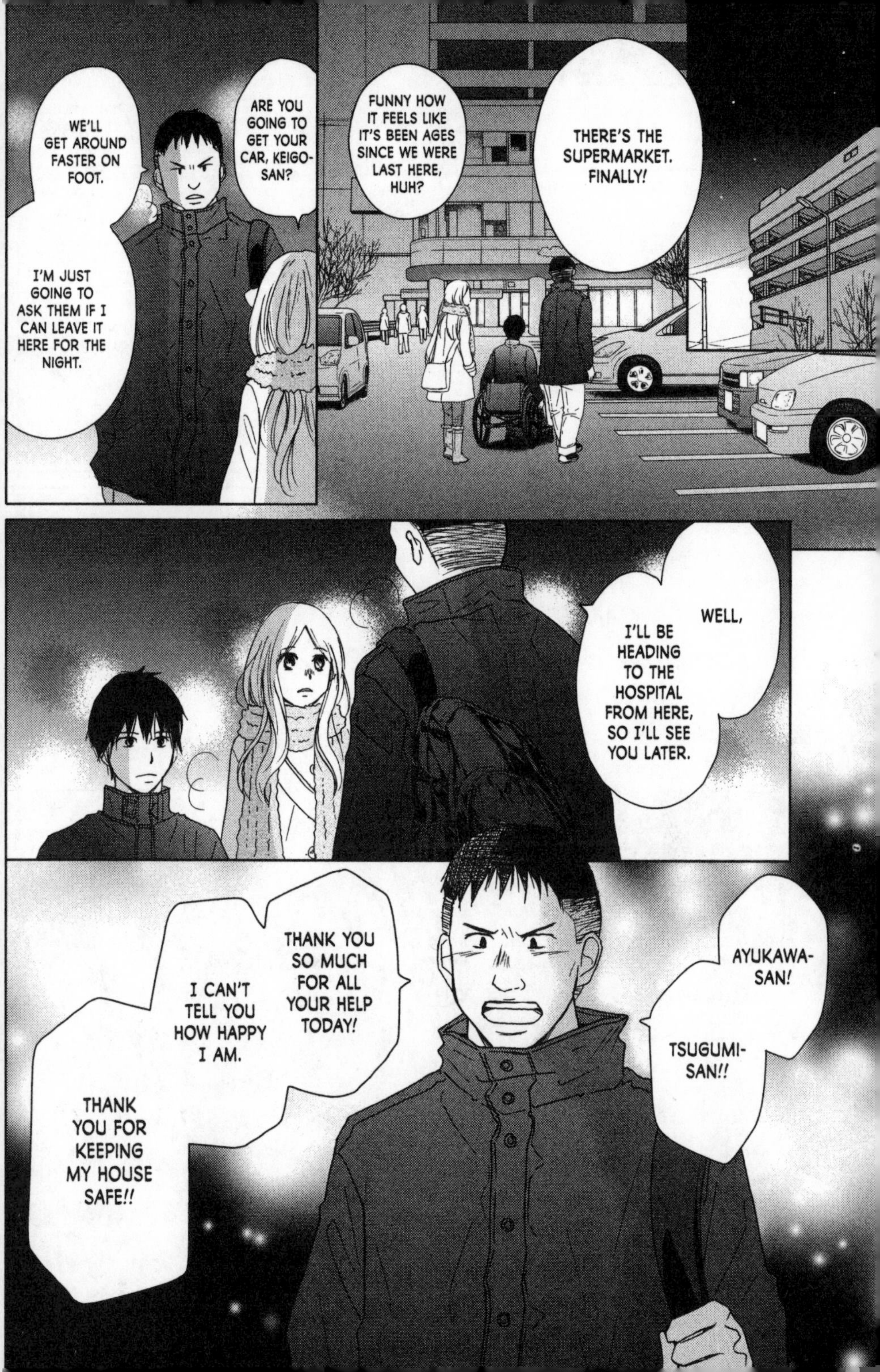
THERE'S THE SUPERMARKET. FINALLY!
FUNNY HOW IT FEELS LIKE IT'S BEEN AGES SINCE WE WERE LAST HERE, HUH?
ARE YOU GOING TO GET YOUR CAR, KEIGO-SAN?
WE'LL GET AROUND FASTER ON FOOT.
I'M JUST GOING TO ASK THEM IF I CAN LEAVE IT HERE FOR THE NIGHT.
WELL, I'LL BE HEADING TO THE HOSPITAL FROM HERE, SO I'LL SEE YOU LATER.
AYUKAWA-SAN!
TSUGUMI-SAN!!
THANK YOU SO MUCH FOR ALL YOUR HELP TODAY!
I CAN'T TELL YOU HOW HAPPY I AM.
THANK YOU FOR KEEPING MY HOUSE SAFE!!

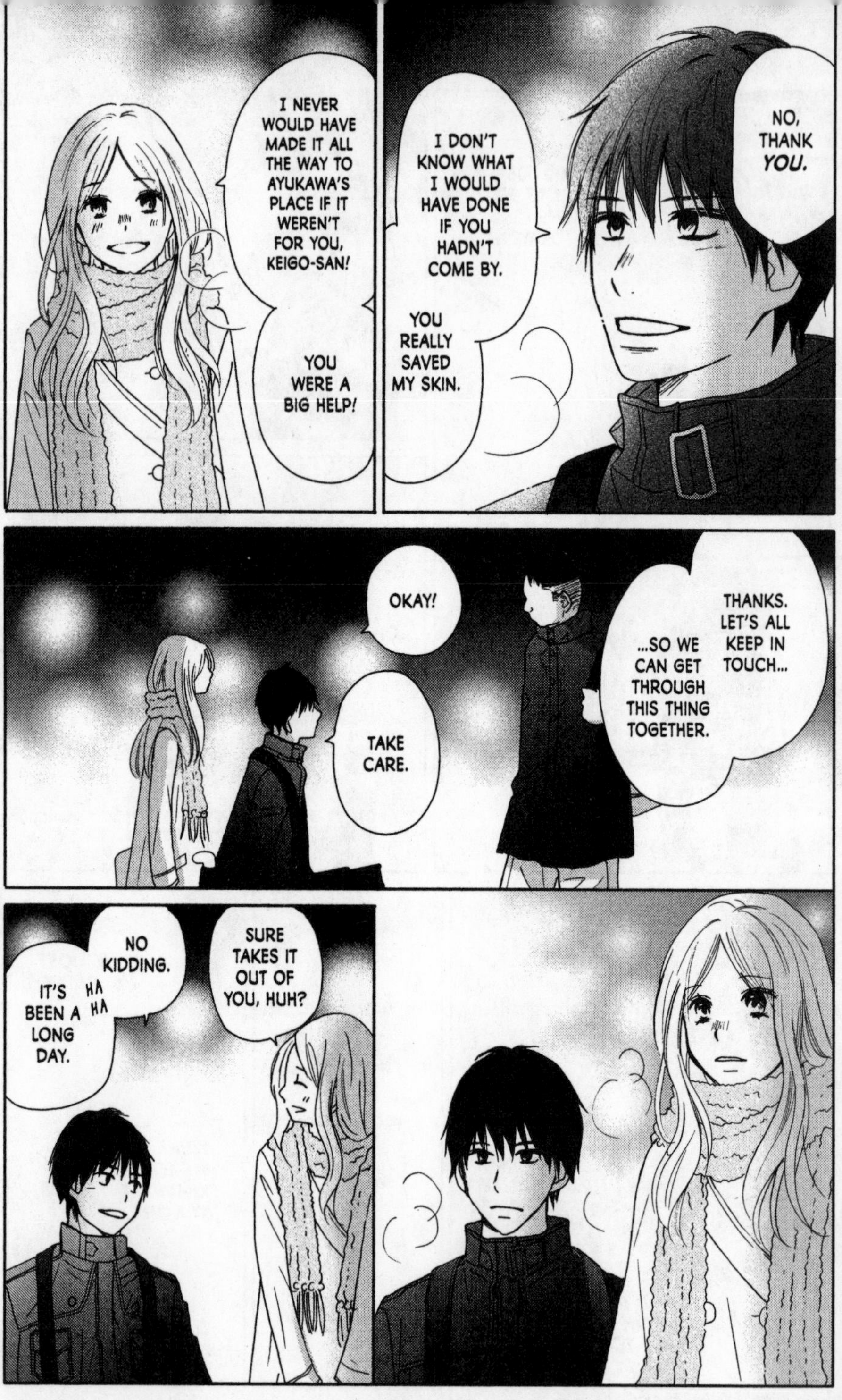
NO, THANK *YOU.*
I DON'T KNOW WHAT I WOULD HAVE DONE IF YOU HADN'T COME BY.
YOU REALLY SAVED MY SKIN.
I NEVER WOULD HAVE MADE IT ALL THE WAY TO AYUKAWA'S PLACE IF IT WEREN'T FOR YOU, KEIGO-SAN!
YOU WERE A BIG HELP!
THANKS. LET'S ALL KEEP IN TOUCH...
...SO WE CAN GET THROUGH THIS THING TOGETHER.
OKAY!
TAKE CARE.
SURE TAKES IT OUT OF YOU, HUH?
NO KIDDING.
HA HA
IT'S BEEN A LONG DAY.

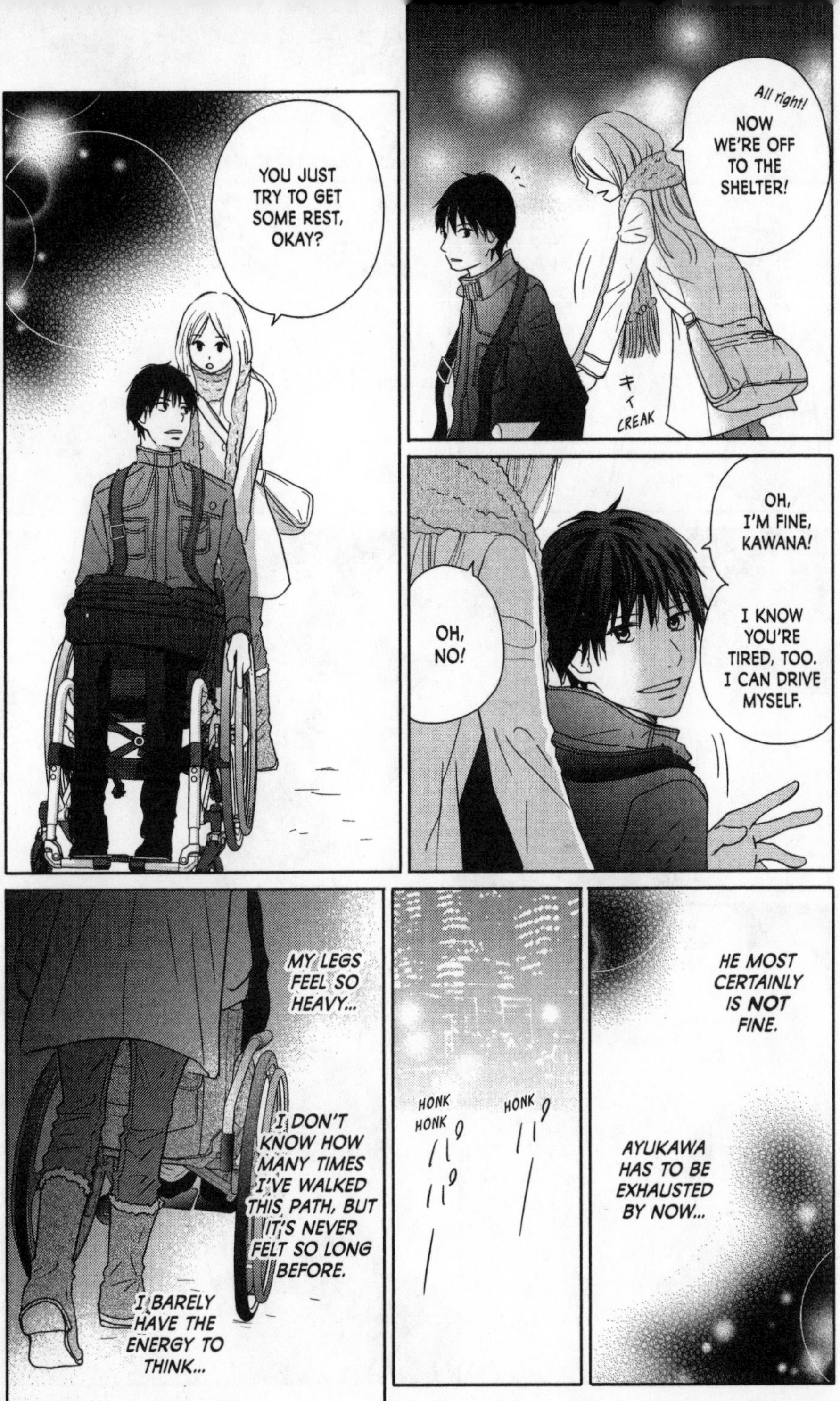
All right!
NOW WE'RE OFF TO THE SHELTER!
キイ
CREAK
OH, I'M FINE, KAWANA!
I KNOW YOU'RE TIRED, TOO. I CAN DRIVE MYSELF.
OH, NO!
YOU JUST TRY TO GET SOME REST, OKAY?
HE MOST CERTAINLY IS **NOT** FINE.
AYUKAWA HAS TO BE EXHAUSTED BY NOW...
HONK HONK
HONK
MY LEGS FEEL SO HEAVY...
I DON'T KNOW HOW MANY TIMES I'VE WALKED THIS PATH, BUT IT'S NEVER FELT SO LONG BEFORE.
I BARELY HAVE THE ENERGY TO THINK...

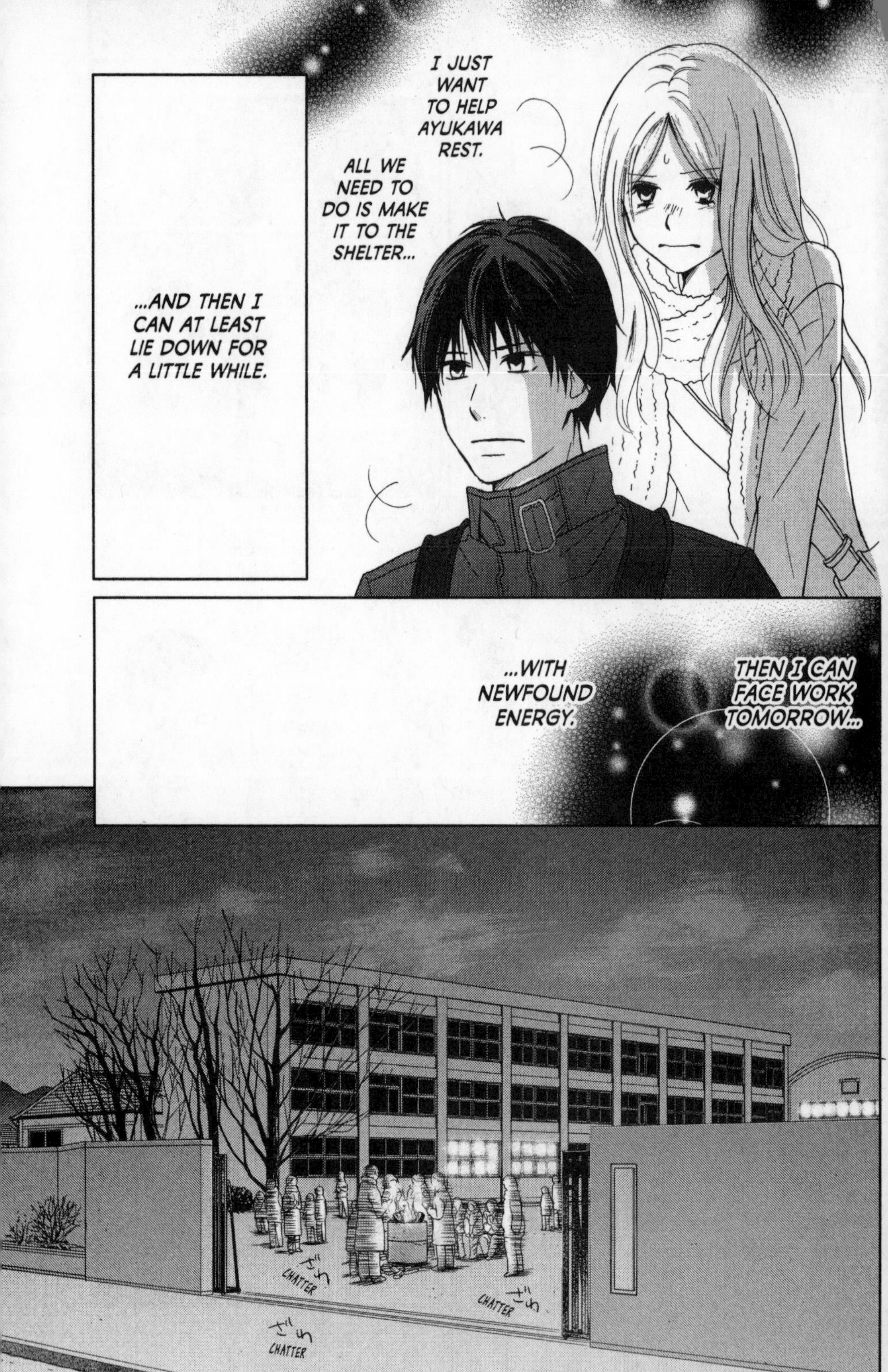
I JUST WANT TO HELP AYUKAWA REST.
ALL WE NEED TO DO IS MAKE IT TO THE SHELTER...
...AND THEN I CAN AT LEAST LIE DOWN FOR A LITTLE WHILE.
THEN I CAN FACE WORK TOMORROW...
...WITH NEWFOUND ENERGY.
CHATTER
CHATTER
CHATTER

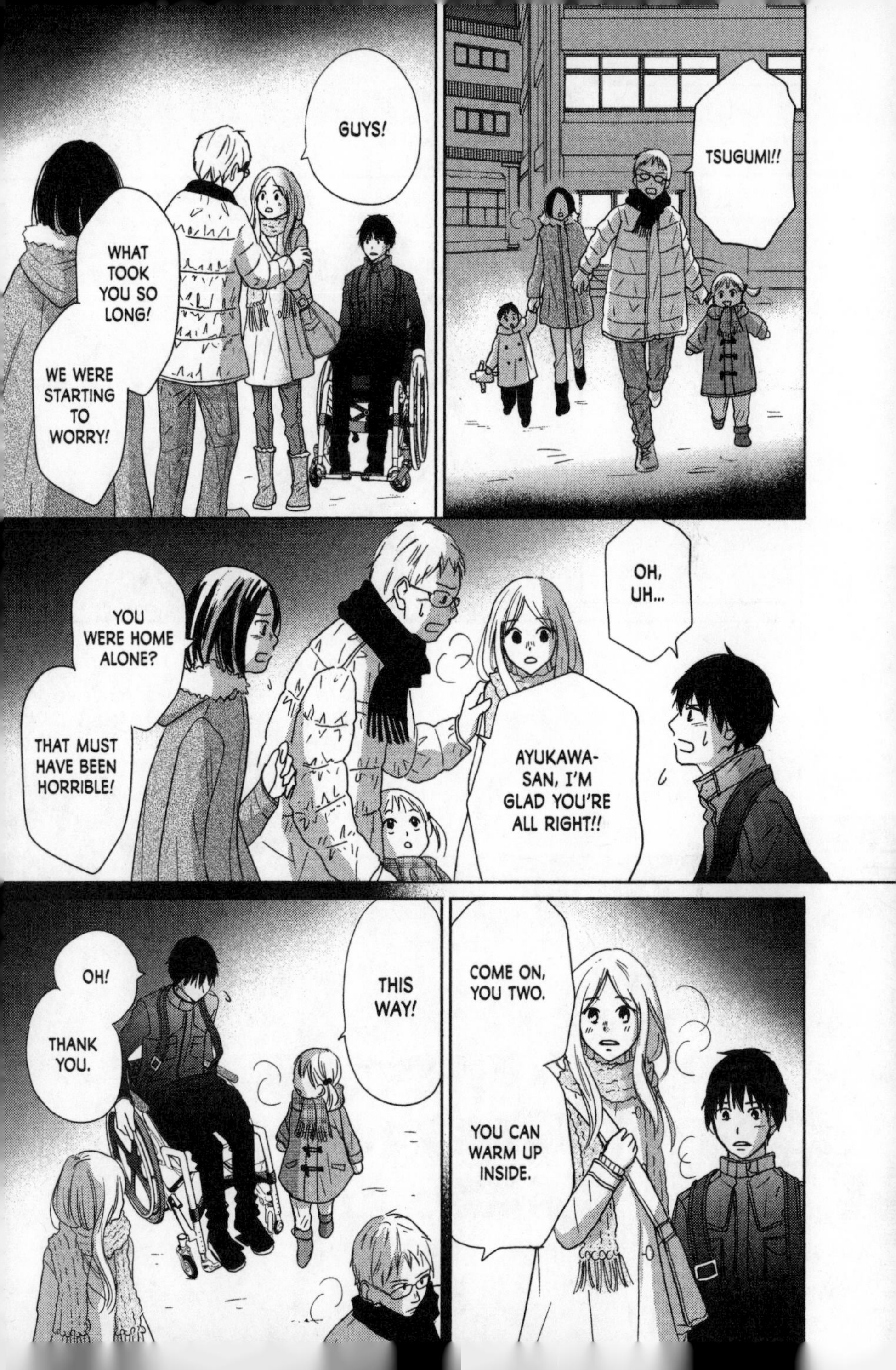
TSUGUMI!!
GUYS!
WHAT TOOK YOU SO LONG!
WE WERE STARTING TO WORRY!
OH, UH...
AYUKAWA-SAN, I'M GLAD YOU'RE ALL RIGHT!!
YOU WERE HOME ALONE?
THAT MUST HAVE BEEN HORRIBLE!
COME ON, YOU TWO.
YOU CAN WARM UP INSIDE.
THIS WAY!
OH!
THANK YOU.

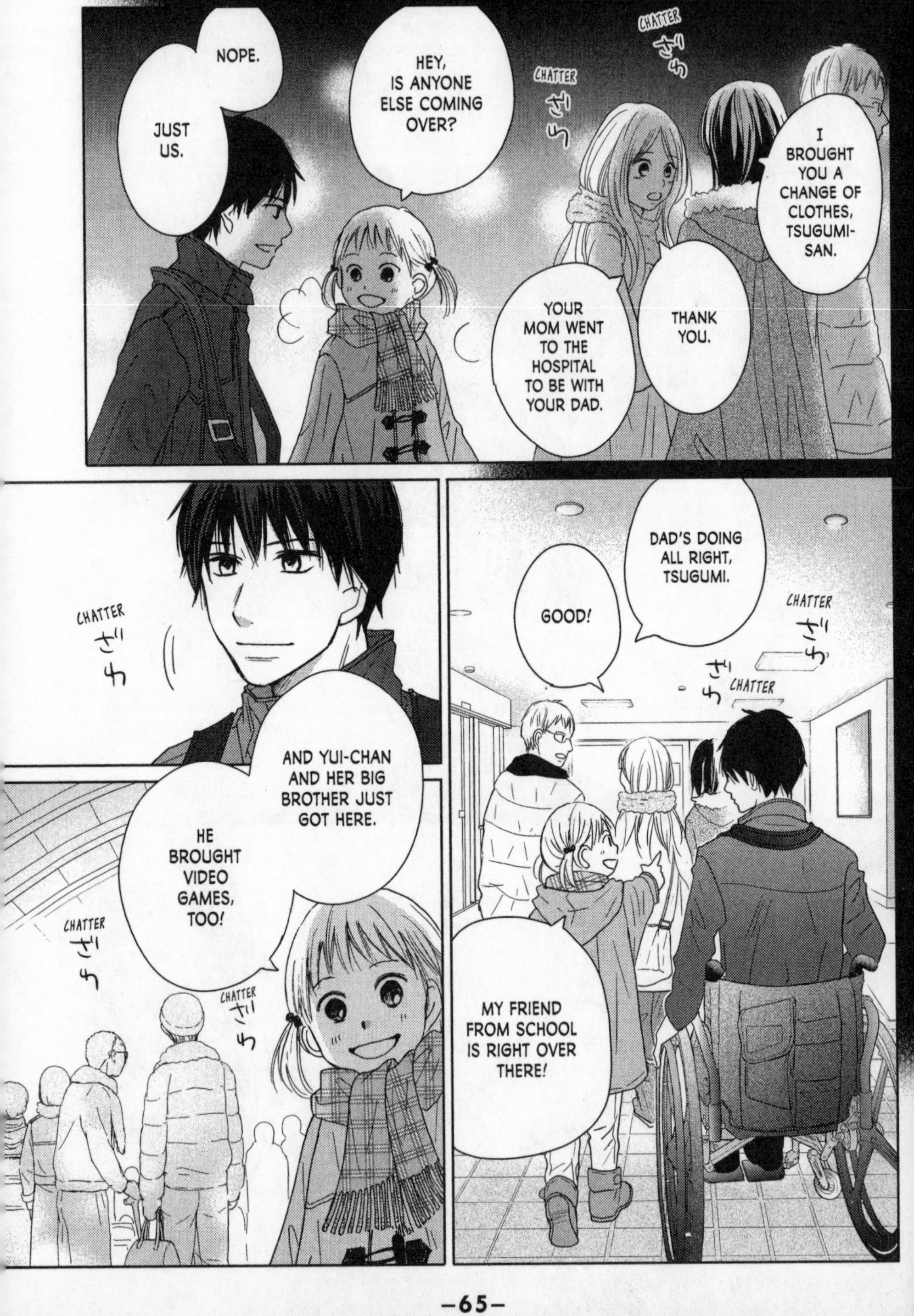
CHATTER
ざわ
CHATTER
ざわ
I BROUGHT YOU A CHANGE OF CLOTHES, TSUGUMI-SAN.
THANK YOU.
YOUR MOM WENT TO THE HOSPITAL TO BE WITH YOUR DAD.
HEY, IS ANYONE ELSE COMING OVER?
NOPE.
JUST US.
DAD'S DOING ALL RIGHT, TSUGUMI.
GOOD!
CHATTER
ざわ
CHATTER
ざわ
MY FRIEND FROM SCHOOL IS RIGHT OVER THERE!
CHATTER
ざわ
AND YUI-CHAN AND HER BIG BROTHER JUST GOT HERE.
HE BROUGHT VIDEO GAMES, TOO!
CHATTER
ざわ
CHATTER
ざわ

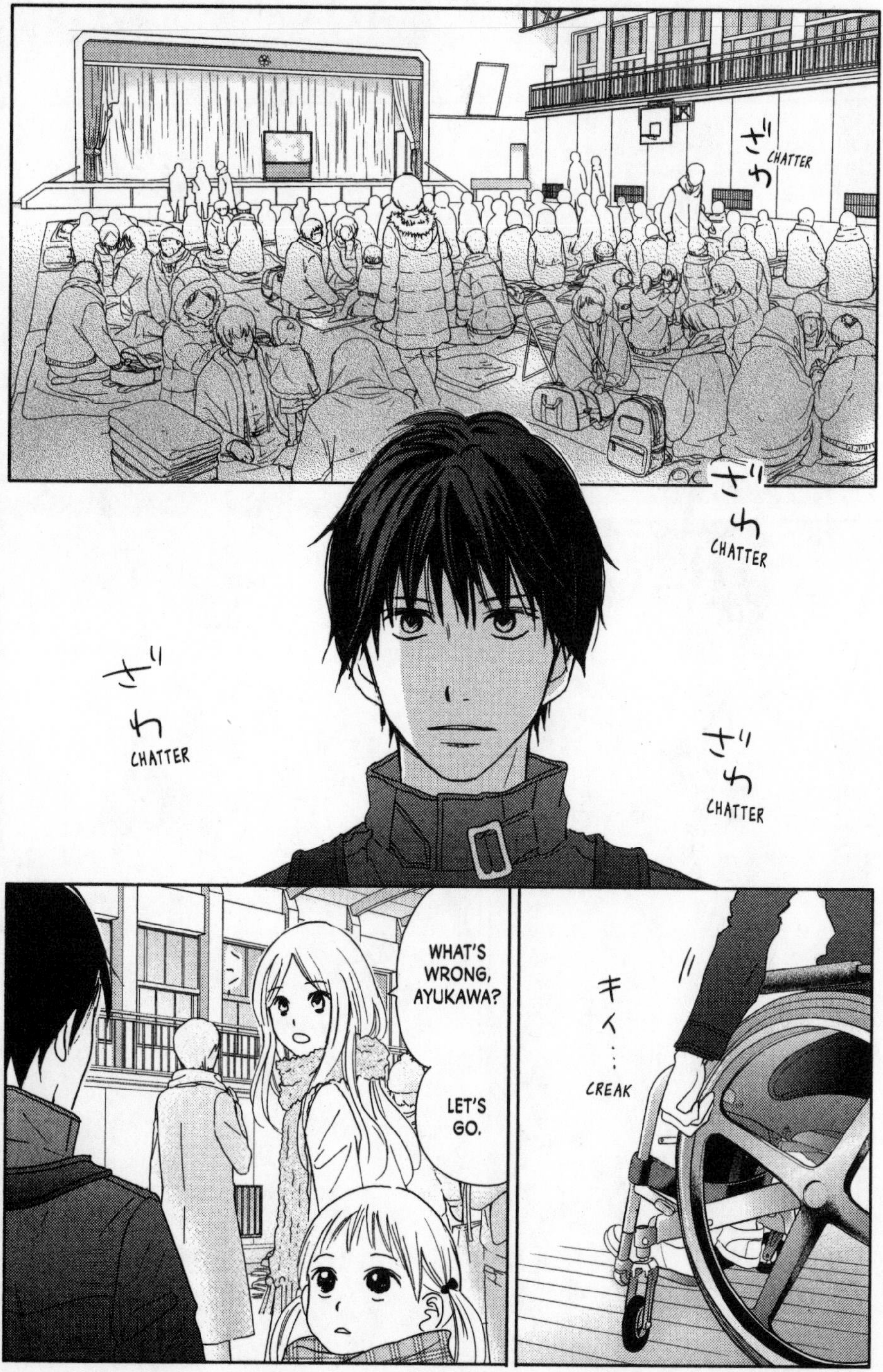
ざわ
CHATTER
ざわ
CHATTER
ざわ
CHATTER
ざわ
CHATTER
キィ…
CREAK
WHAT'S WRONG, AYUKAWA?
LET'S GO.

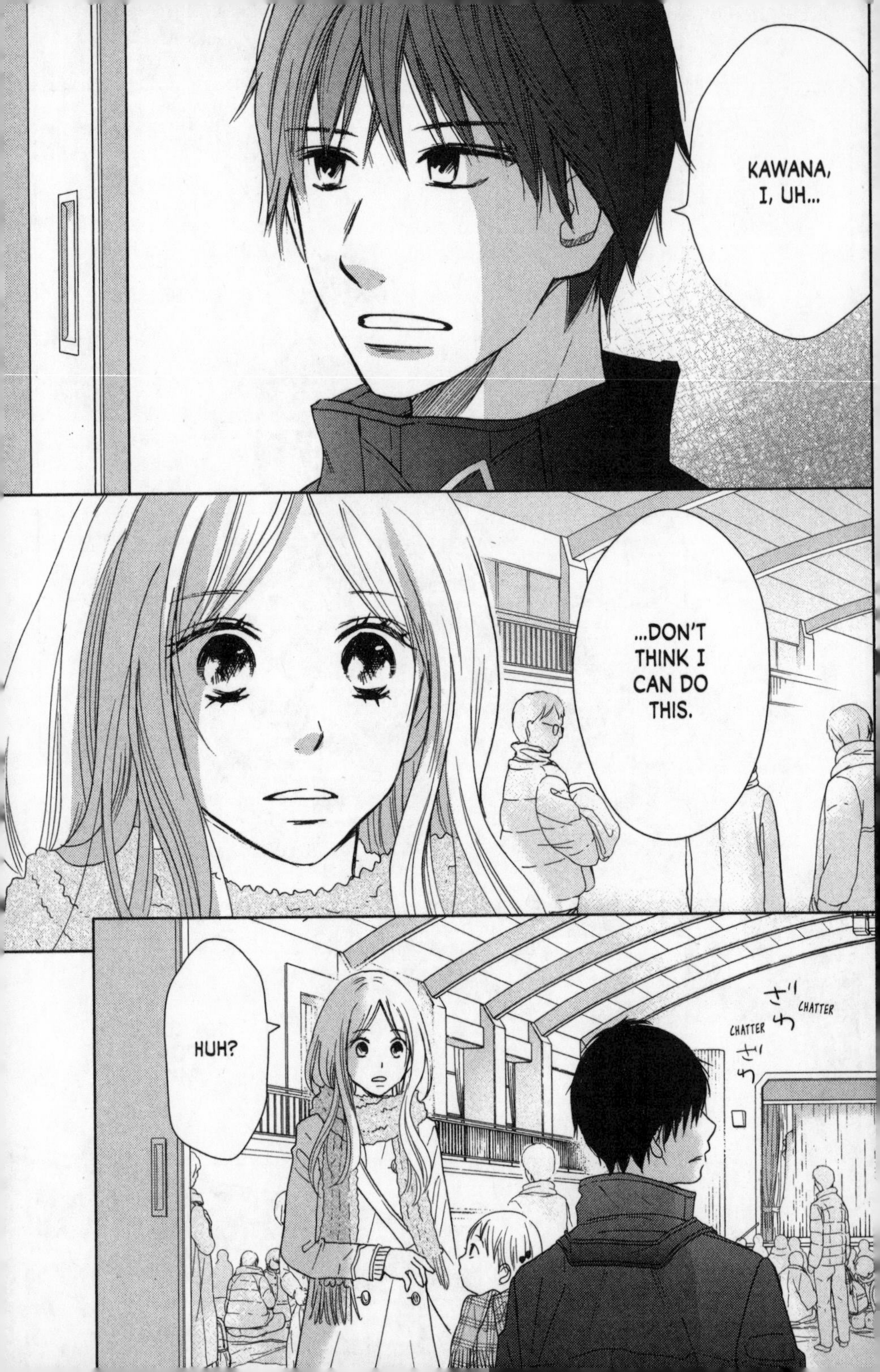
KAWANA, I, UH...
...DON'T THINK I CAN DO THIS.
ざわ
CHATTER
ざわ
CHATTER
HUH?

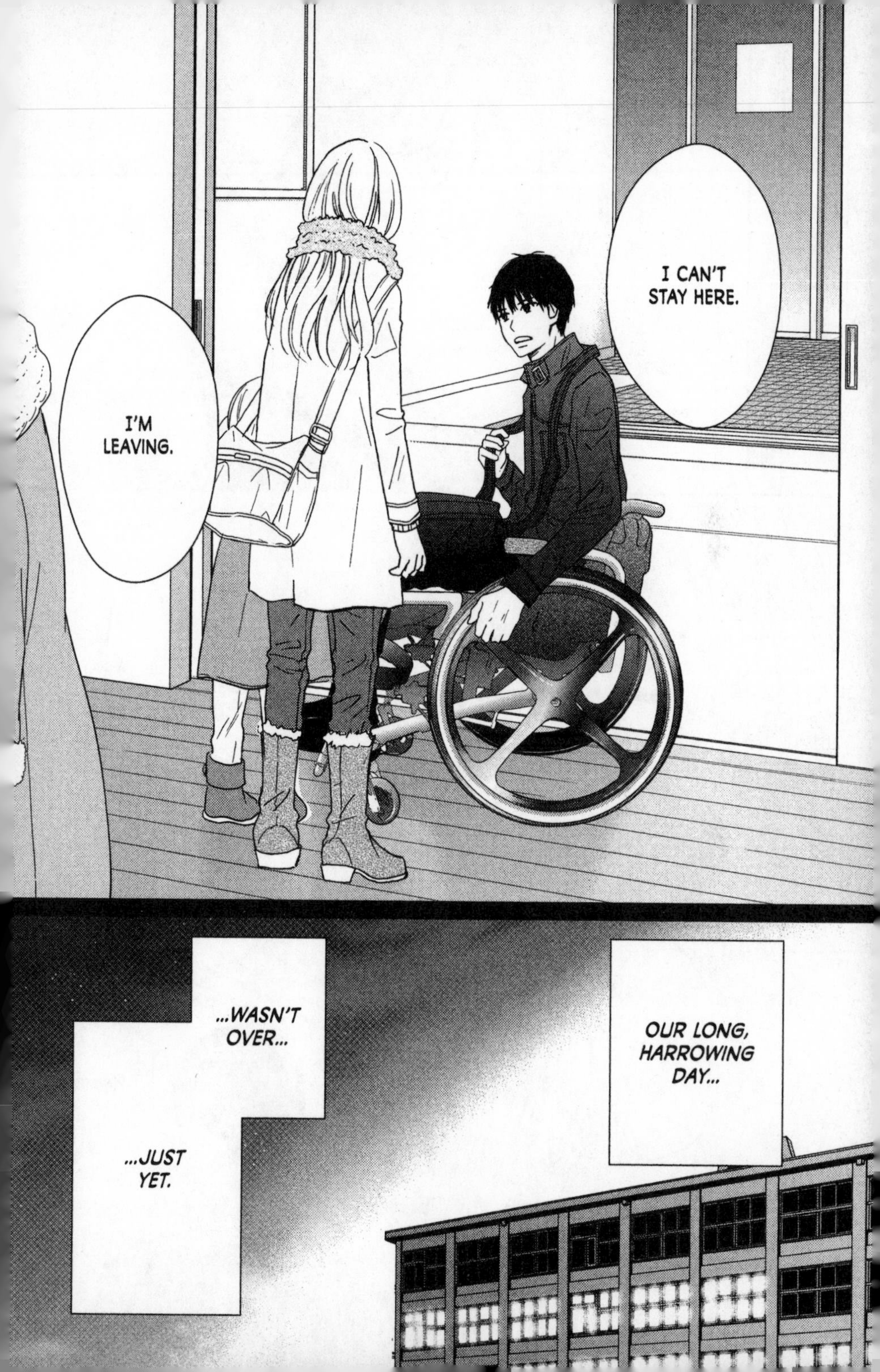
I CAN'T STAY HERE.
I'M LEAVING.
OUR LONG, HARROWING DAY...
...WASN'T OVER...
...JUST YET.

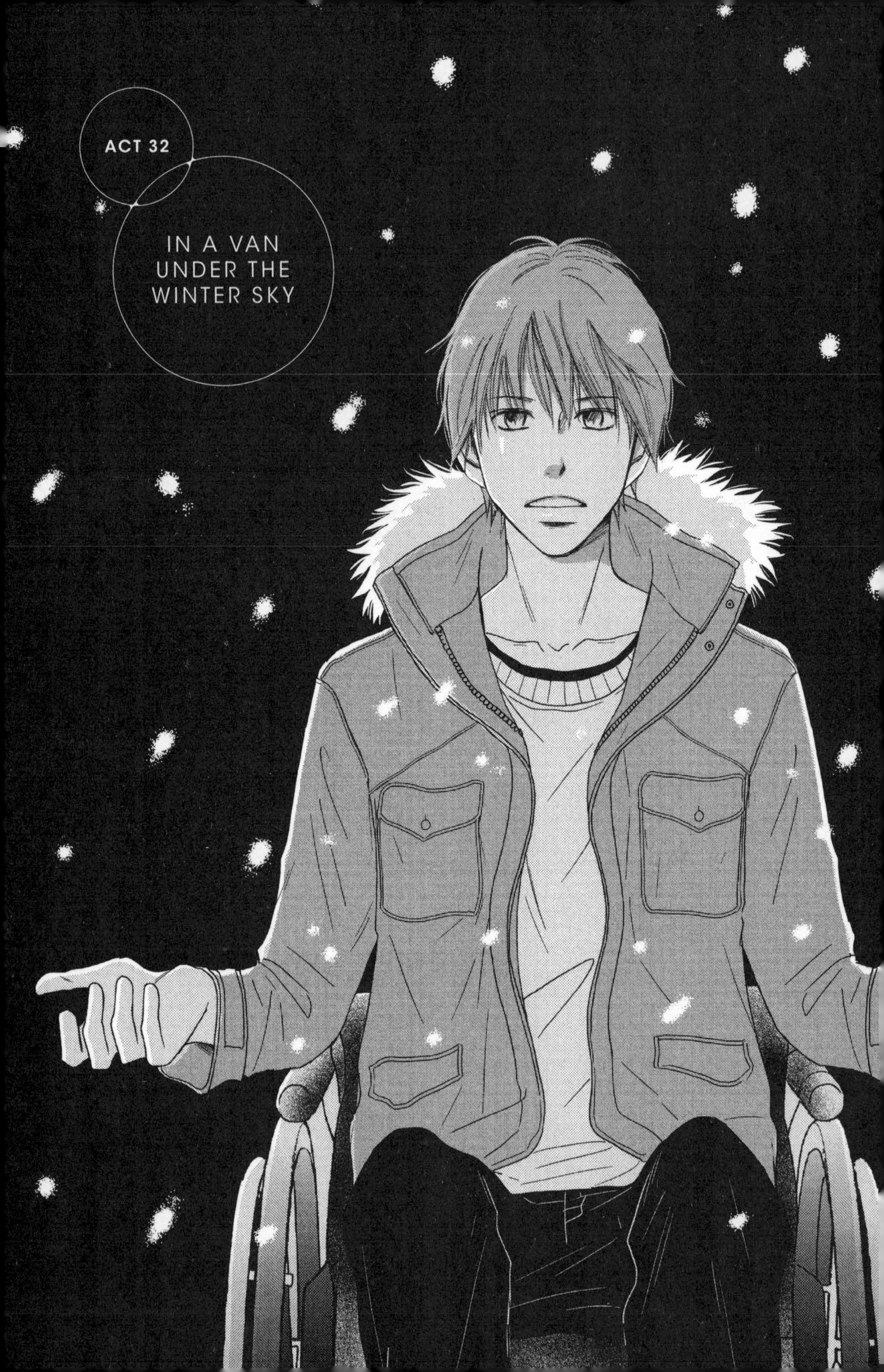
ACT 32
IN A VAN
UNDER THE
WINTER SKY

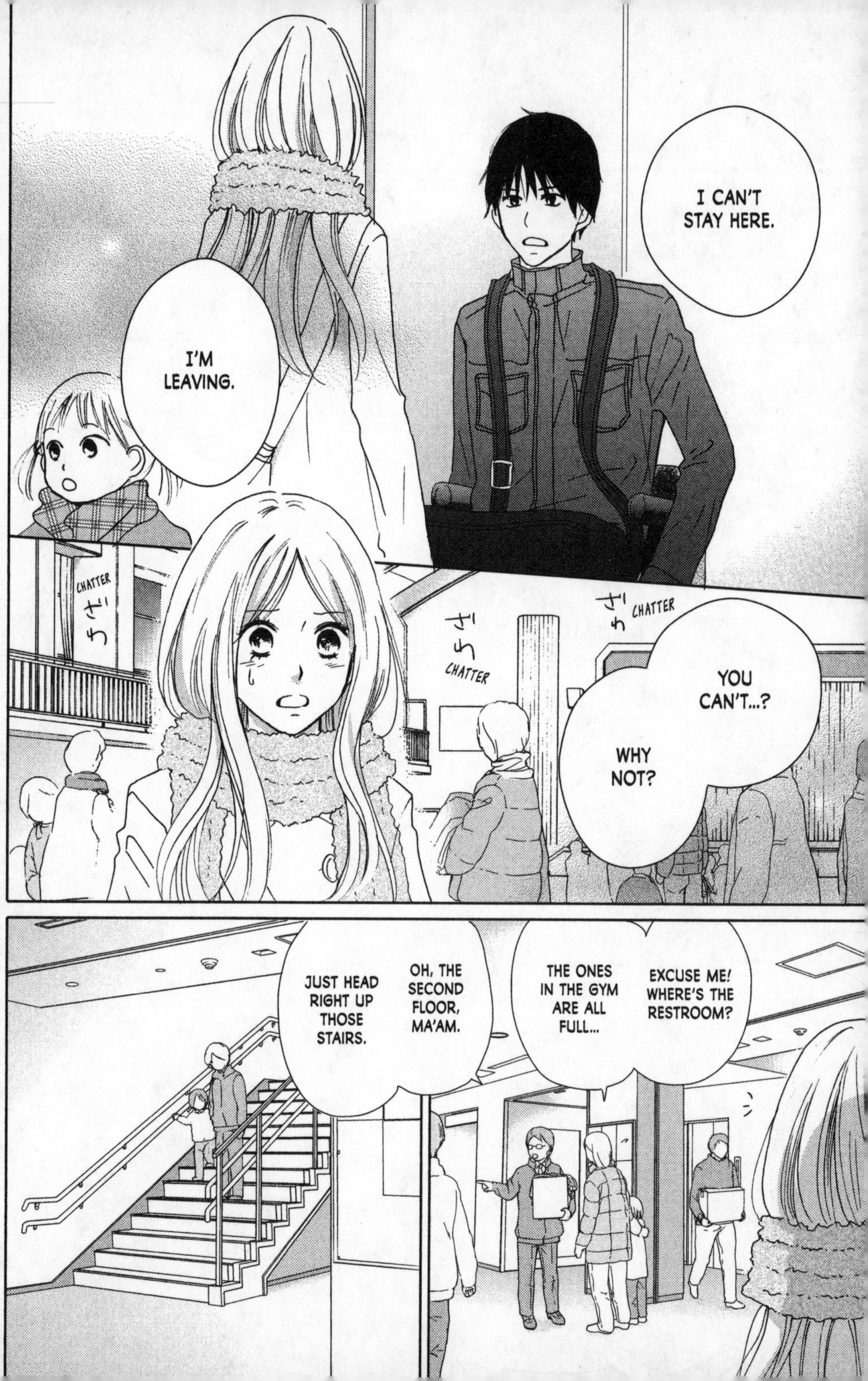
I CAN'T STAY HERE.
I'M LEAVING.
ざわ CHATTER
ざわ CHATTER
ざわ CHATTER
YOU CAN'T...?
WHY NOT?
EXCUSE ME! WHERE'S THE RESTROOM?
THE ONES IN THE GYM ARE ALL FULL...
OH, THE SECOND FLOOR, MA'AM.
JUST HEAD RIGHT UP THOSE STAIRS.

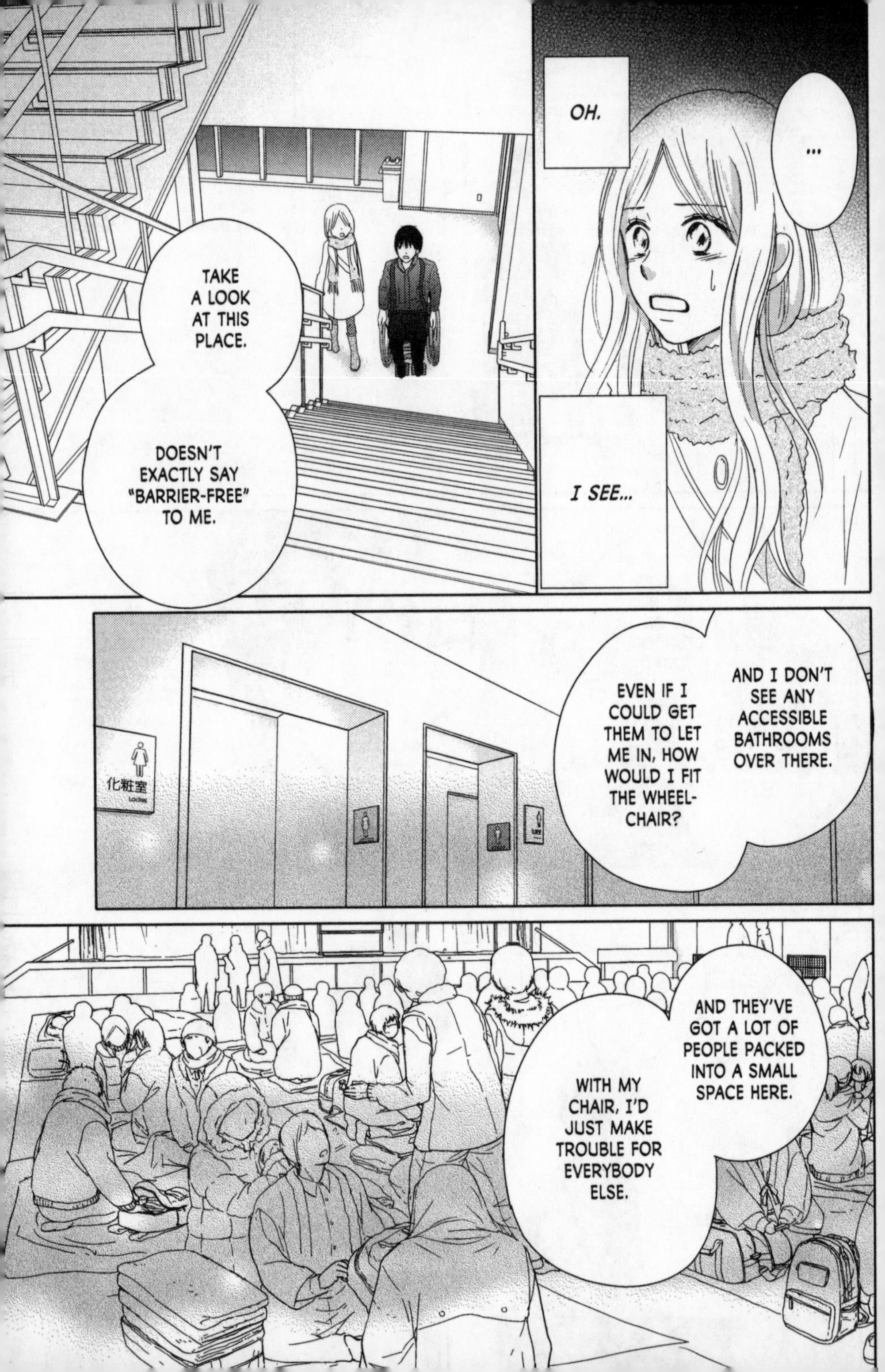
...
OH.
I SEE...
TAKE A LOOK AT THIS PLACE.
DOESN'T EXACTLY SAY "BARRIER-FREE" TO ME.
AND I DON'T SEE ANY ACCESSIBLE BATHROOMS OVER THERE.
EVEN IF I COULD GET THEM TO LET ME IN, HOW WOULD I FIT THE WHEEL-CHAIR?
化粧室
AND THEY'VE GOT A LOT OF PEOPLE PACKED INTO A SMALL SPACE HERE.
WITH MY CHAIR, I'D JUST MAKE TROUBLE FOR EVERYBODY ELSE.

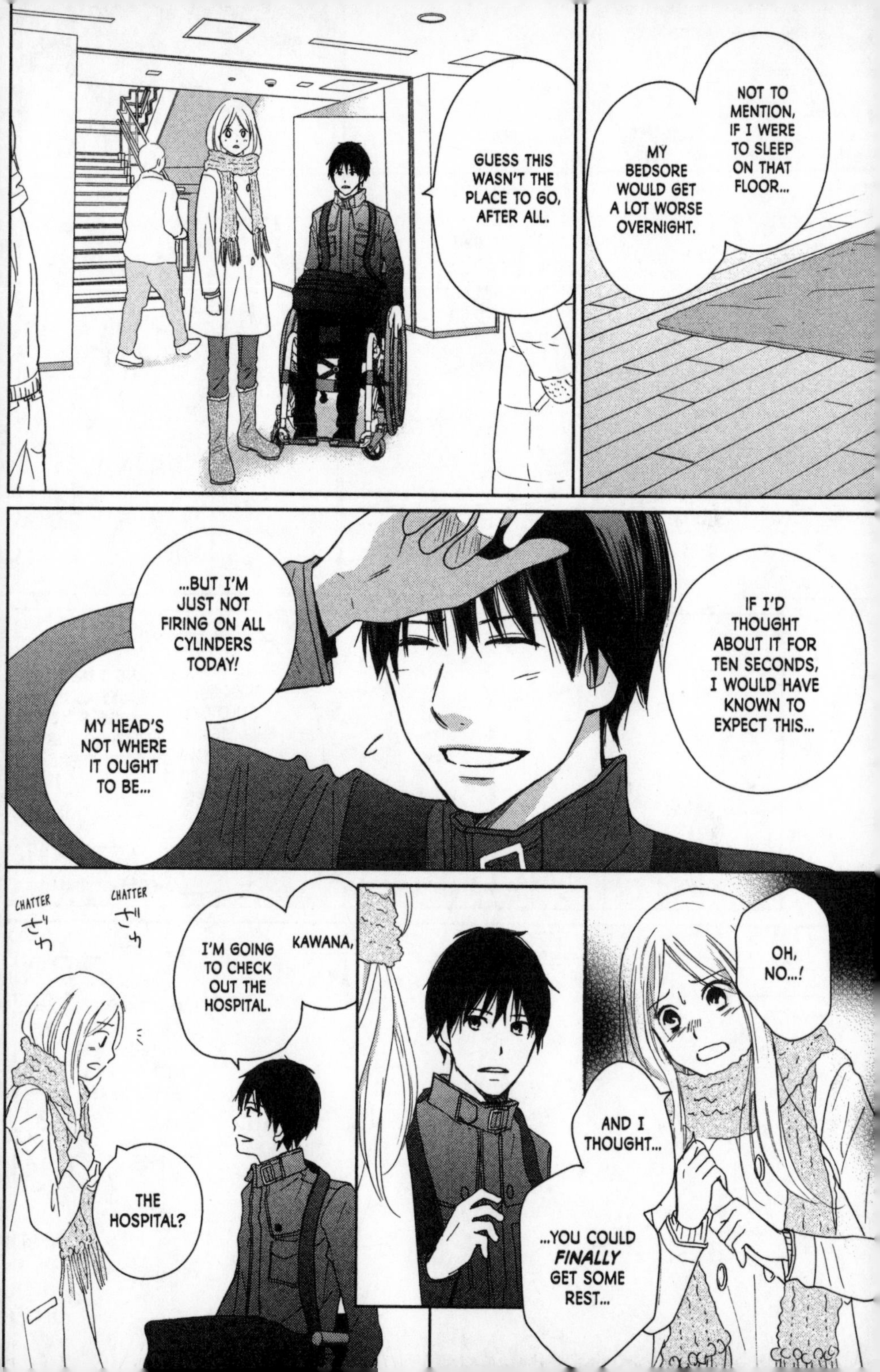
GUESS THIS WASN'T THE PLACE TO GO, AFTER ALL.
NOT TO MENTION, IF I WERE TO SLEEP ON THAT FLOOR...
MY BEDSORE WOULD GET A LOT WORSE OVERNIGHT.
IF I'D THOUGHT ABOUT IT FOR TEN SECONDS, I WOULD HAVE KNOWN TO EXPECT THIS...
...BUT I'M JUST NOT FIRING ON ALL CYLINDERS TODAY!
MY HEAD'S NOT WHERE IT OUGHT TO BE...
OH, NO...!
AND I THOUGHT...
...YOU COULD *FINALLY* GET SOME REST...
KAWANA,
I'M GOING TO CHECK OUT THE HOSPITAL.
CHATTER ざわ
CHATTER ざわ
THE HOSPITAL?

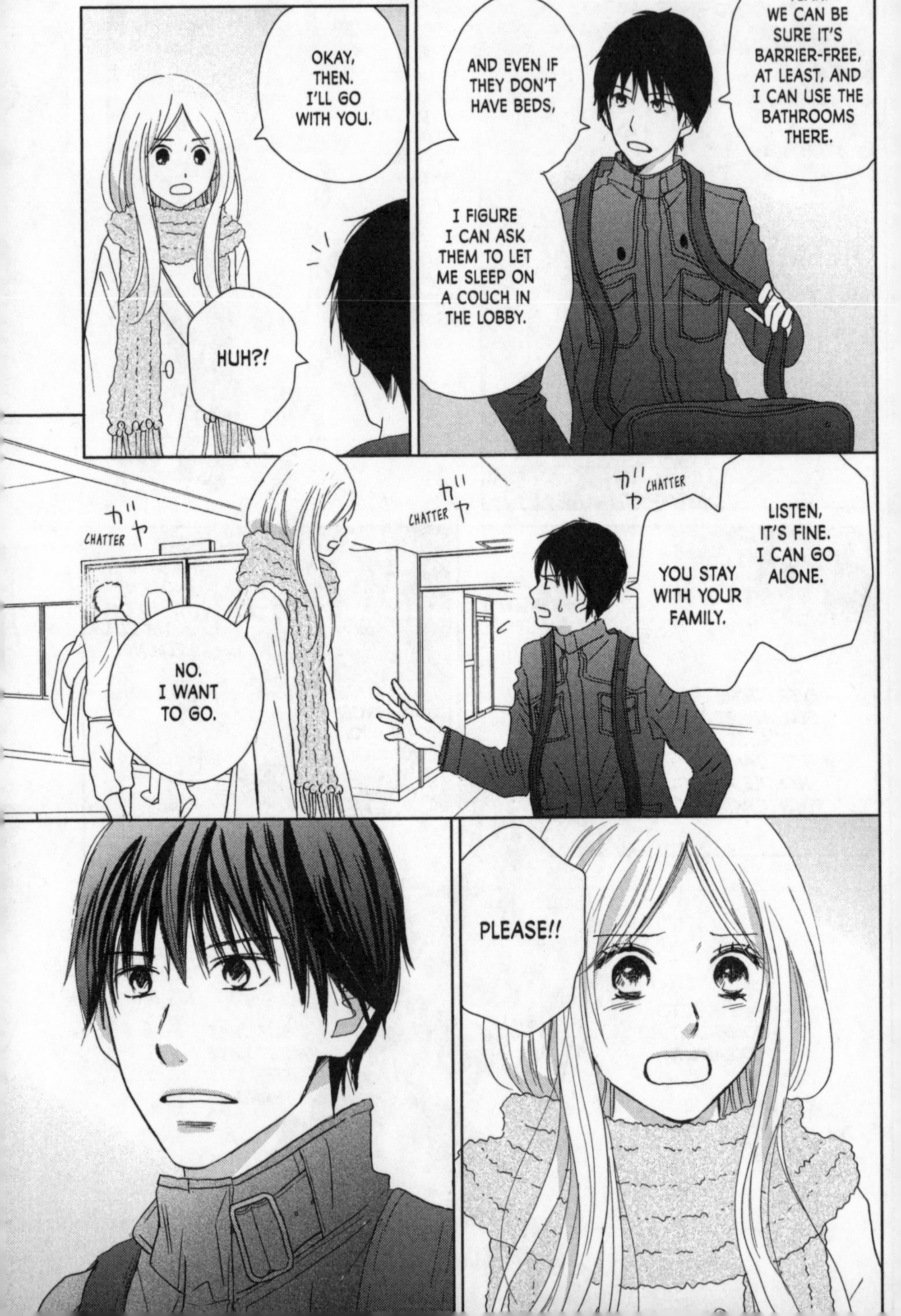
YEAH. WE CAN BE SURE IT'S BARRIER-FREE, AT LEAST, AND I CAN USE THE BATHROOMS THERE.
AND EVEN IF THEY DON'T HAVE BEDS,
I FIGURE I CAN ASK THEM TO LET ME SLEEP ON A COUCH IN THE LOBBY.
OKAY, THEN. I'LL GO WITH YOU.
HUH?!
ガヤ CHATTER
ガヤ CHATTER
ガヤ CHATTER
LISTEN, IT'S FINE. I CAN GO ALONE.
YOU STAY WITH YOUR FAMILY.
NO. I WANT TO GO.
PLEASE!!

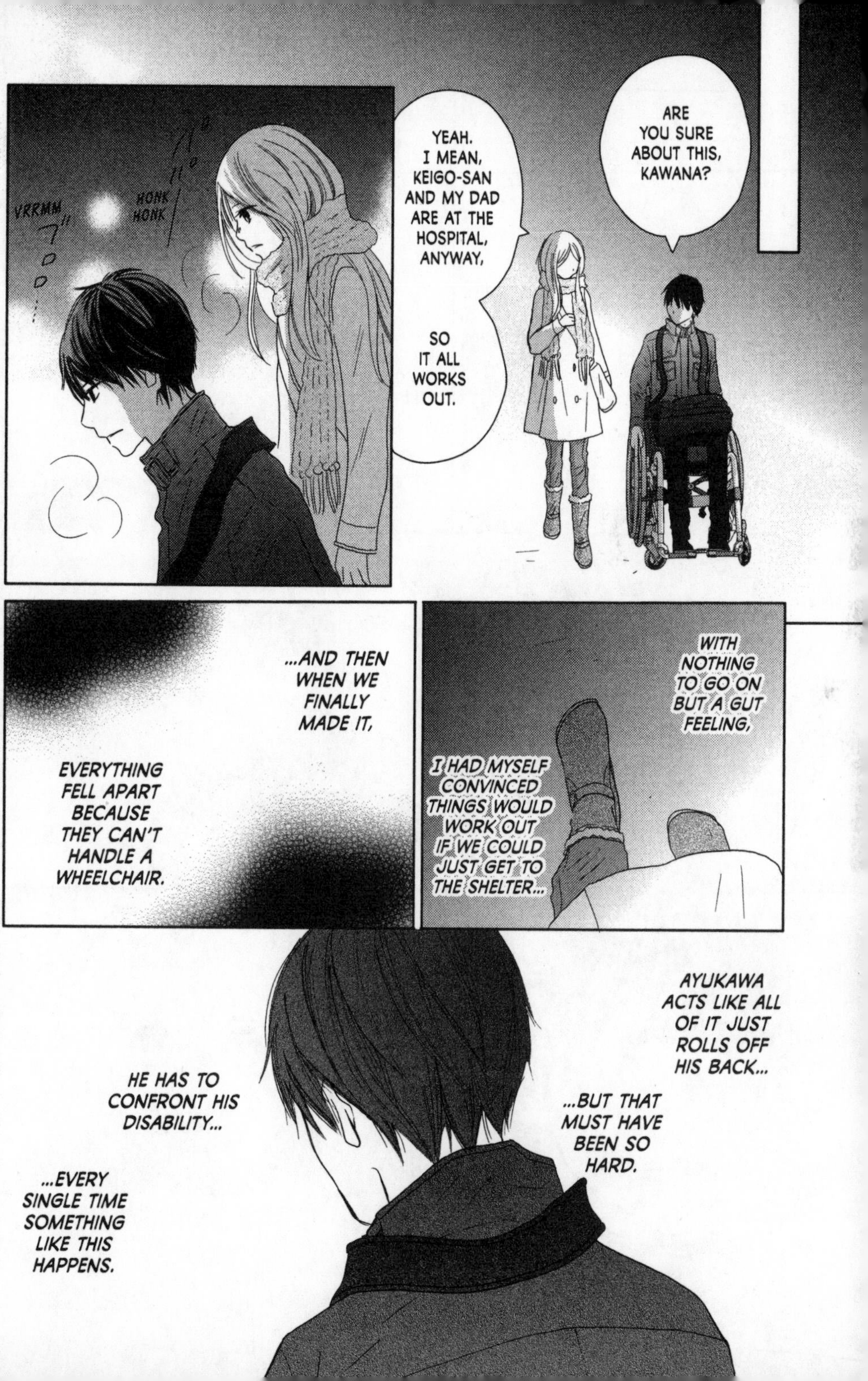
ARE YOU SURE ABOUT THIS, KAWANA?
YEAH. I MEAN, KEIGO-SAN AND MY DAD ARE AT THE HOSPITAL, ANYWAY,
SO IT ALL WORKS OUT.
HONK HONK
VRKMM
WITH NOTHING TO GO ON BUT A GUT FEELING,
I HAD MYSELF CONVINCED THINGS WOULD WORK OUT IF WE COULD JUST GET TO THE SHELTER...
...AND THEN WHEN WE FINALLY MADE IT,
EVERYTHING FELL APART BECAUSE THEY CAN'T HANDLE A WHEELCHAIR.
AYUKAWA ACTS LIKE ALL OF IT JUST ROLLS OFF HIS BACK...
...BUT THAT MUST HAVE BEEN SO HARD.
HE HAS TO CONFRONT HIS DISABILITY...
...EVERY SINGLE TIME SOMETHING LIKE THIS HAPPENS.

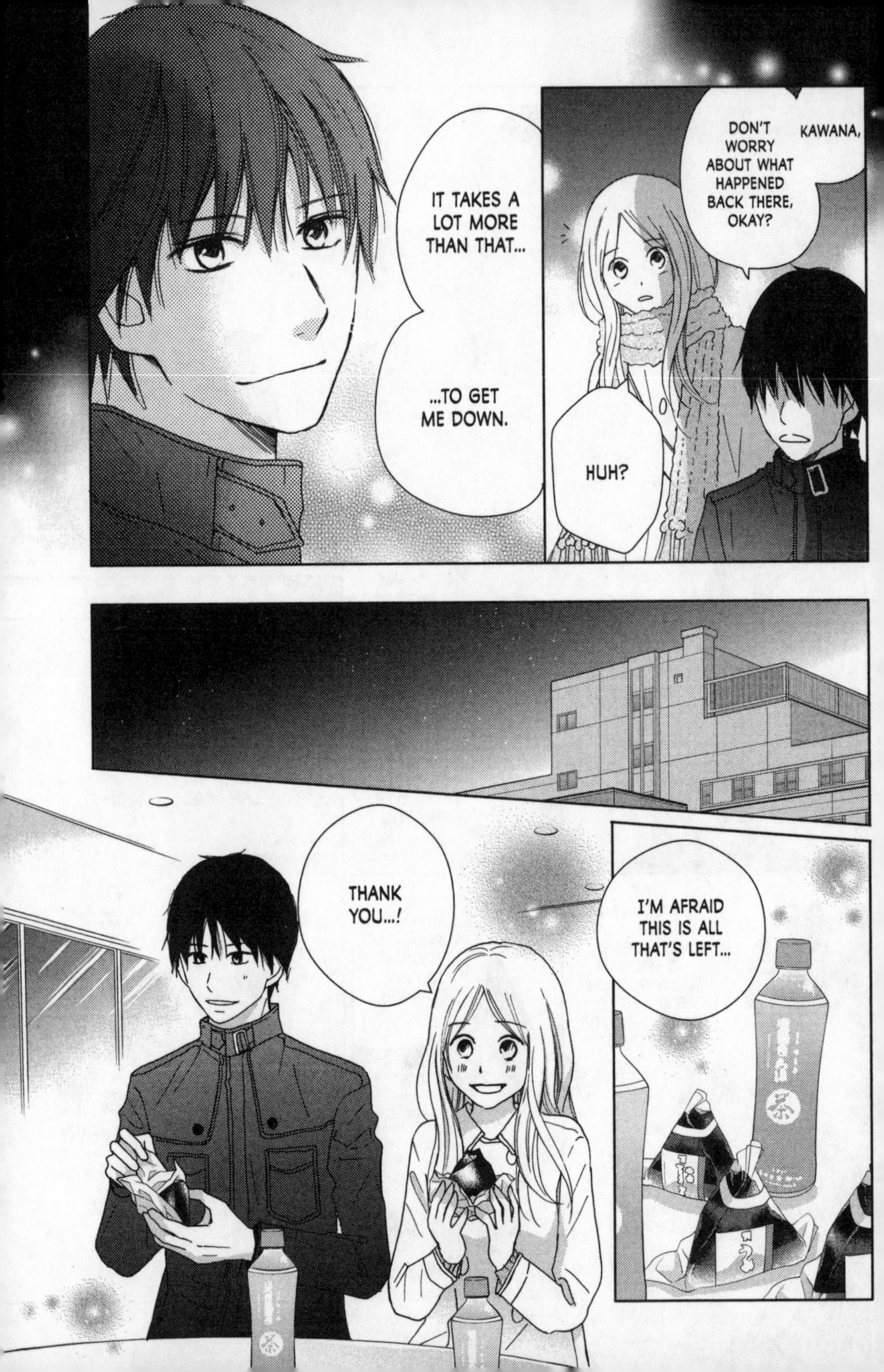
KAWANA, DON'T WORRY ABOUT WHAT HAPPENED BACK THERE, OKAY?
HUH?
IT TAKES A LOT MORE THAN THAT...
...TO GET ME DOWN.
I'M AFRAID THIS IS ALL THAT'S LEFT...
THANK YOU...!

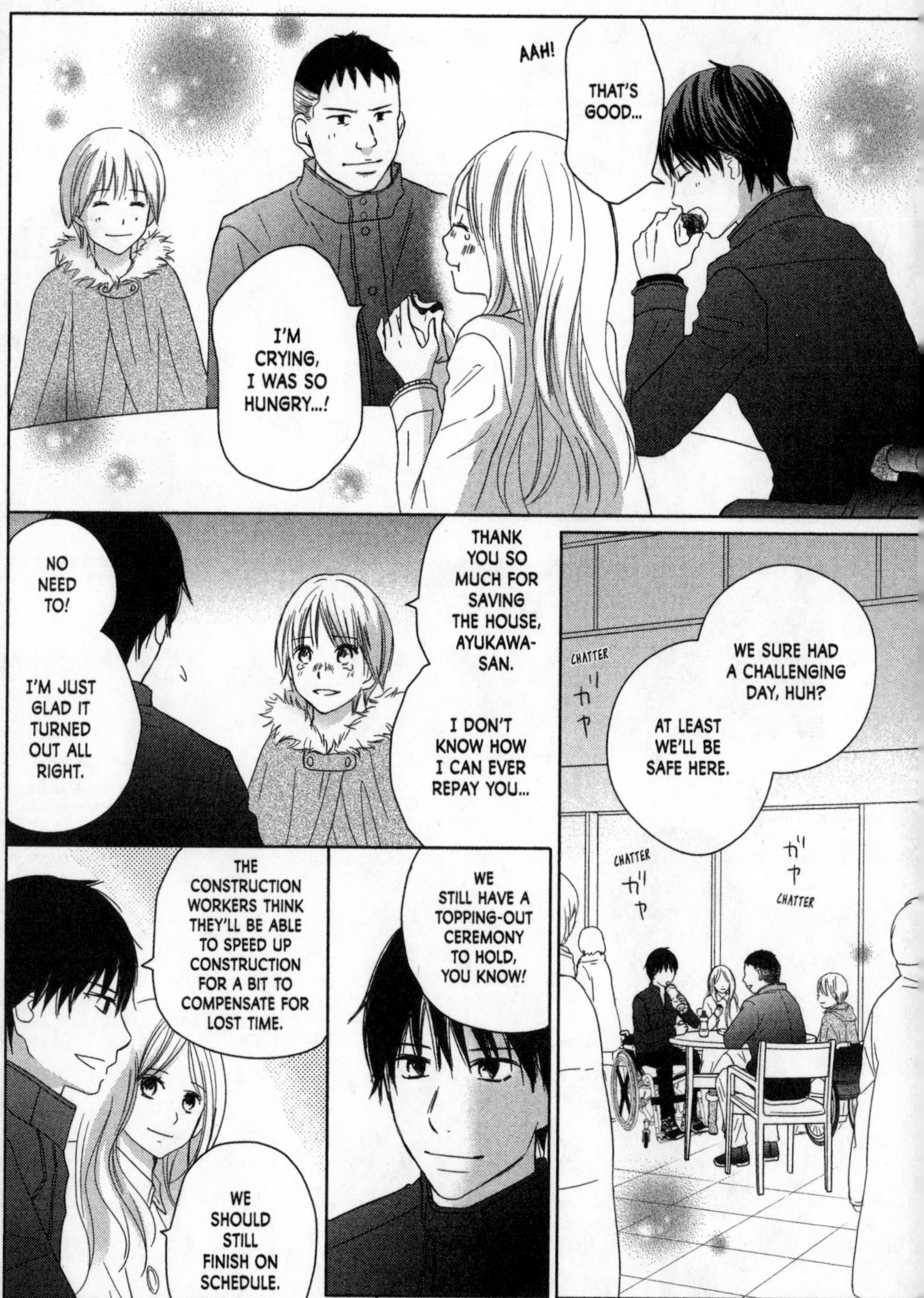
AAH!
THAT'S GOOD...
I'M CRYING, I WAS SO HUNGRY...!
CHATTER ガヤ
WE SURE HAD A CHALLENGING DAY, HUH?
AT LEAST WE'LL BE SAFE HERE.
ガヤ CHATTER
CHATTER ガヤ
THANK YOU SO MUCH FOR SAVING THE HOUSE, AYUKAWA-SAN.
I DON'T KNOW HOW I CAN EVER REPAY YOU...
NO NEED TO!
I'M JUST GLAD IT TURNED OUT ALL RIGHT.
WE STILL HAVE A TOPPING-OUT CEREMONY TO HOLD, YOU KNOW!
THE CONSTRUCTION WORKERS THINK THEY'LL BE ABLE TO SPEED UP CONSTRUCTION FOR A BIT TO COMPENSATE FOR LOST TIME.
WE SHOULD STILL FINISH ON SCHEDULE.

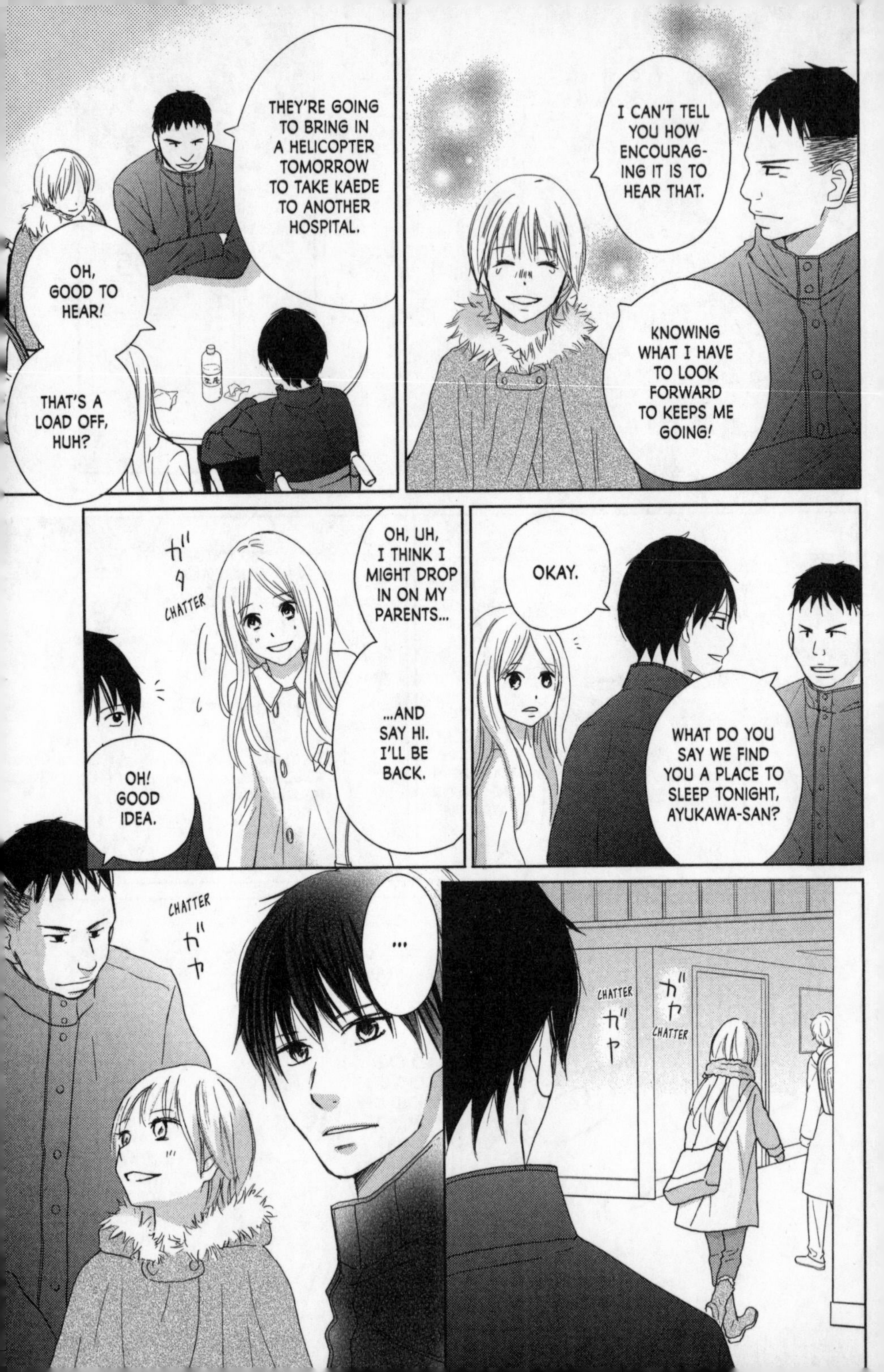
I CAN'T TELL YOU HOW ENCOURAG-ING IT IS TO HEAR THAT.
KNOWING WHAT I HAVE TO LOOK FORWARD TO KEEPS ME GOING!
THEY'RE GOING TO BRING IN A HELICOPTER TOMORROW TO TAKE KAEDE TO ANOTHER HOSPITAL.
OH, GOOD TO HEAR!
THAT'S A LOAD OFF, HUH?
OKAY.
WHAT DO YOU SAY WE FIND YOU A PLACE TO SLEEP TONIGHT, AYUKAWA-SAN?
OH, UH, I THINK I MIGHT DROP IN ON MY PARENTS...
ガタ
CHATTER
...AND SAY HI. I'LL BE BACK.
OH! GOOD IDEA.
ガヤ
CHATTER
ガヤ
CHATTER
...
CHATTER
ガヤ

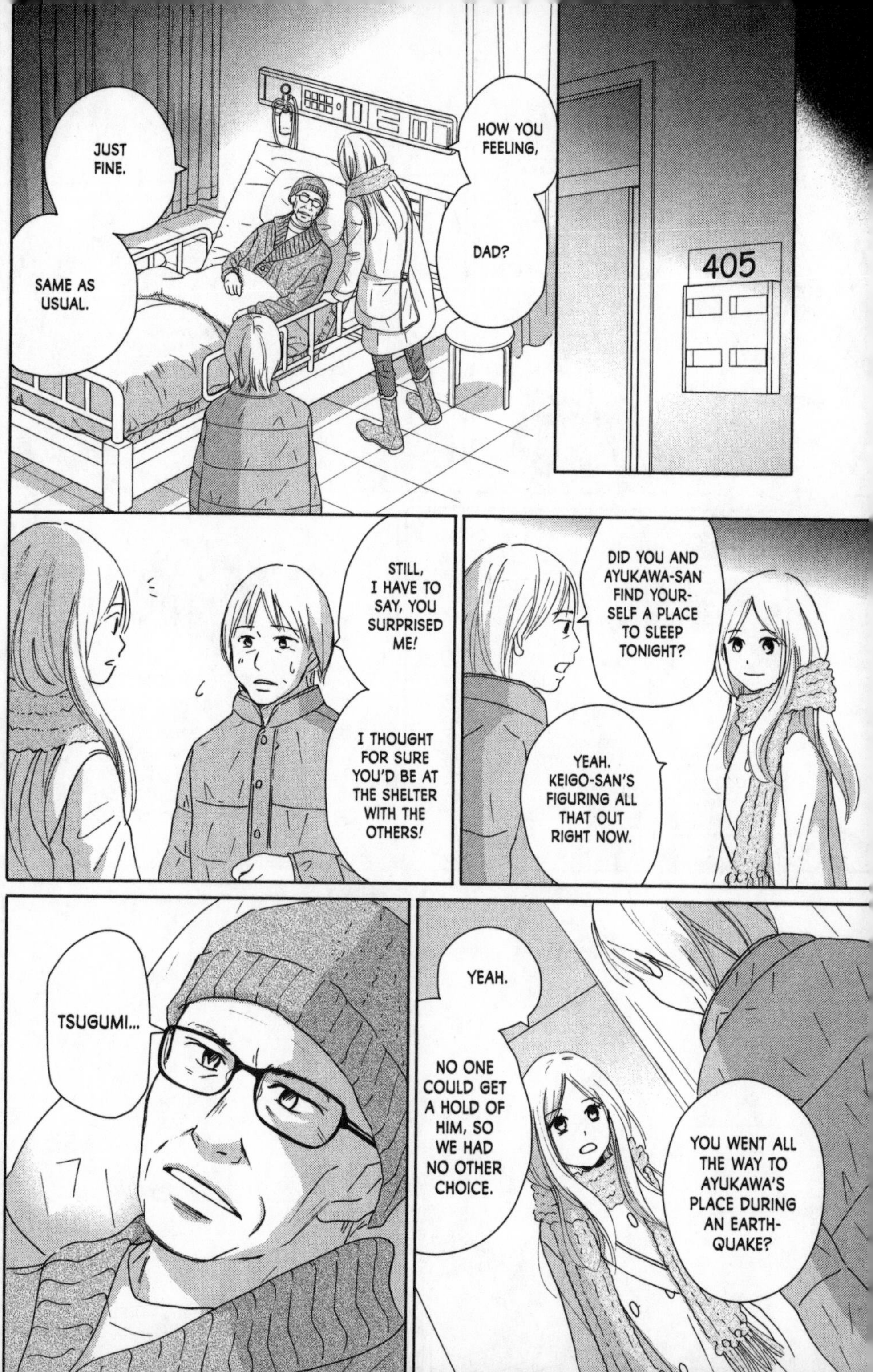
HOW YOU FEELING,
DAD?
405
JUST FINE.
SAME AS USUAL.
DID YOU AND AYUKAWA-SAN FIND YOUR-SELF A PLACE TO SLEEP TONIGHT?
YEAH. KEIGO-SAN'S FIGURING ALL THAT OUT RIGHT NOW.
STILL, I HAVE TO SAY, YOU SURPRISED ME!
I THOUGHT FOR SURE YOU'D BE AT THE SHELTER WITH THE OTHERS!
YOU WENT ALL THE WAY TO AYUKAWA'S PLACE DURING AN EARTH-QUAKE?
YEAH.
NO ONE COULD GET A HOLD OF HIM, SO WE HAD NO OTHER CHOICE.
TSUGUMI...

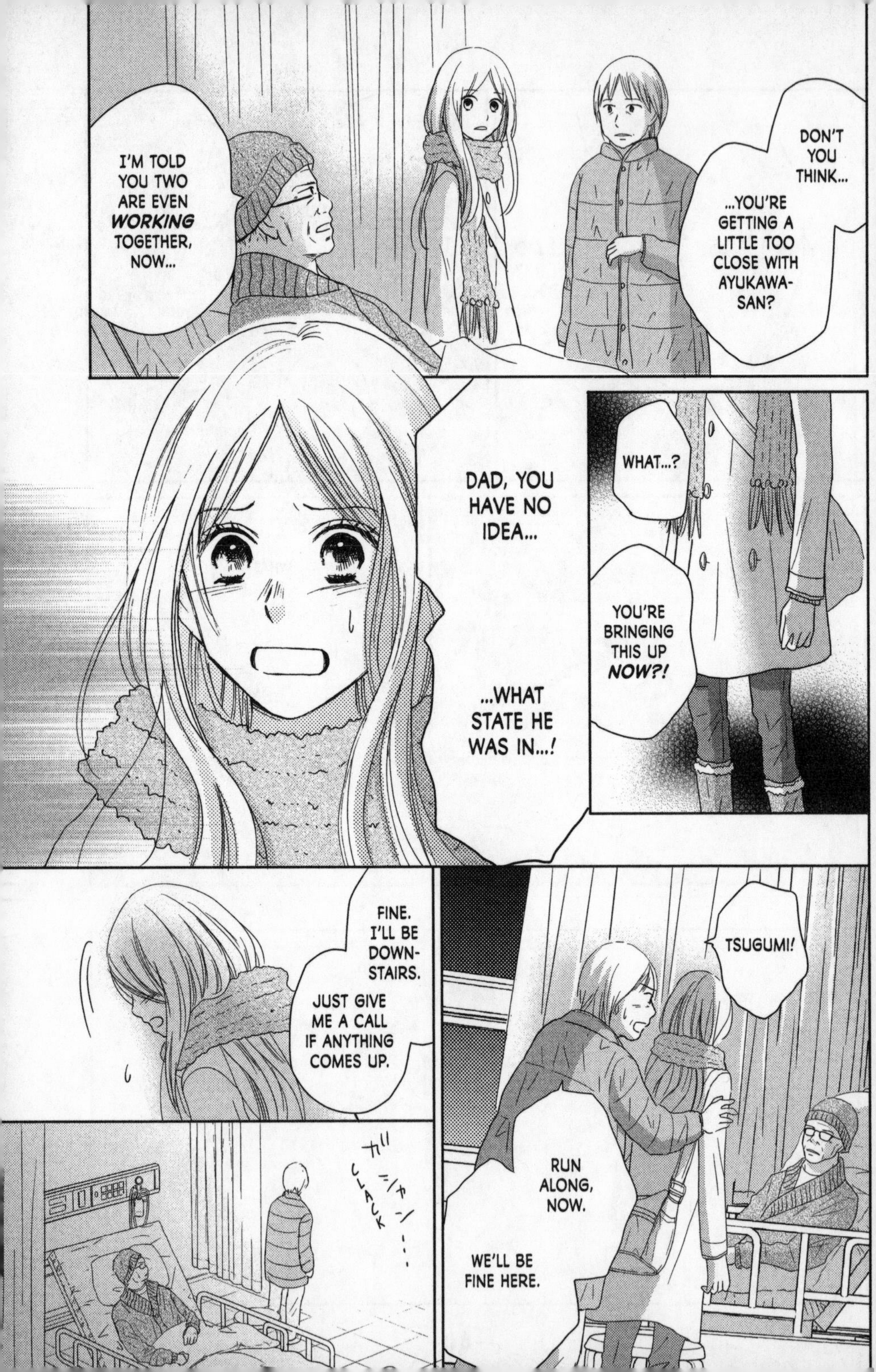
DON'T YOU THINK...
...YOU'RE GETTING A LITTLE TOO CLOSE WITH AYUKAWA-SAN?
I'M TOLD YOU TWO ARE EVEN *WORKING* TOGETHER, NOW...
WHAT...?
YOU'RE BRINGING THIS UP *NOW?!*
DAD, YOU HAVE NO IDEA...
...WHAT STATE HE WAS IN...!
TSUGUMI!
RUN ALONG, NOW.
WE'LL BE FINE HERE.
FINE. I'LL BE DOWN-STAIRS.
JUST GIVE ME A CALL IF ANYTHING COMES UP.
ガラッ
CLACK

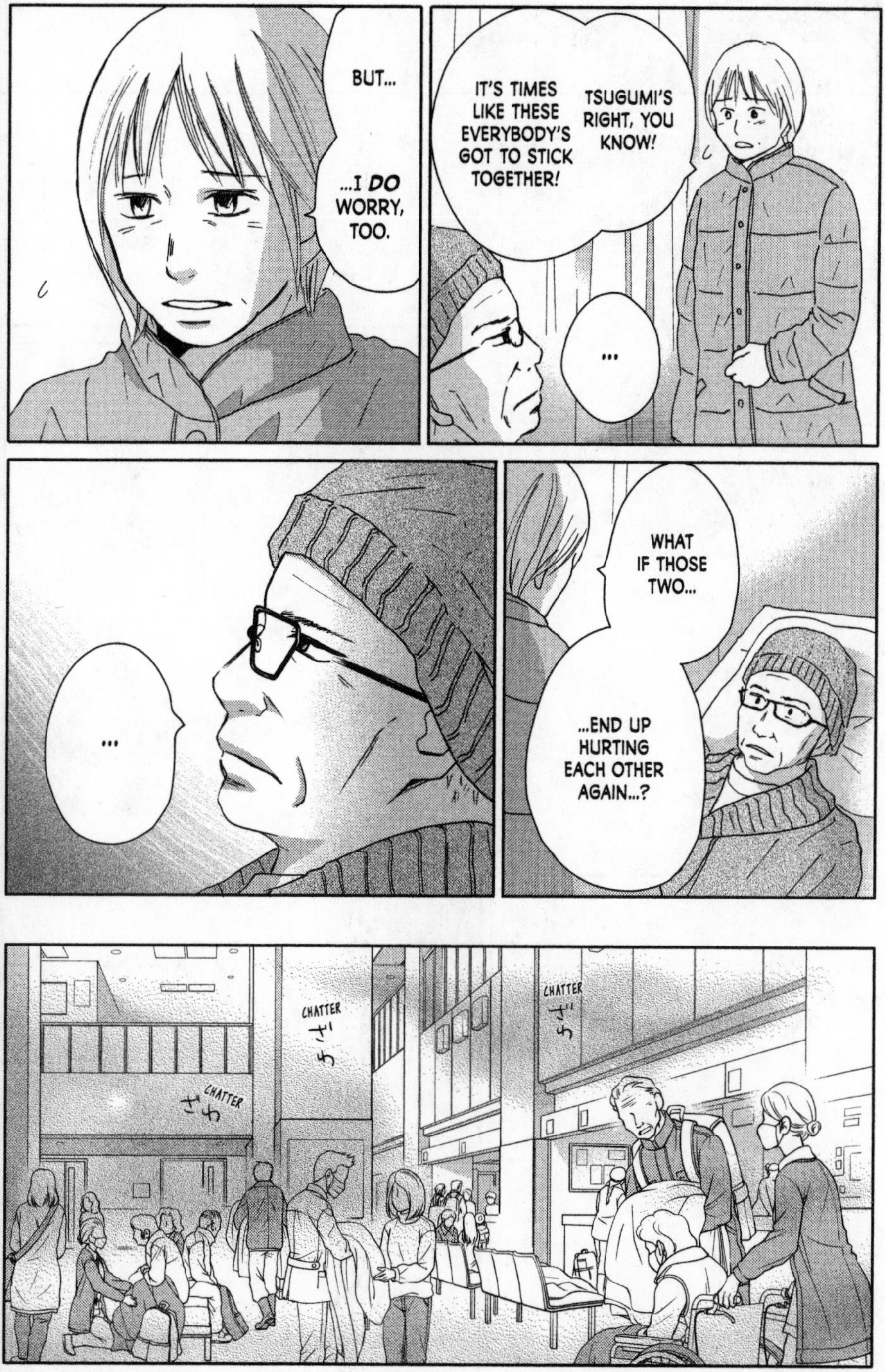
TSUGUMI'S RIGHT, YOU KNOW!
IT'S TIMES LIKE THESE EVERYBODY'S GOT TO STICK TOGETHER!
...
BUT...
...I *DO* WORRY, TOO.
WHAT IF THOSE TWO...
...END UP HURTING EACH OTHER AGAIN...?
...
CHATTER
CHATTER
CHATTER

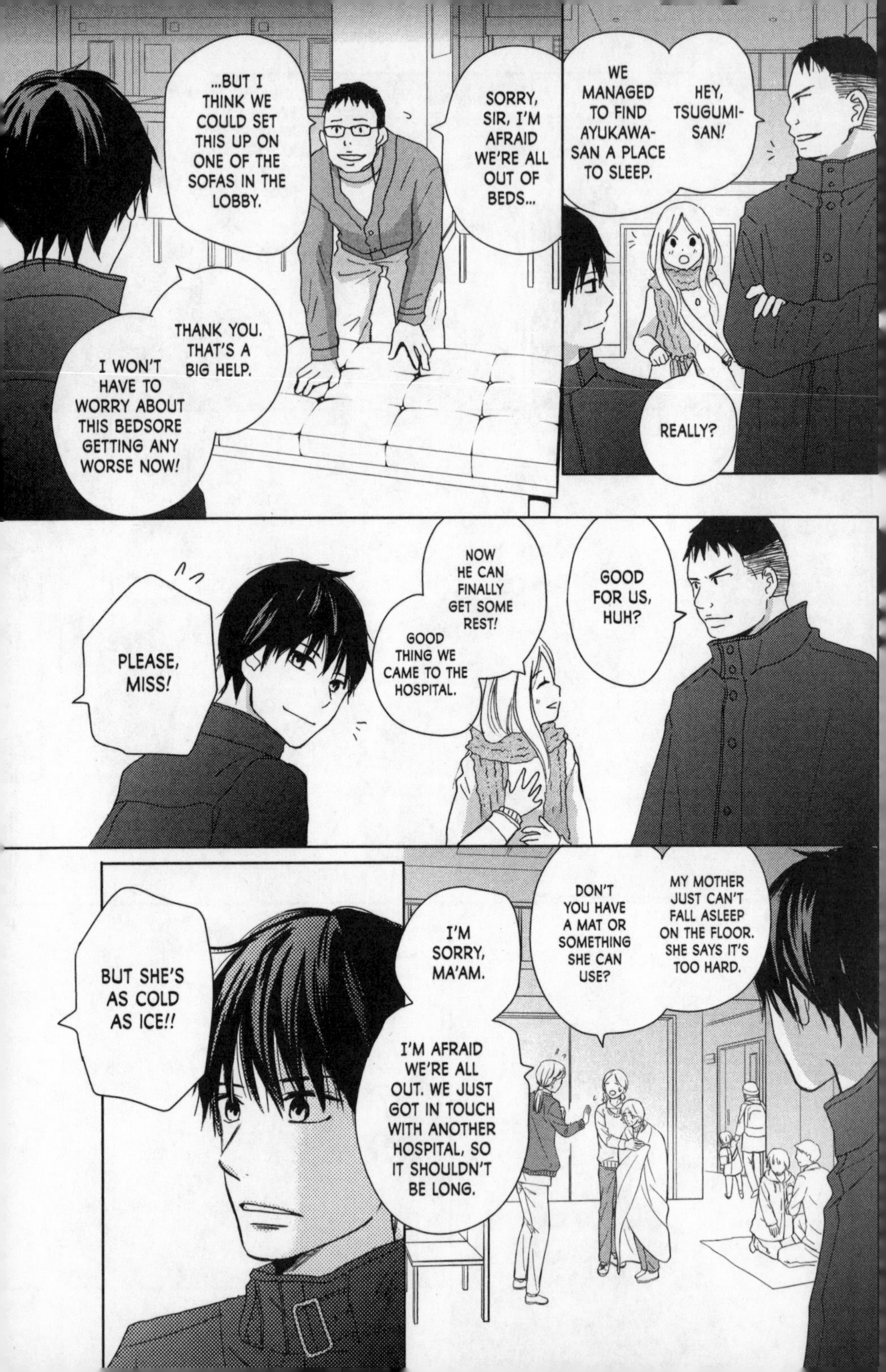
HEY, TSUGUMI-SAN!
WE MANAGED TO FIND AYUKAWA-SAN A PLACE TO SLEEP.
REALLY?
SORRY, SIR, I'M AFRAID WE'RE ALL OUT OF BEDS...
...BUT I THINK WE COULD SET THIS UP ON ONE OF THE SOFAS IN THE LOBBY.
THANK YOU. THAT'S A BIG HELP.
I WON'T HAVE TO WORRY ABOUT THIS BEDSORE GETTING ANY WORSE NOW!
GOOD FOR US, HUH?
NOW HE CAN FINALLY GET SOME REST!
GOOD THING WE CAME TO THE HOSPITAL.
PLEASE, MISS!
MY MOTHER JUST CAN'T FALL ASLEEP ON THE FLOOR. SHE SAYS IT'S TOO HARD.
DON'T YOU HAVE A MAT OR SOMETHING SHE CAN USE?
I'M SORRY, MA'AM.
I'M AFRAID WE'RE ALL OUT. WE JUST GOT IN TOUCH WITH ANOTHER HOSPITAL, SO IT SHOULDN'T BE LONG.
BUT SHE'S AS COLD AS ICE!!

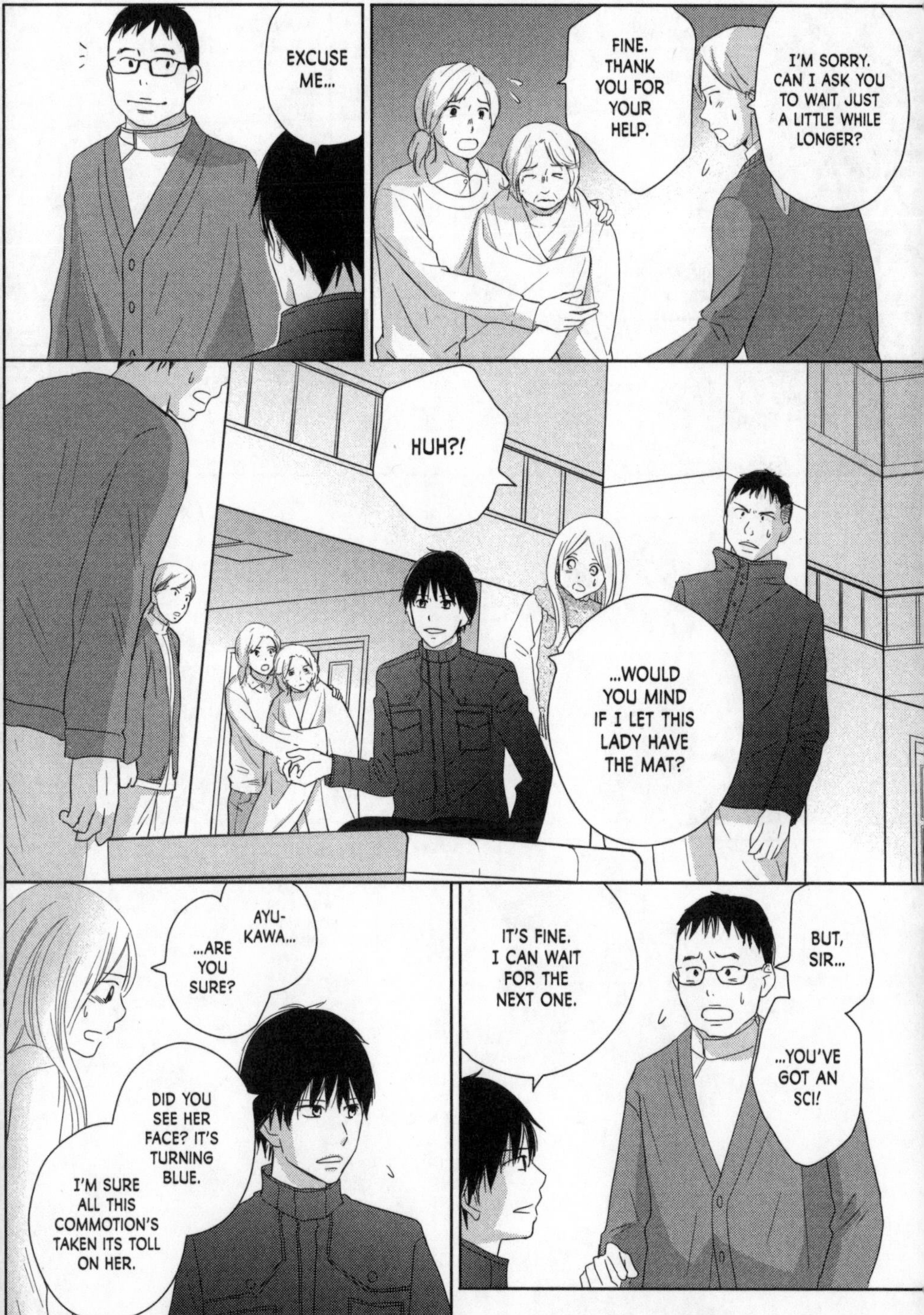
I'M SORRY. CAN I ASK YOU TO WAIT JUST A LITTLE WHILE LONGER?
FINE. THANK YOU FOR YOUR HELP.
EXCUSE ME...
HUH?!
...WOULD YOU MIND IF I LET THIS LADY HAVE THE MAT?
BUT, SIR...
...YOU'VE GOT AN SCI!
IT'S FINE. I CAN WAIT FOR THE NEXT ONE.
AYU-KAWA...
...ARE YOU SURE?
DID YOU SEE HER FACE? IT'S TURNING BLUE.
I'M SURE ALL THIS COMMOTION'S TAKEN ITS TOLL ON HER.

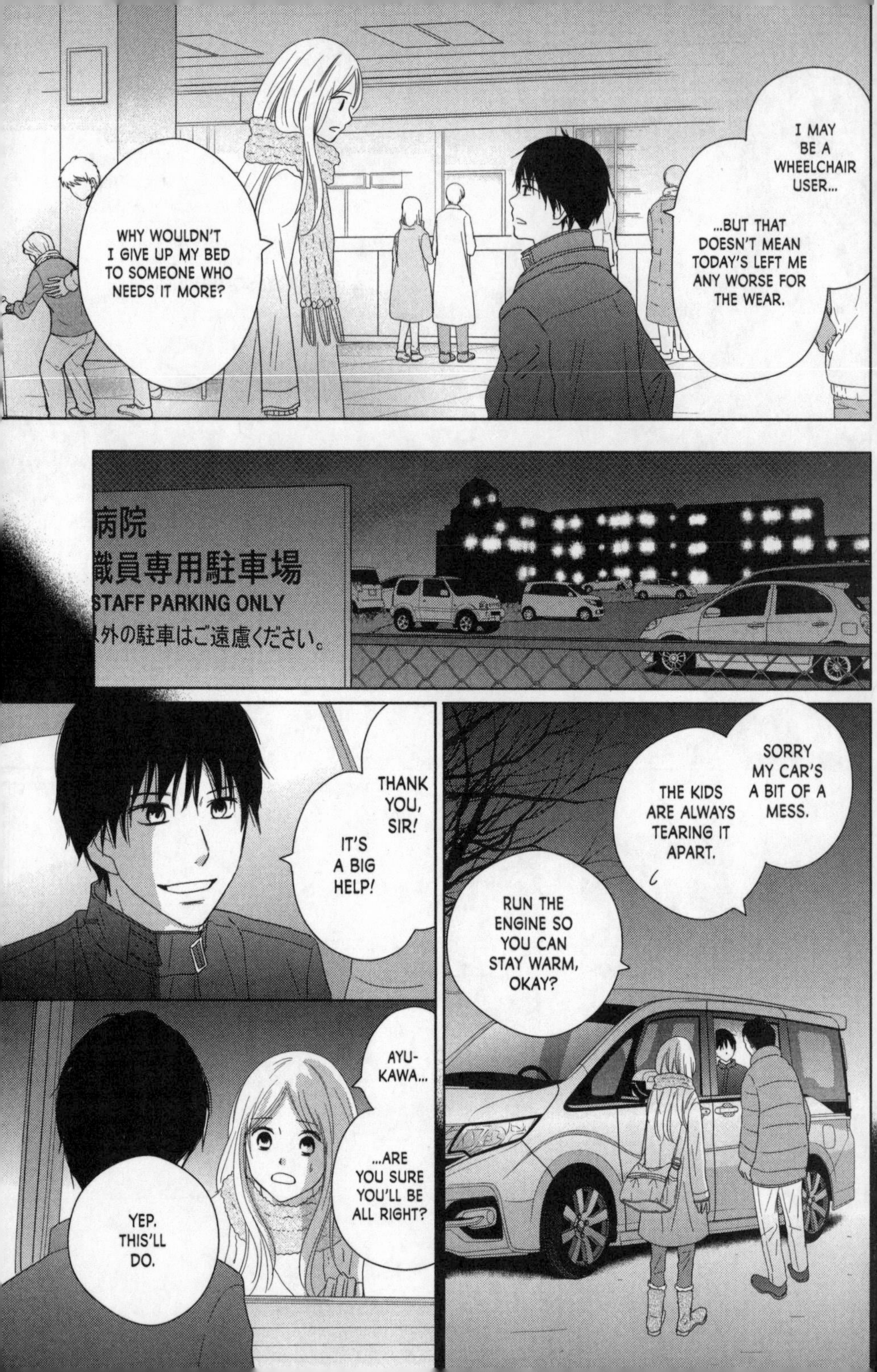
I MAY BE A WHEELCHAIR USER...
...BUT THAT DOESN'T MEAN TODAY'S LEFT ME ANY WORSE FOR THE WEAR.
WHY WOULDN'T I GIVE UP MY BED TO SOMEONE WHO NEEDS IT MORE?
病院
職員専用駐車場
STAFF PARKING ONLY
外の駐車はご遠慮ください。
SORRY MY CAR'S A BIT OF A MESS.
THE KIDS ARE ALWAYS TEARING IT APART.
RUN THE ENGINE SO YOU CAN STAY WARM, OKAY?
THANK YOU, SIR!
IT'S A BIG HELP!
AYU-KAWA...
...ARE YOU SURE YOU'LL BE ALL RIGHT?
YEP. THIS'LL DO.

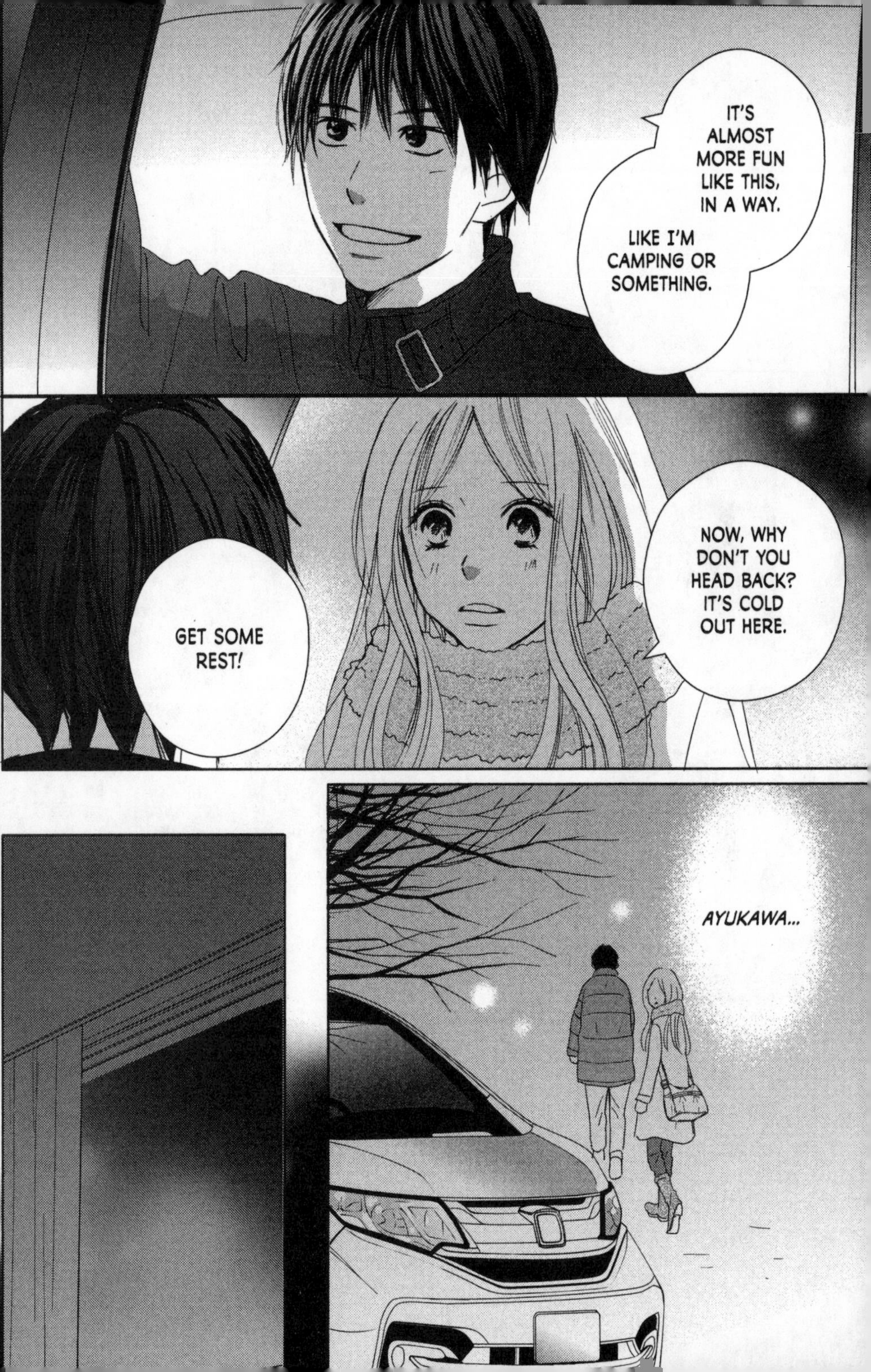
IT'S ALMOST MORE FUN LIKE THIS, IN A WAY.
LIKE I'M CAMPING OR SOMETHING.
NOW, WHY DON'T YOU HEAD BACK? IT'S COLD OUT HERE.
GET SOME REST!
AYUKAWA...

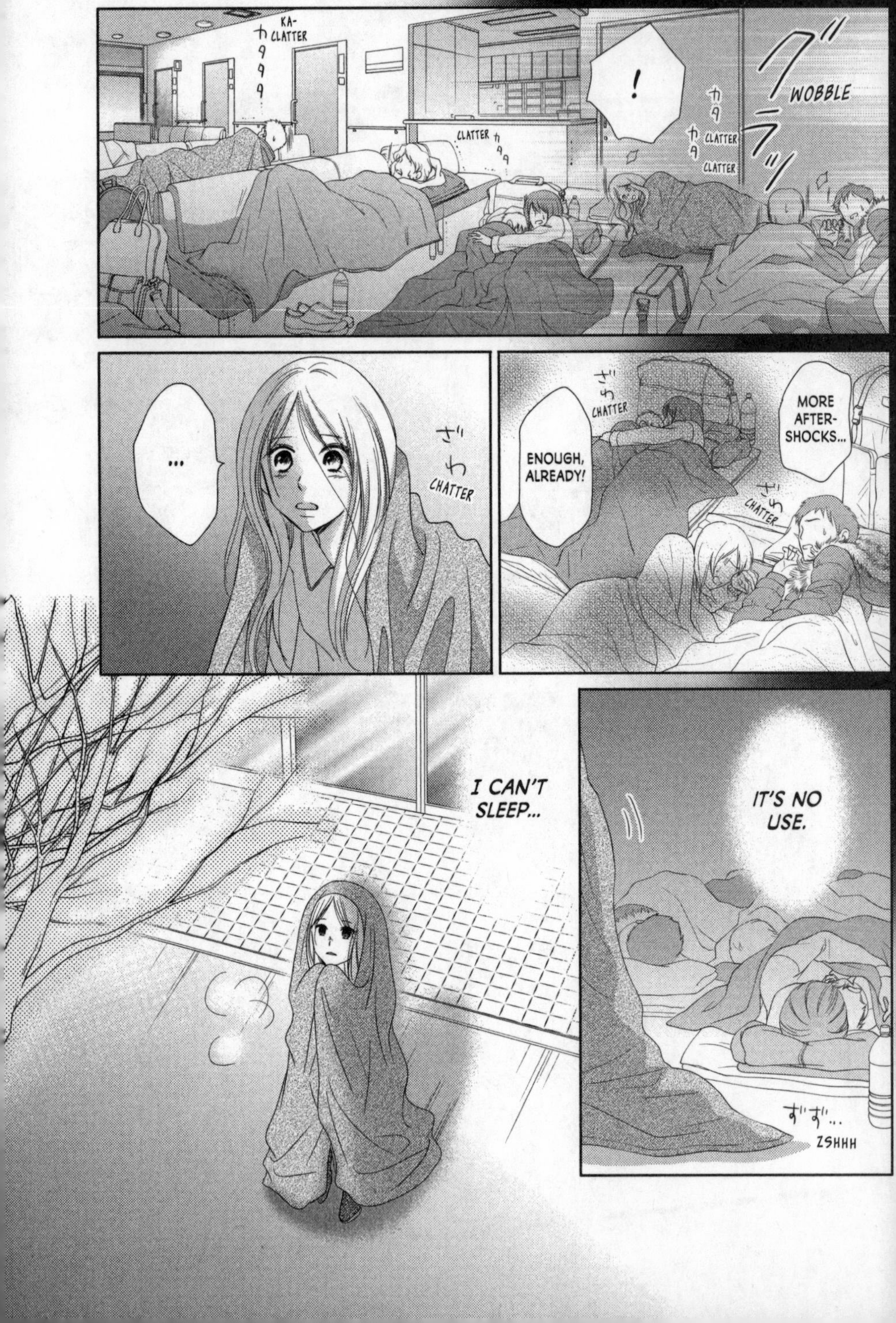
グラッ WOBBLE
カタ CLATTER
カタ CLATTER
!
CLATTER カタタ
KA-CLATTER カタタタ...
MORE AFTER-SHOCKS...
ざわ CHATTER
ENOUGH, ALREADY!
ざわ CHATTER
ざわ CHATTER
...
IT'S NO USE.
ずず... ZSHHH
I CAN'T SLEEP...

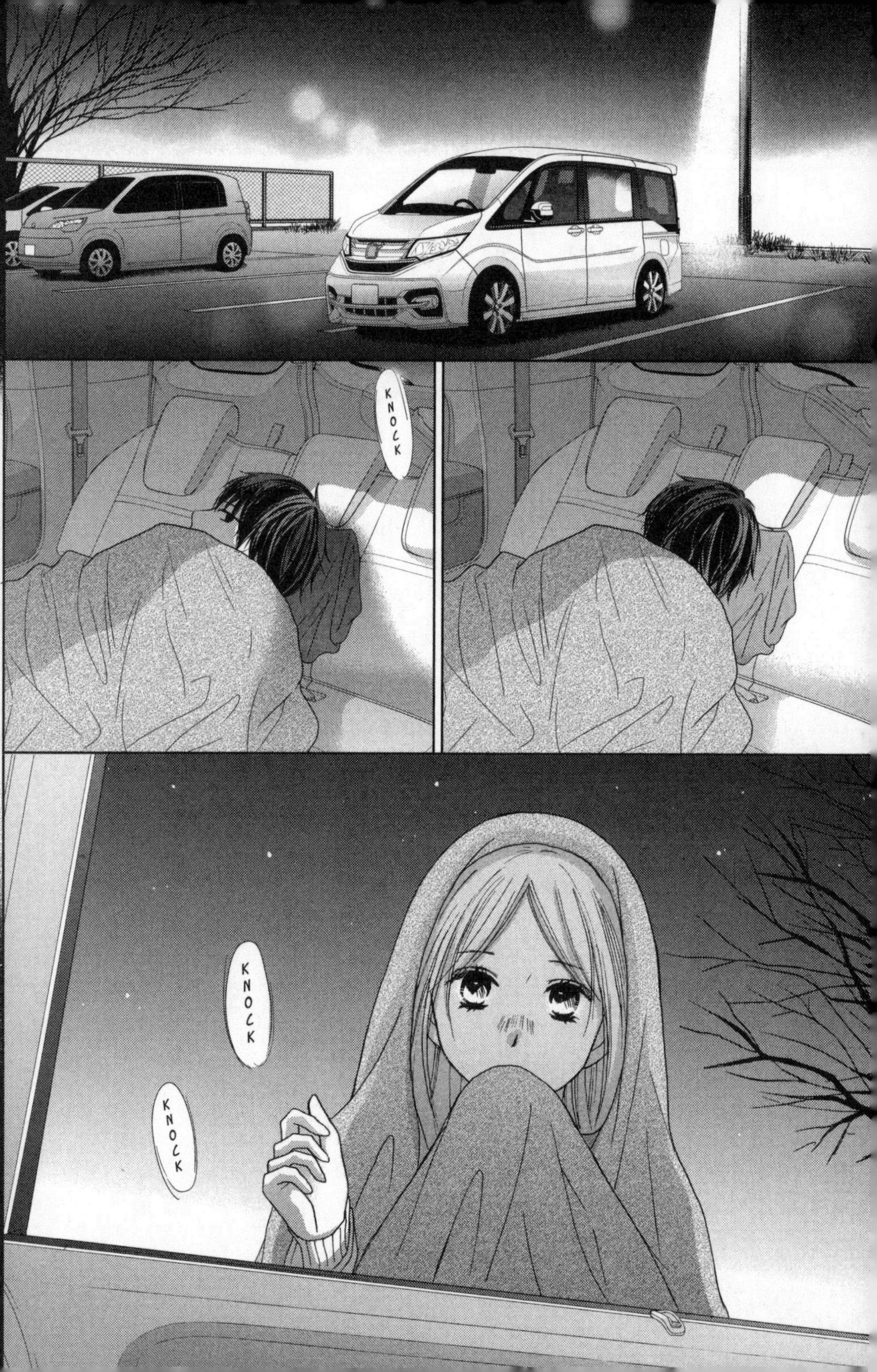
KNOCK
KNOCK
KNOCK

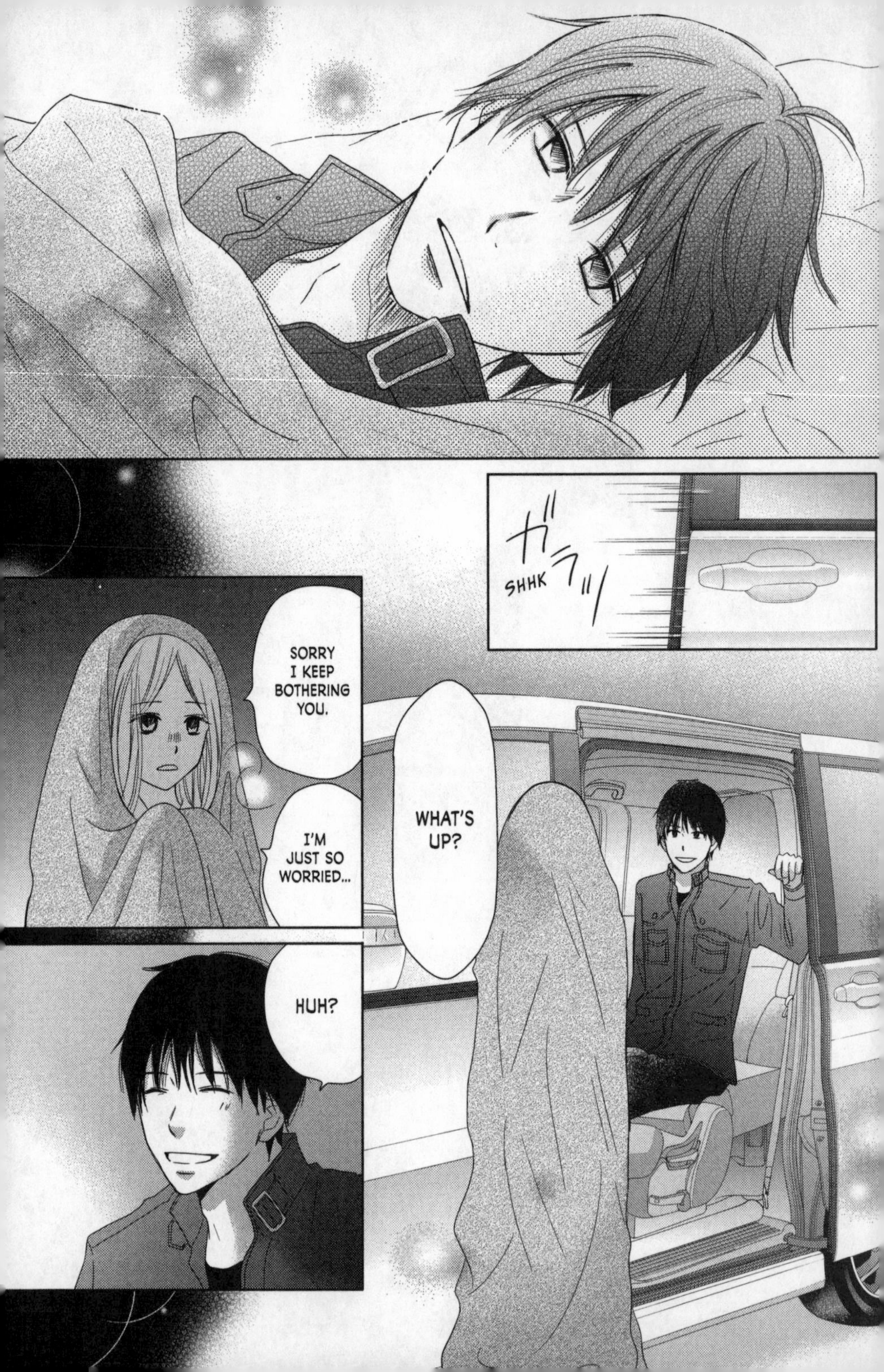
ガラッ
SHHK
WHAT'S UP?
SORRY I KEEP BOTHERING YOU.
I'M JUST SO WORRIED...
HUH?

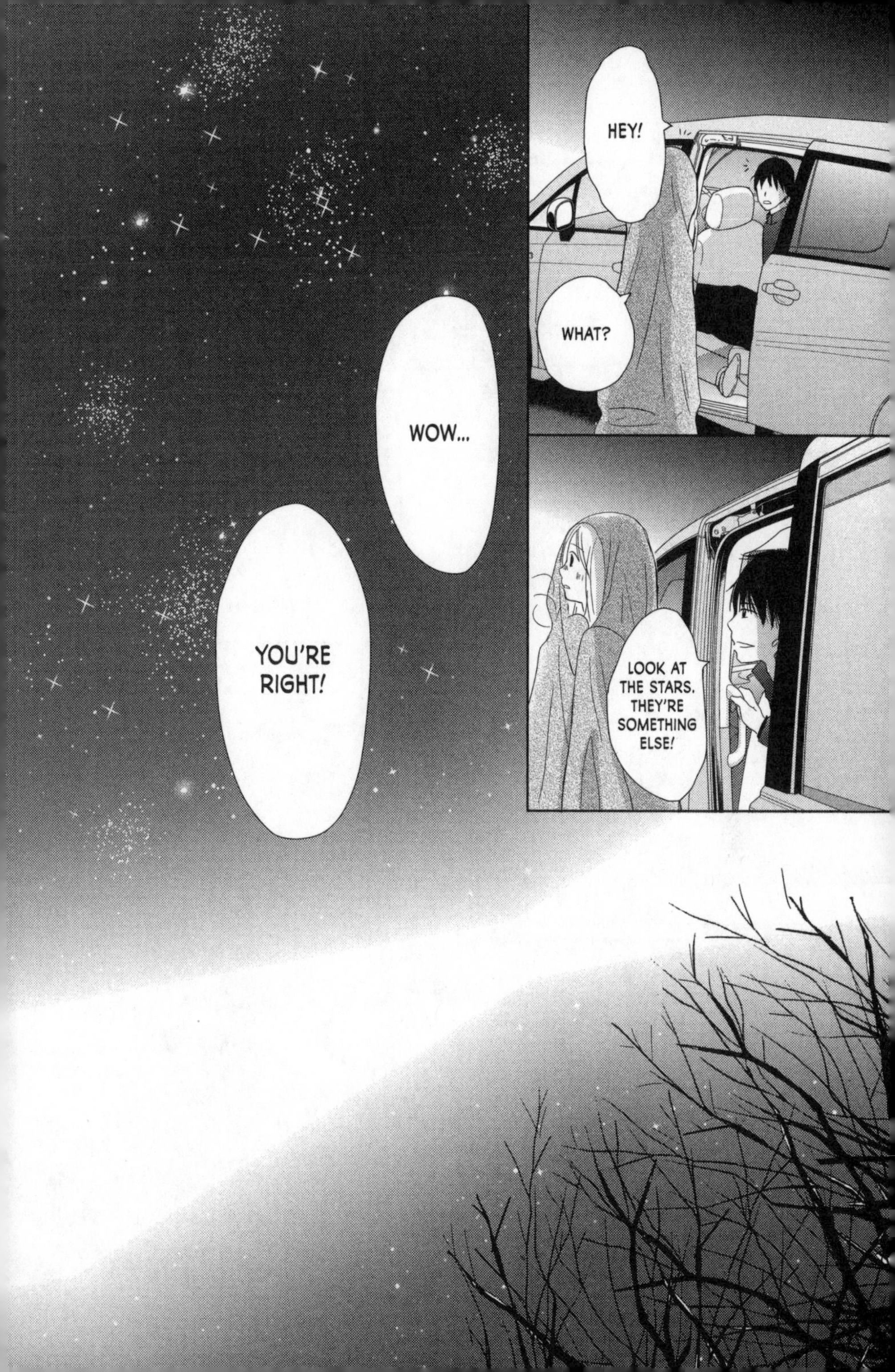
HEY!
WHAT?
LOOK AT THE STARS. THEY'RE SOMETHING ELSE!
WOW...
YOU'RE RIGHT!

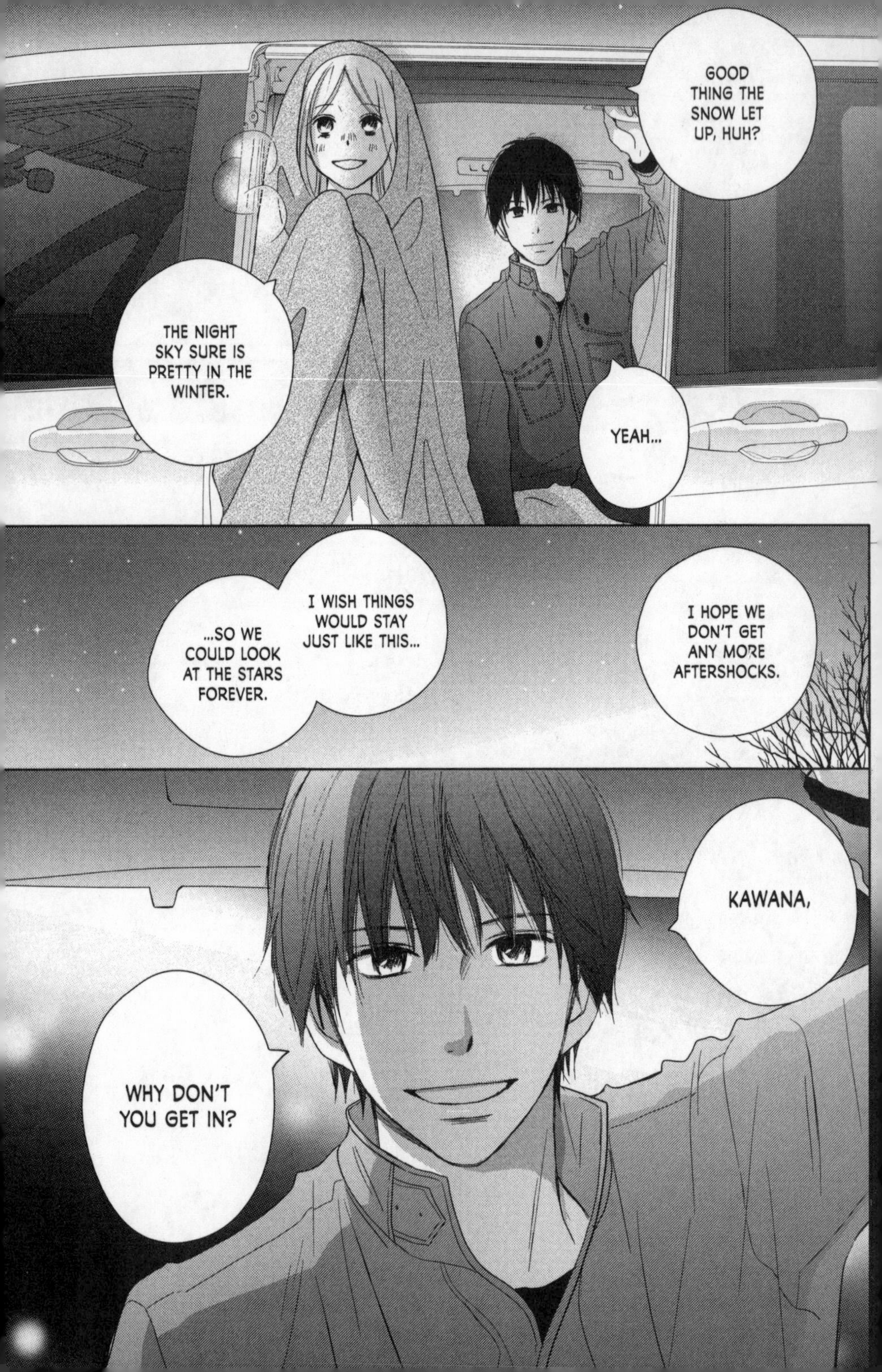
GOOD THING THE SNOW LET UP, HUH?
THE NIGHT SKY SURE IS PRETTY IN THE WINTER.
YEAH...
I HOPE WE DON'T GET ANY MORE AFTERSHOCKS.
I WISH THINGS WOULD STAY JUST LIKE THIS...
...SO WE COULD LOOK AT THE STARS FOREVER.
KAWANA,
WHY DON'T YOU GET IN?

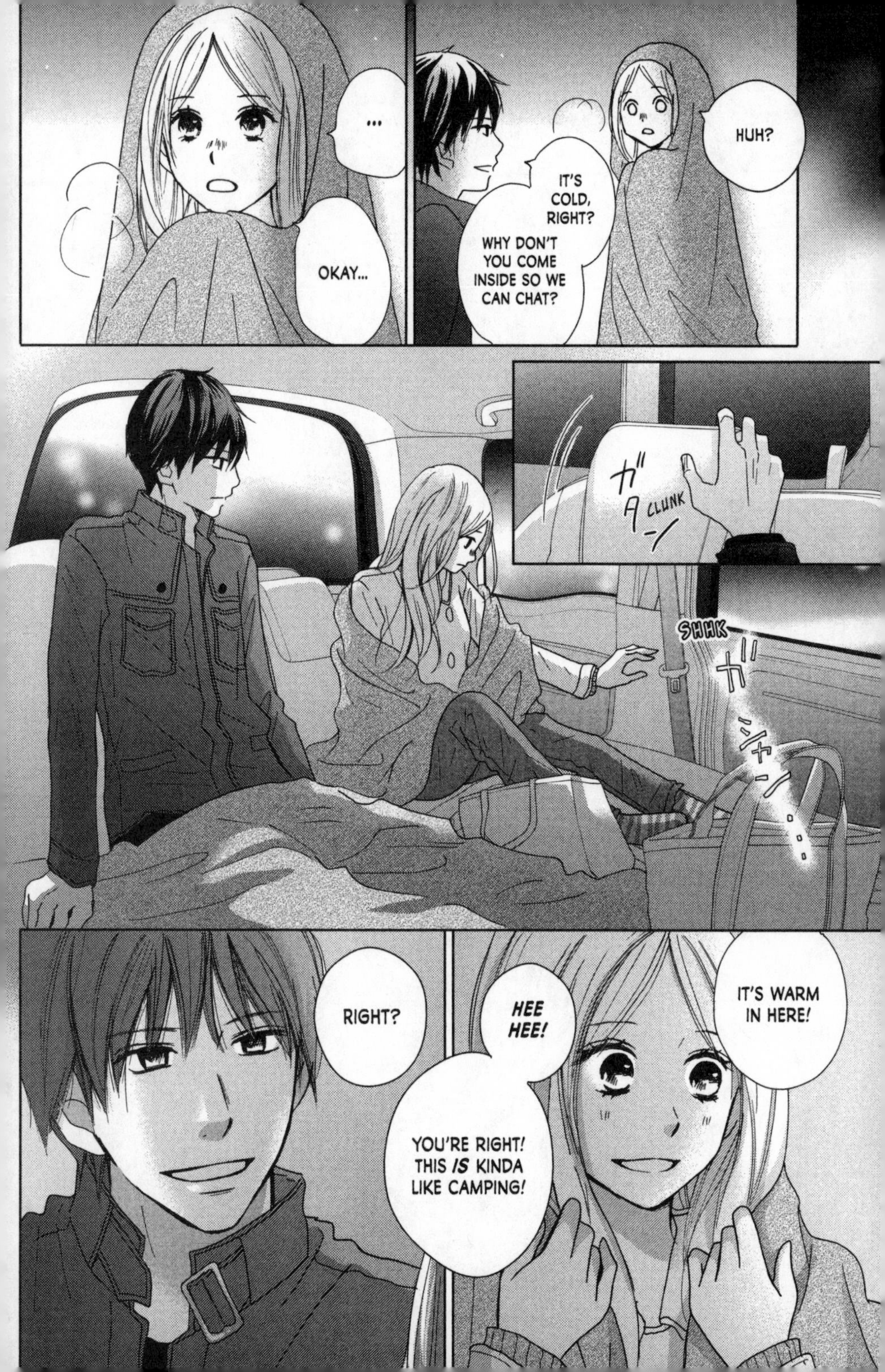
HUH?
IT'S COLD, RIGHT?
WHY DON'T YOU COME INSIDE SO WE CAN CHAT?
...
OKAY...
ガタン
CLUNK
SHHK
ガシャン...
IT'S WARM IN HERE!
HEE HEE!
YOU'RE RIGHT! THIS *IS* KINDA LIKE CAMPING!
RIGHT?

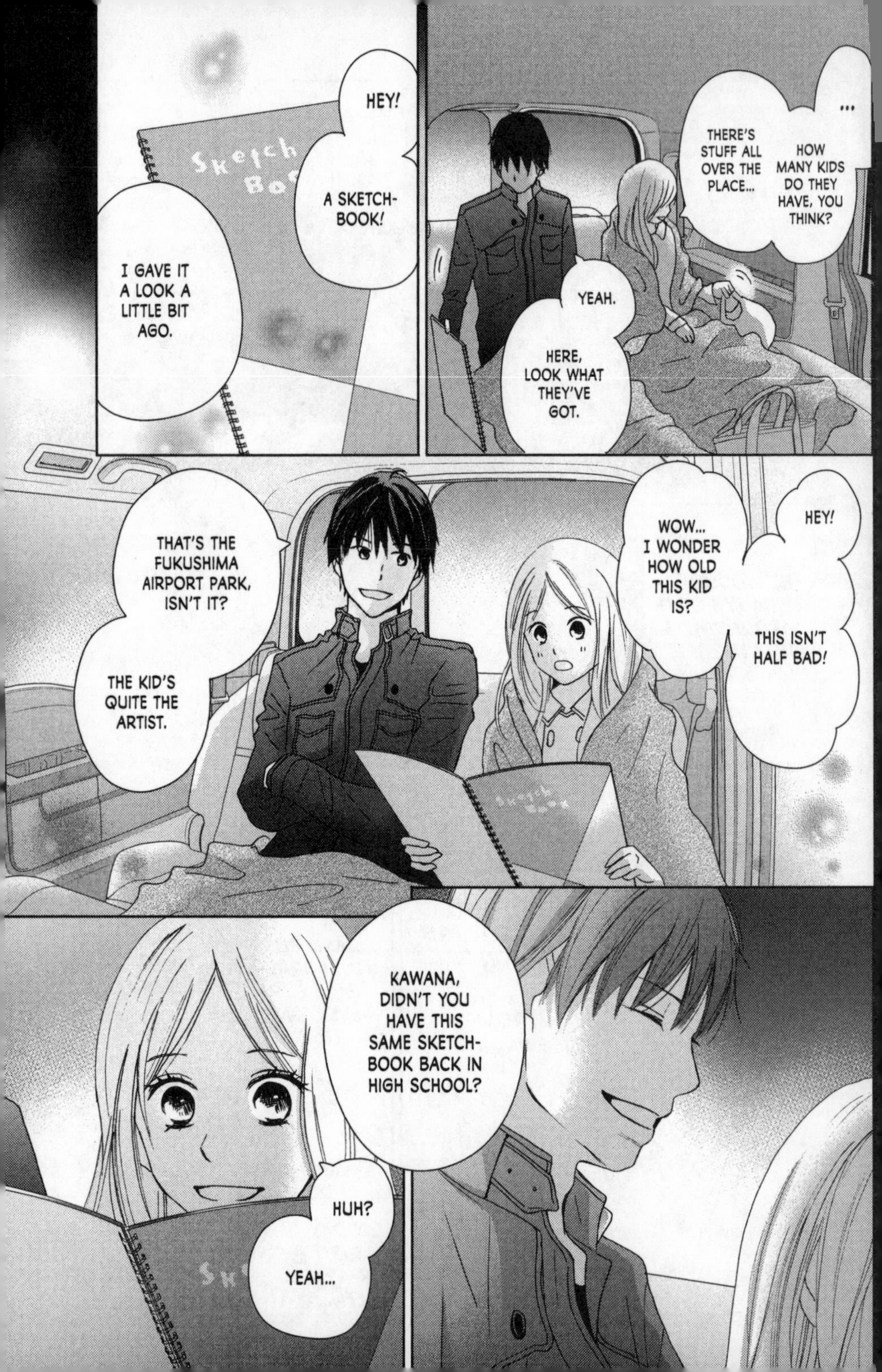
...
HOW MANY KIDS DO THEY HAVE, YOU THINK?
THERE'S STUFF ALL OVER THE PLACE...
YEAH.
HERE, LOOK WHAT THEY'VE GOT.
HEY!
A SKETCH-BOOK!
I GAVE IT A LOOK A LITTLE BIT AGO.
Sketch Book
HEY!
THIS ISN'T HALF BAD!
WOW... I WONDER HOW OLD THIS KID IS?
THAT'S THE FUKUSHIMA AIRPORT PARK, ISN'T IT?
THE KID'S QUITE THE ARTIST.
KAWANA, DIDN'T YOU HAVE THIS SAME SKETCH-BOOK BACK IN HIGH SCHOOL?
HUH?
YEAH...

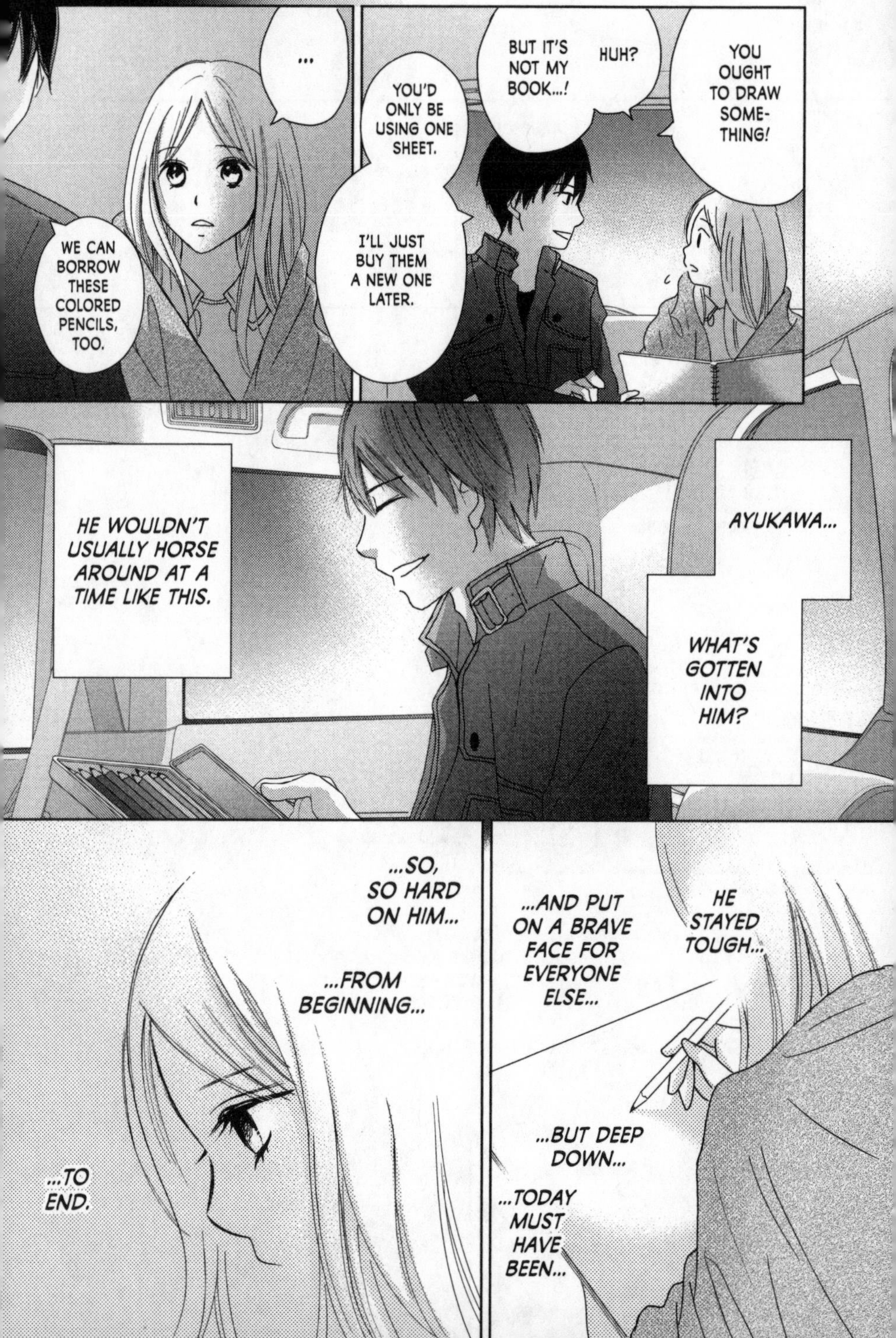
YOU OUGHT TO DRAW SOMETHING!
HUH?
BUT IT'S NOT MY BOOK...!
YOU'D ONLY BE USING ONE SHEET.
I'LL JUST BUY THEM A NEW ONE LATER.
...
WE CAN BORROW THESE COLORED PENCILS, TOO.
AYUKAWA...
WHAT'S GOTTEN INTO HIM?
HE WOULDN'T USUALLY HORSE AROUND AT A TIME LIKE THIS.
HE STAYED TOUGH...
...AND PUT ON A BRAVE FACE FOR EVERYONE ELSE...
...BUT DEEP DOWN...
...TODAY MUST HAVE BEEN...
...SO, SO HARD ON HIM...
...FROM BEGINNING...
...TO END.

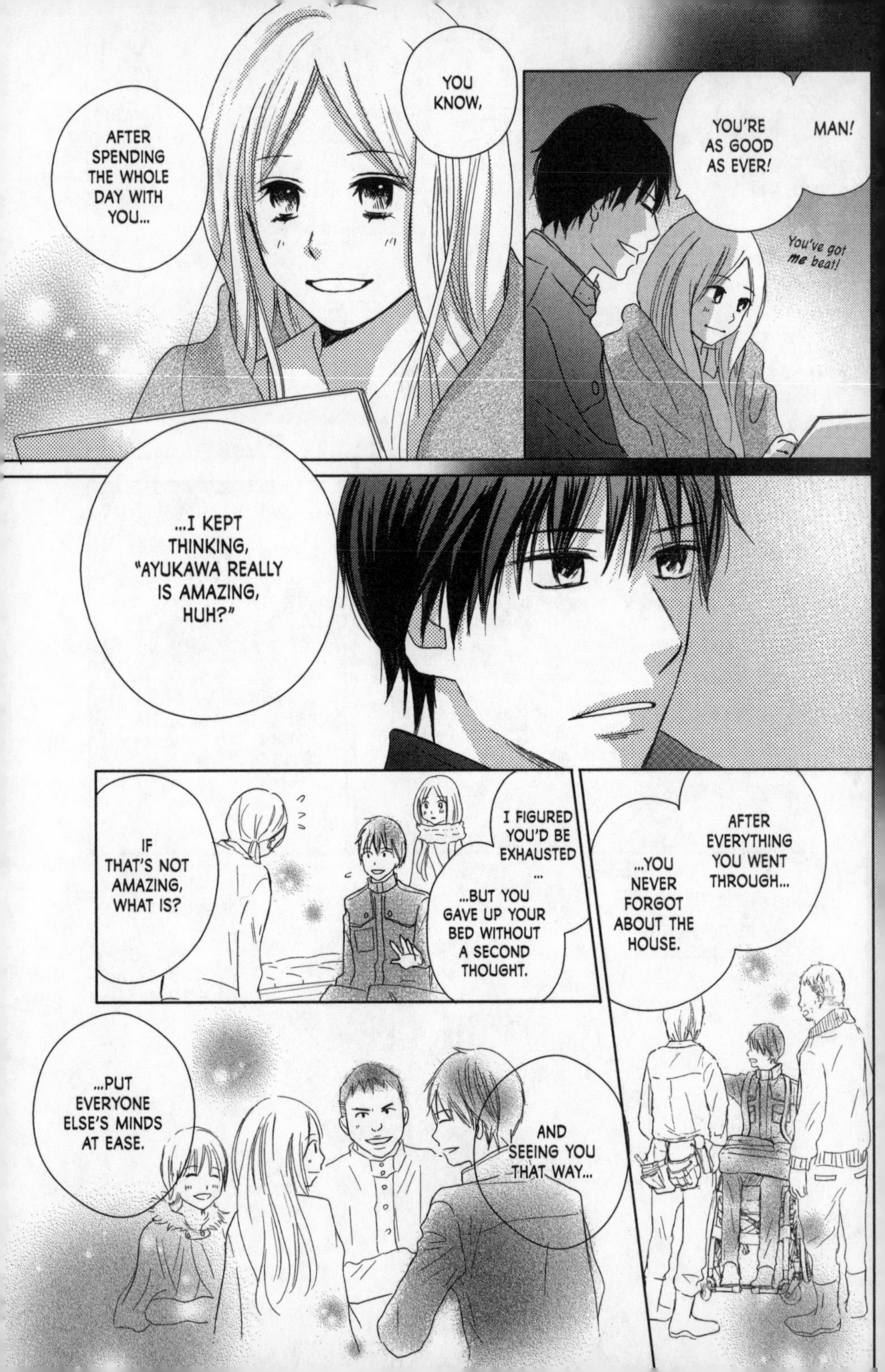
MAN! YOU'RE AS GOOD AS EVER!
You've got me beat!
YOU KNOW,
AFTER SPENDING THE WHOLE DAY WITH YOU...
...I KEPT THINKING, "AYUKAWA REALLY IS AMAZING, HUH?"
AFTER EVERYTHING YOU WENT THROUGH...
...YOU NEVER FORGOT ABOUT THE HOUSE.
I FIGURED YOU'D BE EXHAUSTED ...
...BUT YOU GAVE UP YOUR BED WITHOUT A SECOND THOUGHT.
IF THAT'S NOT AMAZING, WHAT IS?
AND SEEING YOU THAT WAY...
...PUT EVERYONE ELSE'S MINDS AT EASE.

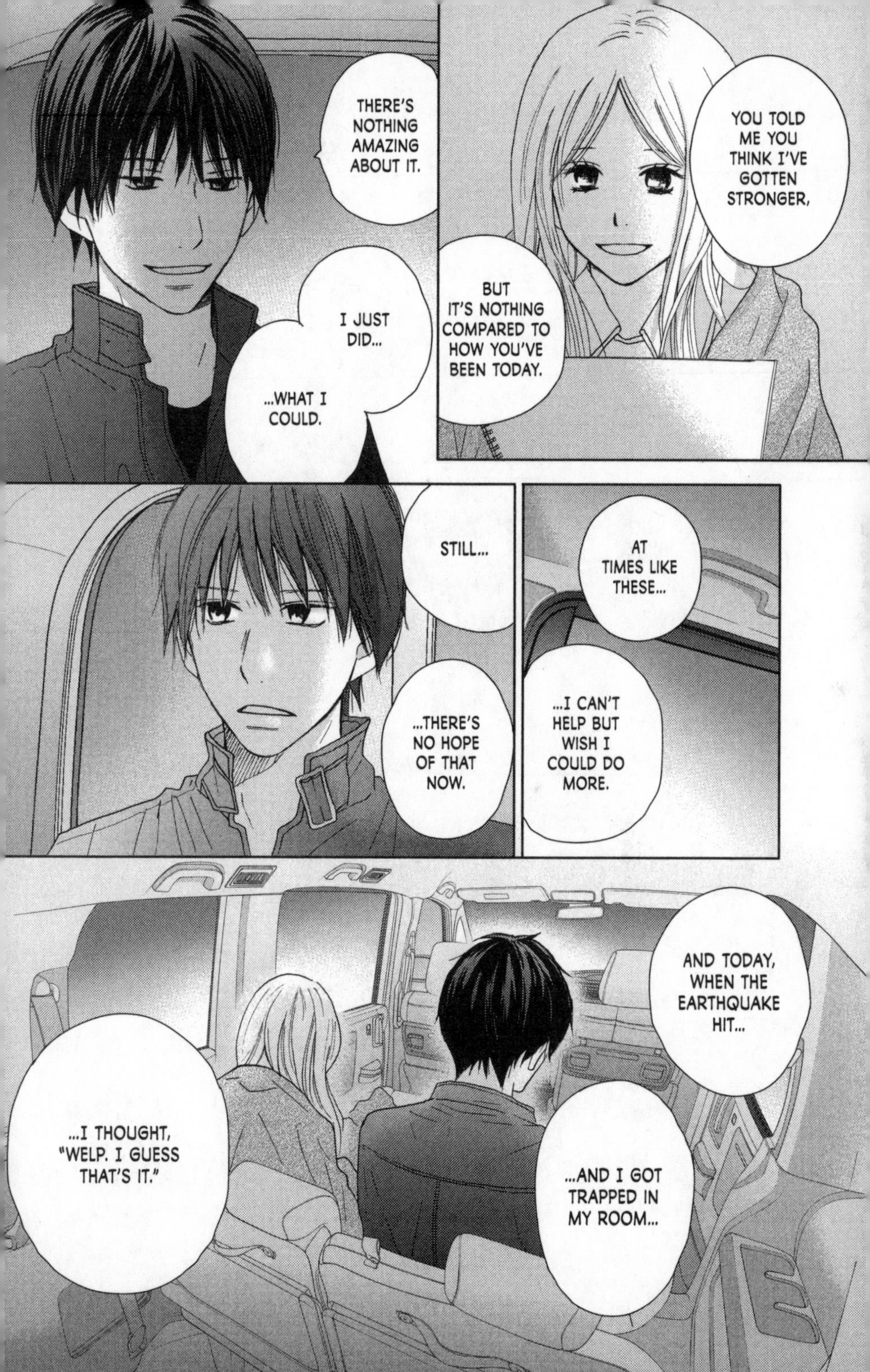
YOU TOLD ME YOU THINK I'VE GOTTEN STRONGER,
BUT IT'S NOTHING COMPARED TO HOW YOU'VE BEEN TODAY.
THERE'S NOTHING AMAZING ABOUT IT.
I JUST DID...
...WHAT I COULD.
AT TIMES LIKE THESE...
...I CAN'T HELP BUT WISH I COULD DO MORE.
STILL...
...THERE'S NO HOPE OF THAT NOW.
AND TODAY, WHEN THE EARTHQUAKE HIT...
...AND I GOT TRAPPED IN MY ROOM...
...I THOUGHT, "WELP. I GUESS THAT'S IT."

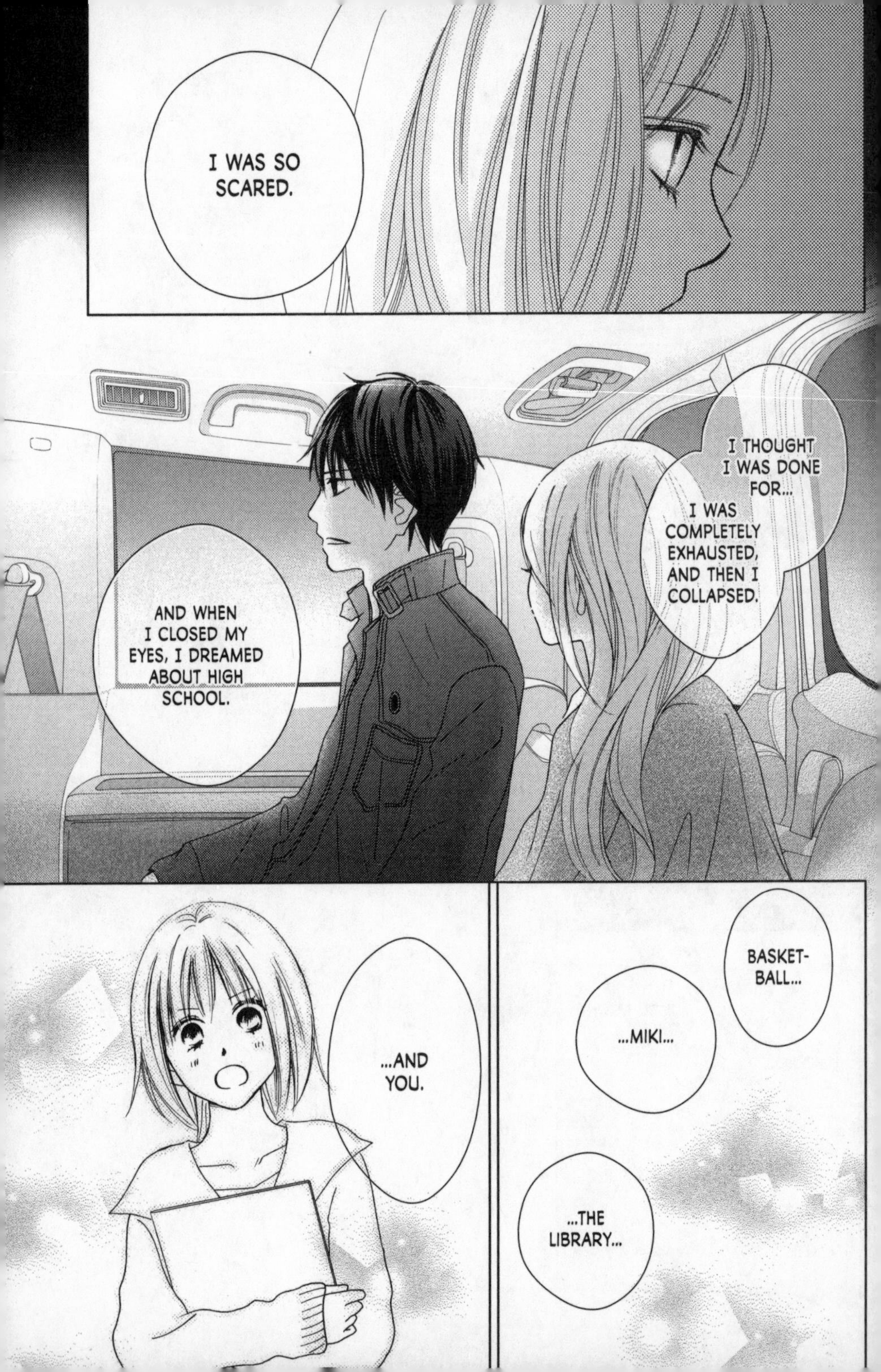
I WAS SO SCARED.
I THOUGHT I WAS DONE FOR...
I WAS COMPLETELY EXHAUSTED, AND THEN I COLLAPSED.
AND WHEN I CLOSED MY EYES, I DREAMED ABOUT HIGH SCHOOL.
BASKET-BALL...
...MIKI...
...THE LIBRARY...
...AND YOU.

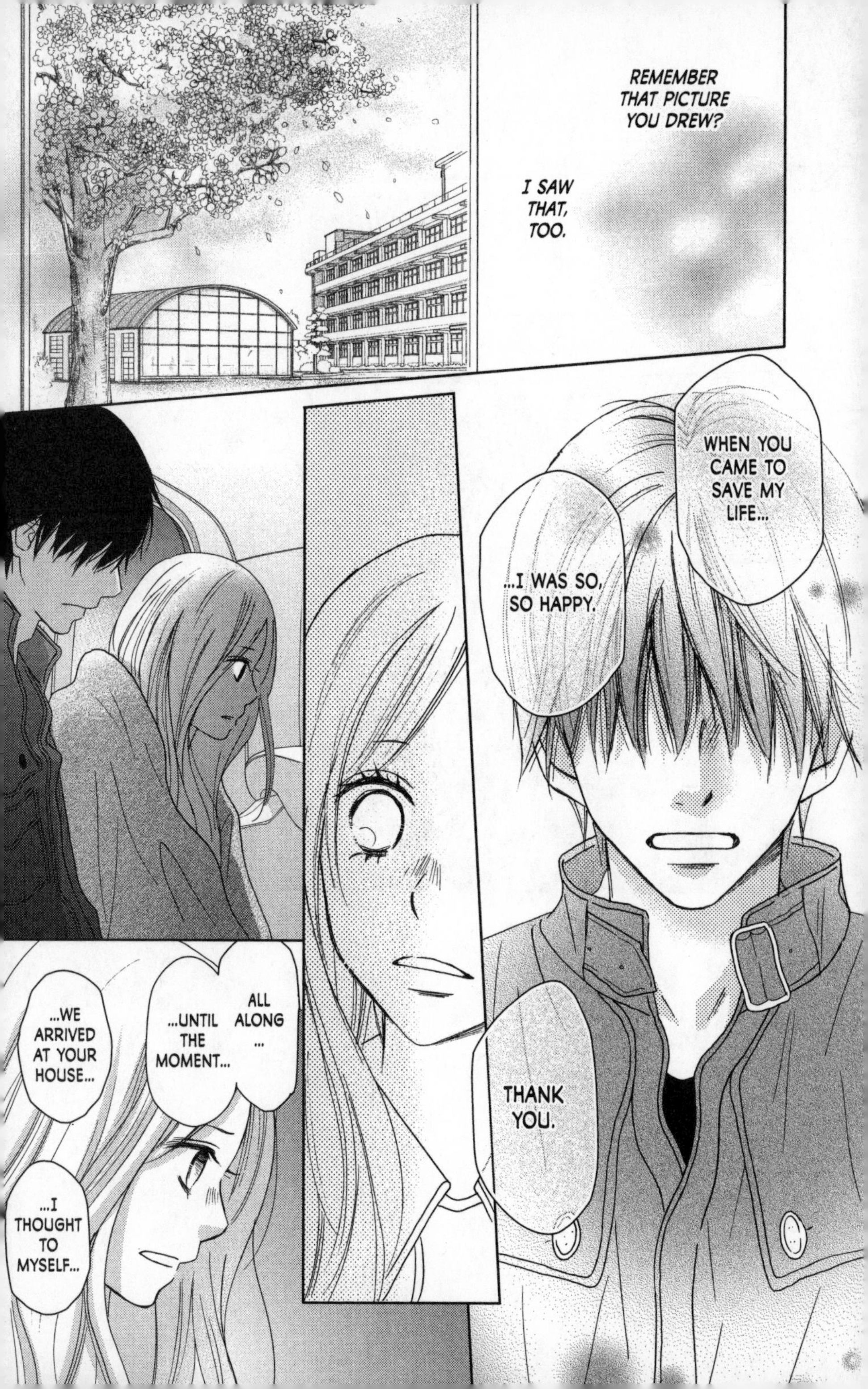
REMEMBER THAT PICTURE YOU DREW?
I SAW THAT, TOO.
WHEN YOU CAME TO SAVE MY LIFE...
...I WAS SO, SO HAPPY.
THANK YOU.
ALL ALONG...
...UNTIL THE MOMENT...
...WE ARRIVED AT YOUR HOUSE...
...I THOUGHT TO MYSELF...

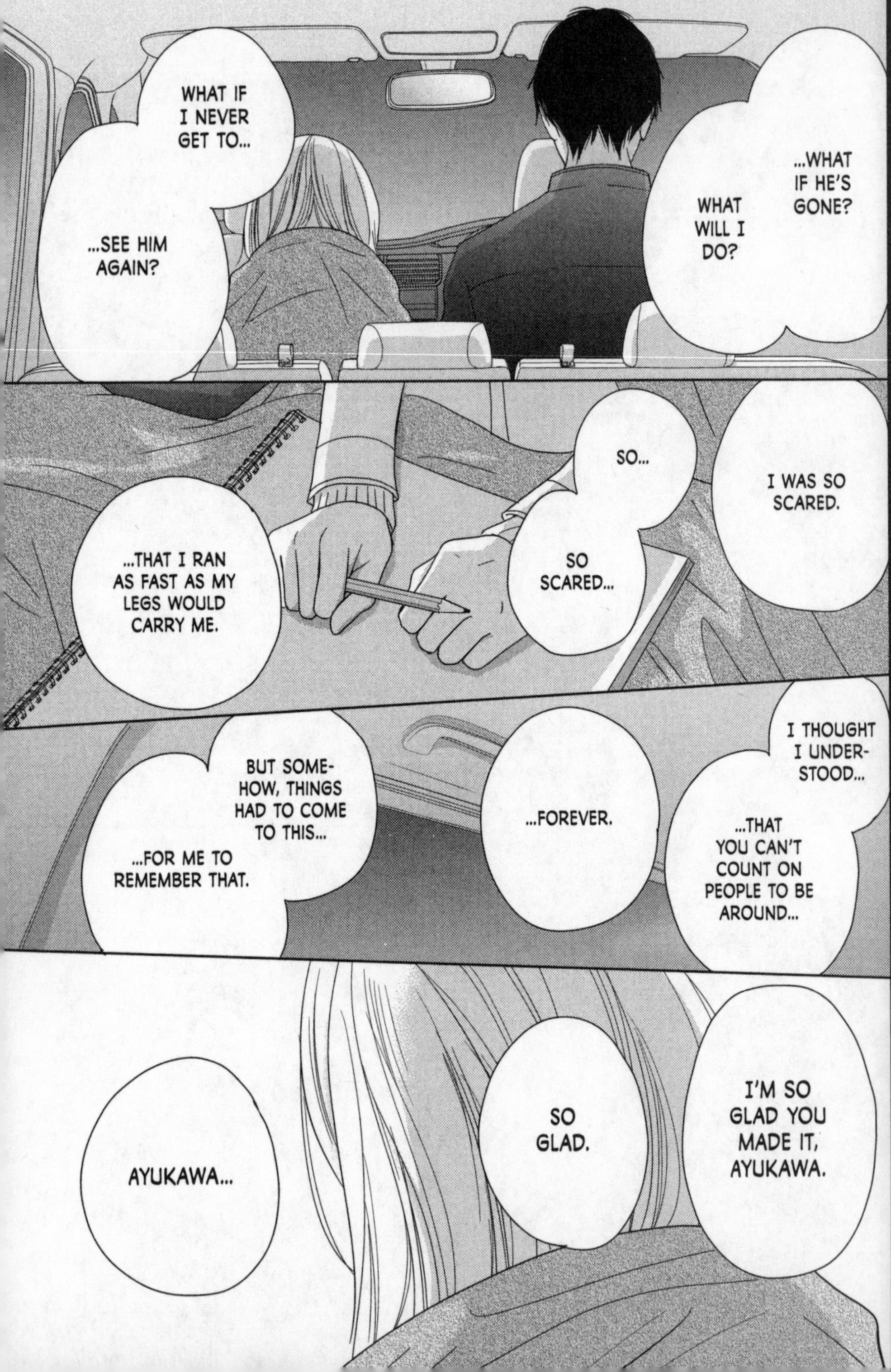
...WHAT IF HE'S GONE?
WHAT WILL I DO?
WHAT IF I NEVER GET TO...
...SEE HIM AGAIN?
I WAS SO SCARED.
SO...
SO SCARED...
...THAT I RAN AS FAST AS MY LEGS WOULD CARRY ME.
I THOUGHT I UNDER-STOOD...
...THAT YOU CAN'T COUNT ON PEOPLE TO BE AROUND...
...FOREVER.
BUT SOME-HOW, THINGS HAD TO COME TO THIS...
...FOR ME TO REMEMBER THAT.
I'M SO GLAD YOU MADE IT, AYUKAWA.
SO GLAD.
AYUKAWA...

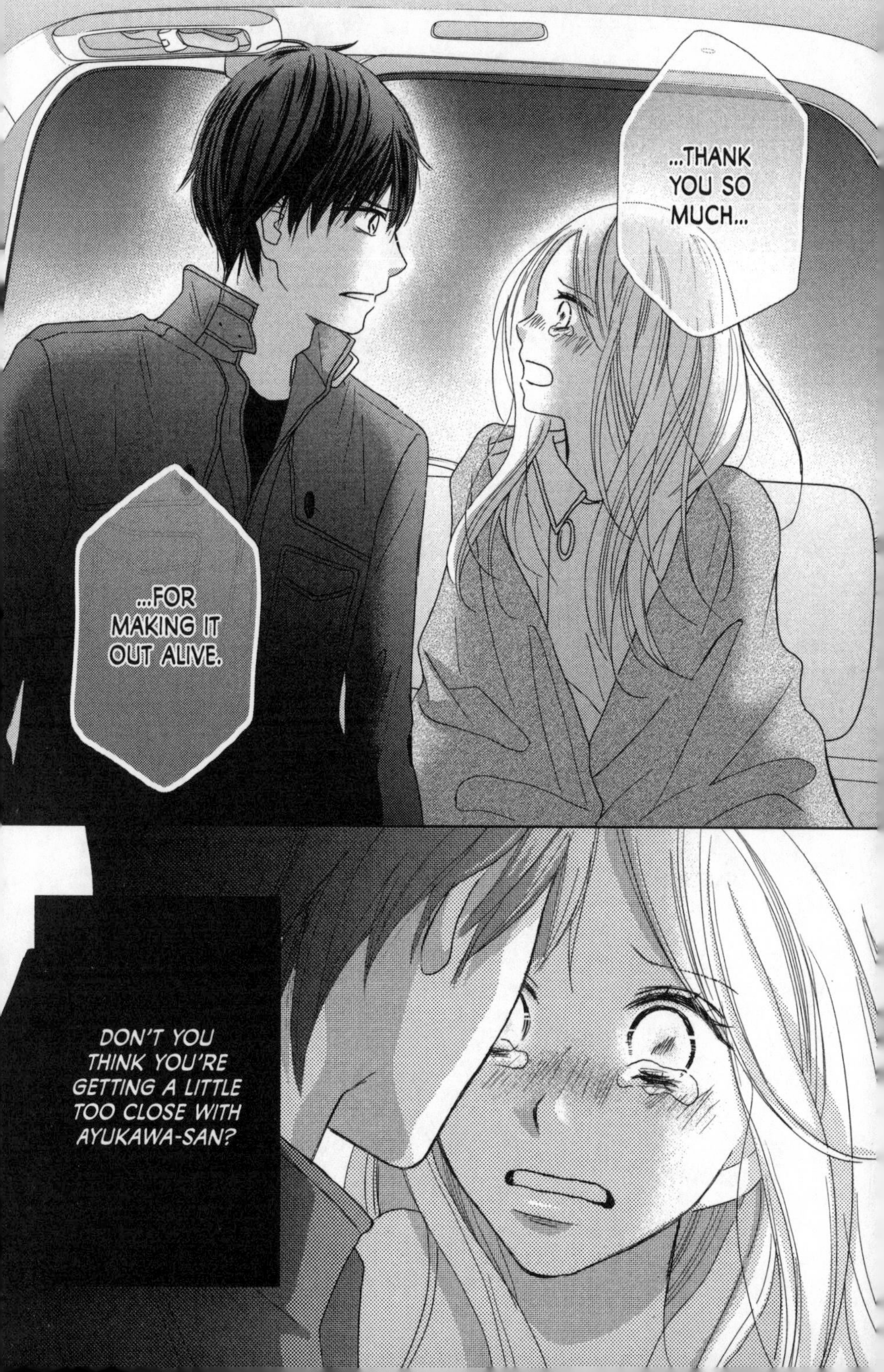
...THANK YOU SO MUCH...
...FOR MAKING IT OUT ALIVE.
DON'T YOU THINK YOU'RE GETTING A LITTLE TOO CLOSE WITH AYUKAWA-SAN?

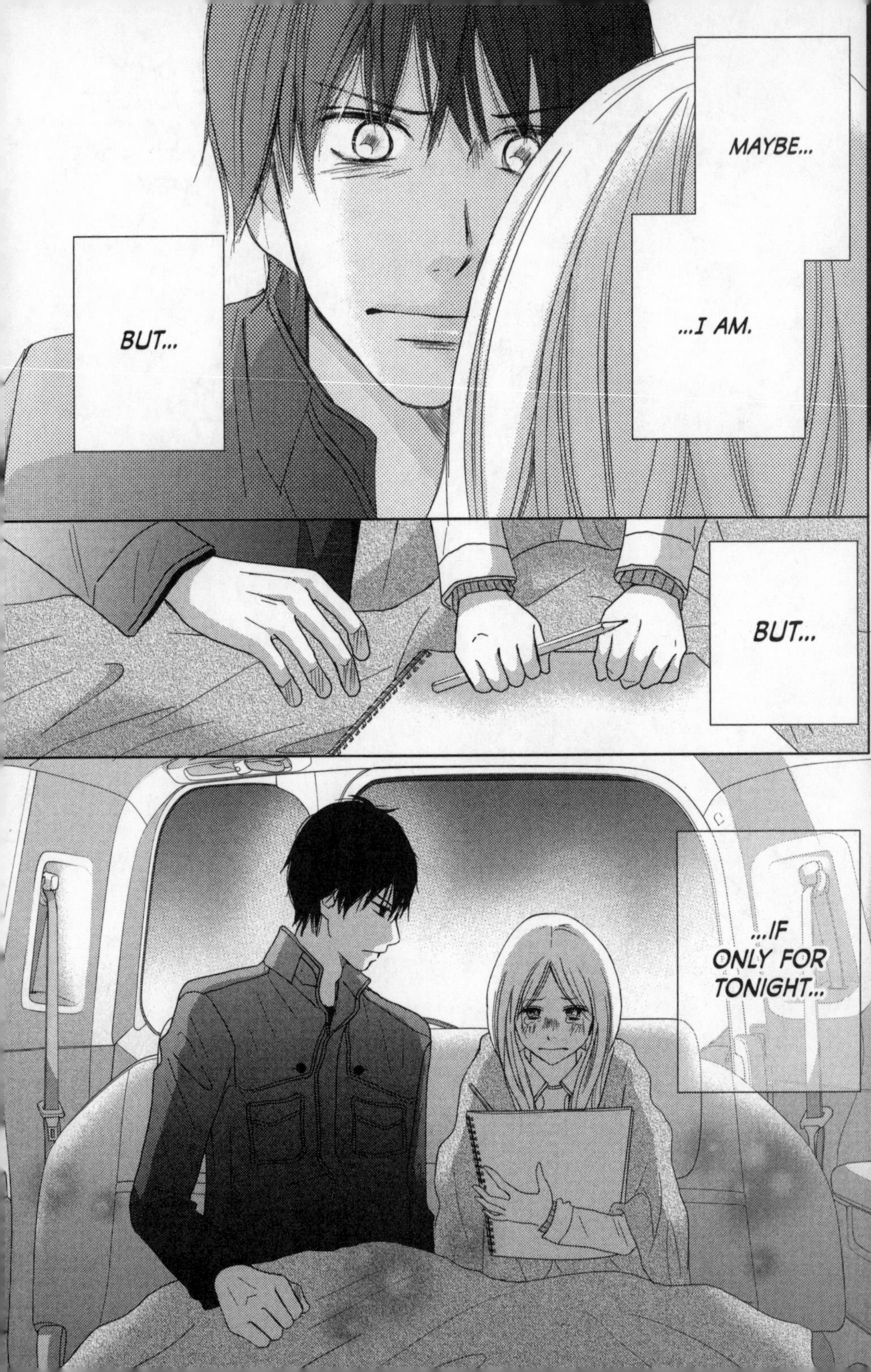
MAYBE...
...I AM.
BUT...
BUT...
...IF ONLY FOR TONIGHT...

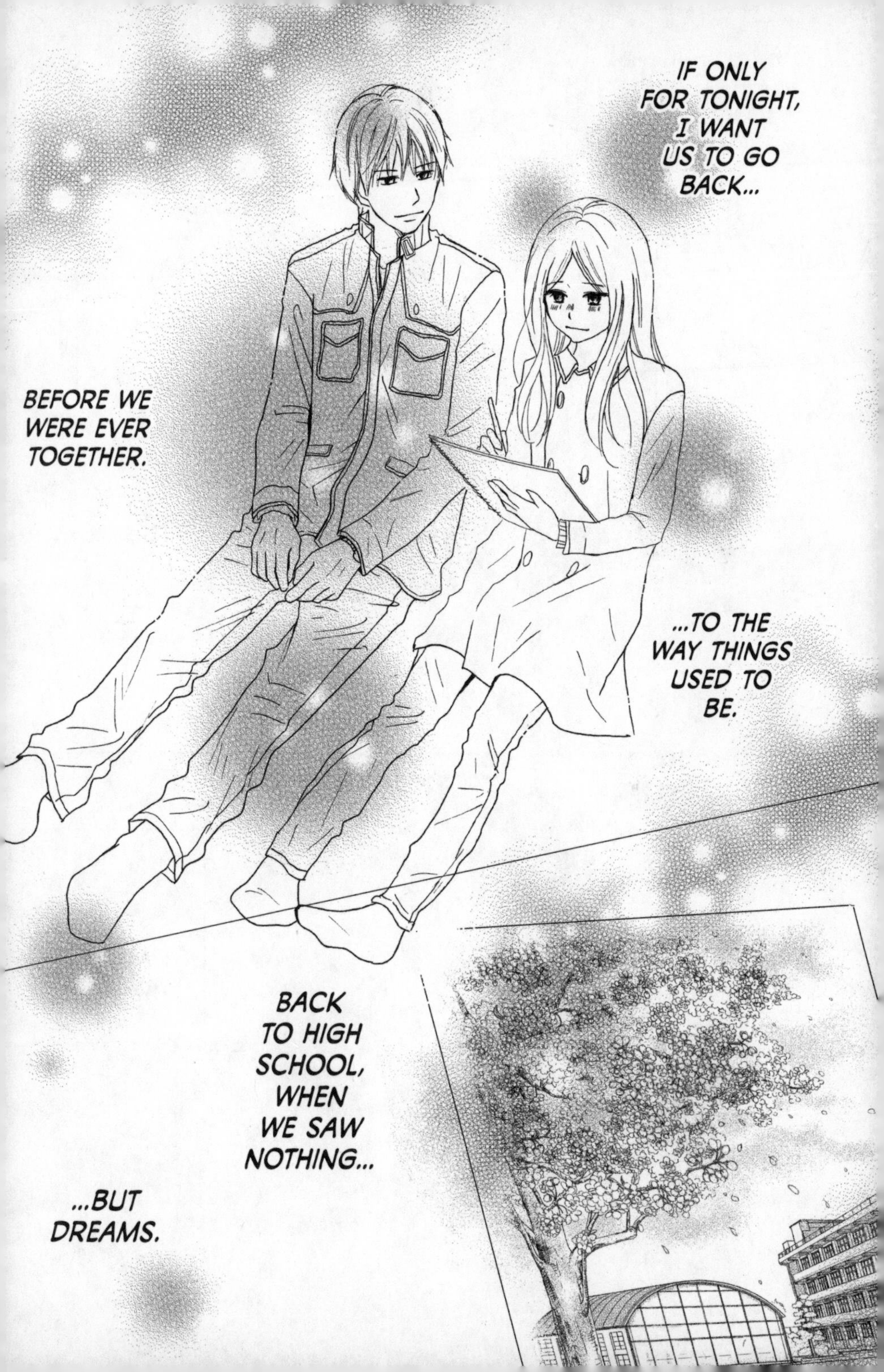
IF ONLY FOR TONIGHT, I WANT US TO GO BACK...
...TO THE WAY THINGS USED TO BE.
BEFORE WE WERE EVER TOGETHER.
BACK TO HIGH SCHOOL, WHEN WE SAW NOTHING...
...BUT DREAMS.

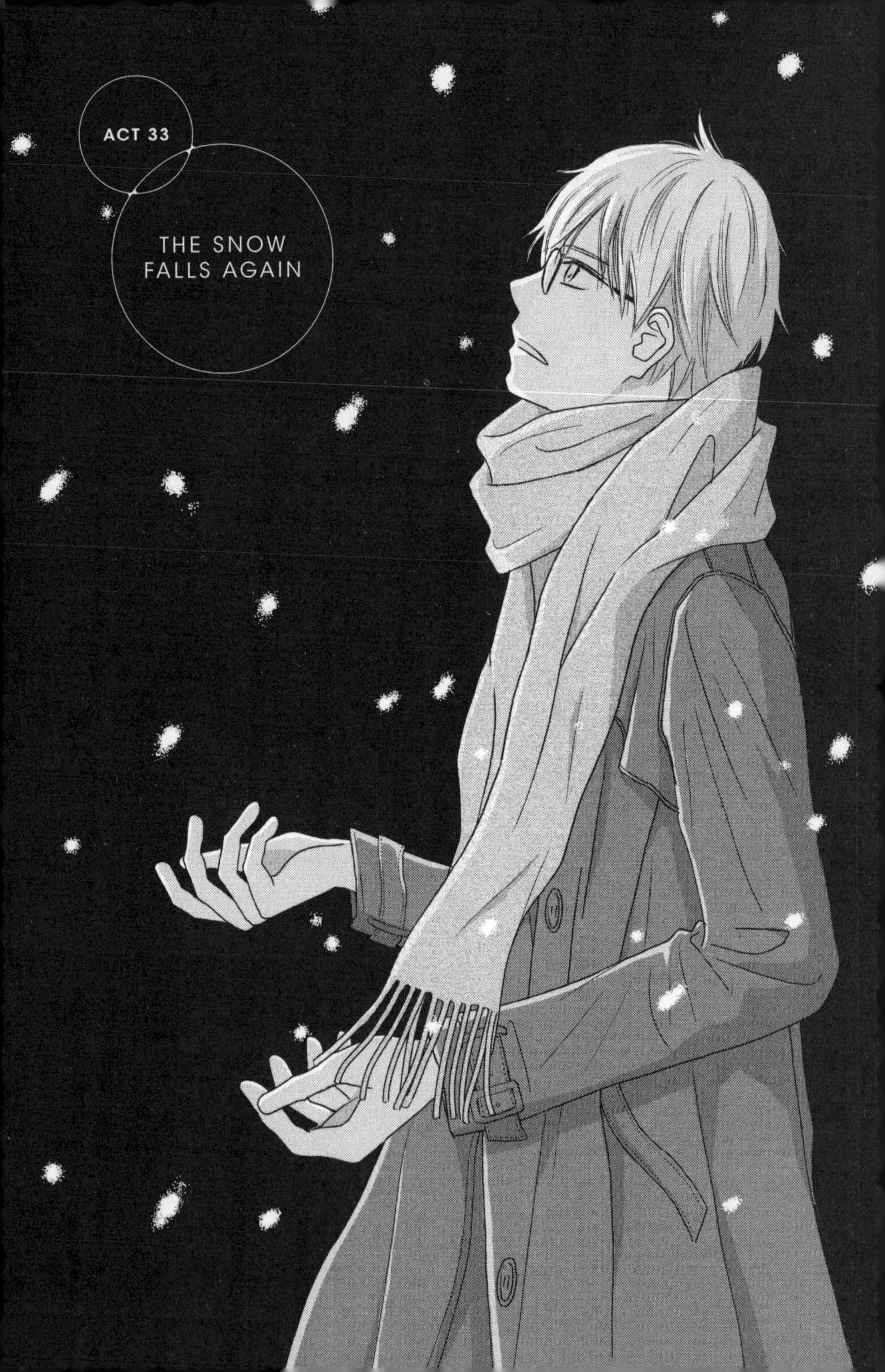
ACT 33
THE SNOW FALLS AGAIN

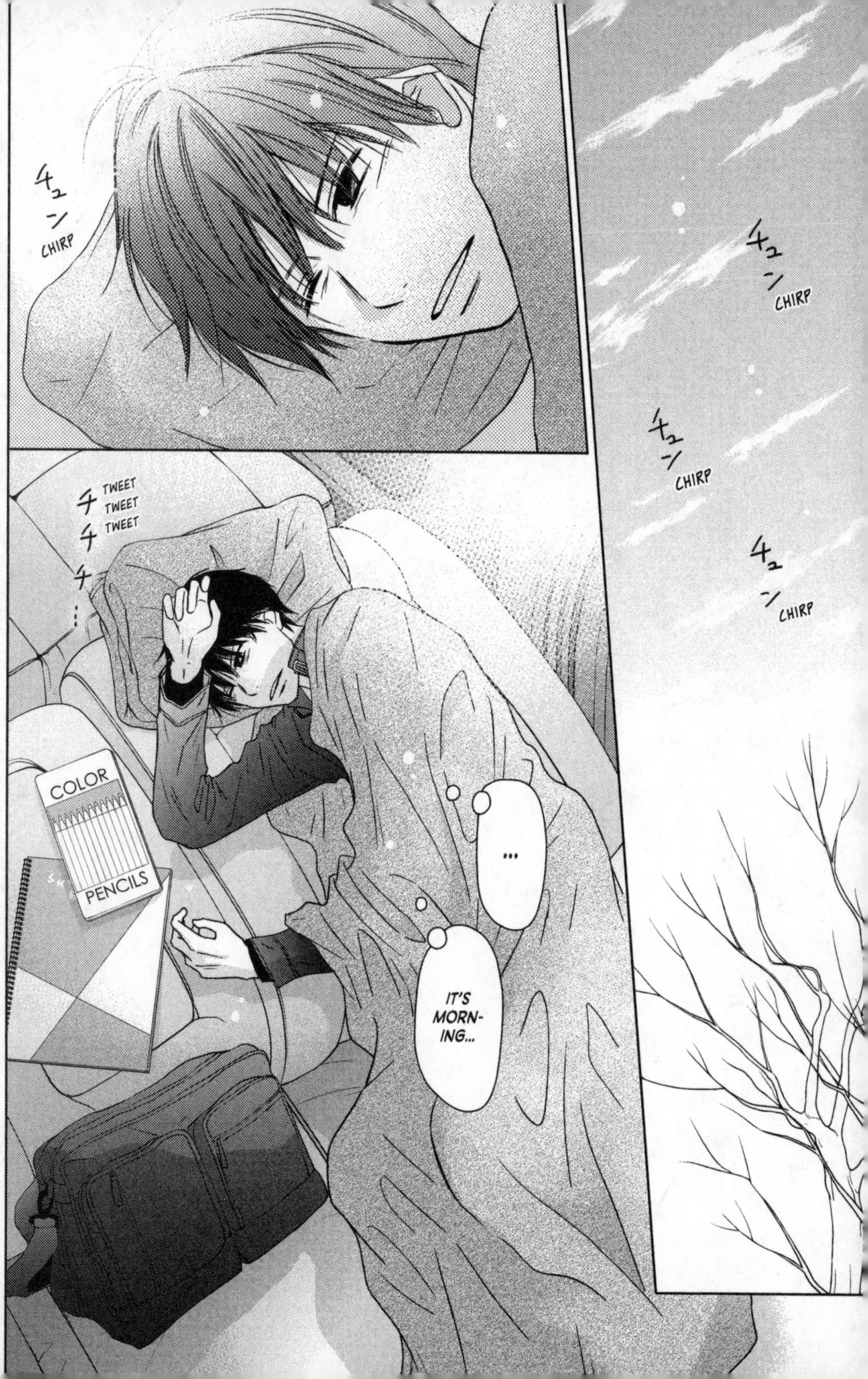
チュン CHIRP
チュン CHIRP
チュン CHIRP
チュン CHIRP
チチチ… TWEET TWEET TWEET
COLOR PENCILS
…
IT'S MORNING...

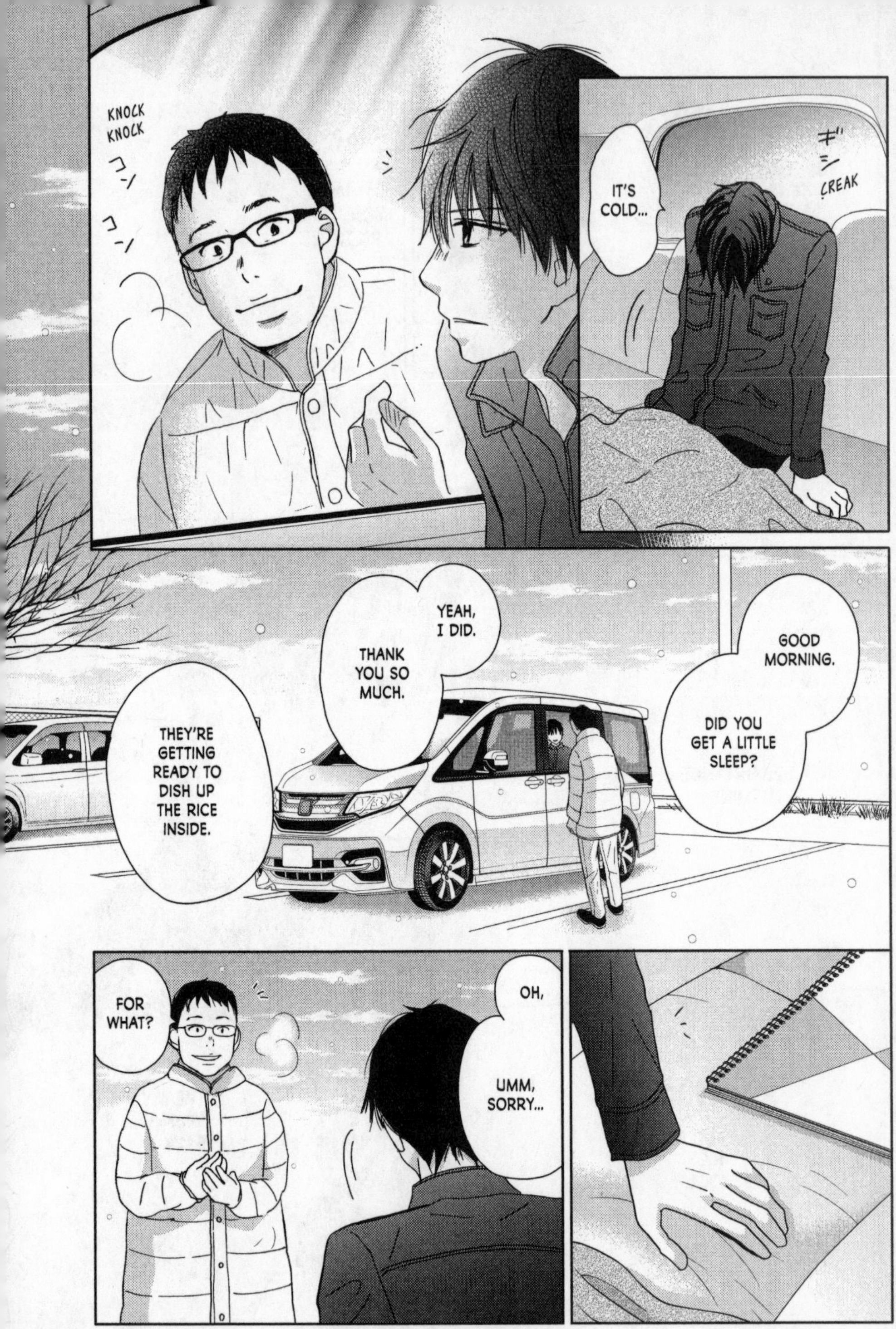
IT'S COLD...
ギシ
CREAK
KNOCK KNOCK
コン
コン
GOOD MORNING.
DID YOU GET A LITTLE SLEEP?
YEAH, I DID.
THANK YOU SO MUCH.
THEY'RE GETTING READY TO DISH UP THE RICE INSIDE.
OH,
UMM, SORRY...
FOR WHAT?

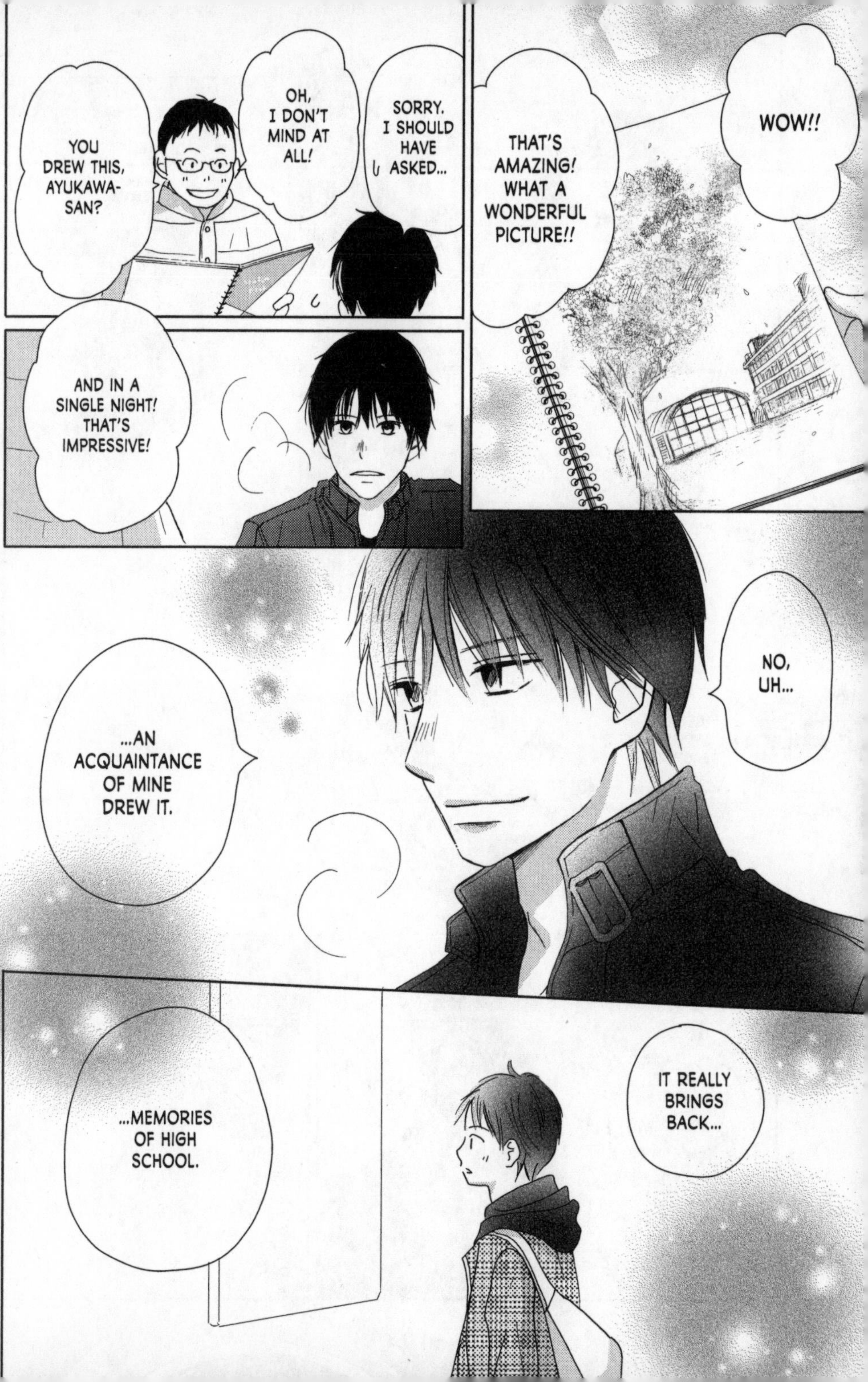
WOW!!
THAT'S AMAZING! WHAT A WONDERFUL PICTURE!!
SORRY. I SHOULD HAVE ASKED...
OH, I DON'T MIND AT ALL!
YOU DREW THIS, AYUKAWA-SAN?
AND IN A SINGLE NIGHT! THAT'S IMPRESSIVE!
NO, UH...
...AN ACQUAINTANCE OF MINE DREW IT.
IT REALLY BRINGS BACK...
...MEMORIES OF HIGH SCHOOL.

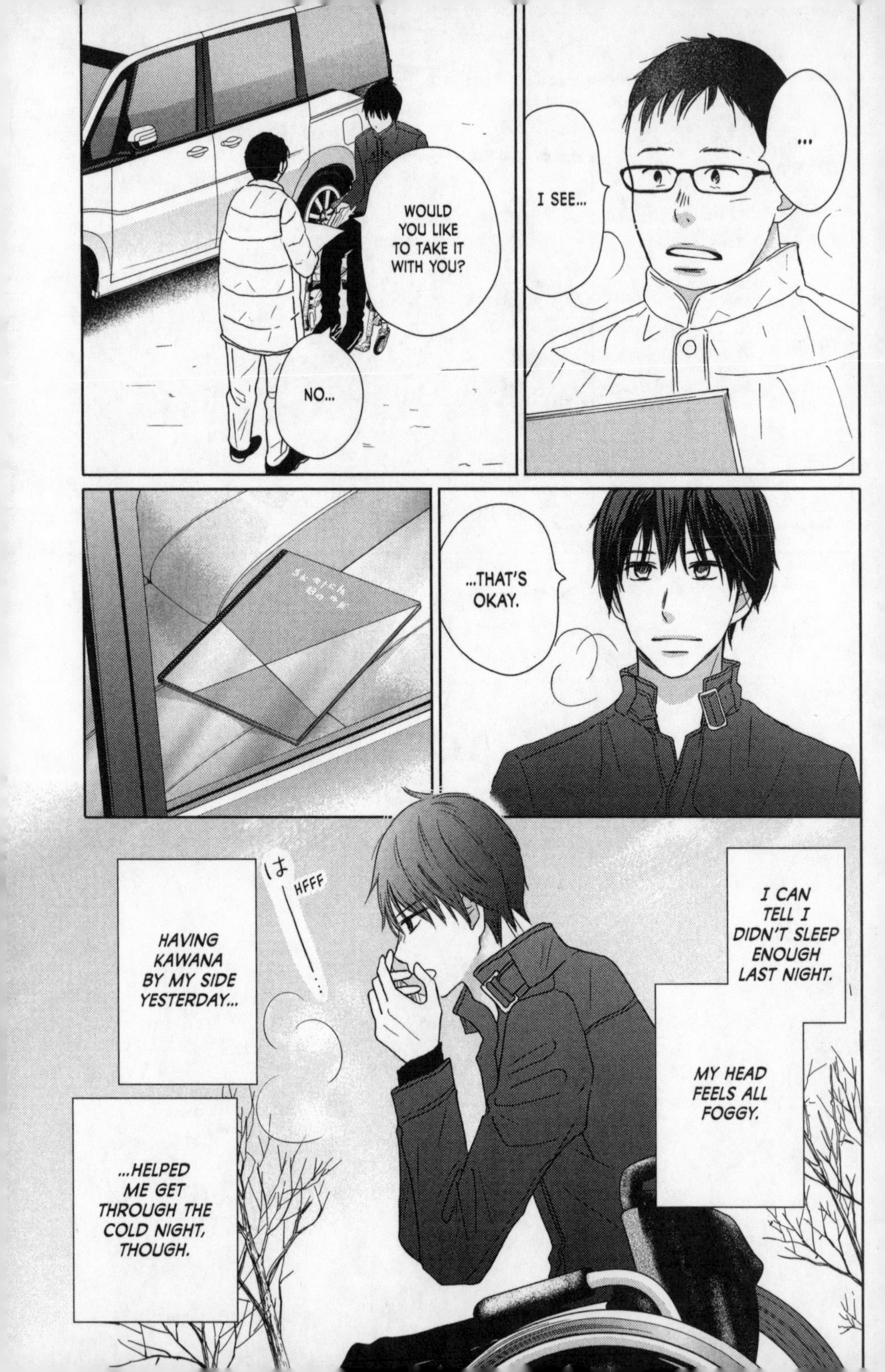
...
I SEE...
WOULD YOU LIKE TO TAKE IT WITH YOU?
NO...
...THAT'S OKAY.
I CAN TELL I DIDN'T SLEEP ENOUGH LAST NIGHT.
MY HEAD FEELS ALL FOGGY.
は HFFF
HAVING KAWANA BY MY SIDE YESTERDAY...
...HELPED ME GET THROUGH THE COLD NIGHT, THOUGH.

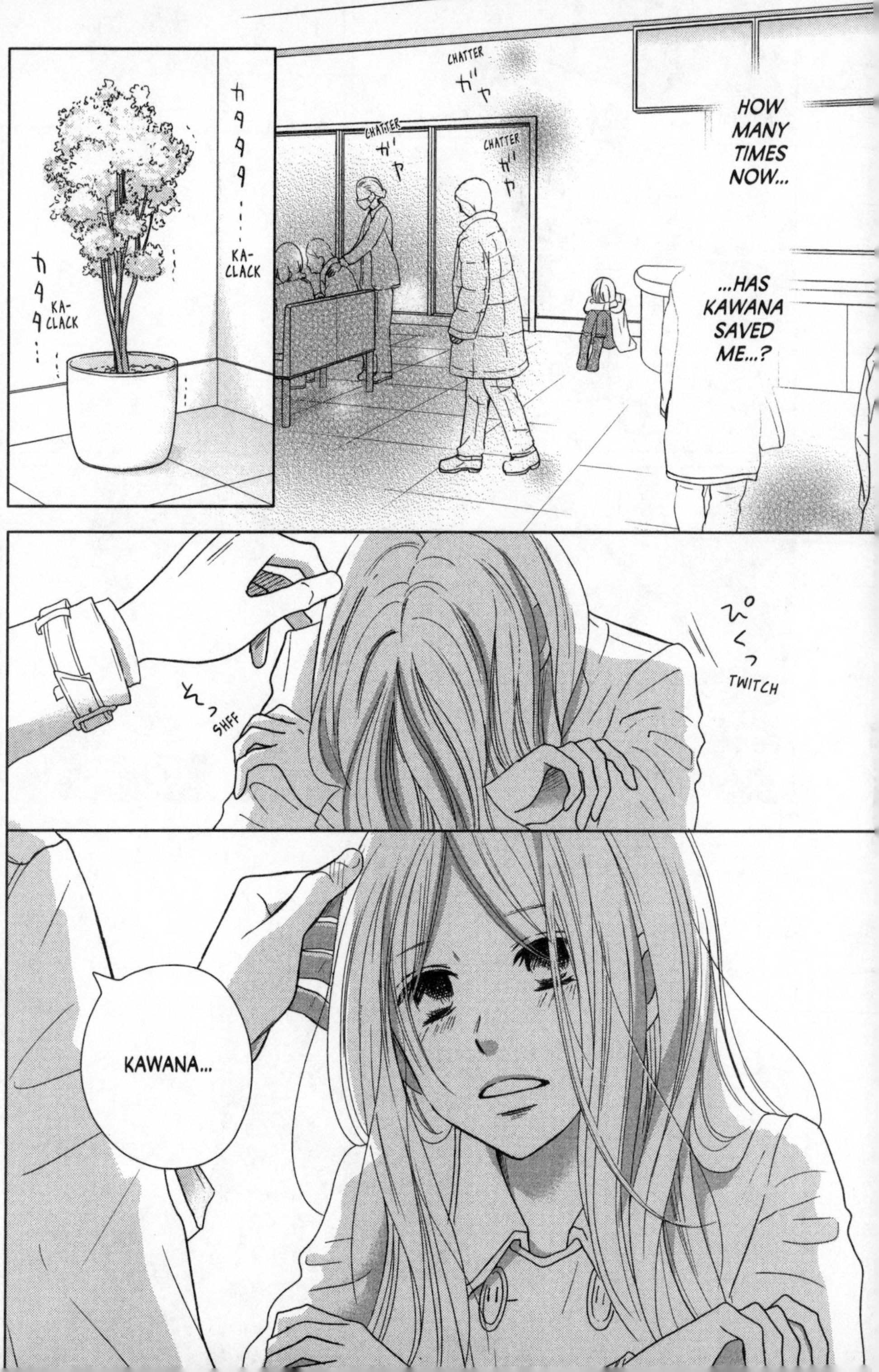
HOW MANY TIMES NOW...
...HAS KAWANA SAVED ME...?
CHATTER
ガヤ
CHATTER
ガヤ
CHATTER
ガヤ
KA-CLACK
カタタタ…
KA-CLACK
カタタ…
ぴくっ
TWITCH
SHFF
KAWANA...

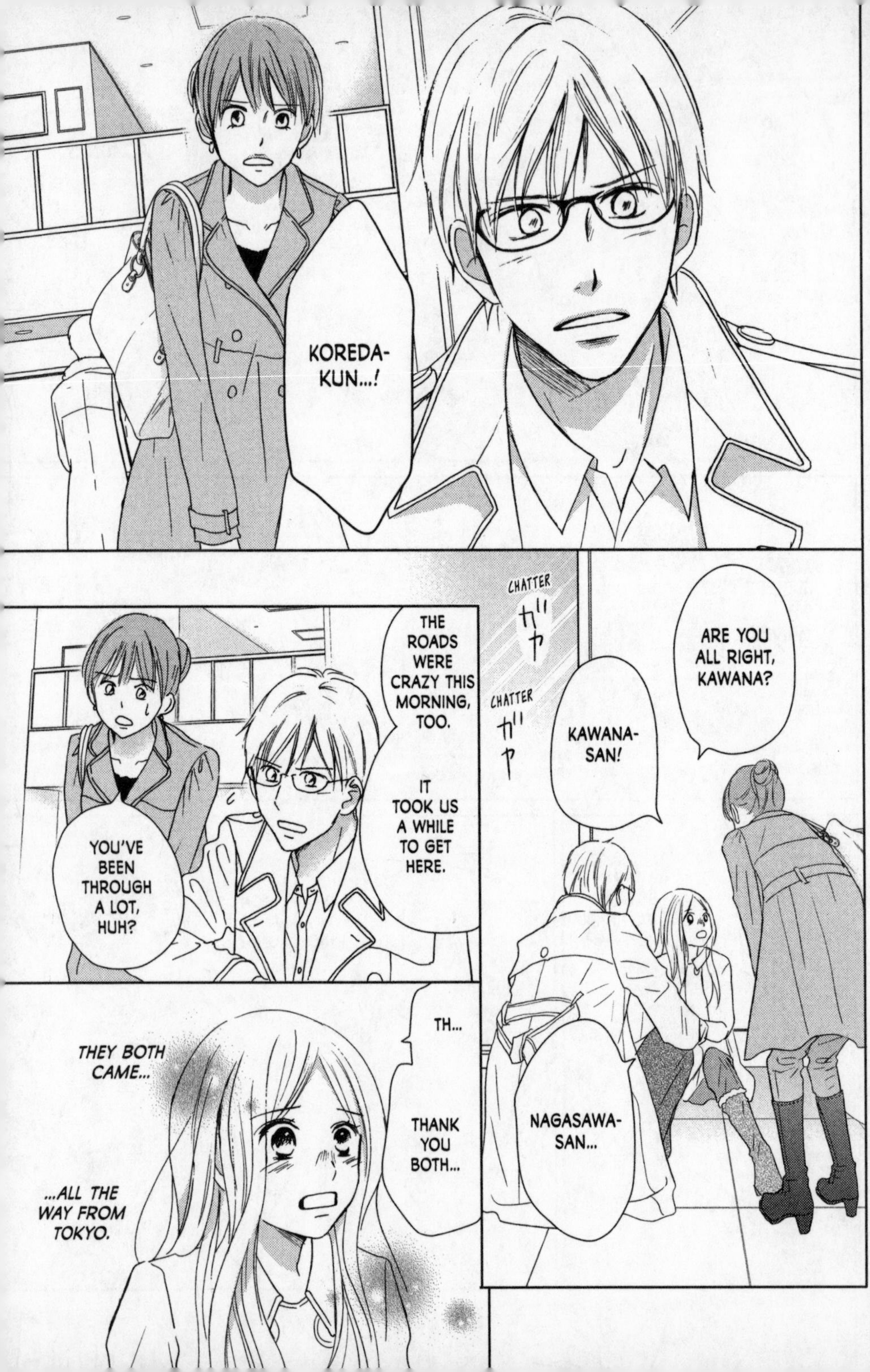
KOREDA-KUN...!
ARE YOU ALL RIGHT, KAWANA?
KAWANA-SAN!
CHATTER ガヤ
CHATTER ガヤ
NAGASAWA-SAN...
THE ROADS WERE CRAZY THIS MORNING, TOO.
IT TOOK US A WHILE TO GET HERE.
YOU'VE BEEN THROUGH A LOT, HUH?
TH...
THANK YOU BOTH...
THEY BOTH CAME...
...ALL THE WAY FROM TOKYO.

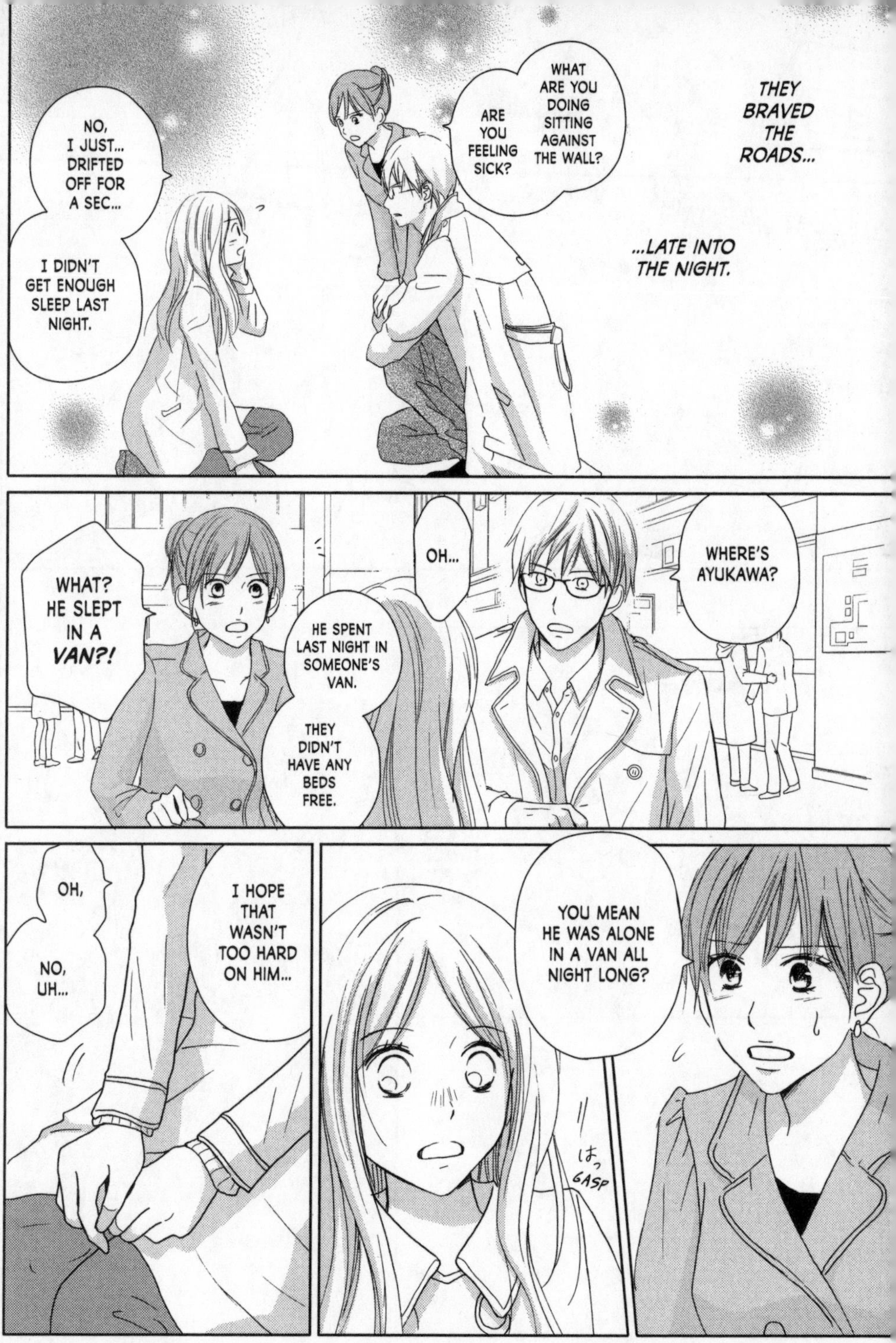
THEY BRAVED THE ROADS...
...LATE INTO THE NIGHT.
WHAT ARE YOU DOING SITTING AGAINST THE WALL?
ARE YOU FEELING SICK?
NO, I JUST... DRIFTED OFF FOR A SEC...
I DIDN'T GET ENOUGH SLEEP LAST NIGHT.
WHERE'S AYUKAWA?
OH...
HE SPENT LAST NIGHT IN SOMEONE'S VAN.
THEY DIDN'T HAVE ANY BEDS FREE.
WHAT? HE SLEPT IN A *VAN?!*
YOU MEAN HE WAS ALONE IN A VAN ALL NIGHT LONG?
はっ
GASP
I HOPE THAT WASN'T TOO HARD ON HIM...
OH,
NO, UH...

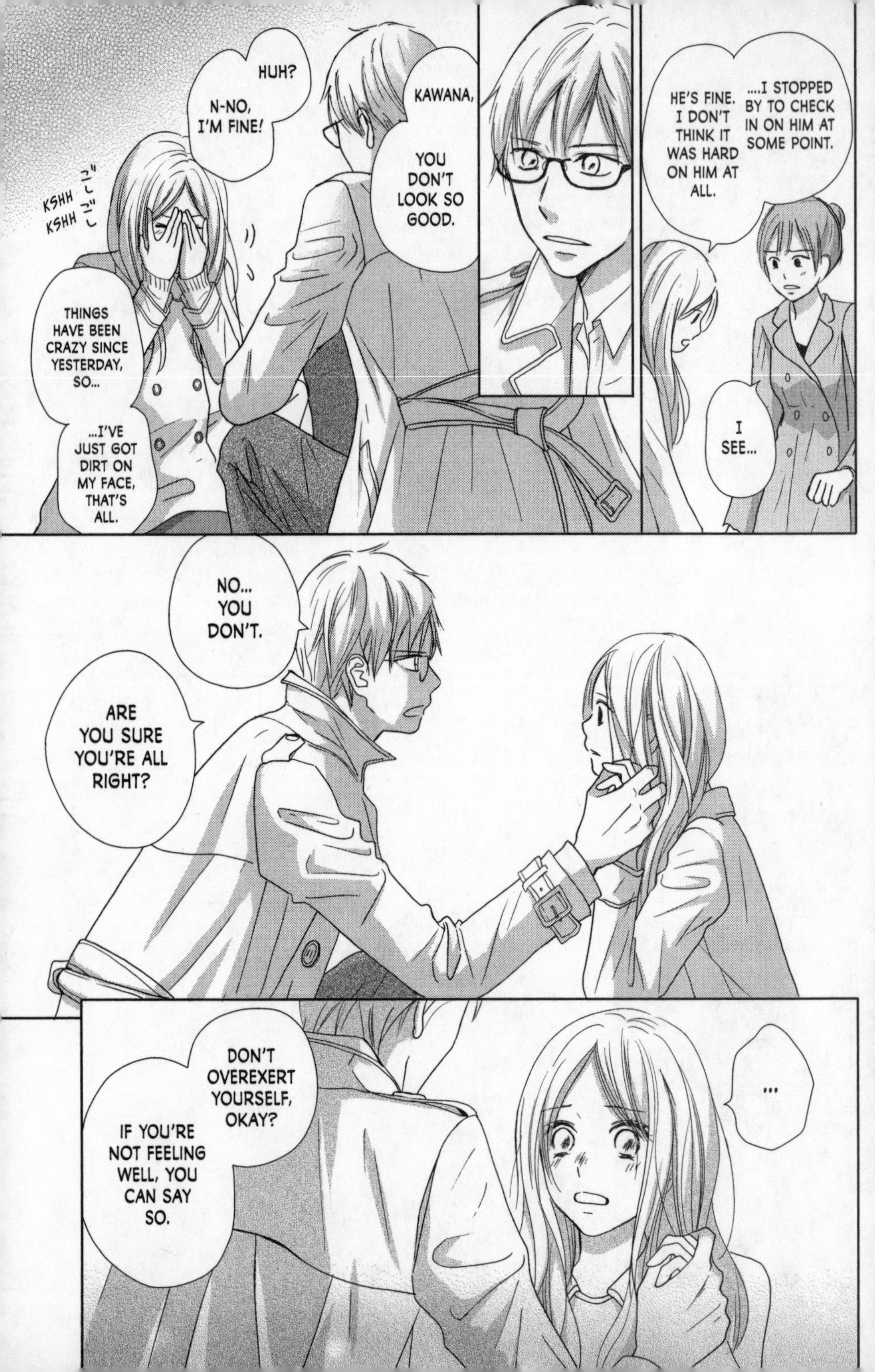
....I STOPPED BY TO CHECK IN ON HIM AT SOME POINT.
HE'S FINE. I DON'T THINK IT WAS HARD ON HIM AT ALL.
I SEE...
KAWANA,
YOU DON'T LOOK SO GOOD.
HUH?
N-NO, I'M FINE!
KSHH KSHH
ごしごし
THINGS HAVE BEEN CRAZY SINCE YESTERDAY, SO...
...I'VE JUST GOT DIRT ON MY FACE, THAT'S ALL.
NO... YOU DON'T.
ARE YOU SURE YOU'RE ALL RIGHT?
...
DON'T OVEREXERT YOURSELF, OKAY?
IF YOU'RE NOT FEELING WELL, YOU CAN SAY SO.

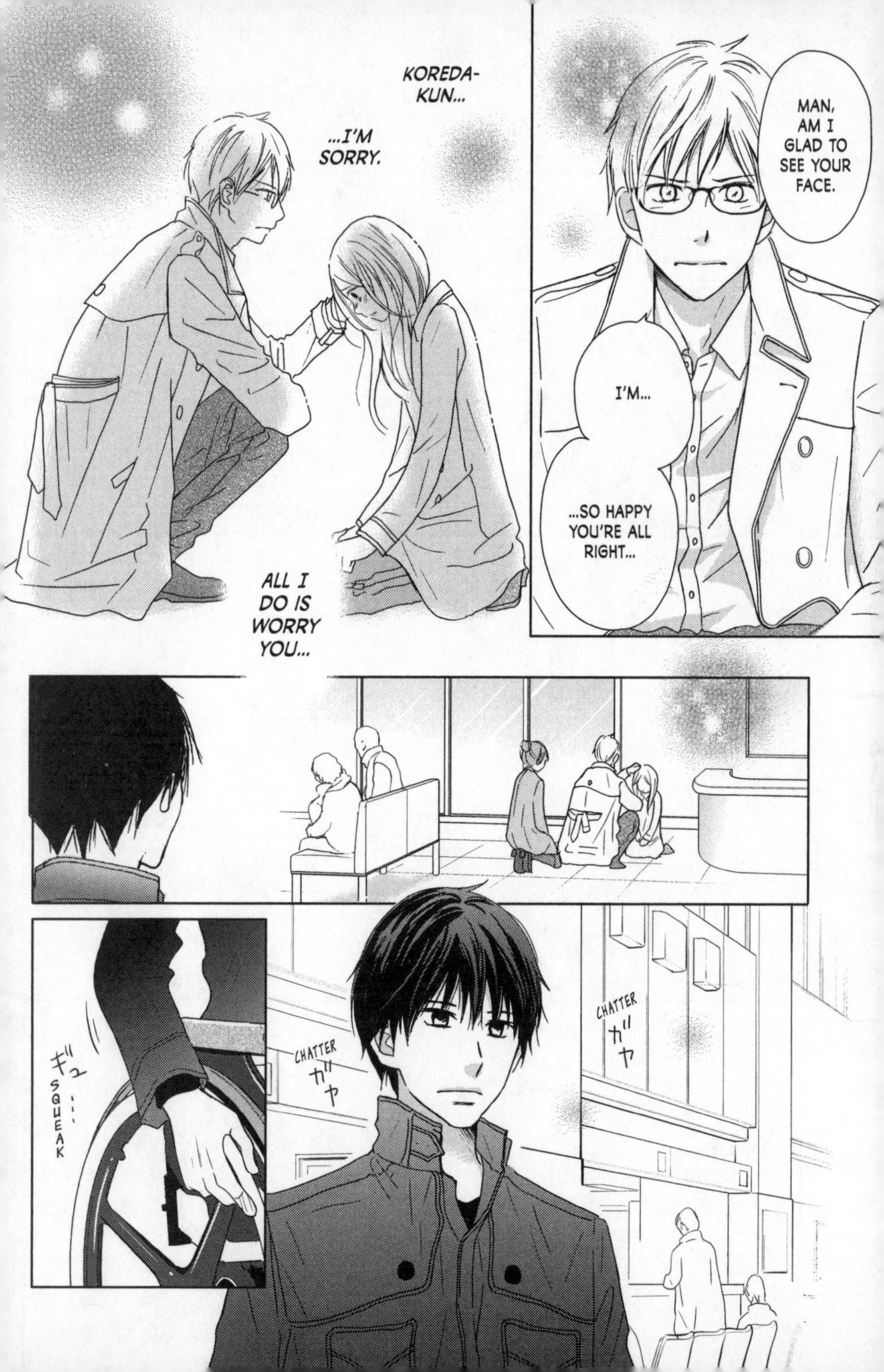
MAN, AM I GLAD TO SEE YOUR FACE.
I'M...
...SO HAPPY YOU'RE ALL RIGHT...
KOREDA-KUN...
...I'M SORRY.
ALL I DO IS WORRY YOU...
CHATTER
ガヤ
CHATTER
ガヤ
ギュ
SQUEAK
...

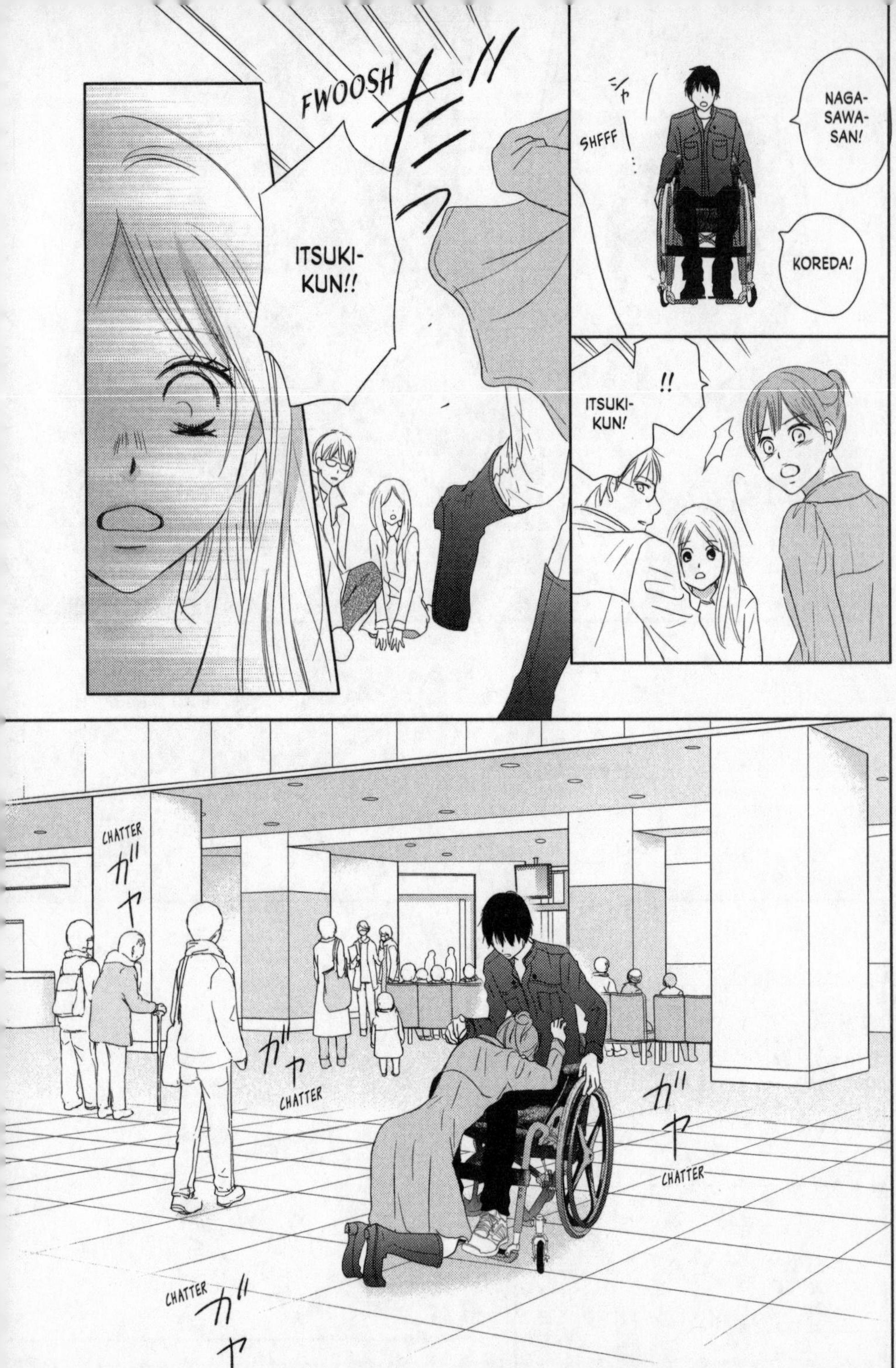
NAGA-SAWA-SAN!
KOREDA!
シャ
SHFFF
ITSUKI-KUN!
!!
ダッ
FWOOSH
ITSUKI-KUN!!
ガヤ
CHATTER
ガヤ
CHATTER
ガヤ
CHATTER
ガヤ
CHATTER

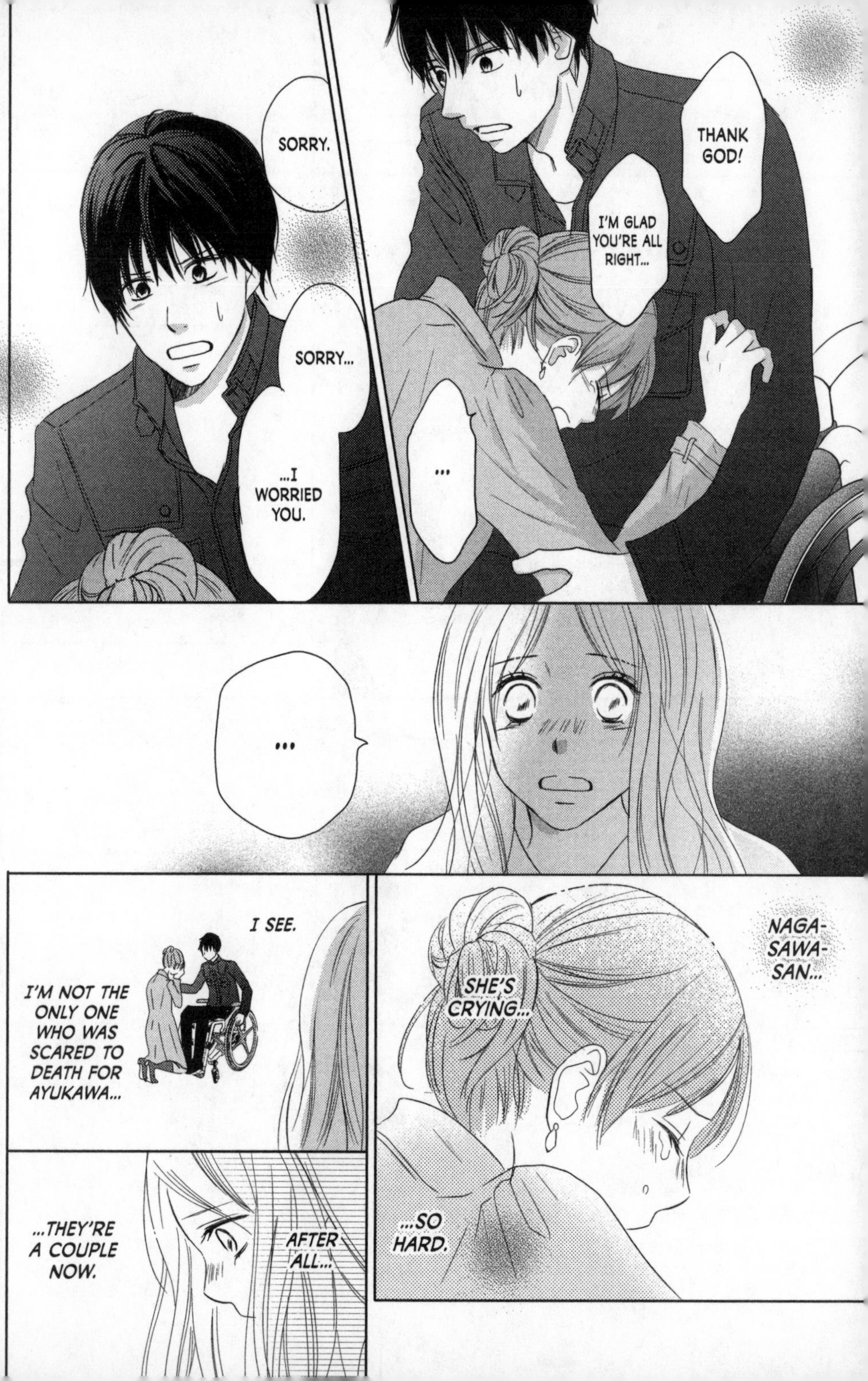
THANK GOD!
I'M GLAD YOU'RE ALL RIGHT...
...
SORRY.
SORRY...
...I WORRIED YOU.
...
NAGA-SAWA-SAN...
SHE'S CRYING...
...SO HARD.
I SEE.
I'M NOT THE ONLY ONE WHO WAS SCARED TO DEATH FOR AYUKAWA...
AFTER ALL...
...THEY'RE A COUPLE NOW.

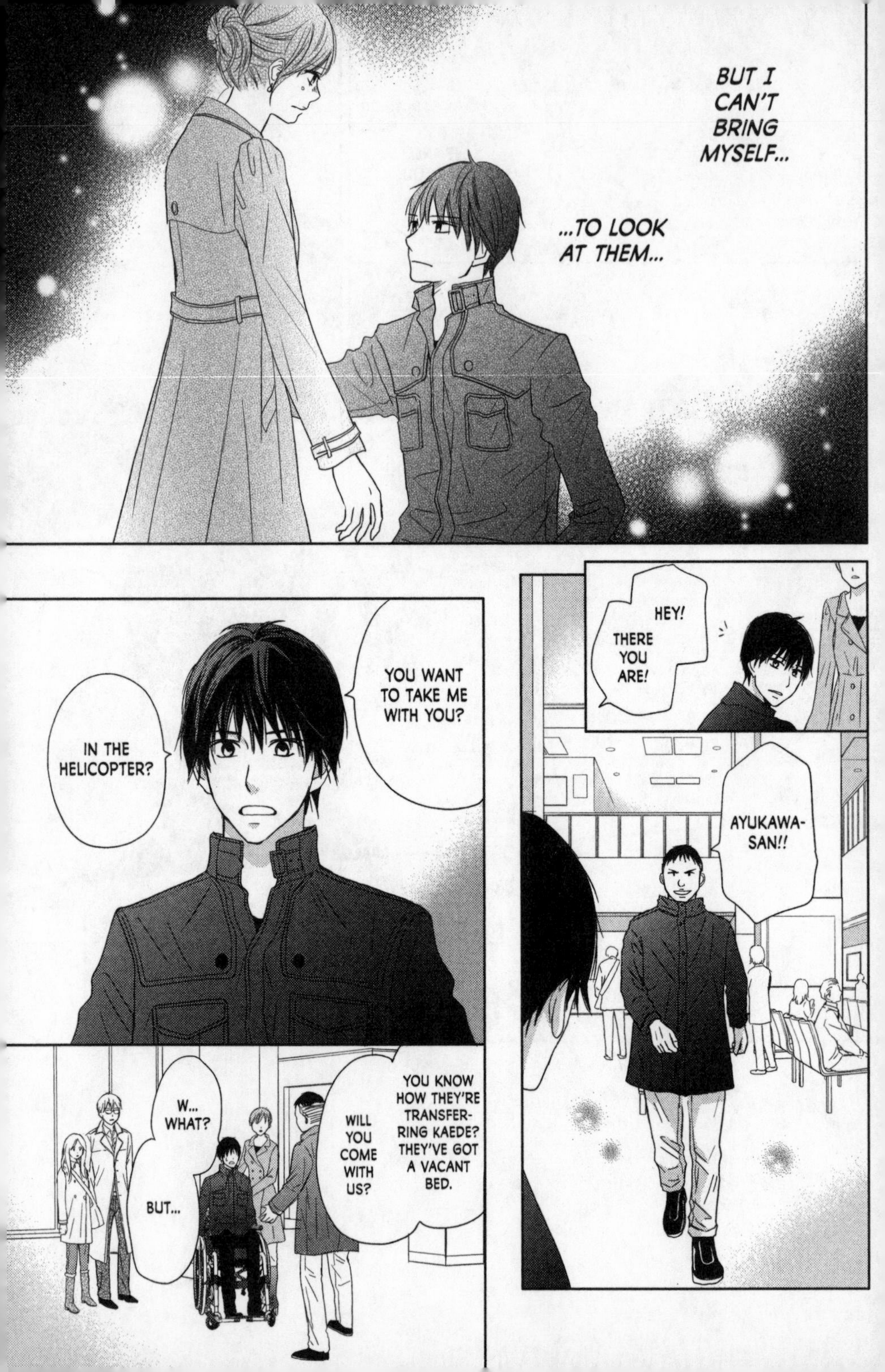
BUT I CAN'T BRING MYSELF...
...TO LOOK AT THEM...
HEY! THERE YOU ARE!
AYUKAWA-SAN!!
YOU WANT TO TAKE ME WITH YOU?
IN THE HELICOPTER?
YOU KNOW HOW THEY'RE TRANSFER-RING KAEDE? THEY'VE GOT A VACANT BED.
WILL YOU COME WITH US?
W... WHAT?
BUT...

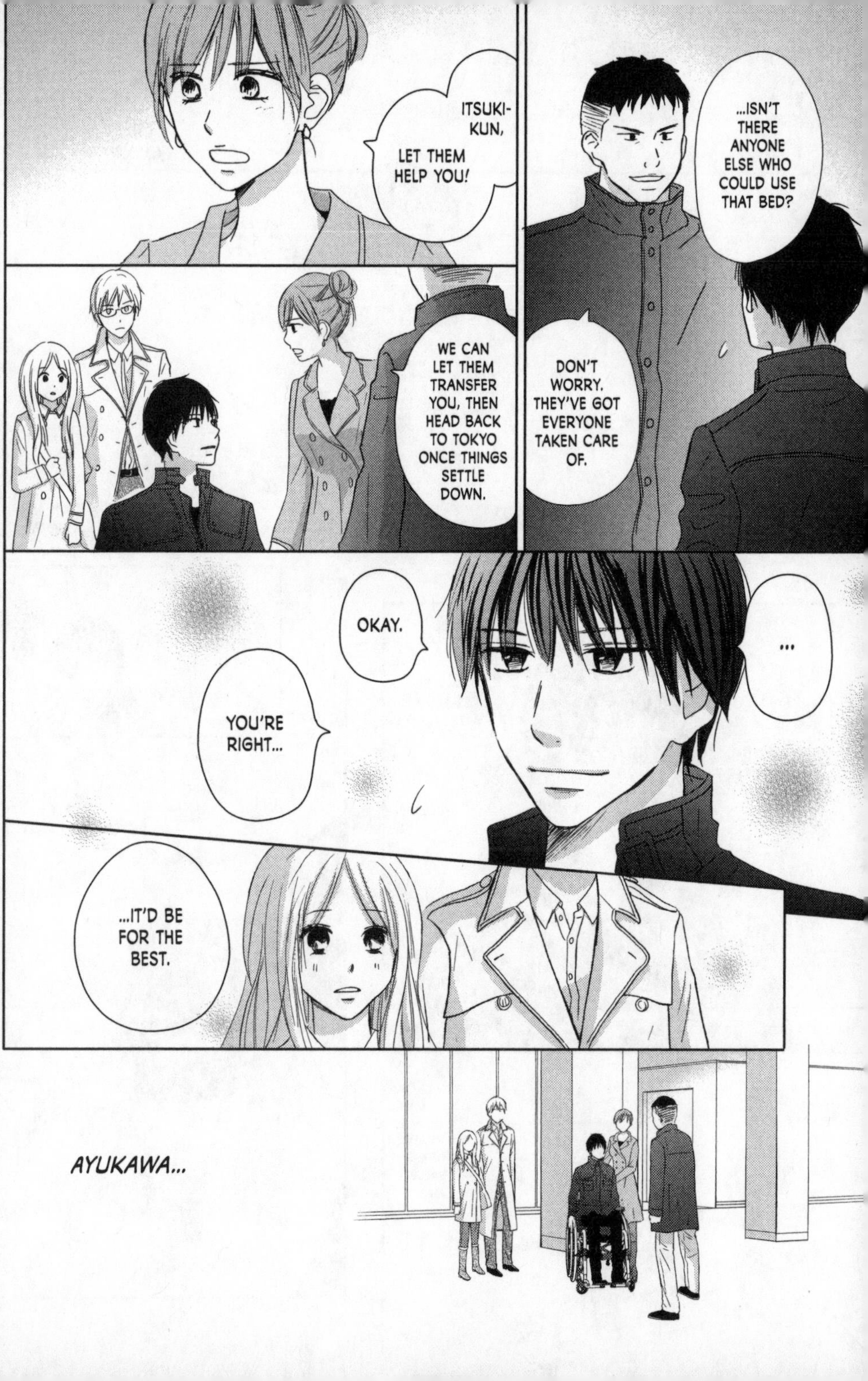
...ISN'T THERE ANYONE ELSE WHO COULD USE THAT BED?
DON'T WORRY. THEY'VE GOT EVERYONE TAKEN CARE OF.
ITSUKI-KUN,
LET THEM HELP YOU!
WE CAN LET THEM TRANSFER YOU, THEN HEAD BACK TO TOKYO ONCE THINGS SETTLE DOWN.
...
OKAY.
YOU'RE RIGHT...
...IT'D BE FOR THE BEST.
AYUKAWA...

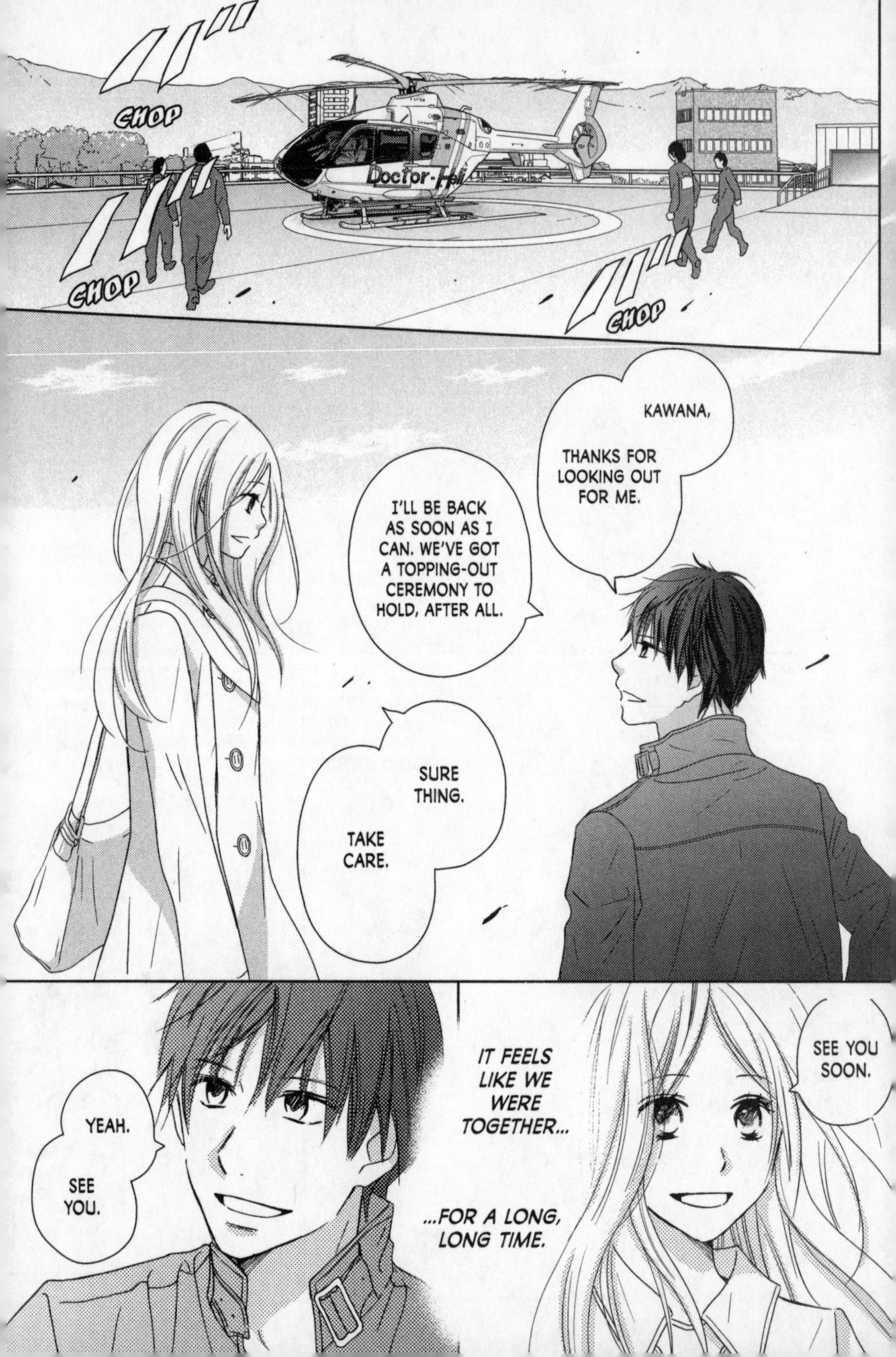
CHOP
CHOP
CHOP
KAWANA,
THANKS FOR LOOKING OUT FOR ME.
I'LL BE BACK AS SOON AS I CAN. WE'VE GOT A TOPPING-OUT CEREMONY TO HOLD, AFTER ALL.
SURE THING.
TAKE CARE.
SEE YOU SOON.
IT FEELS LIKE WE WERE TOGETHER...
...FOR A LONG, LONG TIME.
YEAH.
SEE YOU.

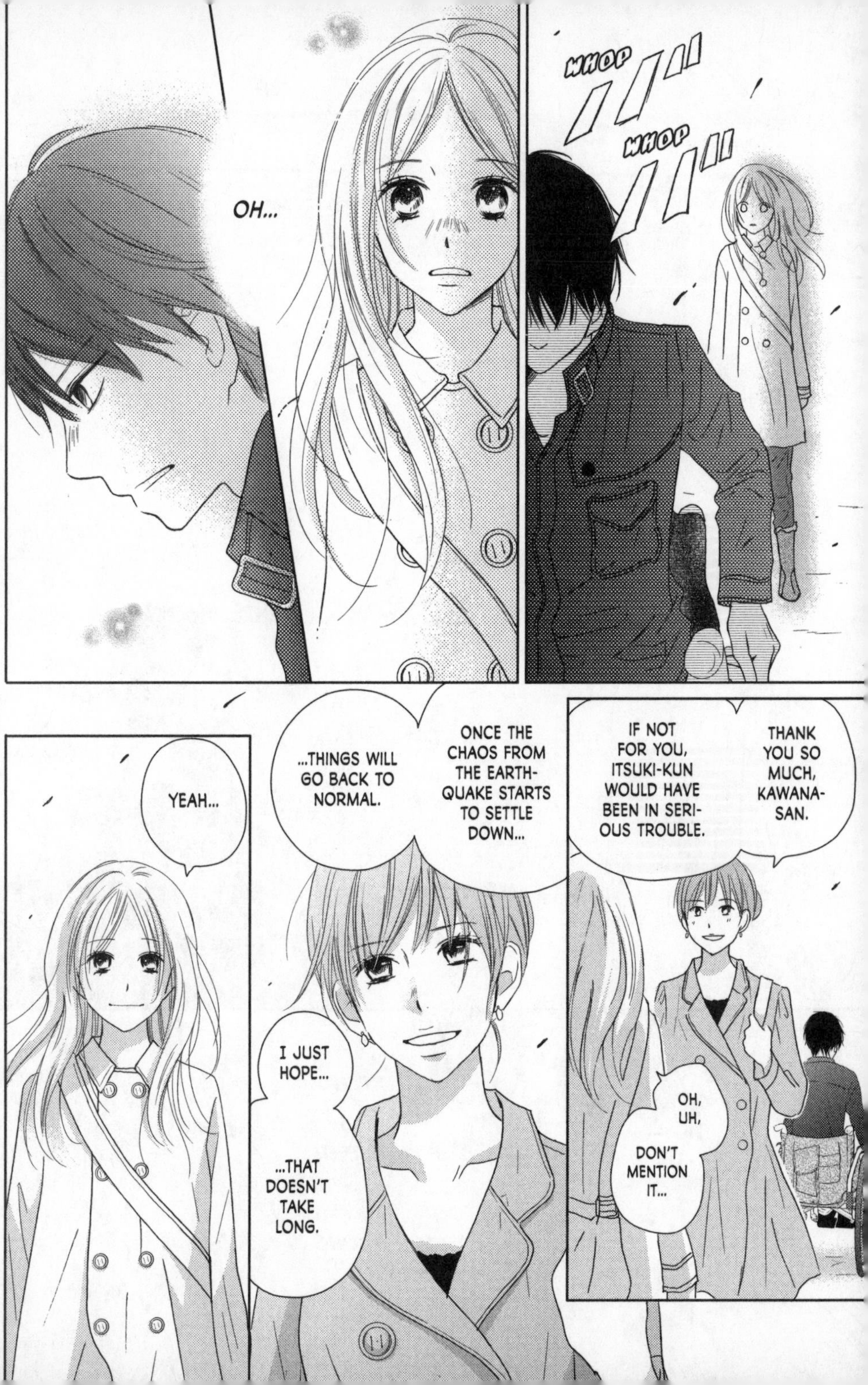
WHOP
WHOP
OH...
THANK YOU SO MUCH, KAWANA-SAN.
IF NOT FOR YOU, ITSUKI-KUN WOULD HAVE BEEN IN SERI-OUS TROUBLE.
OH, UH, DON'T MENTION IT...
ONCE THE CHAOS FROM THE EARTH-QUAKE STARTS TO SETTLE DOWN...
...THINGS WILL GO BACK TO NORMAL.
I JUST HOPE...
...THAT DOESN'T TAKE LONG.
YEAH...

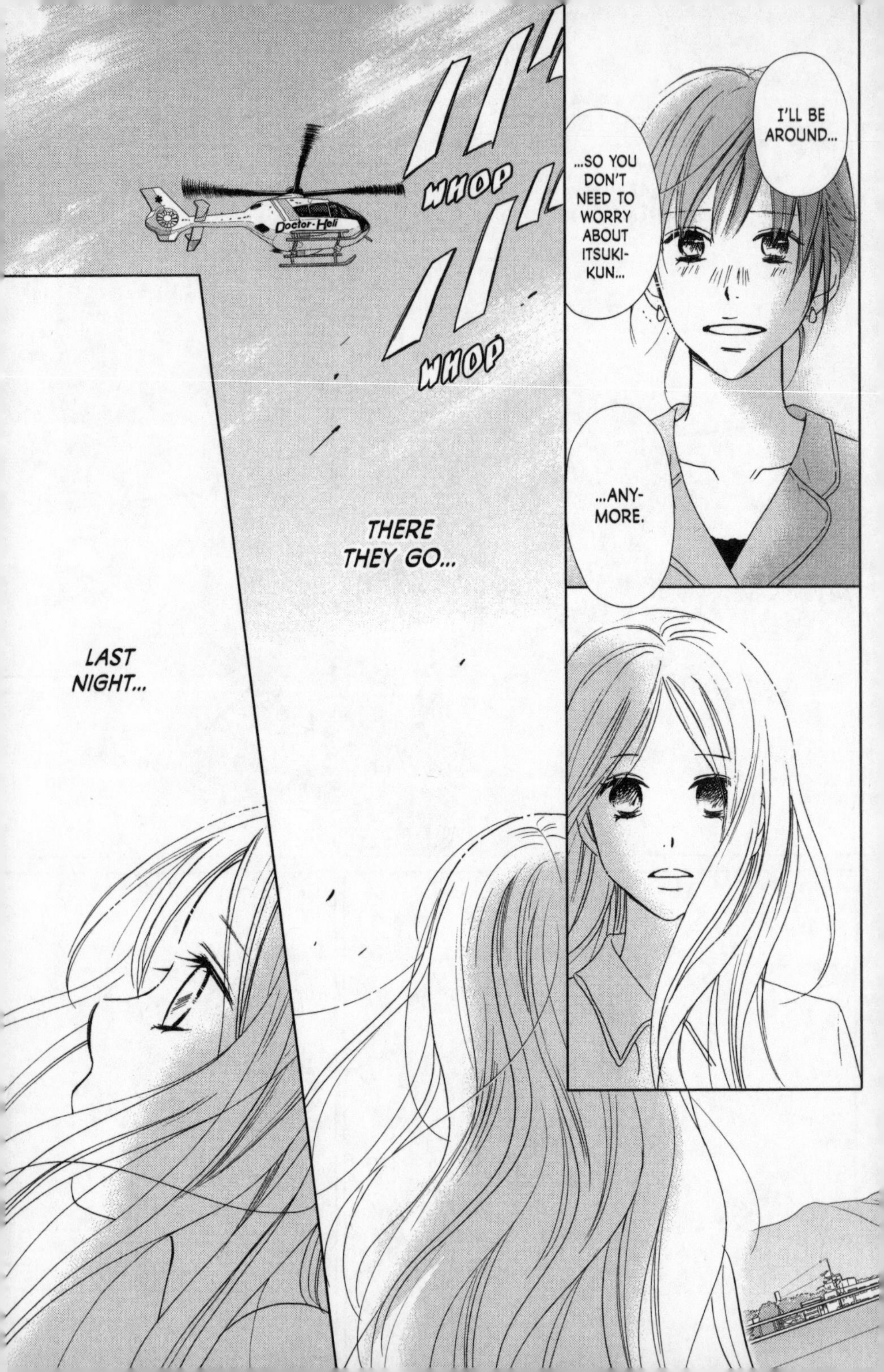
I'LL BE AROUND...
...SO YOU DON'T NEED TO WORRY ABOUT ITSUKI-KUN...
...ANY-MORE.
Doctor-Heli
WHOP
WHOP
THERE THEY GO...
LAST NIGHT...

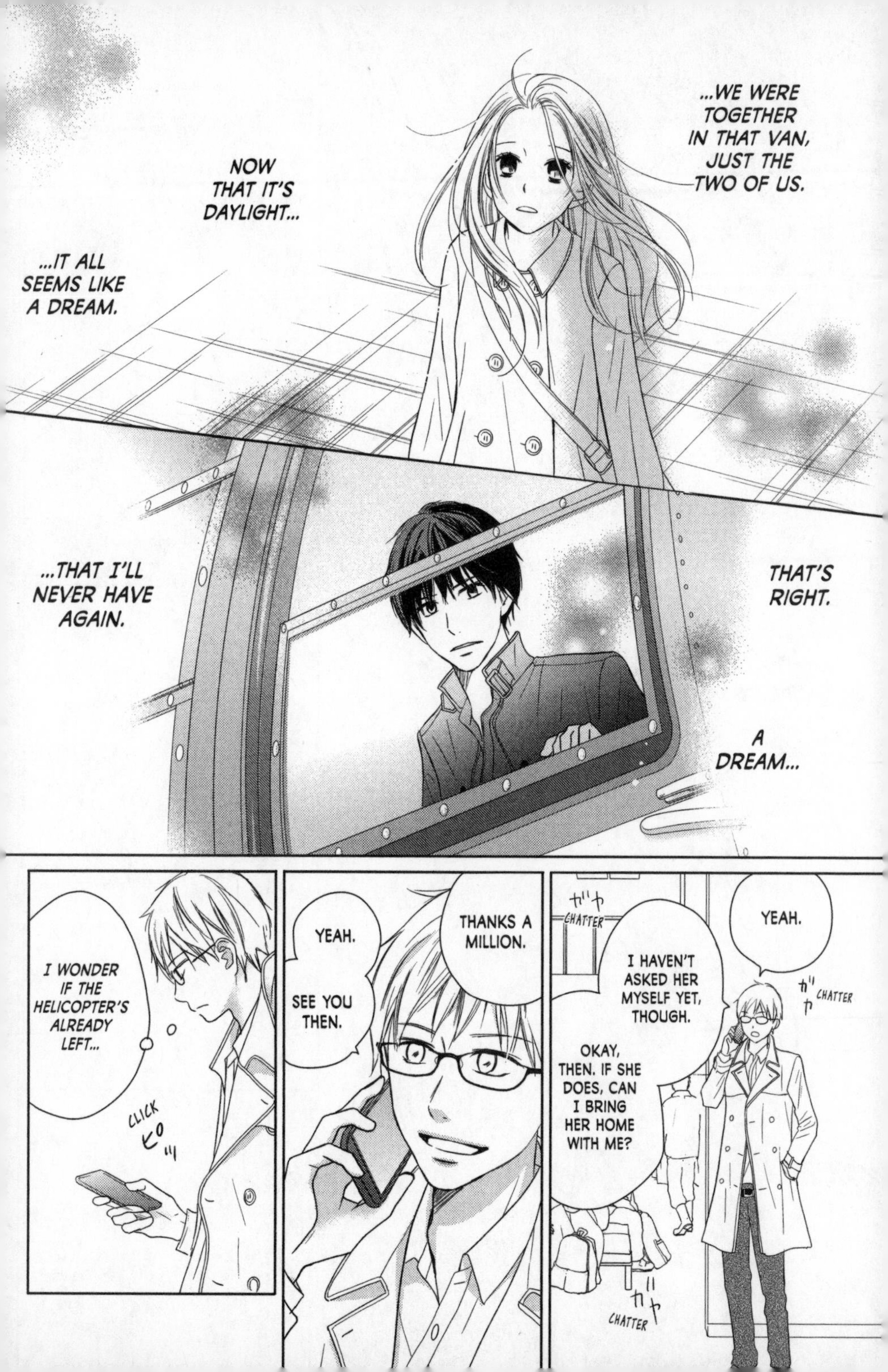
...WE WERE TOGETHER IN THAT VAN, JUST THE TWO OF US.
NOW THAT IT'S DAYLIGHT...
...IT ALL SEEMS LIKE A DREAM.
THAT'S RIGHT.
A DREAM...
...THAT I'LL NEVER HAVE AGAIN.
YEAH.
CHATTER
CHATTER
I HAVEN'T ASKED HER MYSELF YET, THOUGH.
OKAY, THEN. IF SHE DOES, CAN I BRING HER HOME WITH ME?
CHATTER
THANKS A MILLION.
YEAH.
SEE YOU THEN.
I WONDER IF THE HELICOPTER'S ALREADY LEFT...
CLICK

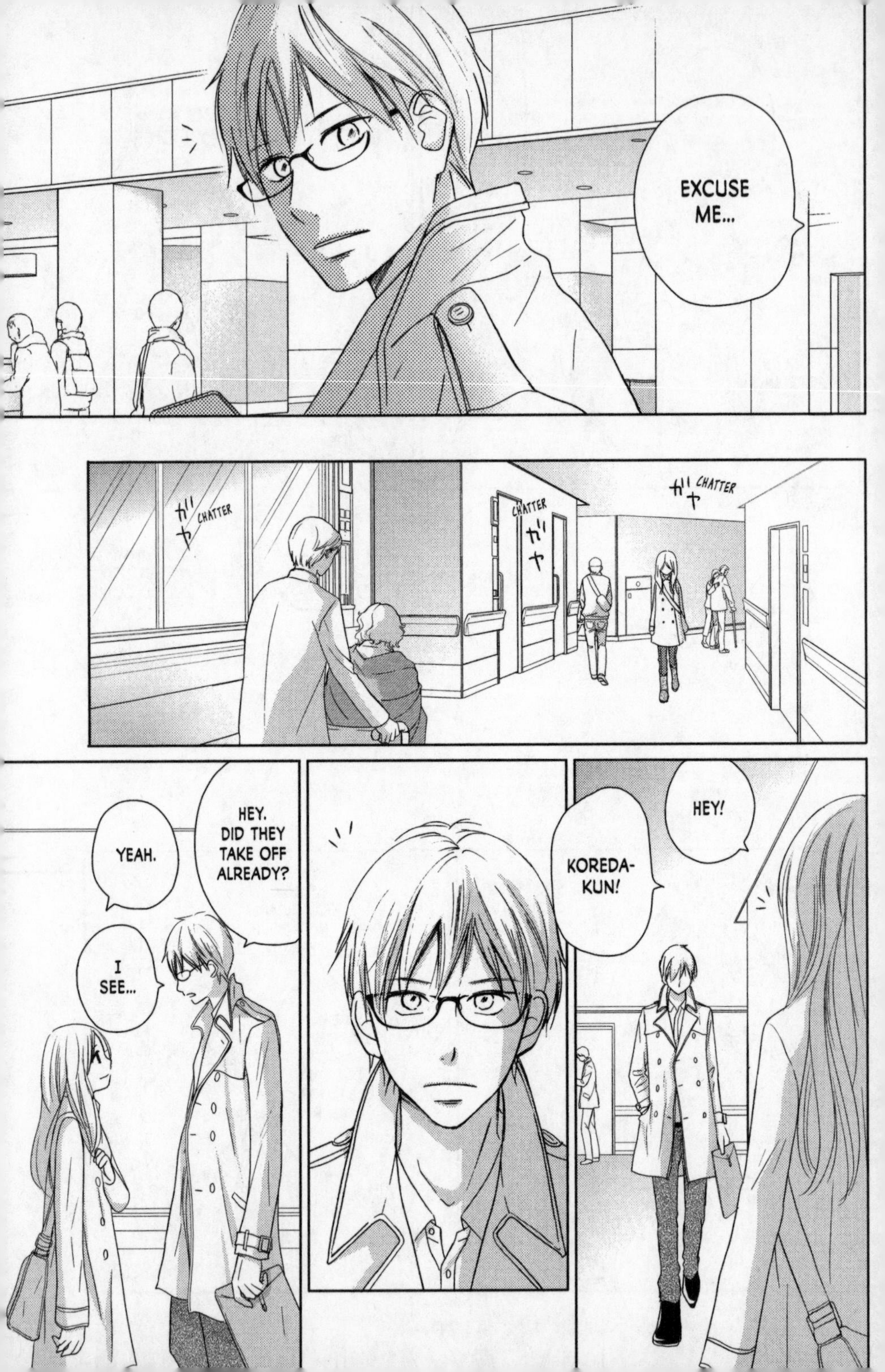
EXCUSE ME...
ガヤ CHATTER
ガヤ CHATTER
ガヤ CHATTER
HEY!
KOREDA-KUN!
HEY. DID THEY TAKE OFF ALREADY?
YEAH.
I SEE...

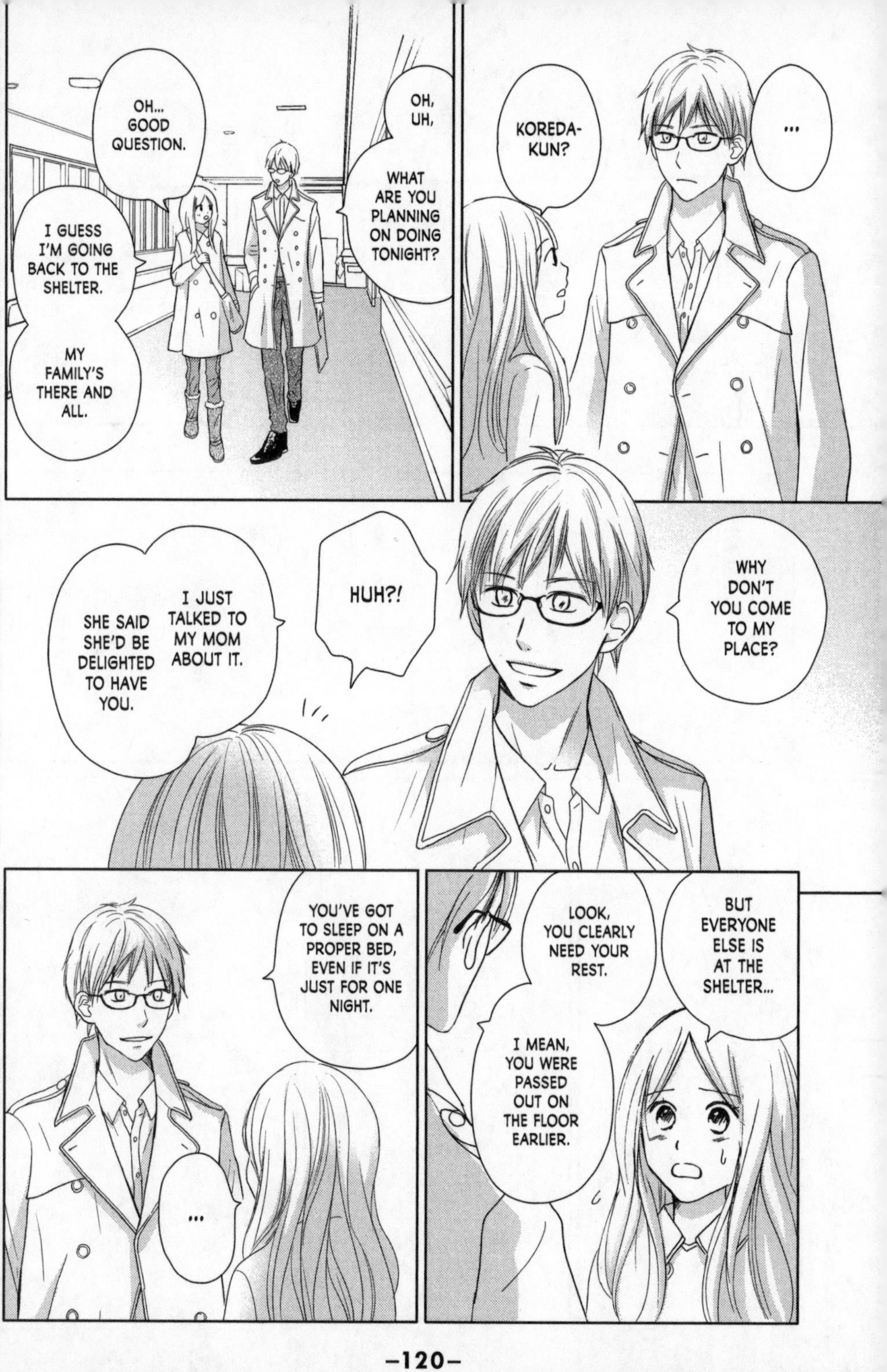
...
KOREDA-KUN?
OH, UH,
WHAT ARE YOU PLANNING ON DOING TONIGHT?
OH... GOOD QUESTION.
I GUESS I'M GOING BACK TO THE SHELTER.
MY FAMILY'S THERE AND ALL.
WHY DON'T YOU COME TO MY PLACE?
HUH?!
I JUST TALKED TO MY MOM ABOUT IT.
SHE SAID SHE'D BE DELIGHTED TO HAVE YOU.
BUT EVERYONE ELSE IS AT THE SHELTER...
LOOK, YOU CLEARLY NEED YOUR REST.
I MEAN, YOU WERE PASSED OUT ON THE FLOOR EARLIER.
YOU'VE GOT TO SLEEP ON A PROPER BED, EVEN IF IT'S JUST FOR ONE NIGHT.
...

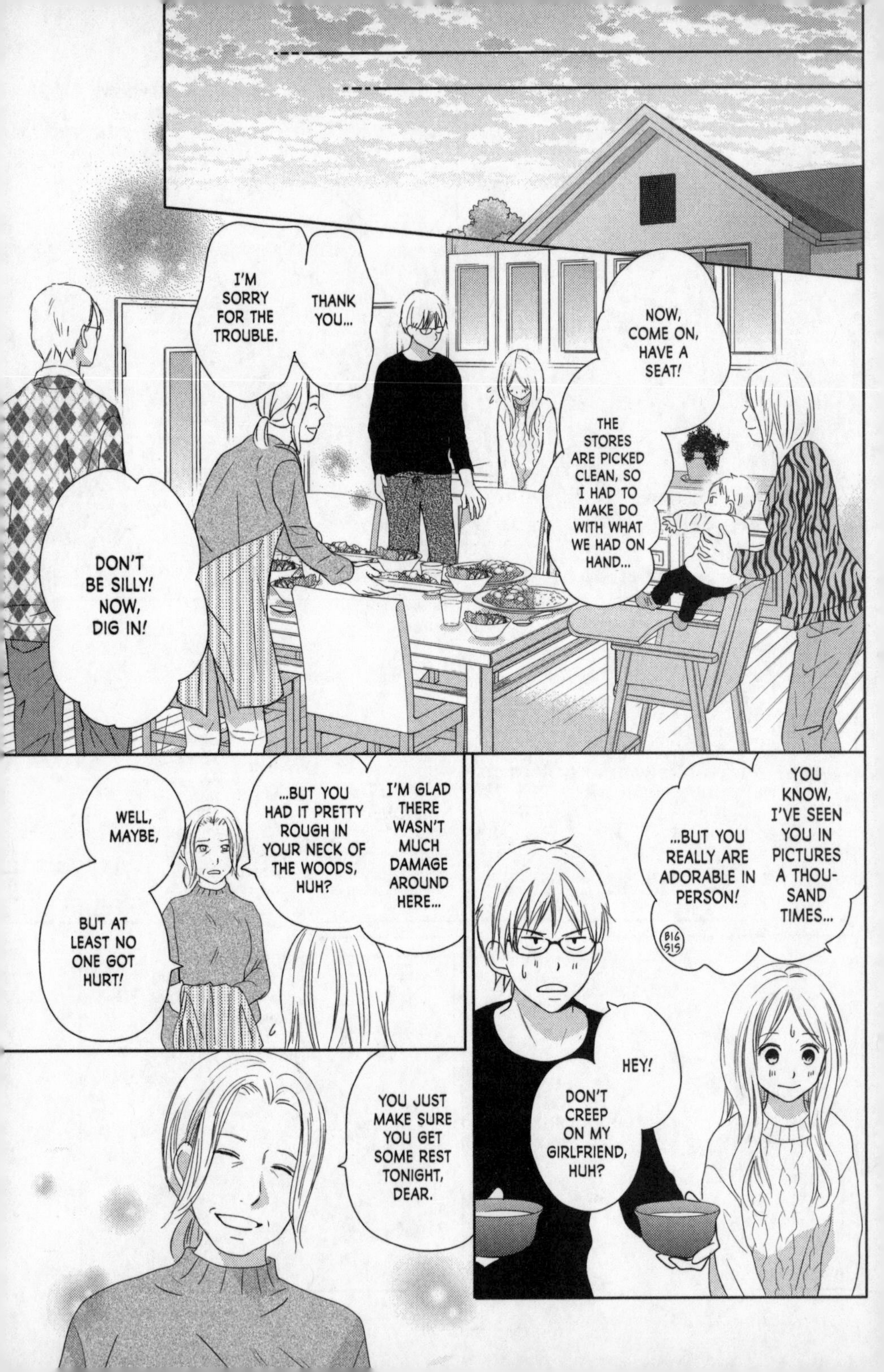
NOW, COME ON, HAVE A SEAT!
THE STORES ARE PICKED CLEAN, SO I HAD TO MAKE DO WITH WHAT WE HAD ON HAND...
THANK YOU...
I'M SORRY FOR THE TROUBLE.
DON'T BE SILLY! NOW, DIG IN!
YOU KNOW, I'VE SEEN YOU IN PICTURES A THOUSAND TIMES...
...BUT YOU REALLY ARE ADORABLE IN PERSON!
BIG SIS
HEY!
DON'T CREEP ON MY GIRLFRIEND, HUH?
I'M GLAD THERE WASN'T MUCH DAMAGE AROUND HERE...
...BUT YOU HAD IT PRETTY ROUGH IN YOUR NECK OF THE WOODS, HUH?
WELL, MAYBE,
BUT AT LEAST NO ONE GOT HURT!
YOU JUST MAKE SURE YOU GET SOME REST TONIGHT, DEAR.

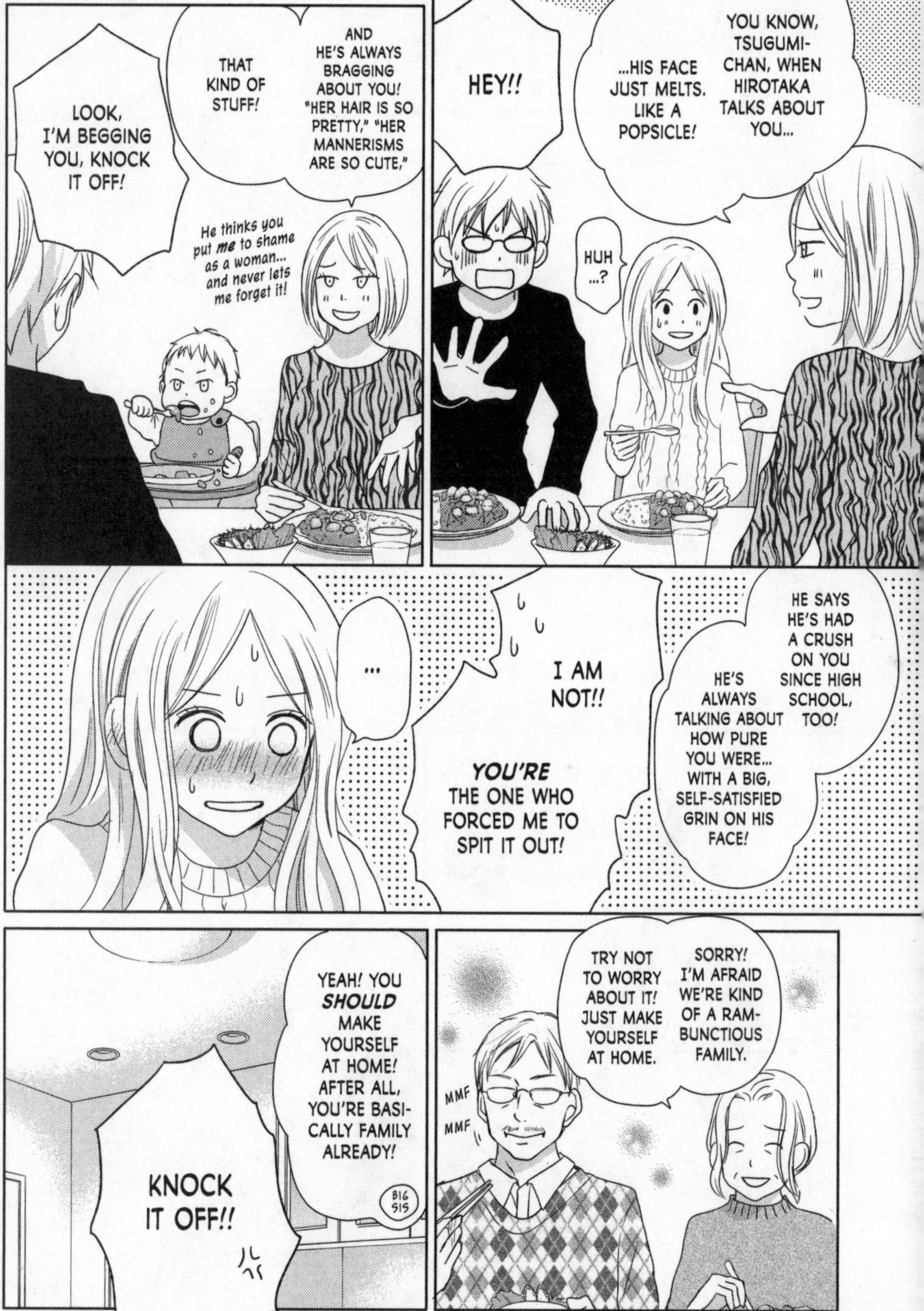
YOU KNOW, TSUGUMI-CHAN, WHEN HIROTAKA TALKS ABOUT YOU...
...HIS FACE JUST MELTS. LIKE A POPSICLE!
HEY!!
HUH ...?
AND HE'S ALWAYS BRAGGING ABOUT YOU! "HER HAIR IS SO PRETTY," "HER MANNERISMS ARE SO CUTE,"
THAT KIND OF STUFF!
He thinks you put *me* to shame as a woman... and never lets me forget it!
LOOK, I'M BEGGING YOU, KNOCK IT OFF!
HE SAYS HE'S HAD A CRUSH ON YOU SINCE HIGH SCHOOL, TOO!
HE'S ALWAYS TALKING ABOUT HOW PURE YOU WERE... WITH A BIG, SELF-SATISFIED GRIN ON HIS FACE!
I AM NOT!!
YOU'RE THE ONE WHO FORCED ME TO SPIT IT OUT!
...
SORRY! I'M AFRAID WE'RE KIND OF A RAM-BUNCTIOUS FAMILY.
TRY NOT TO WORRY ABOUT IT! JUST MAKE YOURSELF AT HOME.
MMF
MMF
YEAH! YOU *SHOULD* MAKE YOURSELF AT HOME! AFTER ALL, YOU'RE BASI-CALLY FAMILY ALREADY!
BIG SIS
KNOCK IT OFF!!

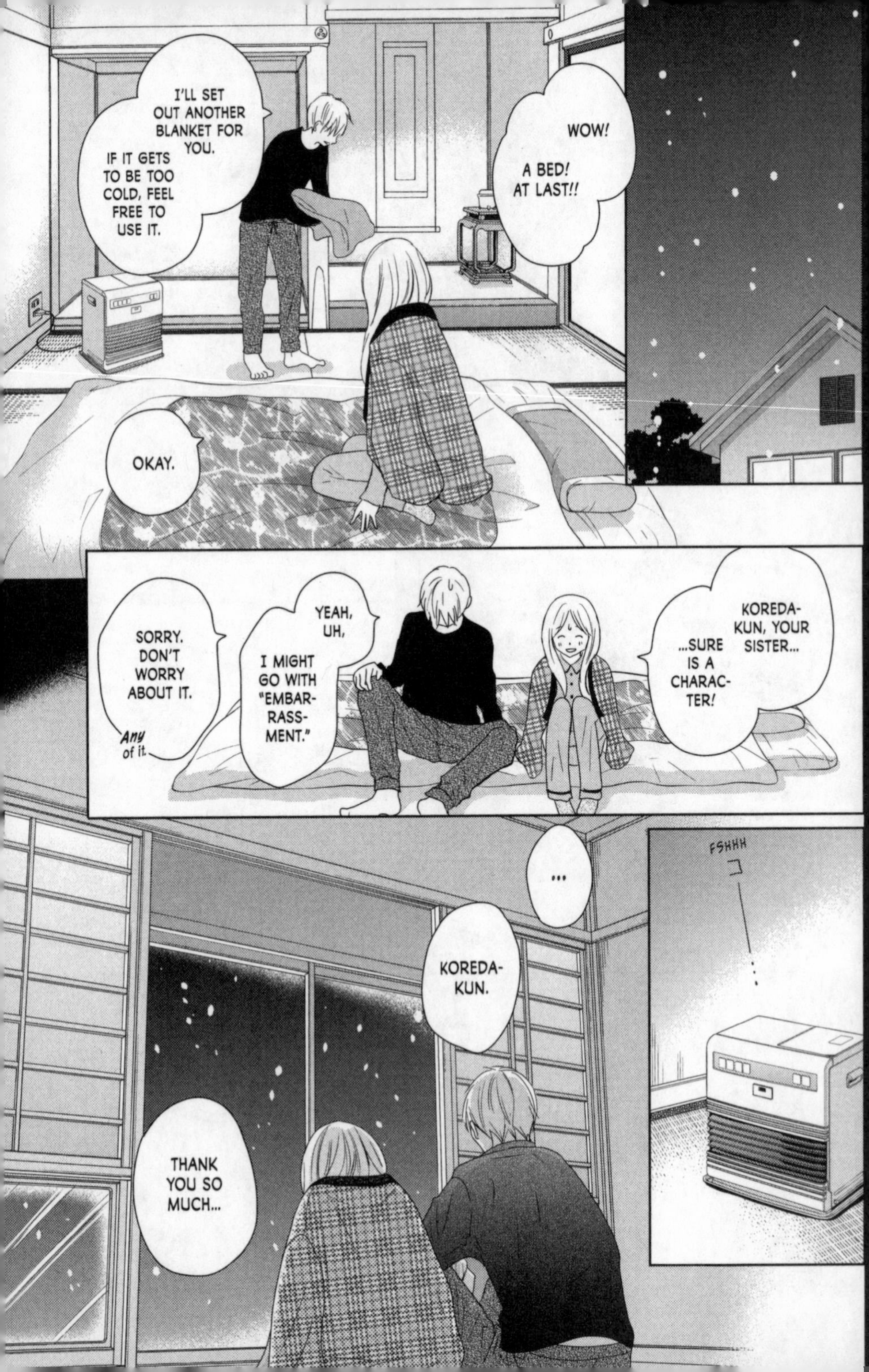
WOW!
A BED! AT LAST!!
I'LL SET OUT ANOTHER BLANKET FOR YOU.
IF IT GETS TO BE TOO COLD, FEEL FREE TO USE IT.
OKAY.
KOREDA-KUN, YOUR SISTER...
...SURE IS A CHARAC-TER!
YEAH, UH,
I MIGHT GO WITH "EMBAR-RASS-MENT."
SORRY. DON'T WORRY ABOUT IT.
Any of it.
FSHHH
...
KOREDA-KUN.
THANK YOU SO MUCH...

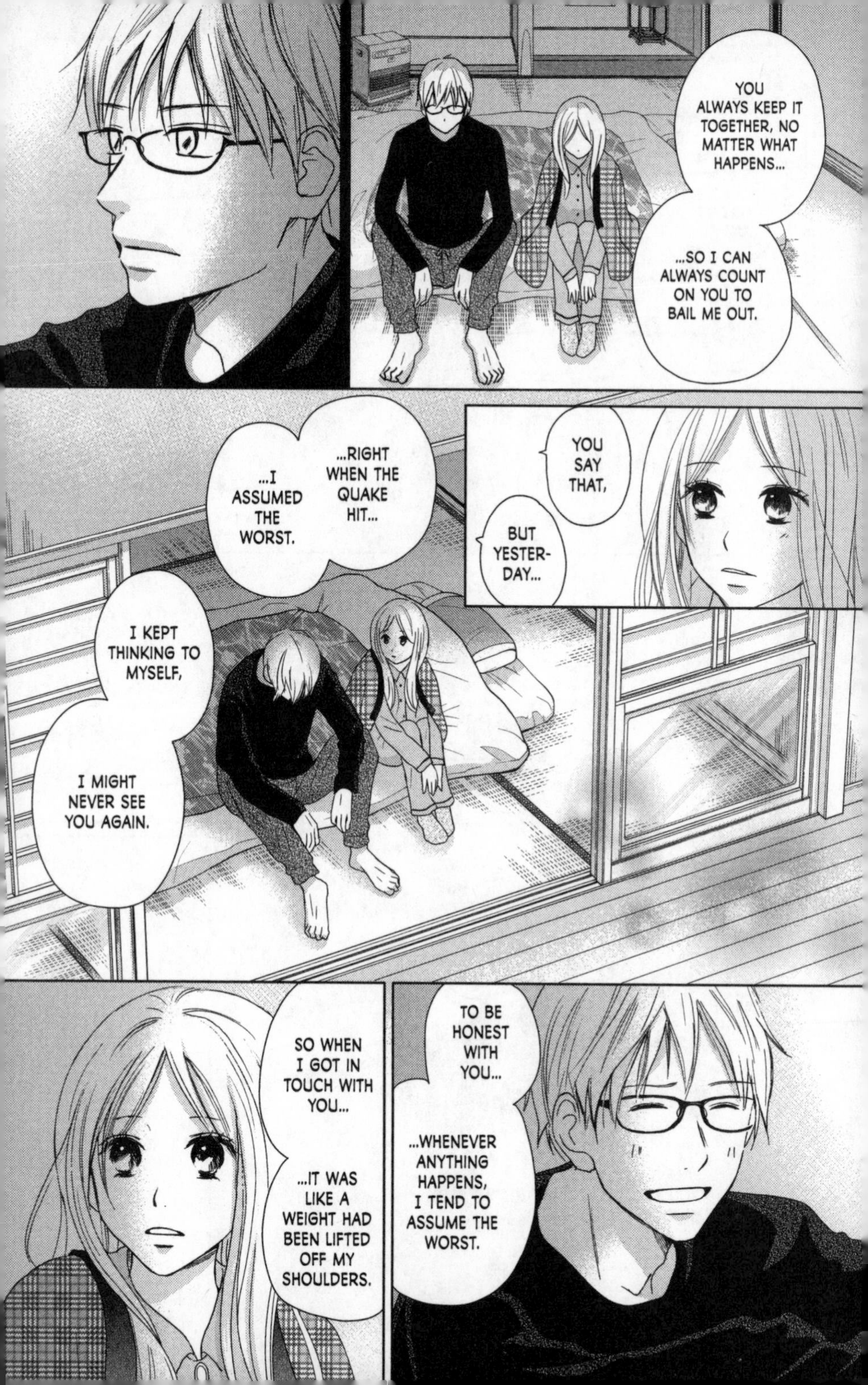
YOU ALWAYS KEEP IT TOGETHER, NO MATTER WHAT HAPPENS...
...SO I CAN ALWAYS COUNT ON YOU TO BAIL ME OUT.
YOU SAY THAT,
BUT YESTER-DAY...
...RIGHT WHEN THE QUAKE HIT...
...I ASSUMED THE WORST.
I KEPT THINKING TO MYSELF,
I MIGHT NEVER SEE YOU AGAIN.
TO BE HONEST WITH YOU...
...WHENEVER ANYTHING HAPPENS, I TEND TO ASSUME THE WORST.
SO WHEN I GOT IN TOUCH WITH YOU...
...IT WAS LIKE A WEIGHT HAD BEEN LIFTED OFF MY SHOULDERS.

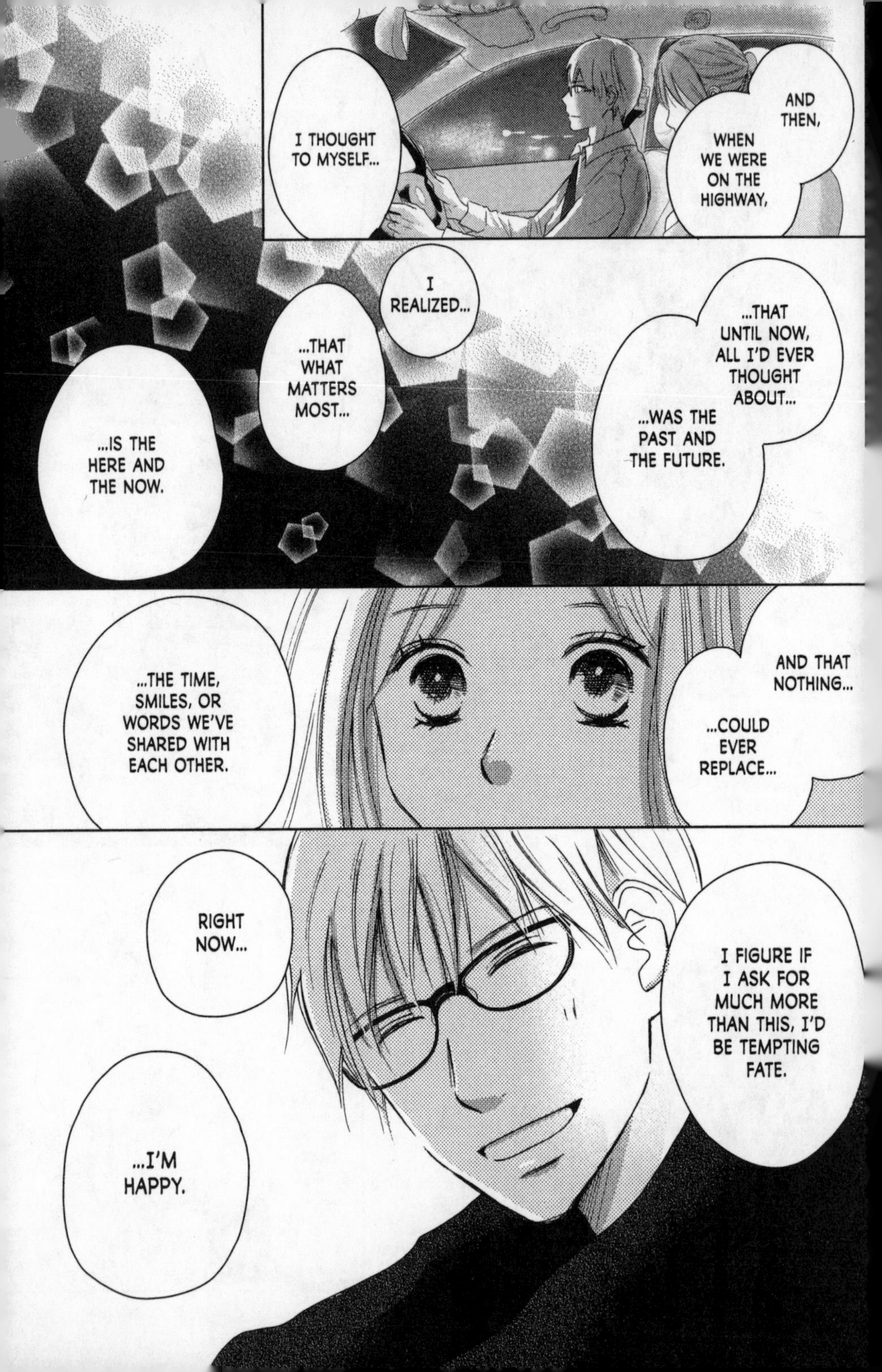
AND THEN, WHEN WE WERE ON THE HIGHWAY,
I THOUGHT TO MYSELF...
...THAT UNTIL NOW, ALL I'D EVER THOUGHT ABOUT...
...WAS THE PAST AND THE FUTURE.
I REALIZED...
...THAT WHAT MATTERS MOST...
...IS THE HERE AND THE NOW.
AND THAT NOTHING...
...COULD EVER REPLACE...
...THE TIME, SMILES, OR WORDS WE'VE SHARED WITH EACH OTHER.
I FIGURE IF I ASK FOR MUCH MORE THAN THIS, I'D BE TEMPTING FATE.
RIGHT NOW...
...I'M HAPPY.

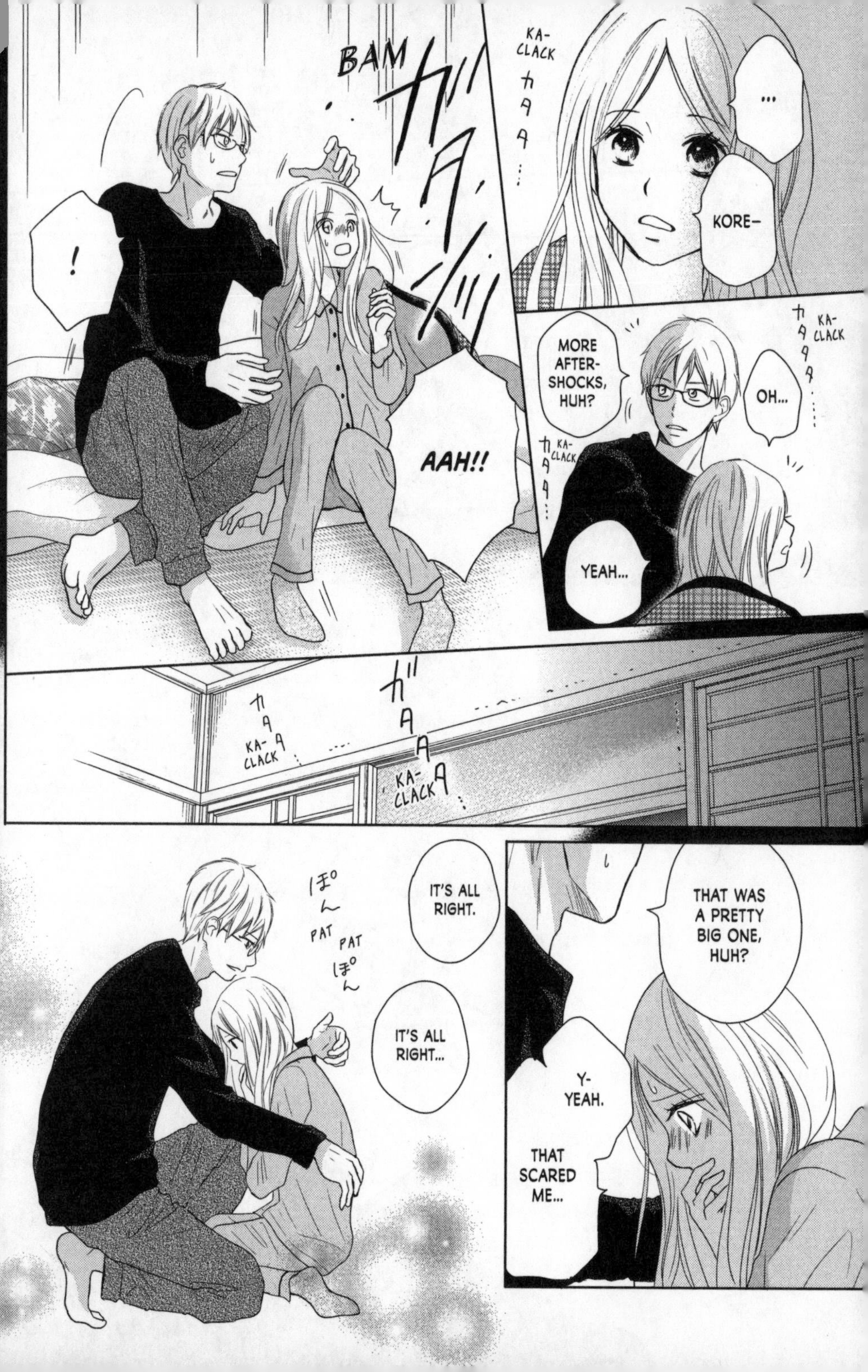
KA-CLACK
カタタ…
...
KORE–
カタタタ… KA-CLACK
OH...
MORE AFTER-SHOCKS, HUH?
カタタ… KA-CLACK
YEAH...
BAM
ガタン
AAH!!
!
ガタタタ… KA-CLACK
カタタ… KA-CLACK
THAT WAS A PRETTY BIG ONE, HUH?
Y-YEAH.
THAT SCARED ME...
IT'S ALL RIGHT.
IT'S ALL RIGHT...
ぽん PAT PAT ぽん

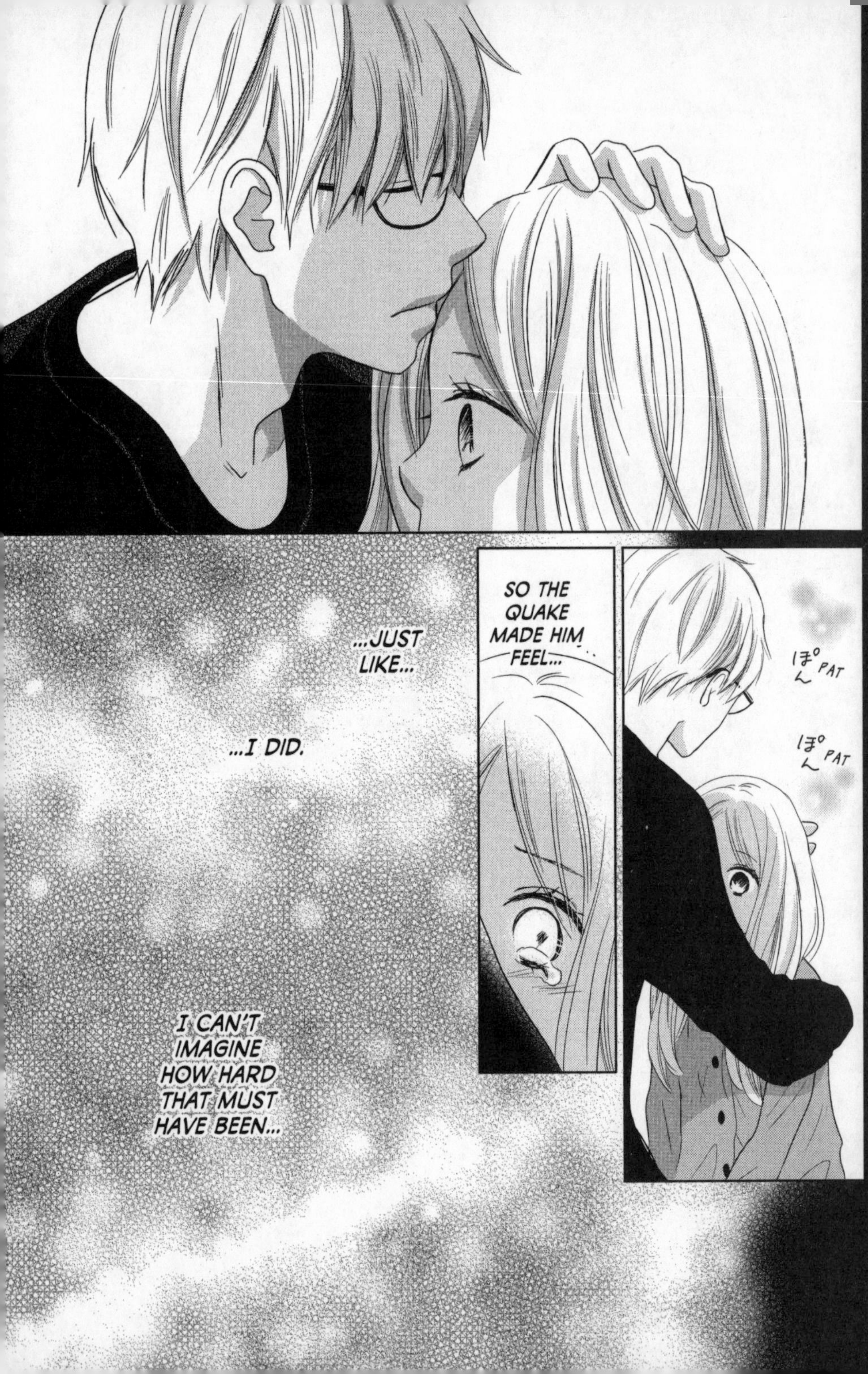
ぽん PAT
ぽん PAT
SO THE QUAKE MADE HIM FEEL...
...JUST LIKE...
...I DID.
I CAN'T IMAGINE HOW HARD THAT MUST HAVE BEEN...

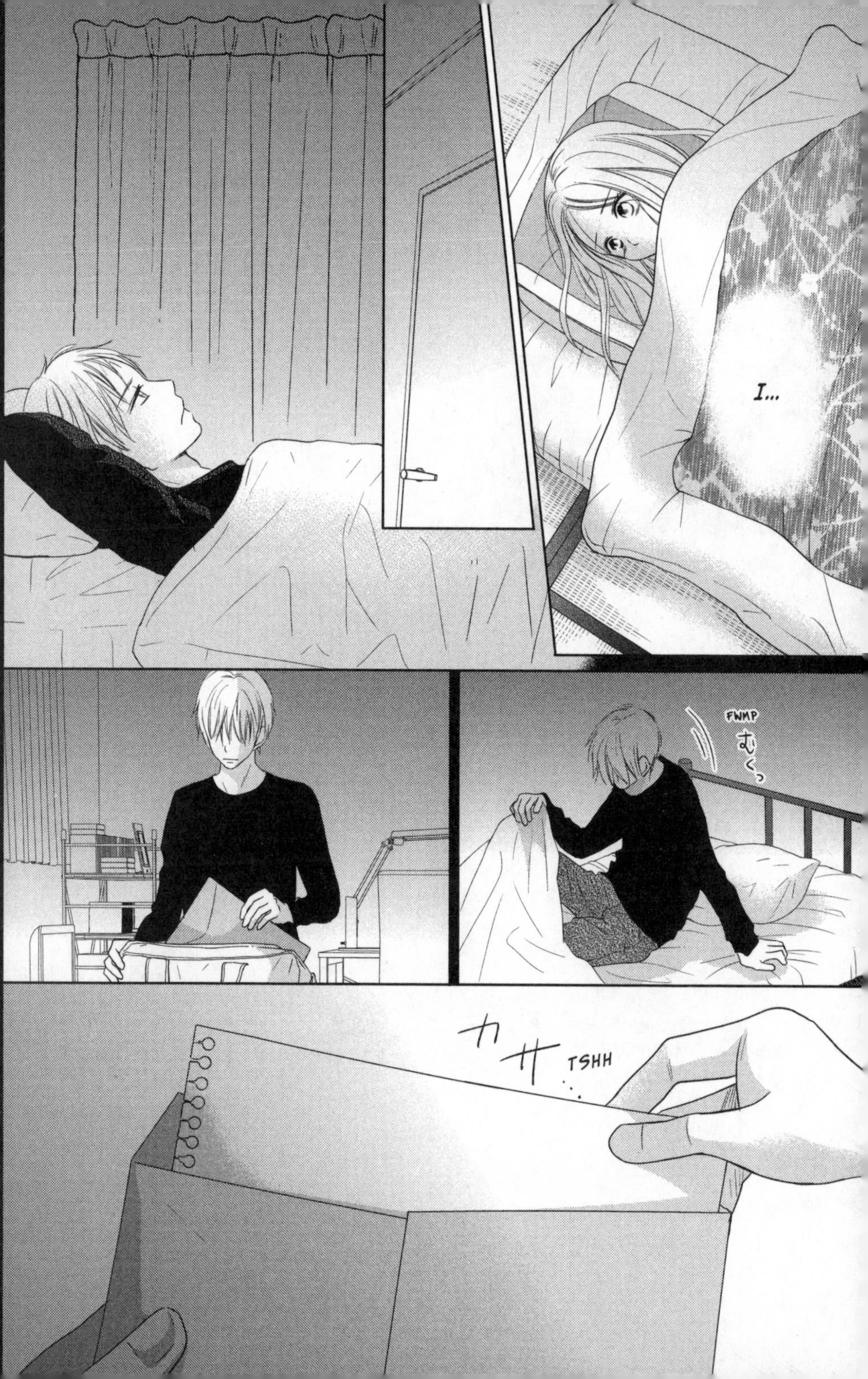
I...
FWMP
むくっ
カサ
TSHH

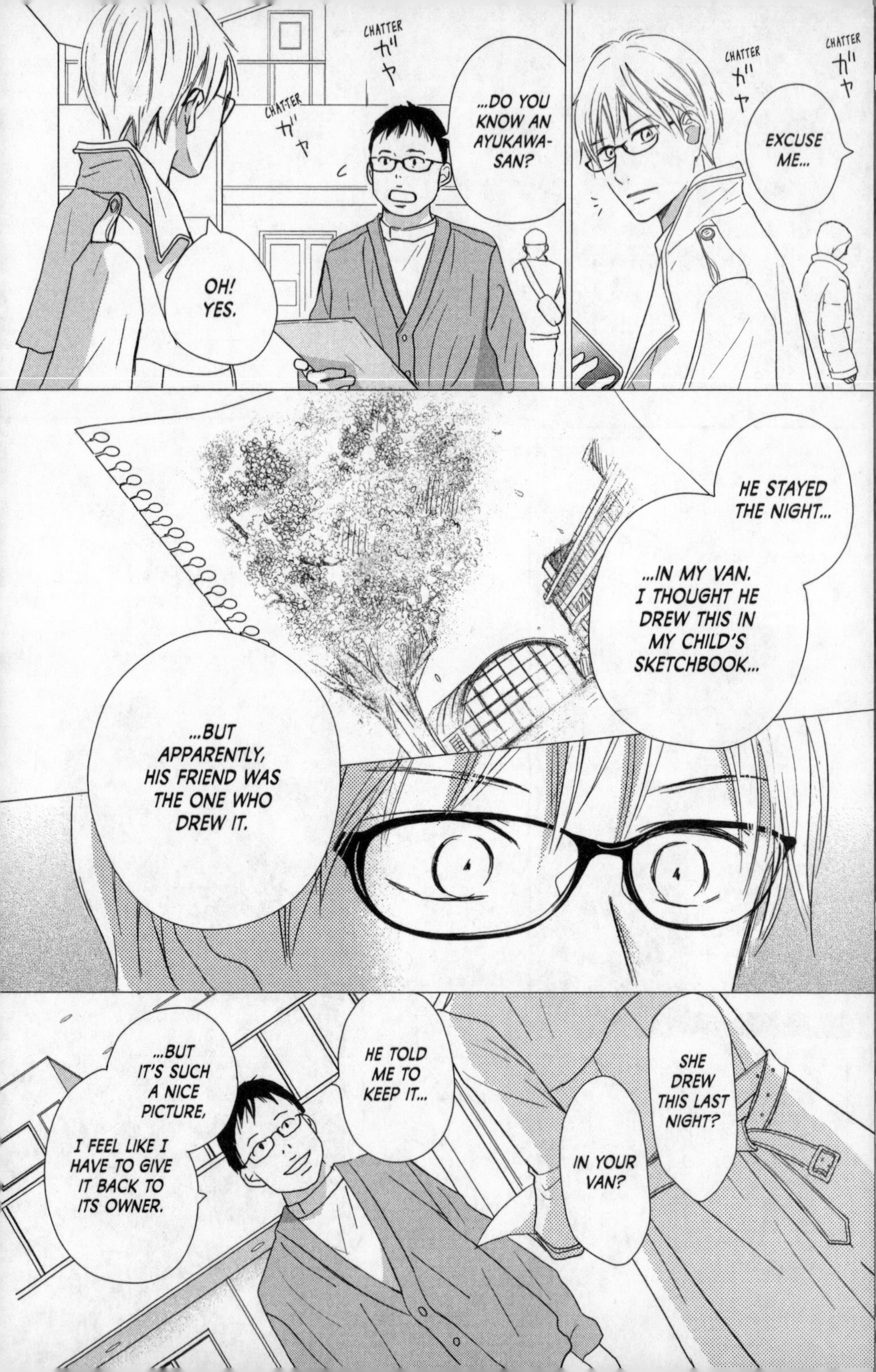
CHATTER ガヤ
CHATTER ガヤ
EXCUSE ME...
...DO YOU KNOW AN AYUKAWA-SAN?
CHATTER ガヤ
CHATTER ガヤ
OH! YES.
HE STAYED THE NIGHT...
...IN MY VAN. I THOUGHT HE DREW THIS IN MY CHILD'S SKETCHBOOK...
...BUT APPARENTLY, HIS FRIEND WAS THE ONE WHO DREW IT.
SHE DREW THIS LAST NIGHT?
IN YOUR VAN?
HE TOLD ME TO KEEP IT...
...BUT IT'S SUCH A NICE PICTURE,
I FEEL LIKE I HAVE TO GIVE IT BACK TO ITS OWNER.

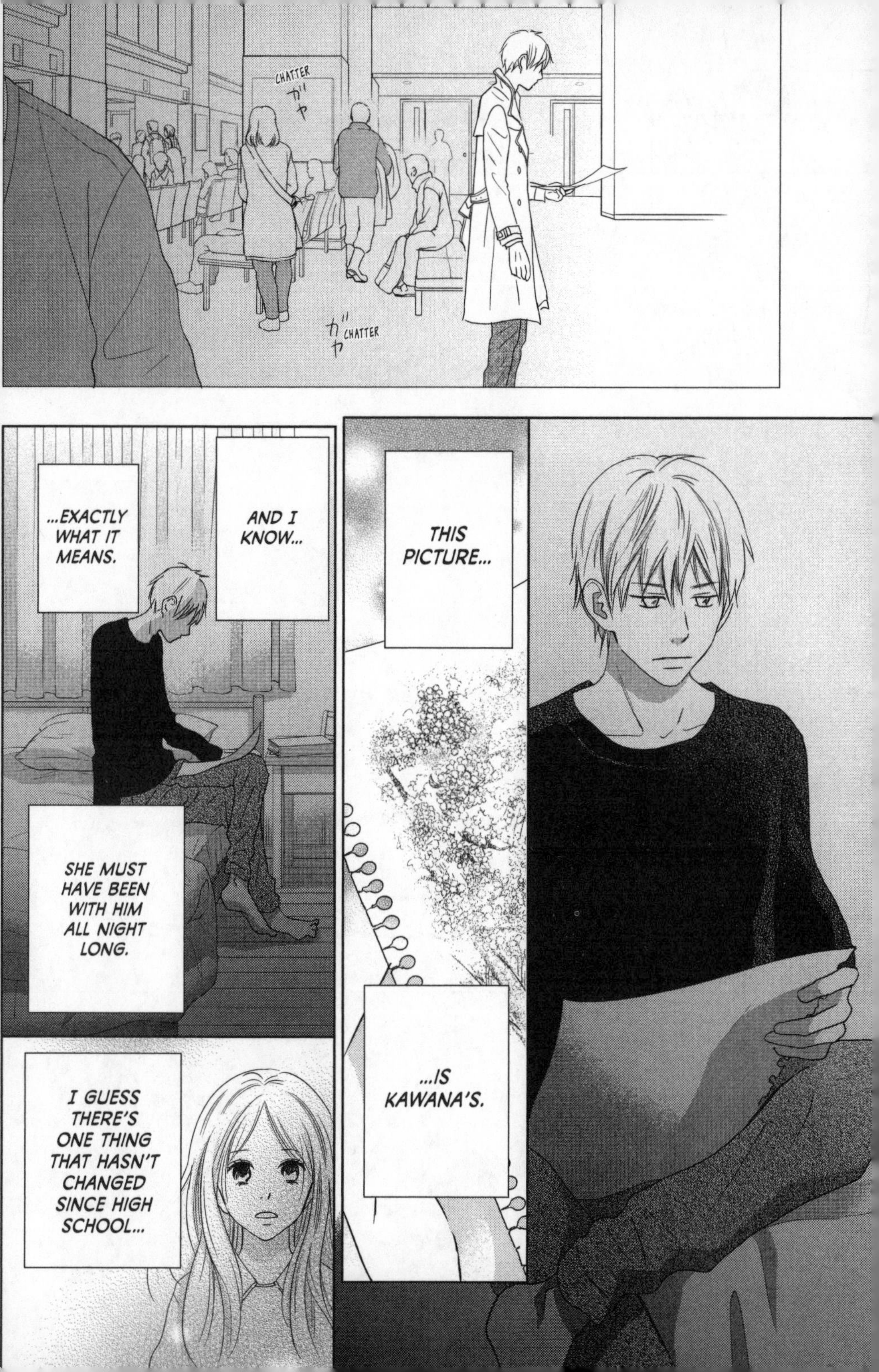
CHATTER
ガヤ
ガヤ
CHATTER
THIS PICTURE...
...IS KAWANA'S.
AND I KNOW...
...EXACTLY WHAT IT MEANS.
SHE MUST HAVE BEEN WITH HIM ALL NIGHT LONG.
I GUESS THERE'S ONE THING THAT HASN'T CHANGED SINCE HIGH SCHOOL...

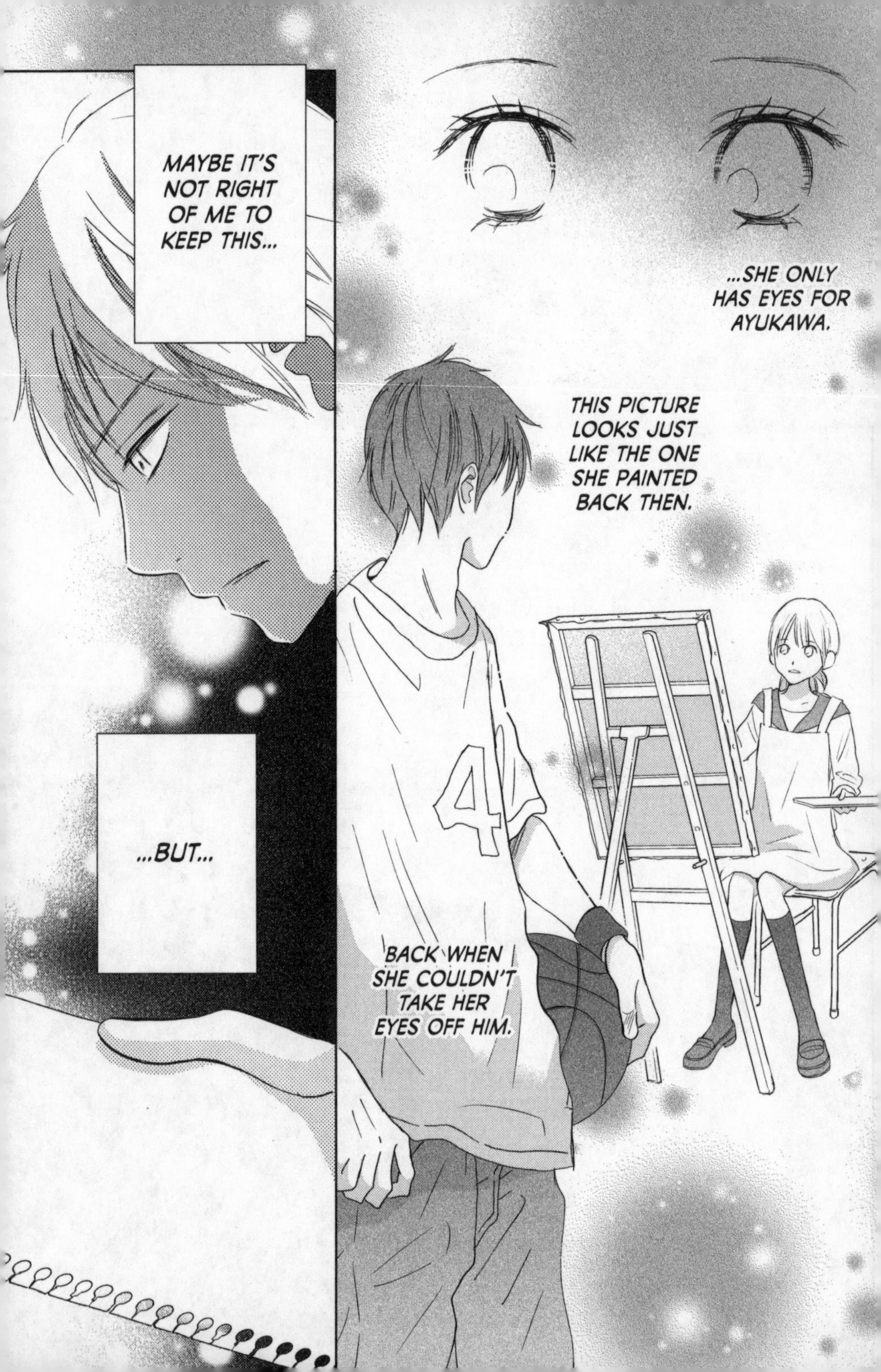
...SHE ONLY HAS EYES FOR AYUKAWA.
THIS PICTURE LOOKS JUST LIKE THE ONE SHE PAINTED BACK THEN.
BACK WHEN SHE COULDN'T TAKE HER EYES OFF HIM.
MAYBE IT'S NOT RIGHT OF ME TO KEEP THIS...
...BUT...

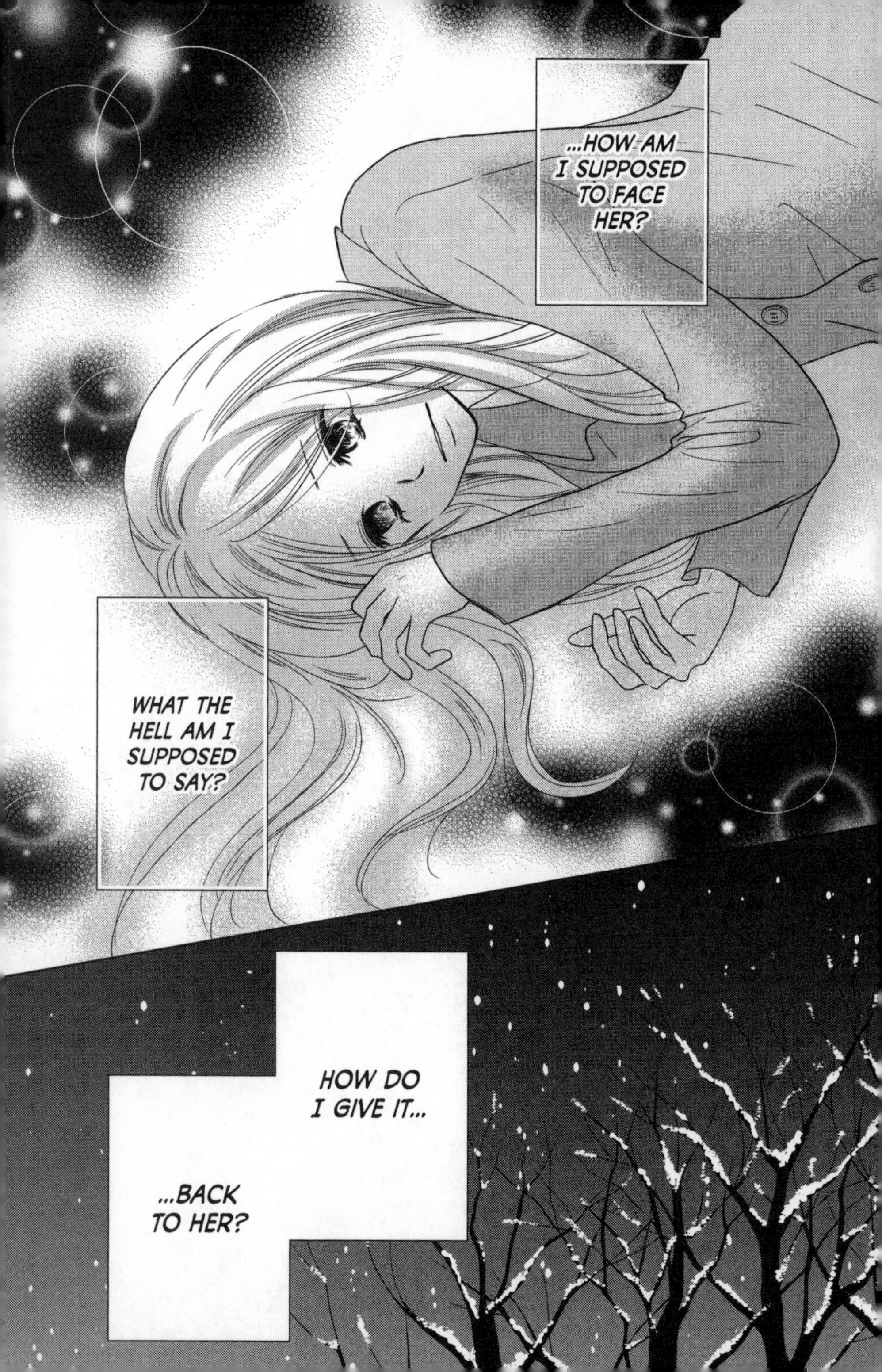
...HOW AM I SUPPOSED TO FACE HER?
WHAT THE HELL AM I SUPPOSED TO SAY?
HOW DO I GIVE IT...
...BACK TO HER?

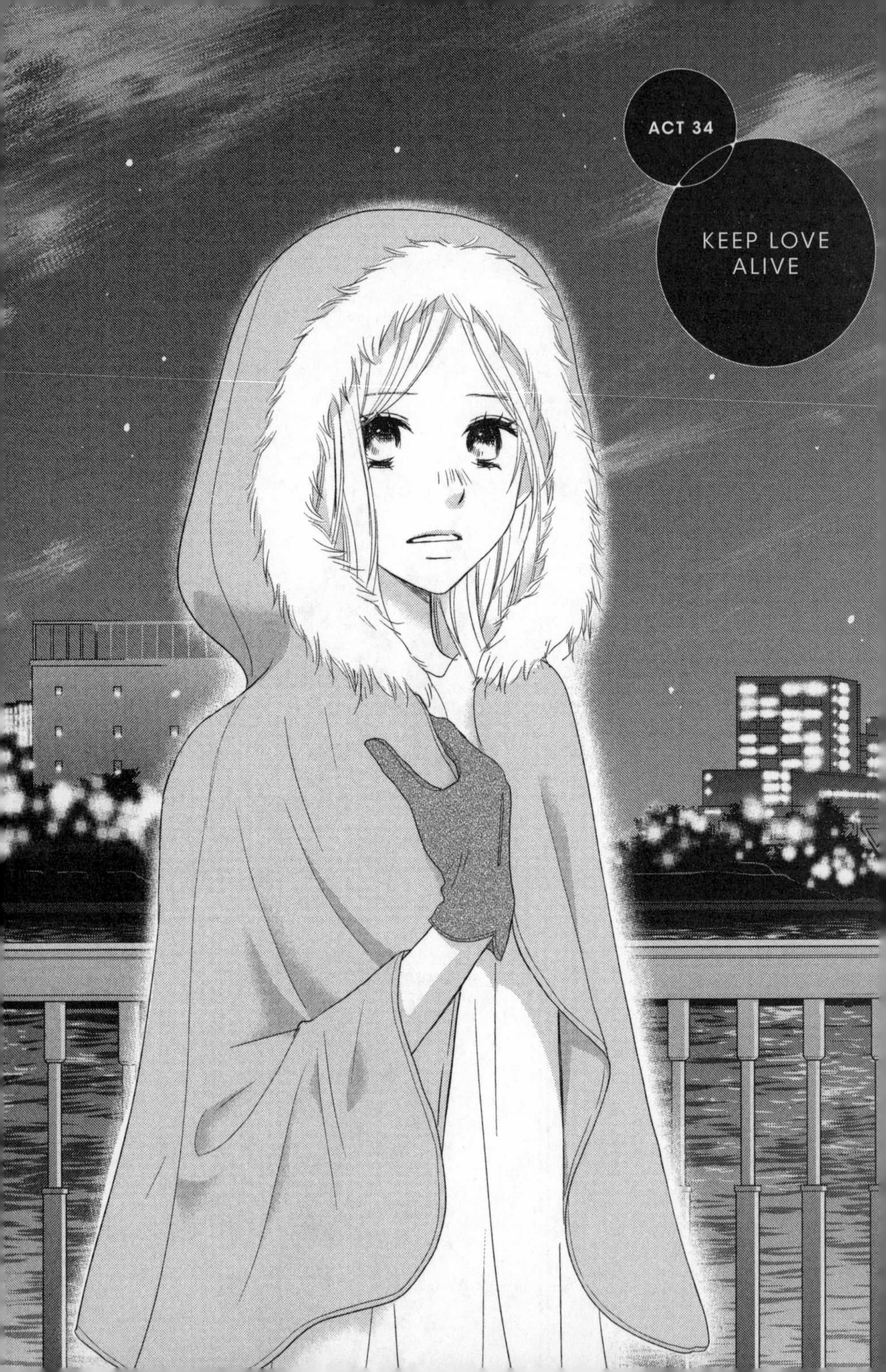
ACT 34
KEEP LOVE
ALIVE

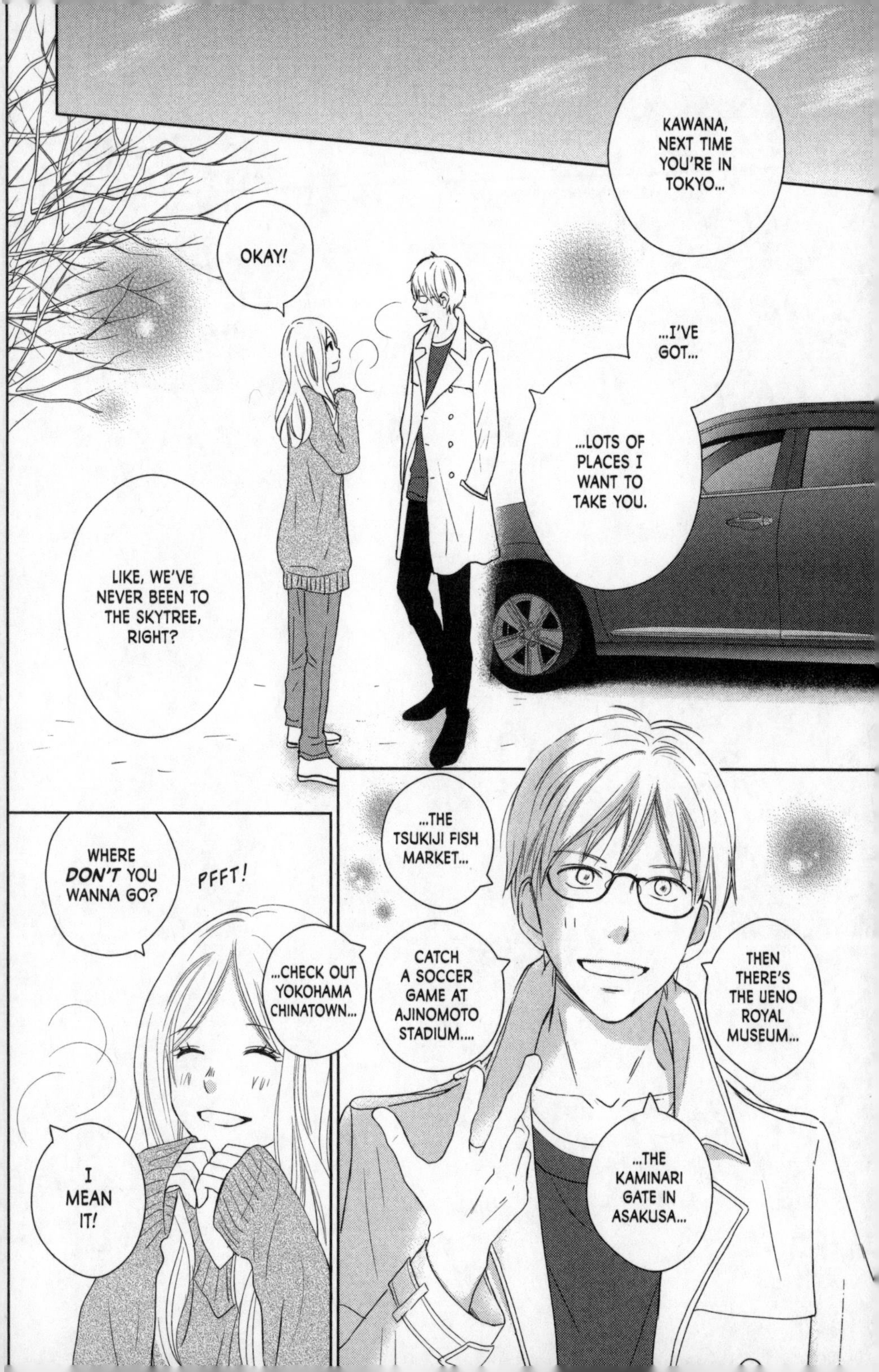
KAWANA, NEXT TIME YOU'RE IN TOKYO...
...I'VE GOT...
...LOTS OF PLACES I WANT TO TAKE YOU.
OKAY!
LIKE, WE'VE NEVER BEEN TO THE SKYTREE, RIGHT?
...THE TSUKIJI FISH MARKET...
THEN THERE'S THE UENO ROYAL MUSEUM...
...THE KAMINARI GATE IN ASAKUSA...
CATCH A SOCCER GAME AT AJINOMOTO STADIUM....
...CHECK OUT YOKOHAMA CHINATOWN...
WHERE ***DON'T*** YOU WANNA GO?
PFFT!
I MEAN IT!

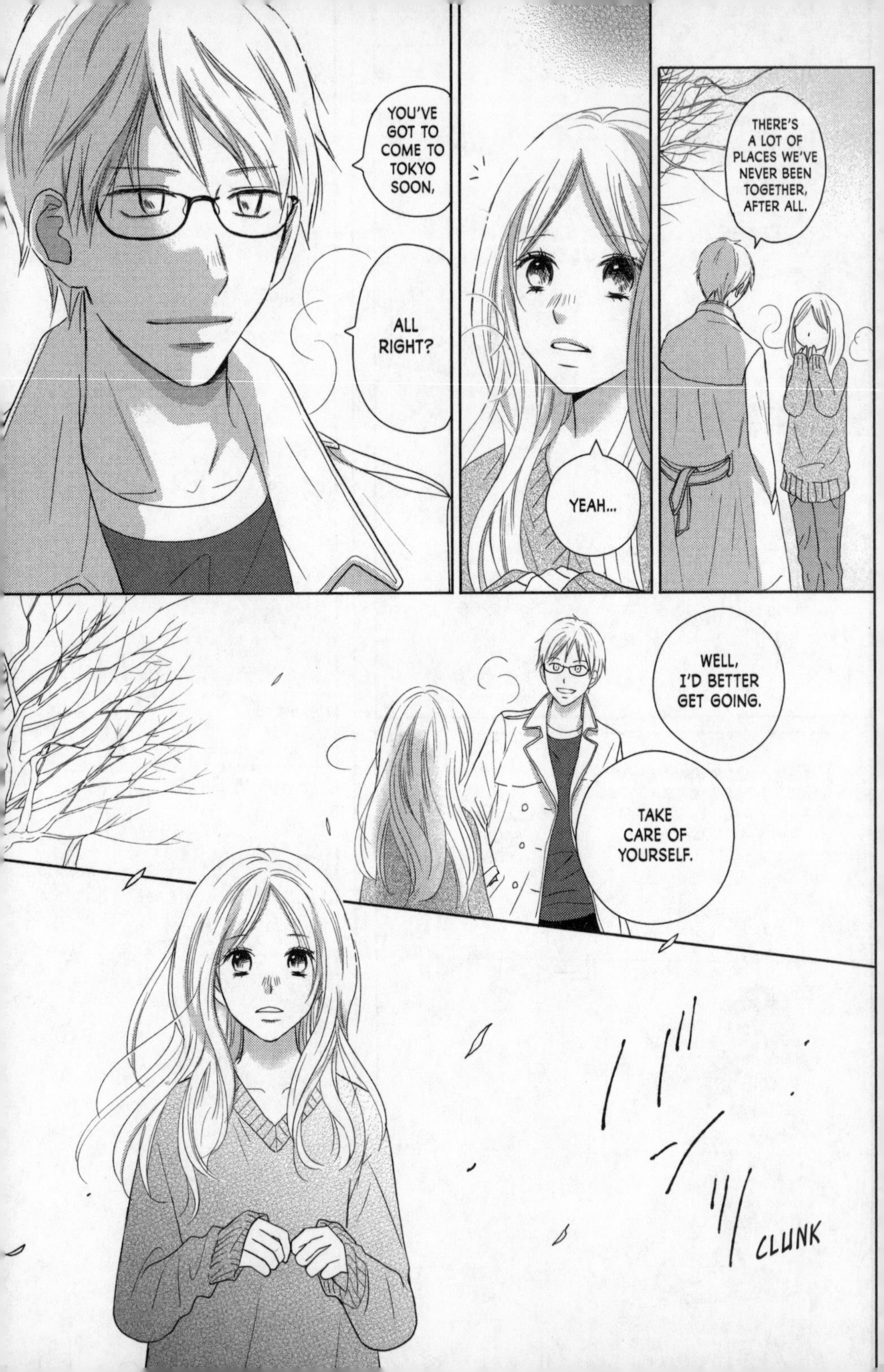
THERE'S A LOT OF PLACES WE'VE NEVER BEEN TOGETHER, AFTER ALL.
YEAH...
YOU'VE GOT TO COME TO TOKYO SOON,
ALL RIGHT?
WELL, I'D BETTER GET GOING.
TAKE CARE OF YOURSELF.
CLUNK

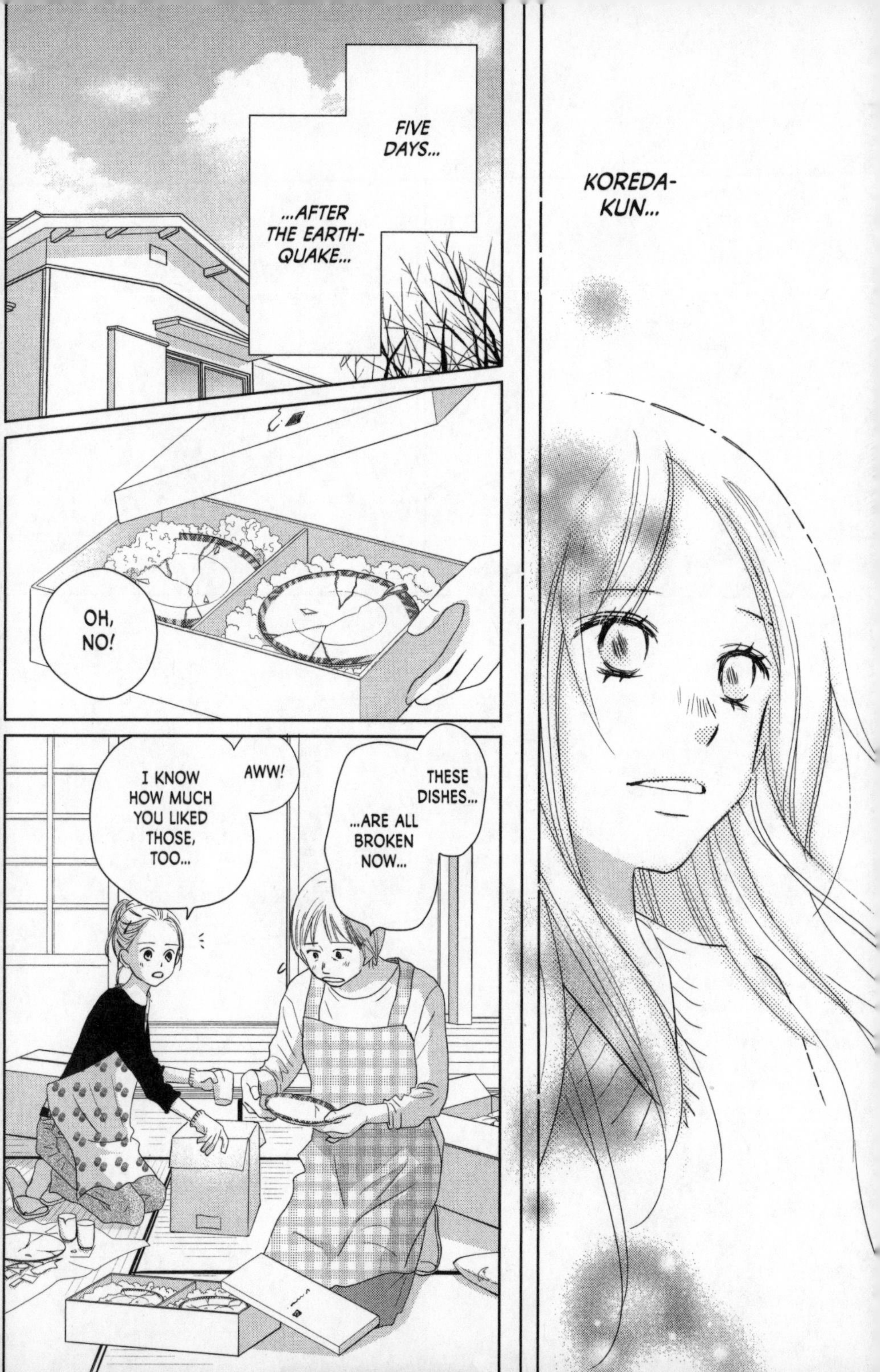
KOREDA-KUN...
FIVE DAYS...
...AFTER THE EARTHQUAKE...
OH, NO!
THESE DISHES...
...ARE ALL BROKEN NOW...
AWW!
I KNOW HOW MUCH YOU LIKED THOSE, TOO...

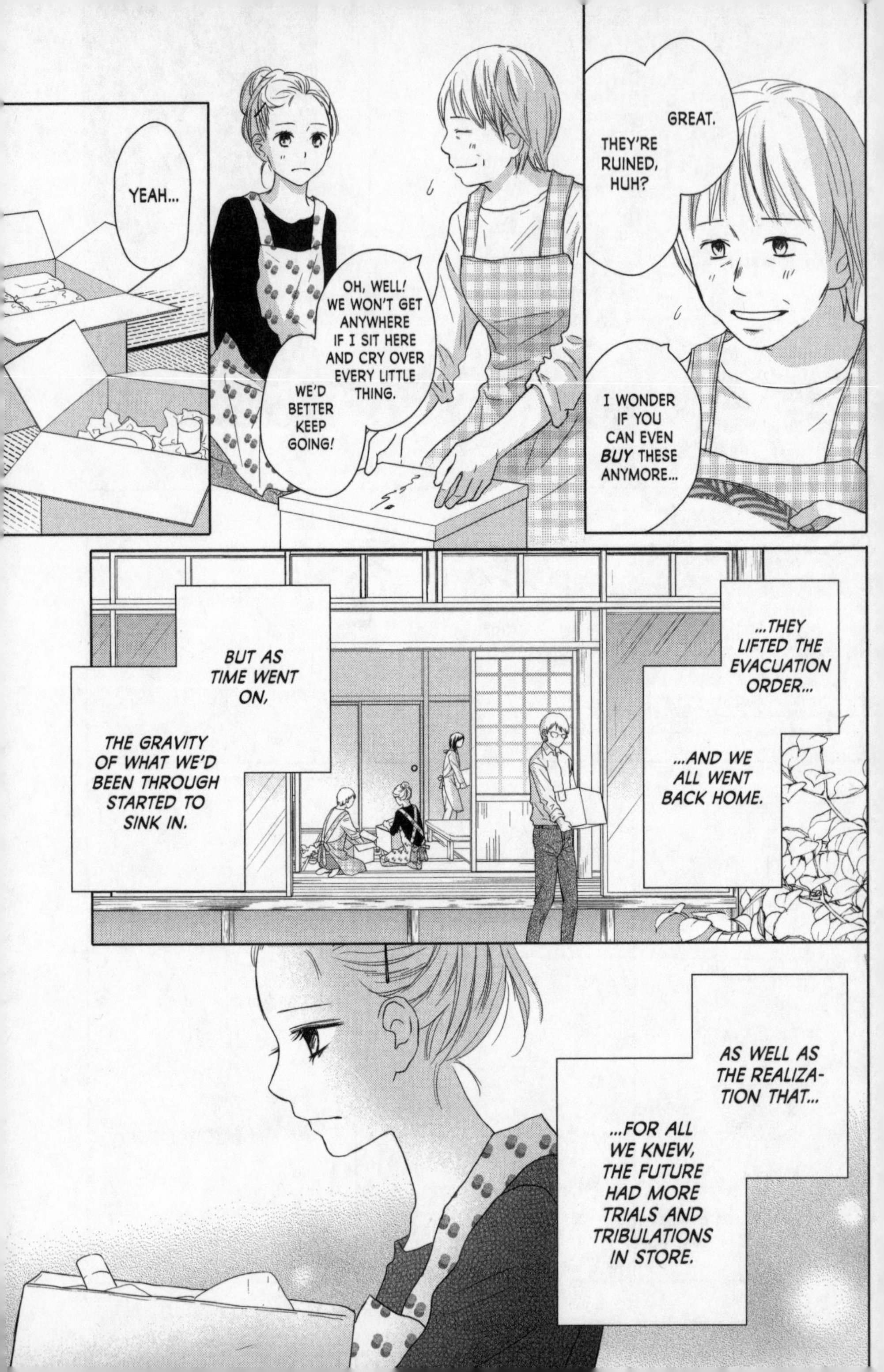
GREAT.
THEY'RE RUINED, HUH?
I WONDER IF YOU CAN EVEN *BUY* THESE ANYMORE...
OH, WELL! WE WON'T GET ANYWHERE IF I SIT HERE AND CRY OVER EVERY LITTLE THING.
WE'D BETTER KEEP GOING!
YEAH...
...THEY LIFTED THE EVACUATION ORDER...
...AND WE ALL WENT BACK HOME.
BUT AS TIME WENT ON,
THE GRAVITY OF WHAT WE'D BEEN THROUGH STARTED TO SINK IN.
AS WELL AS THE REALIZATION THAT...
...FOR ALL WE KNEW, THE FUTURE HAD MORE TRIALS AND TRIBULATIONS IN STORE.

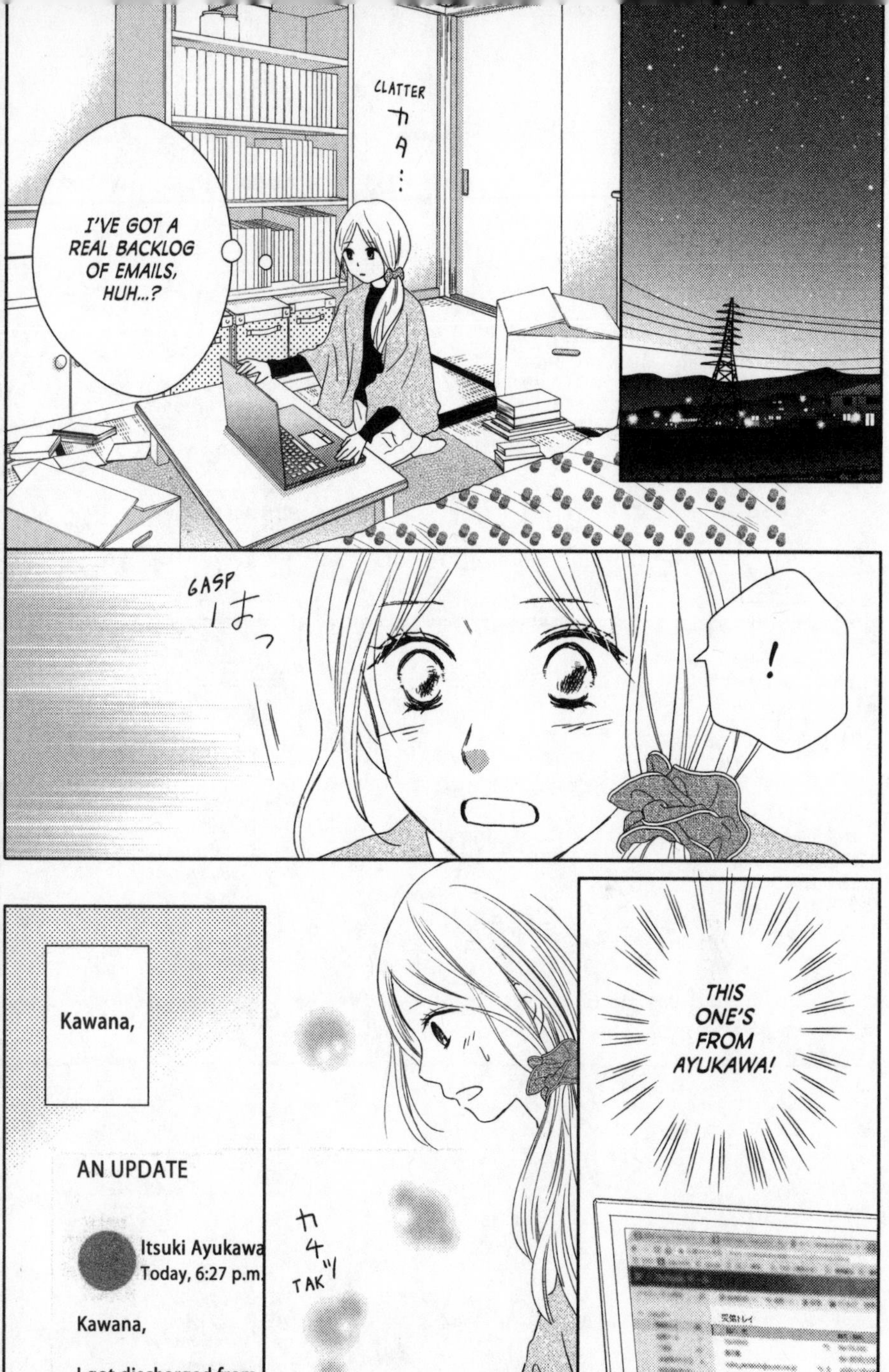
CLATTER
カタ…
I'VE GOT A REAL BACKLOG OF EMAILS, HUH...?
!
GASP
はっ
THIS ONE'S FROM AYUKAWA!
カチッ
TAK
Kawana,
AN UPDATE
Itsuki Ayukawa
Today, 6:27 p.m.
Kawana,
I got discharged from
I'm back in Tokyo now

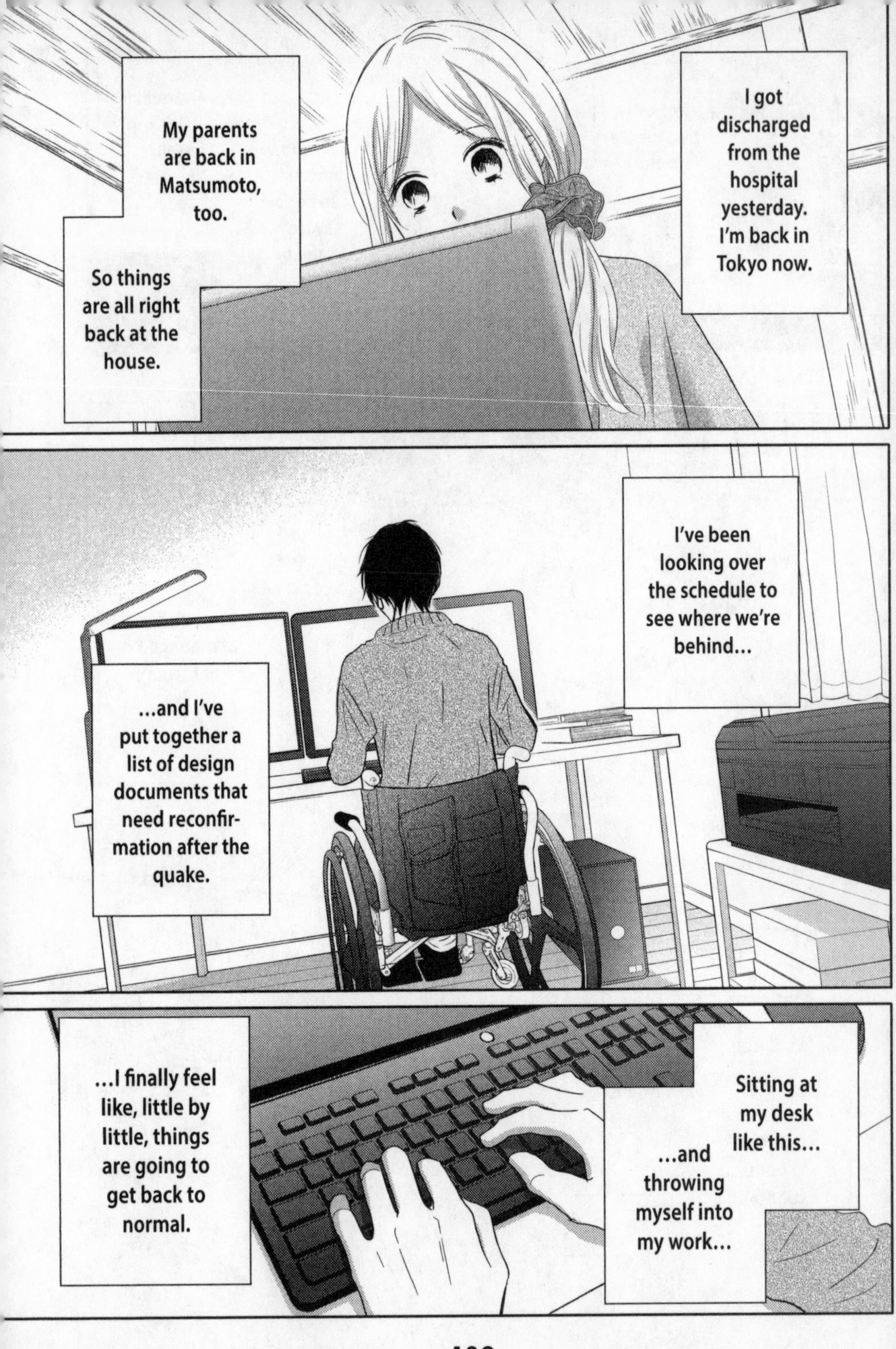
I got discharged from the hospital yesterday. I'm back in Tokyo now.
My parents are back in Matsumoto, too.
So things are all right back at the house.
I've been looking over the schedule to see where we're behind...
...and I've put together a list of design documents that need reconfir-mation after the quake.
Sitting at my desk like this...
...and throwing myself into my work...
...I finally feel like, little by little, things are going to get back to normal.

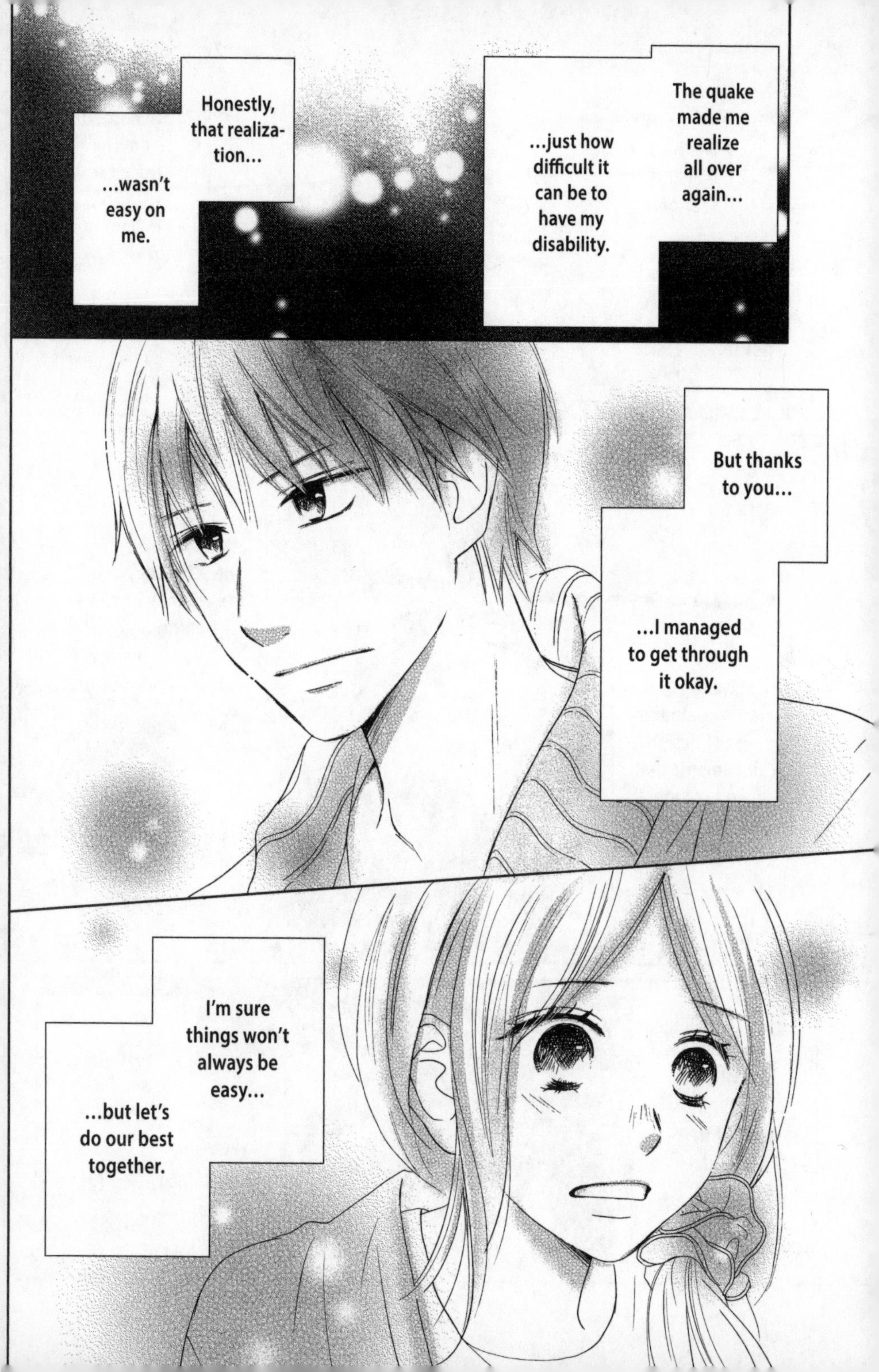
The quake made me realize all over again...
...just how difficult it can be to have my disability.
Honestly, that realization...
...wasn't easy on me.
But thanks to you...
...I managed to get through it okay.
I'm sure things won't always be easy...
...but let's do our best together.

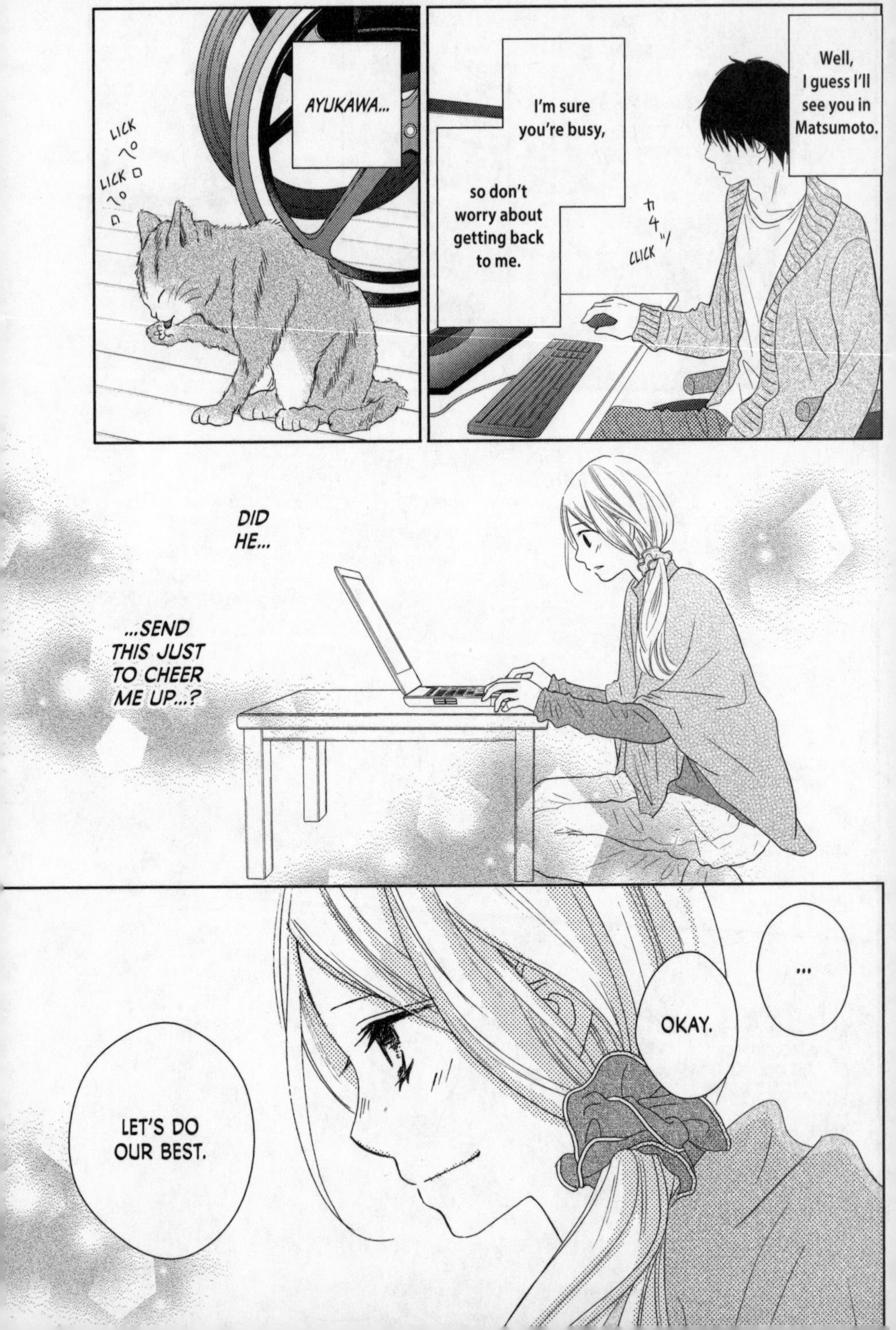
Well, I guess I'll see you in Matsumoto.
I'm sure you're busy,
so don't worry about getting back to me.
CLICK
AYUKAWA...
LICK
LICK
DID HE...
...SEND THIS JUST TO CHEER ME UP...?
...
OKAY.
LET'S DO OUR BEST.

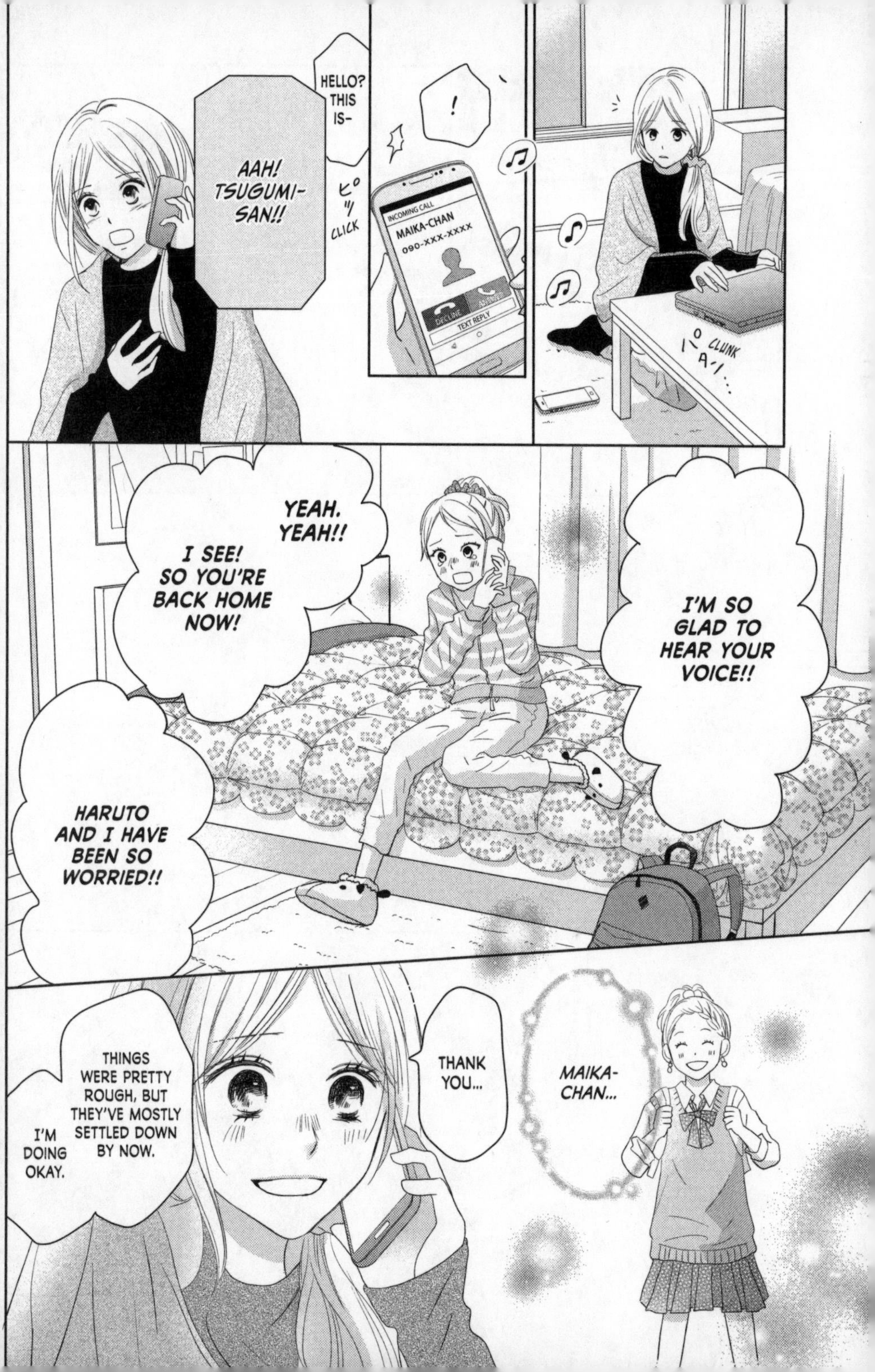

CLUNK
!
INCOMING CALL
MAIKA-CHAN
090-XXX-XXXX
DECLINE
TEXT REPLY
CLICK
HELLO? THIS IS-
AAH! TSUGUMI-SAN!!
I'M SO GLAD TO HEAR YOUR VOICE!!
YEAH. YEAH!!
I SEE! SO YOU'RE BACK HOME NOW!
HARUTO AND I HAVE BEEN SO WORRIED!!
MAIKA-CHAN...
THANK YOU...
THINGS WERE PRETTY ROUGH, BUT THEY'VE MOSTLY SETTLED DOWN BY NOW.
I'M DOING OKAY.

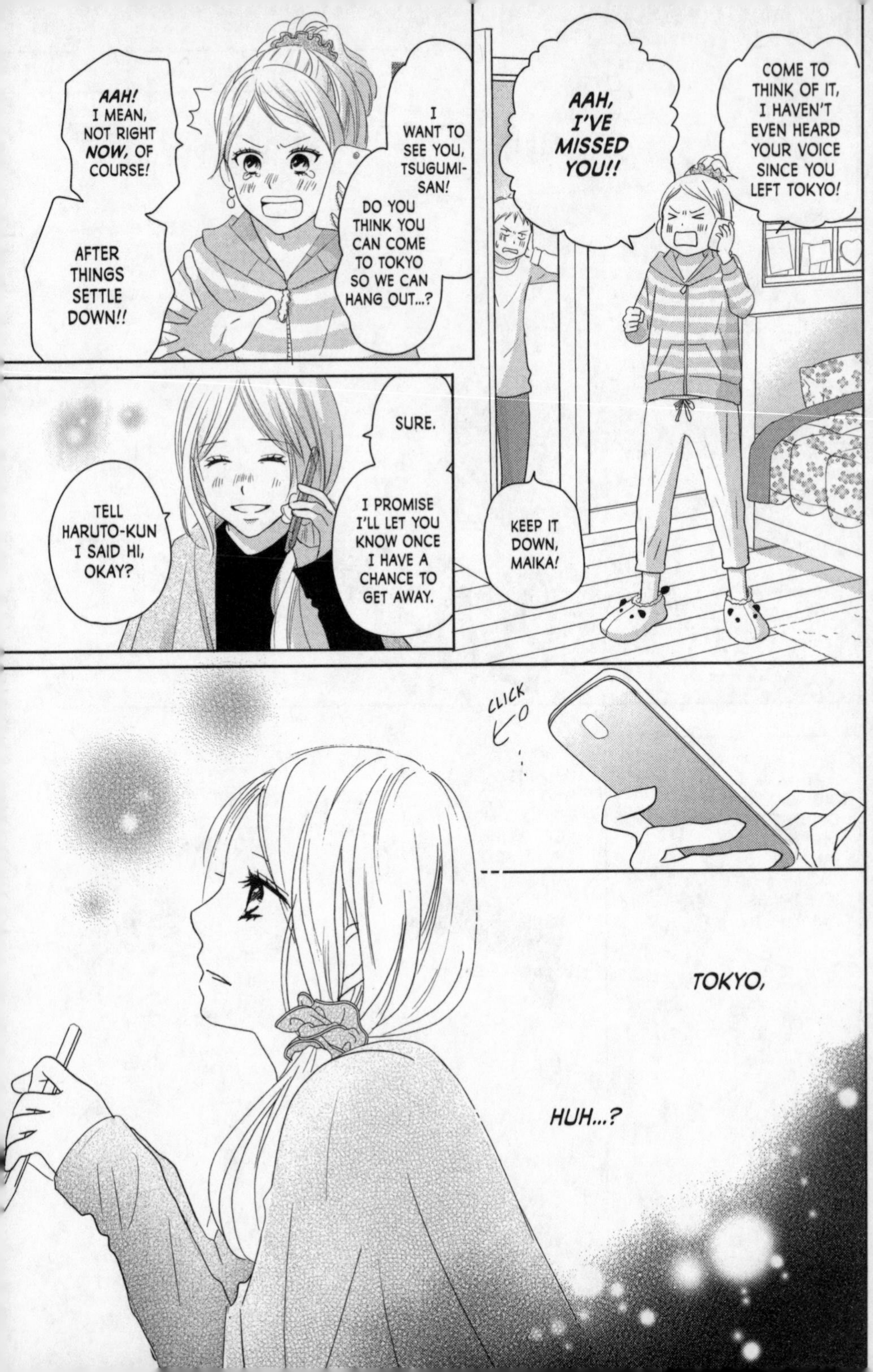
COME TO THINK OF IT, I HAVEN'T EVEN HEARD YOUR VOICE SINCE YOU LEFT TOKYO!
AAH, I'VE MISSED YOU!!
KEEP IT DOWN, MAIKA!
I WANT TO SEE YOU, TSUGUMI-SAN!
DO YOU THINK YOU CAN COME TO TOKYO SO WE CAN HANG OUT...?
AAH! I MEAN, NOT RIGHT NOW, OF COURSE!
AFTER THINGS SETTLE DOWN!!
SURE.
I PROMISE I'LL LET YOU KNOW ONCE I HAVE A CHANCE TO GET AWAY.
TELL HARUTO-KUN I SAID HI, OKAY?
CLICK
TOKYO,
HUH...?

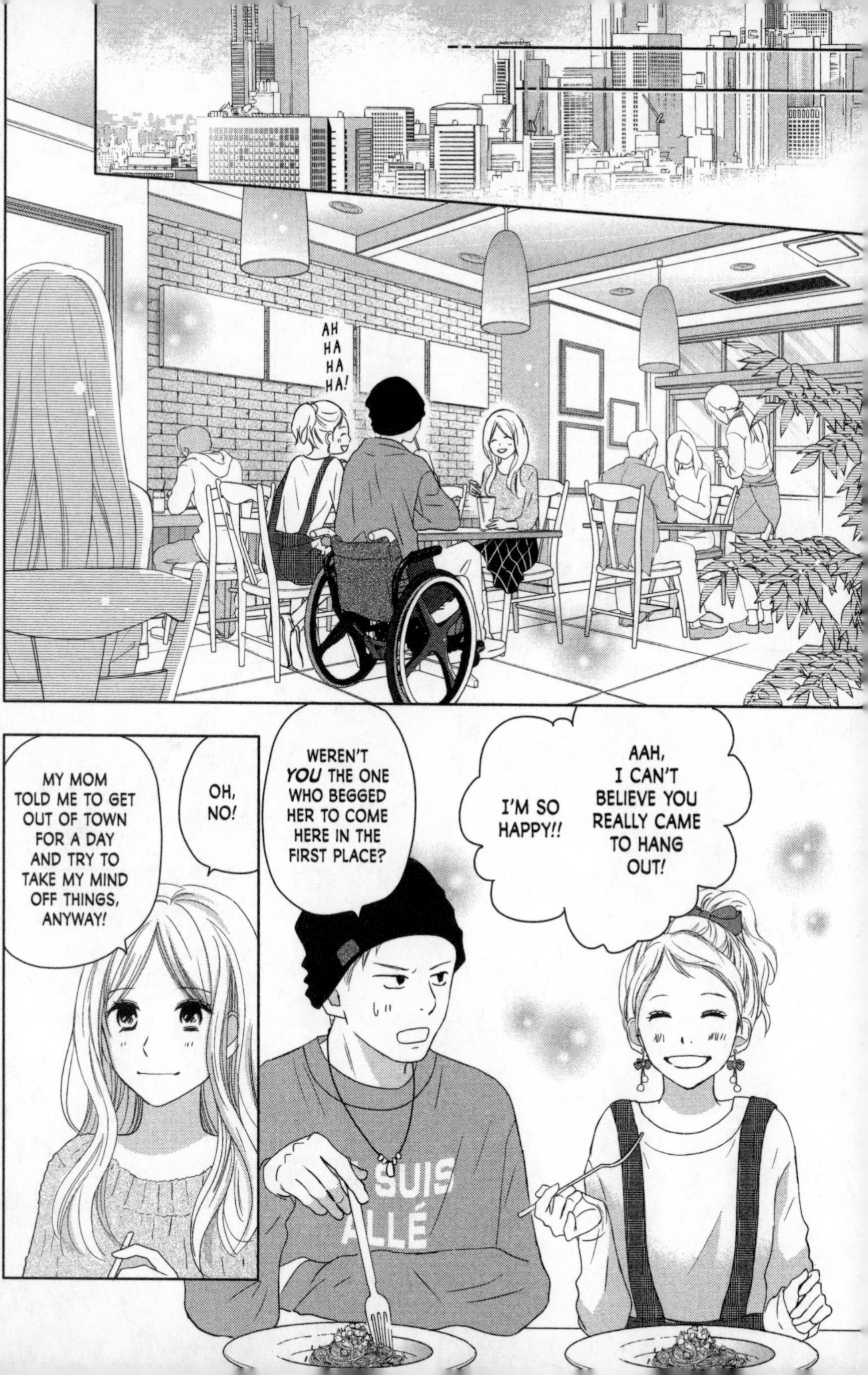
AH HA HA HA!
AAH, I CAN'T BELIEVE YOU REALLY CAME TO HANG OUT!
I'M SO HAPPY!!
WEREN'T *YOU* THE ONE WHO BEGGED HER TO COME HERE IN THE FIRST PLACE?
OH, NO!
MY MOM TOLD ME TO GET OUT OF TOWN FOR A DAY AND TRY TO TAKE MY MIND OFF THINGS, ANYWAY!
JE SUIS ALLÉ

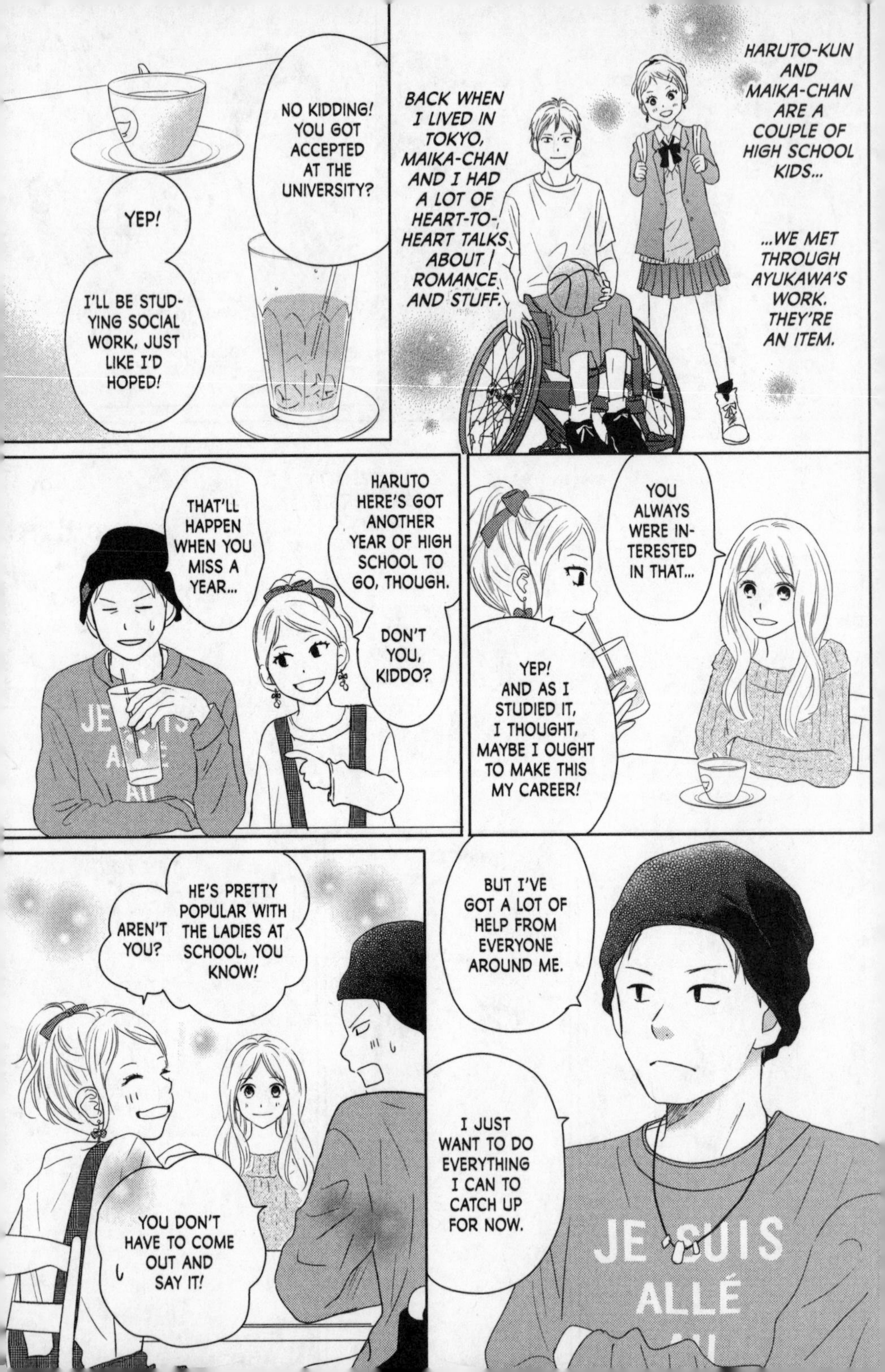
HARUTO-KUN AND MAIKA-CHAN ARE A COUPLE OF HIGH SCHOOL KIDS...
...WE MET THROUGH AYUKAWA'S WORK. THEY'RE AN ITEM.
BACK WHEN I LIVED IN TOKYO, MAIKA-CHAN AND I HAD A LOT OF HEART-TO-HEART TALKS ABOUT ROMANCE AND STUFF.
NO KIDDING! YOU GOT ACCEPTED AT THE UNIVERSITY?
YEP!
I'LL BE STUDYING SOCIAL WORK, JUST LIKE I'D HOPED!
YOU ALWAYS WERE INTERESTED IN THAT...
YEP! AND AS I STUDIED IT, I THOUGHT, MAYBE I OUGHT TO MAKE THIS MY CAREER!
HARUTO HERE'S GOT ANOTHER YEAR OF HIGH SCHOOL TO GO, THOUGH.
DON'T YOU, KIDDO?
THAT'LL HAPPEN WHEN YOU MISS A YEAR...
BUT I'VE GOT A LOT OF HELP FROM EVERYONE AROUND ME.
I JUST WANT TO DO EVERYTHING I CAN TO CATCH UP FOR NOW.
JE SUIS ALLÉ
HE'S PRETTY POPULAR WITH THE LADIES AT SCHOOL, YOU KNOW!
AREN'T YOU?
YOU DON'T HAVE TO COME OUT AND SAY IT!

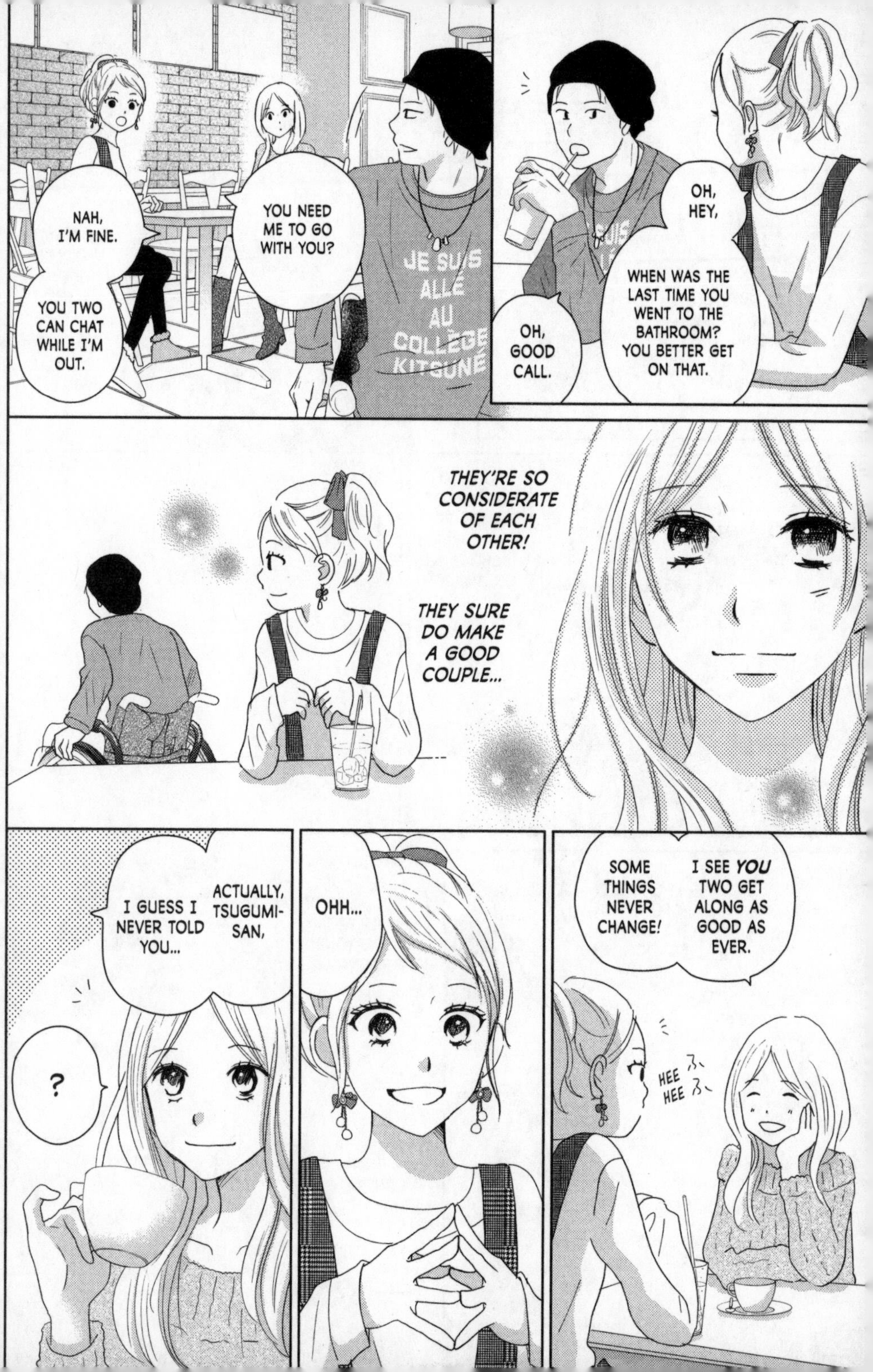
OH, HEY,
WHEN WAS THE LAST TIME YOU WENT TO THE BATHROOM? YOU BETTER GET ON THAT.
OH, GOOD CALL.
YOU NEED ME TO GO WITH YOU?
NAH, I'M FINE.
YOU TWO CAN CHAT WHILE I'M OUT.
JE SUIS ALLÉ AU COLLÈGE KITSUNÉ
THEY'RE SO CONSIDERATE OF EACH OTHER!
THEY SURE DO MAKE A GOOD COUPLE...
I SEE *YOU* TWO GET ALONG AS GOOD AS EVER.
SOME THINGS NEVER CHANGE!
HEE HEE ふふ
OHH...
ACTUALLY, TSUGUMI-SAN,
I GUESS I NEVER TOLD YOU...
?

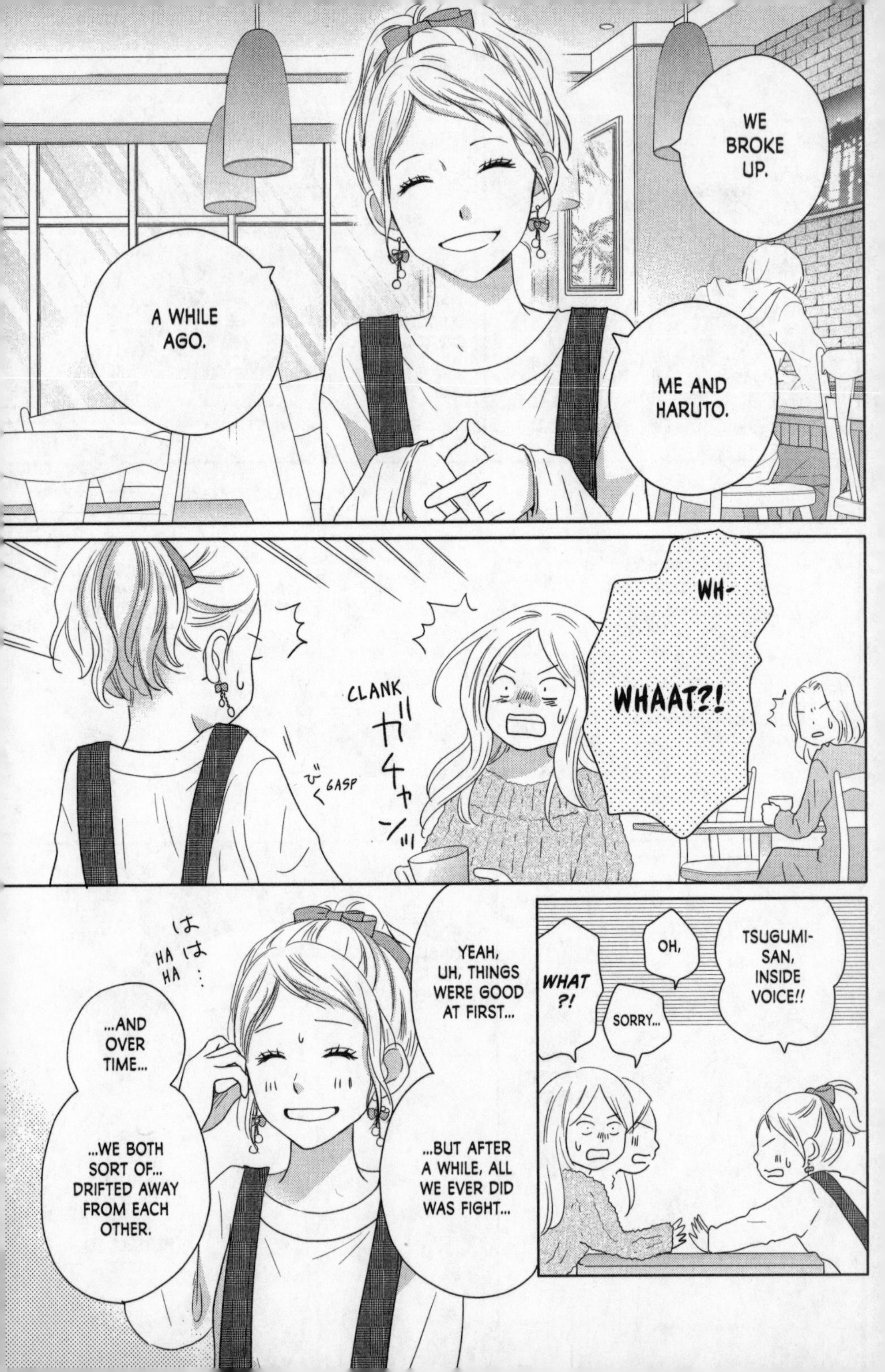
WE BROKE UP.
ME AND HARUTO.
A WHILE AGO.
WH- WHAAT?!
CLANK ガチャンッ
びく GASP
TSUGUMI-SAN, INSIDE VOICE!!
OH,
SORRY...
WHAT?!
YEAH, UH, THINGS WERE GOOD AT FIRST...
...BUT AFTER A WHILE, ALL WE EVER DID WAS FIGHT...
...AND OVER TIME...
...WE BOTH SORT OF... DRIFTED AWAY FROM EACH OTHER.
ははは... HA HA HA

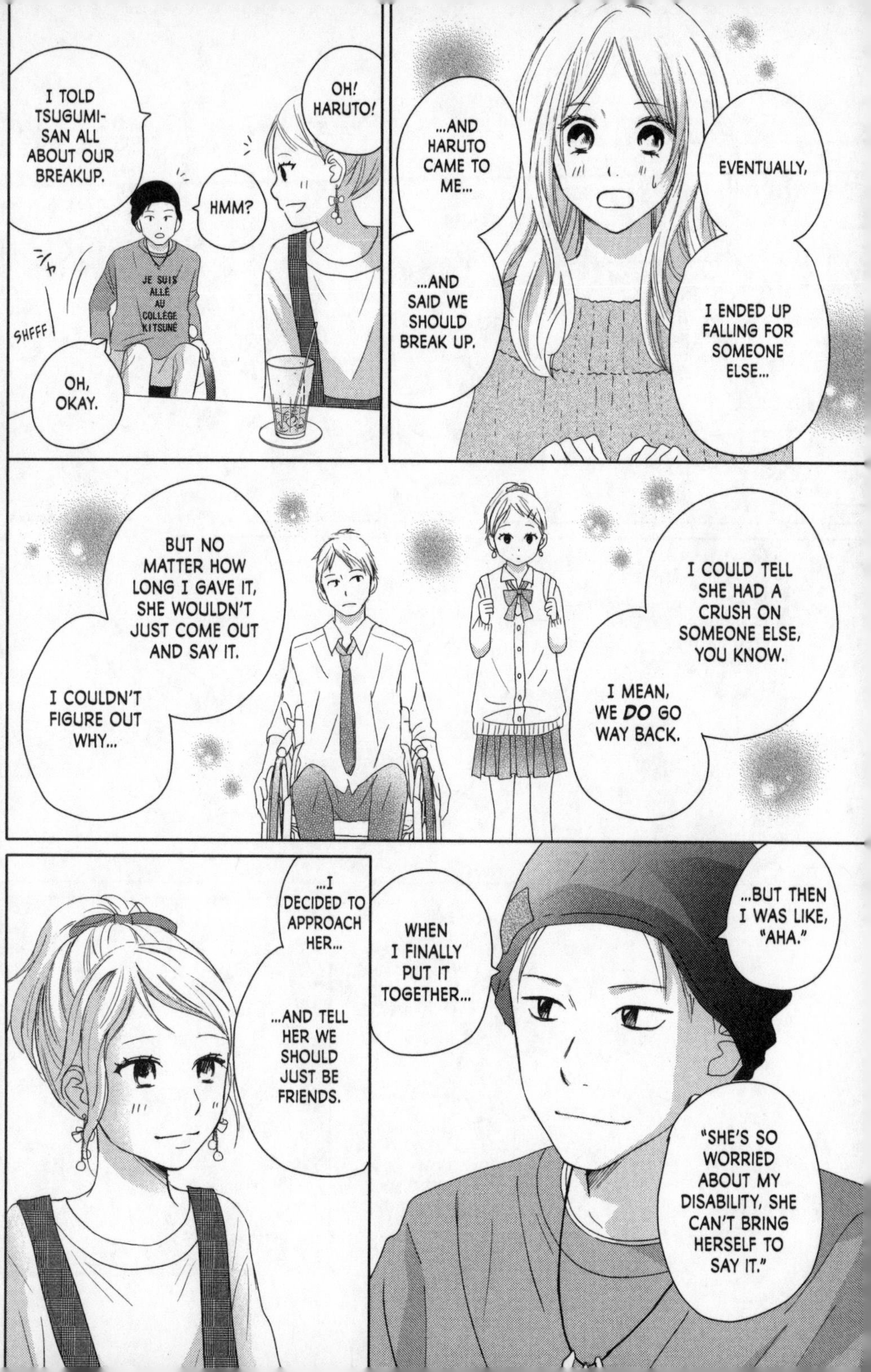
EVENTUALLY,
I ENDED UP FALLING FOR SOMEONE ELSE...
...AND HARUTO CAME TO ME...
...AND SAID WE SHOULD BREAK UP.
OH! HARUTO!
HMM?
I TOLD TSUGUMI-SAN ALL ABOUT OUR BREAKUP.
SHFFF
OH, OKAY.
I COULD TELL SHE HAD A CRUSH ON SOMEONE ELSE, YOU KNOW.
I MEAN, WE *DO* GO WAY BACK.
BUT NO MATTER HOW LONG I GAVE IT, SHE WOULDN'T JUST COME OUT AND SAY IT.
I COULDN'T FIGURE OUT WHY...
...BUT THEN I WAS LIKE, "AHA."
"SHE'S SO WORRIED ABOUT MY DISABILITY, SHE CAN'T BRING HERSELF TO SAY IT."
WHEN I FINALLY PUT IT TOGETHER...
...I DECIDED TO APPROACH HER...
...AND TELL HER WE SHOULD JUST BE FRIENDS.

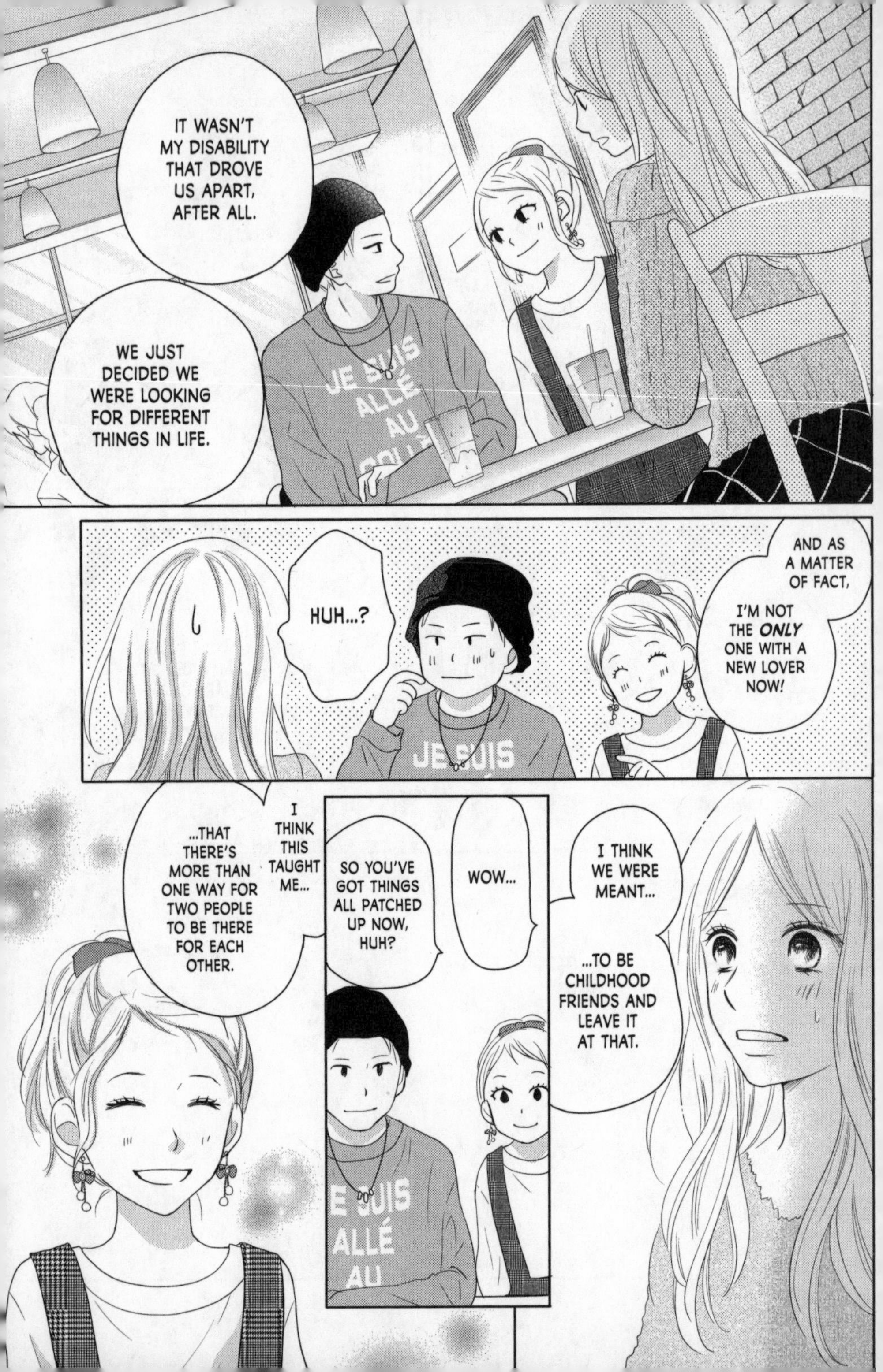
IT WASN'T MY DISABILITY THAT DROVE US APART, AFTER ALL.
WE JUST DECIDED WE WERE LOOKING FOR DIFFERENT THINGS IN LIFE.
AND AS A MATTER OF FACT,
I'M NOT THE *ONLY* ONE WITH A NEW LOVER NOW!
HUH...?
I THINK WE WERE MEANT...
...TO BE CHILDHOOD FRIENDS AND LEAVE IT AT THAT.
WOW...
SO YOU'VE GOT THINGS ALL PATCHED UP NOW, HUH?
I THINK THIS TAUGHT ME...
...THAT THERE'S MORE THAN ONE WAY FOR TWO PEOPLE TO BE THERE FOR EACH OTHER.

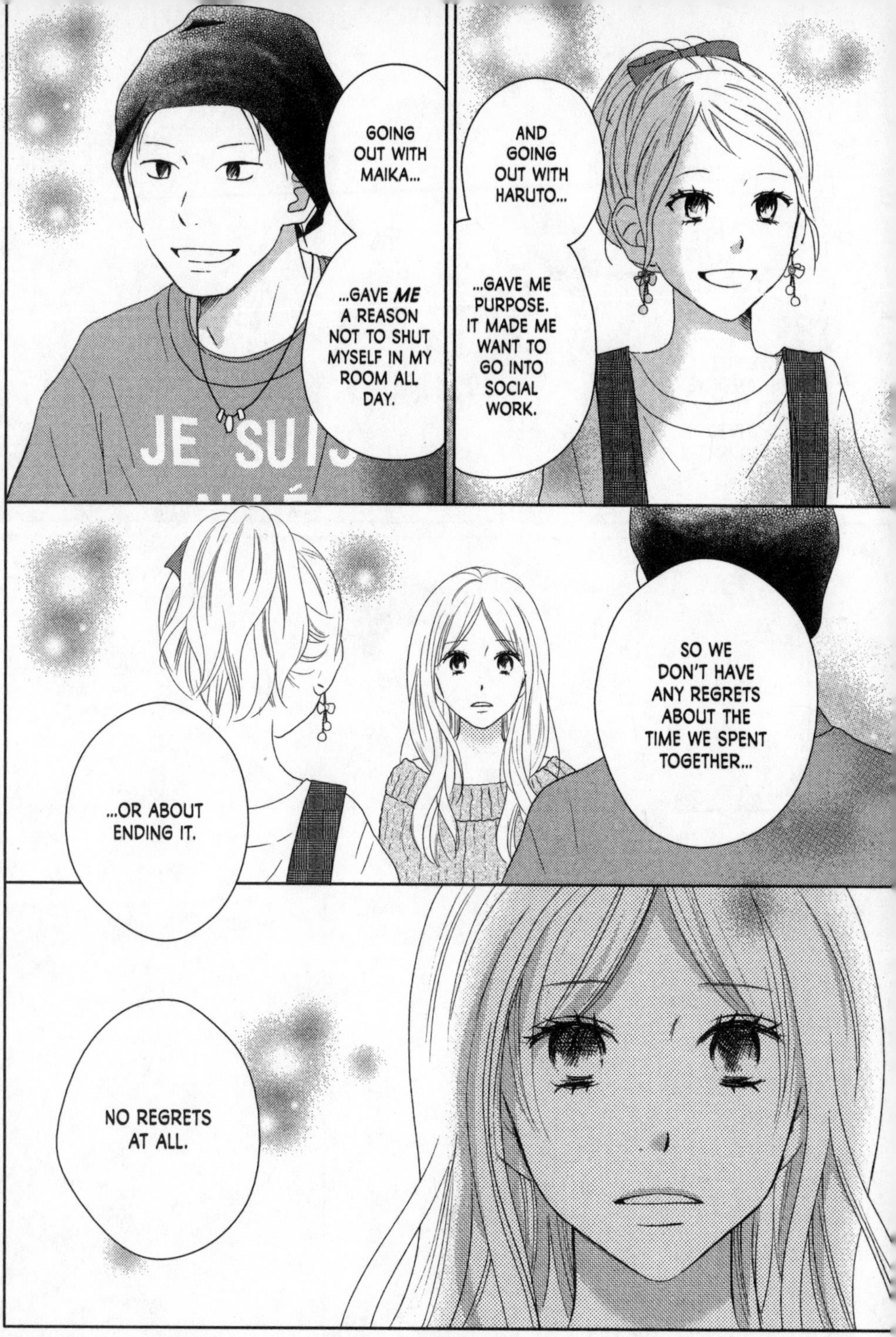
AND GOING OUT WITH HARUTO...
...GAVE ME PURPOSE. IT MADE ME WANT TO GO INTO SOCIAL WORK.
GOING OUT WITH MAIKA...
...GAVE *ME* A REASON NOT TO SHUT MYSELF IN MY ROOM ALL DAY.
JE SUIS
SO WE DON'T HAVE ANY REGRETS ABOUT THE TIME WE SPENT TOGETHER...
...OR ABOUT ENDING IT.
NO REGRETS AT ALL.

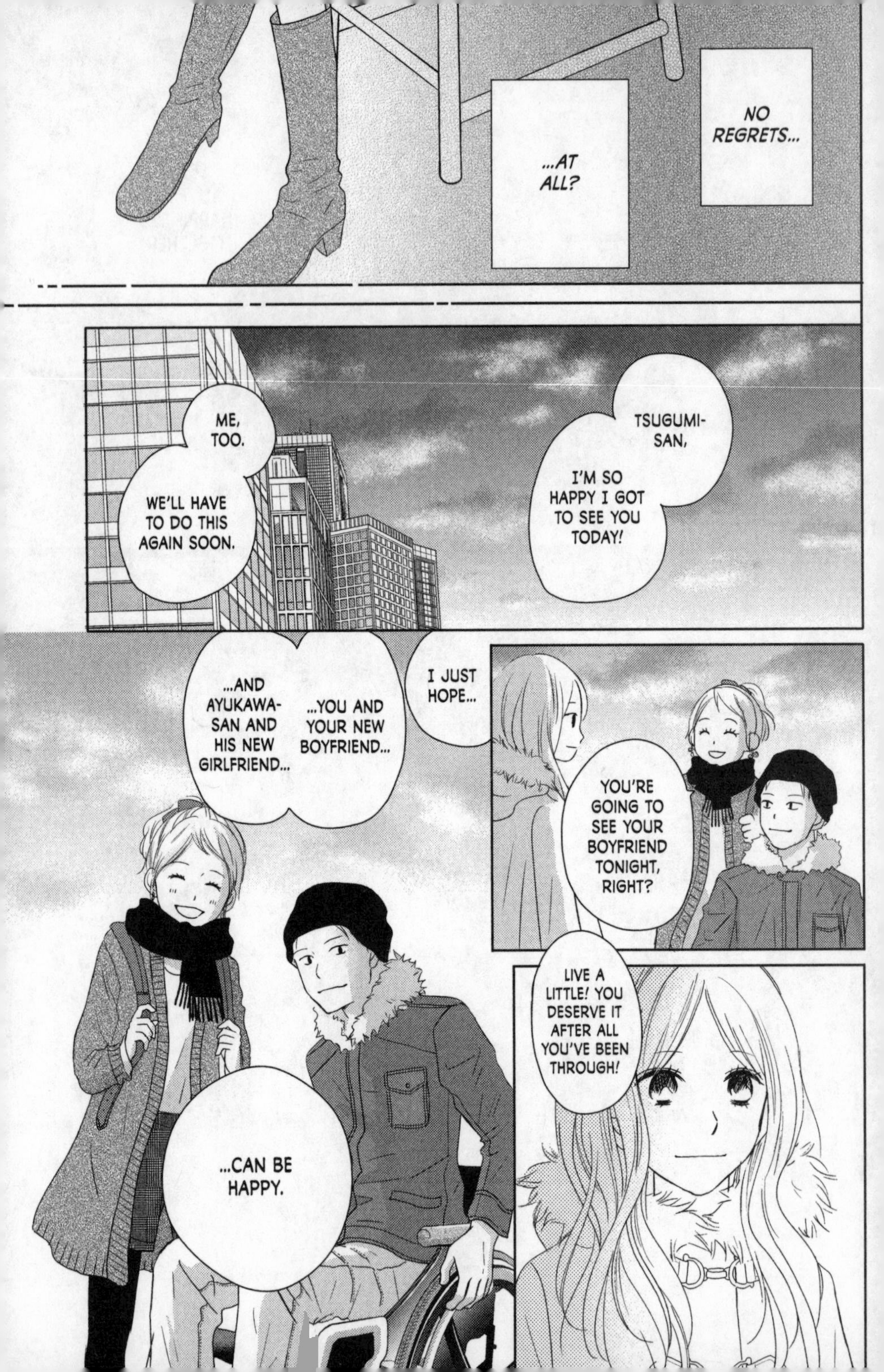
NO REGRETS...
...AT ALL?
TSUGUMI-SAN,
I'M SO HAPPY I GOT TO SEE YOU TODAY!
ME, TOO.
WE'LL HAVE TO DO THIS AGAIN SOON.
YOU'RE GOING TO SEE YOUR BOYFRIEND TONIGHT, RIGHT?
LIVE A LITTLE! YOU DESERVE IT AFTER ALL YOU'VE BEEN THROUGH!
I JUST HOPE...
...YOU AND YOUR NEW BOYFRIEND...
...AND AYUKAWA-SAN AND HIS NEW GIRLFRIEND...
...CAN BE HAPPY.

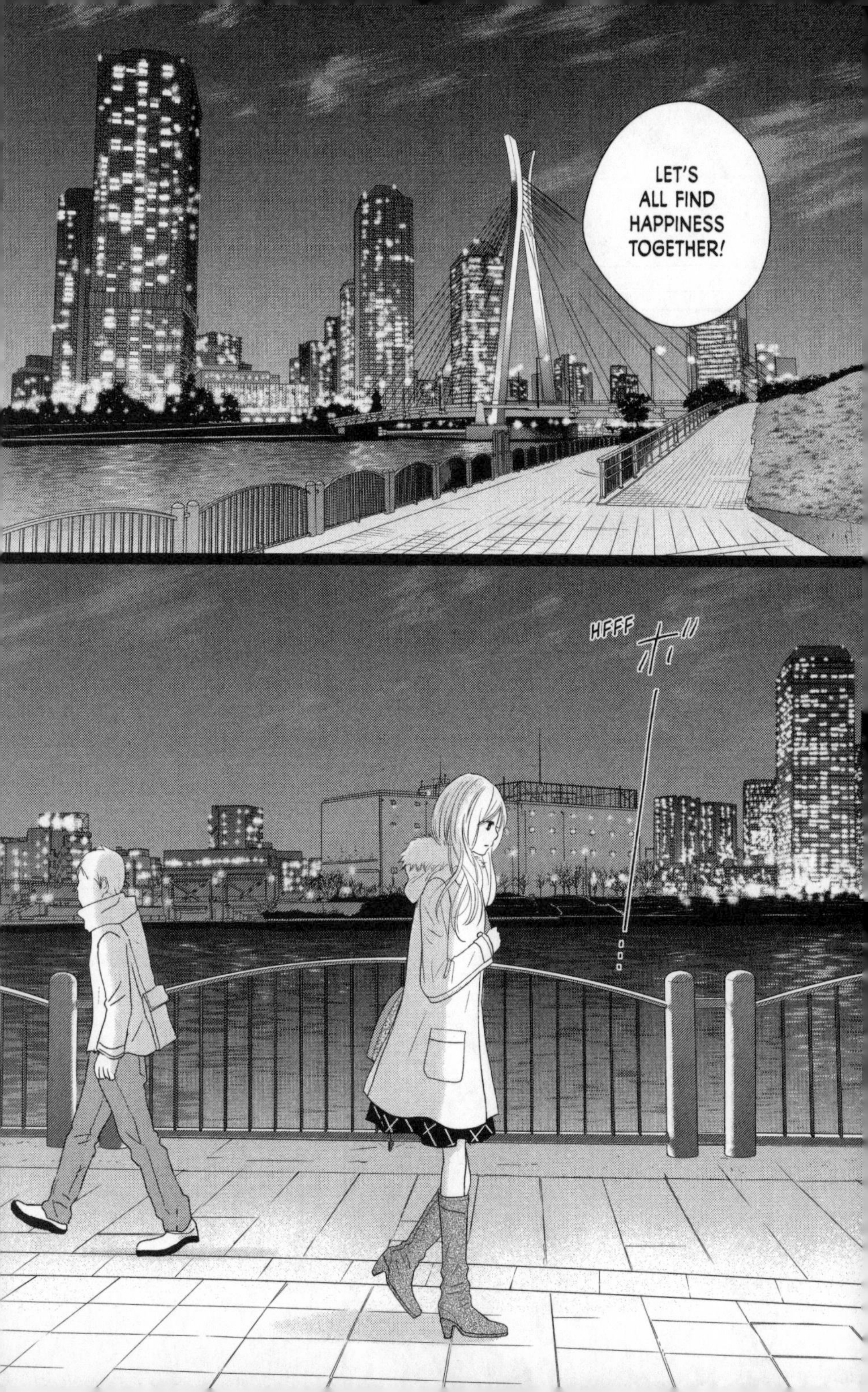
LET'S ALL FIND HAPPINESS TOGETHER!
HFFF

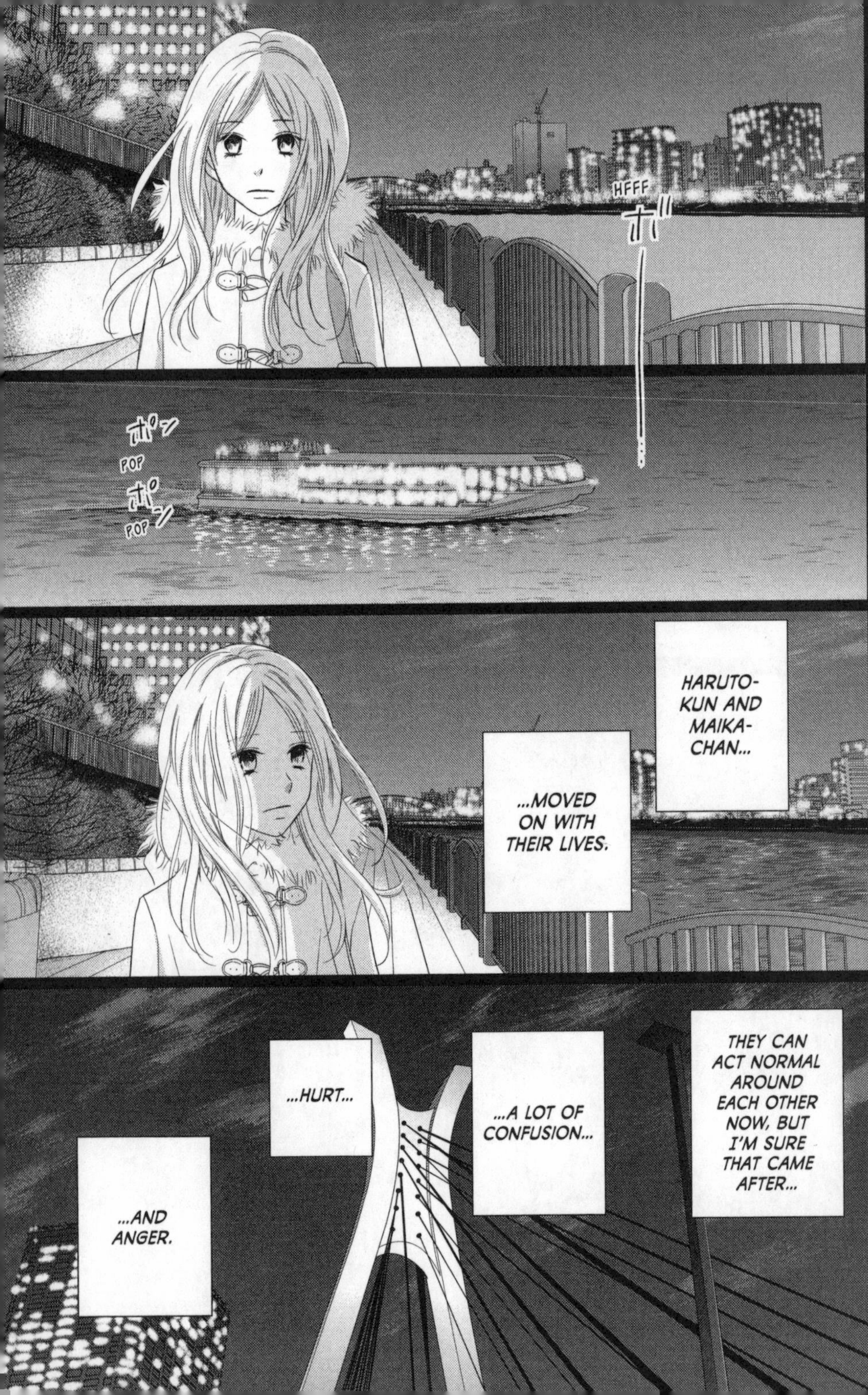
HFFF
POP
POP
HARUTO-KUN AND MAIKA-CHAN...
...MOVED ON WITH THEIR LIVES.
THEY CAN ACT NORMAL AROUND EACH OTHER NOW, BUT I'M SURE THAT CAME AFTER...
...A LOT OF CONFUSION...
...HURT...
...AND ANGER.

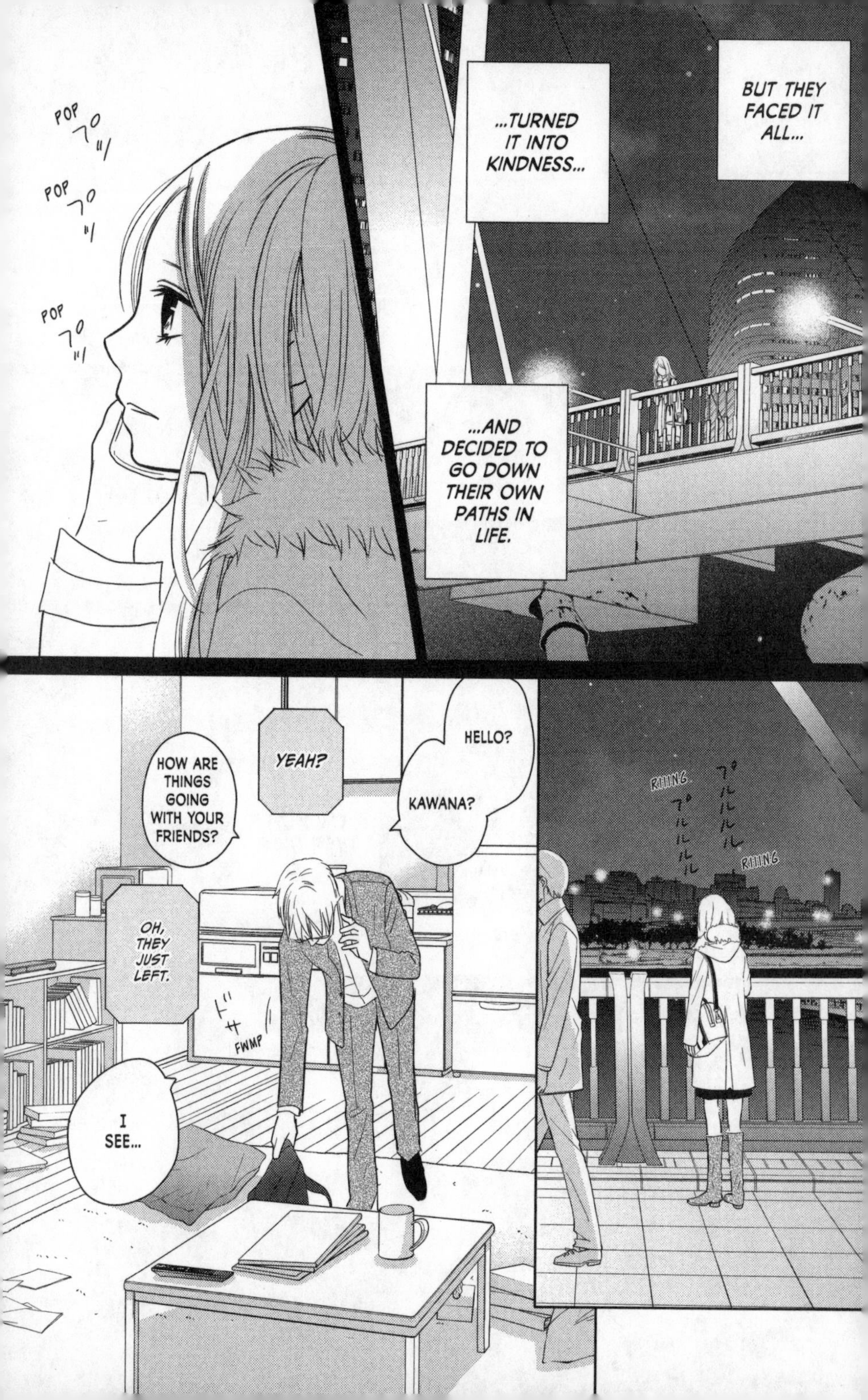
BUT THEY FACED IT ALL...
...TURNED IT INTO KINDNESS...
...AND DECIDED TO GO DOWN THEIR OWN PATHS IN LIFE.
POP
POP
POP
RIIING
RIIING
HELLO?
KAWANA?
YEAH?
HOW ARE THINGS GOING WITH YOUR FRIENDS?
OH, THEY JUST LEFT.
FWMP
I SEE...

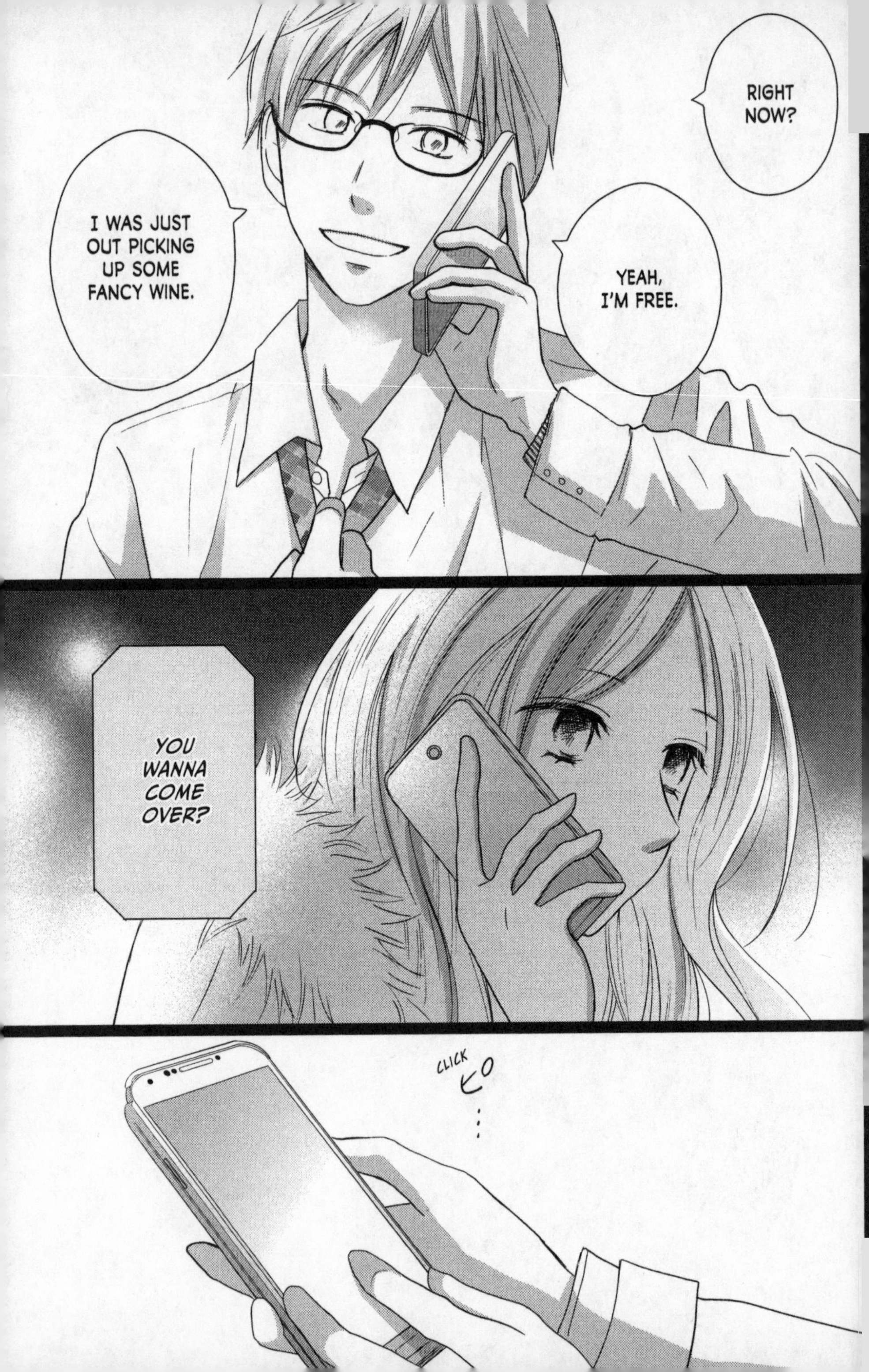
RIGHT NOW?
YEAH, I'M FREE.
I WAS JUST OUT PICKING UP SOME FANCY WINE.
YOU WANNA COME OVER?
CLICK
...

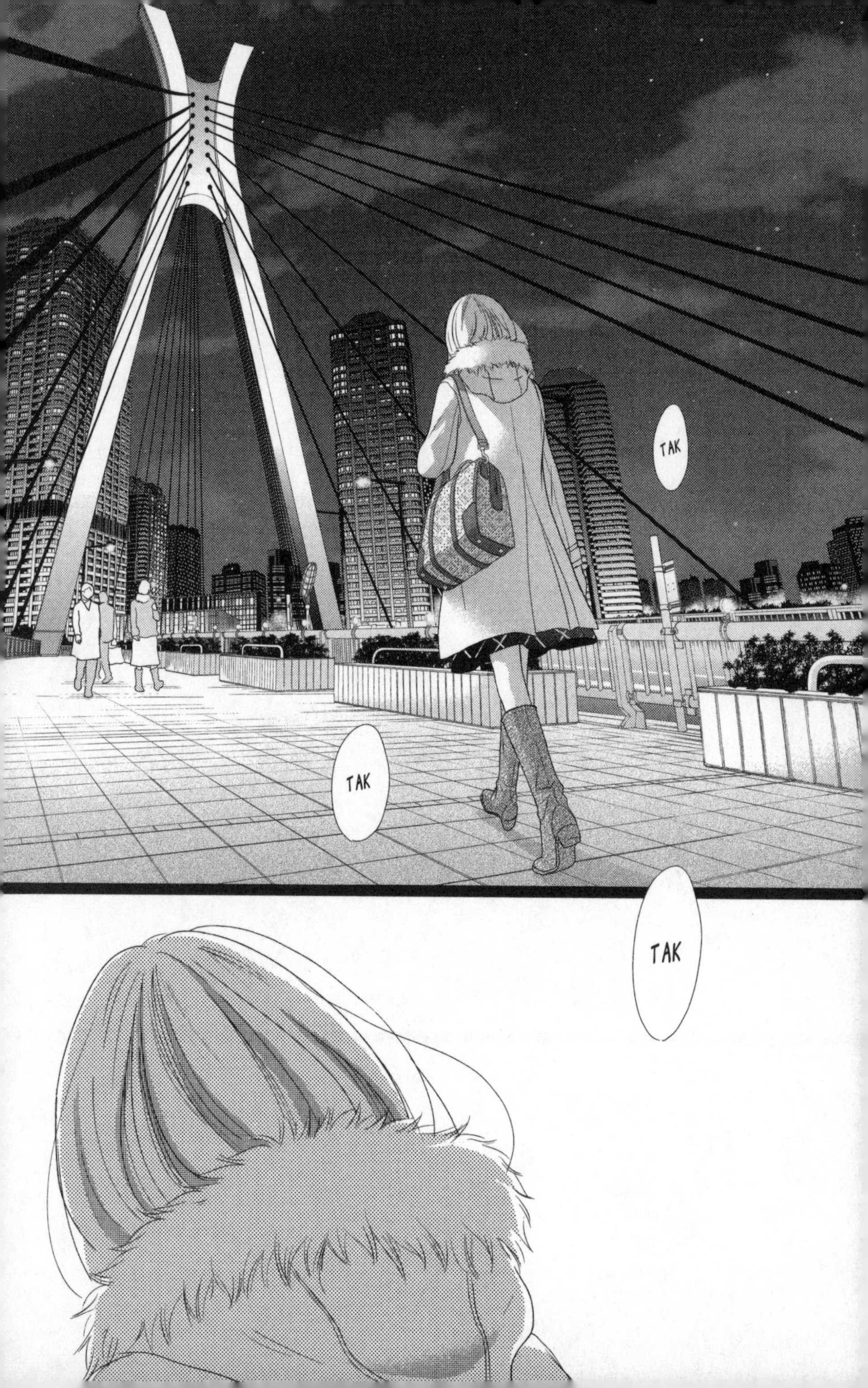
TAK
TAK
TAK

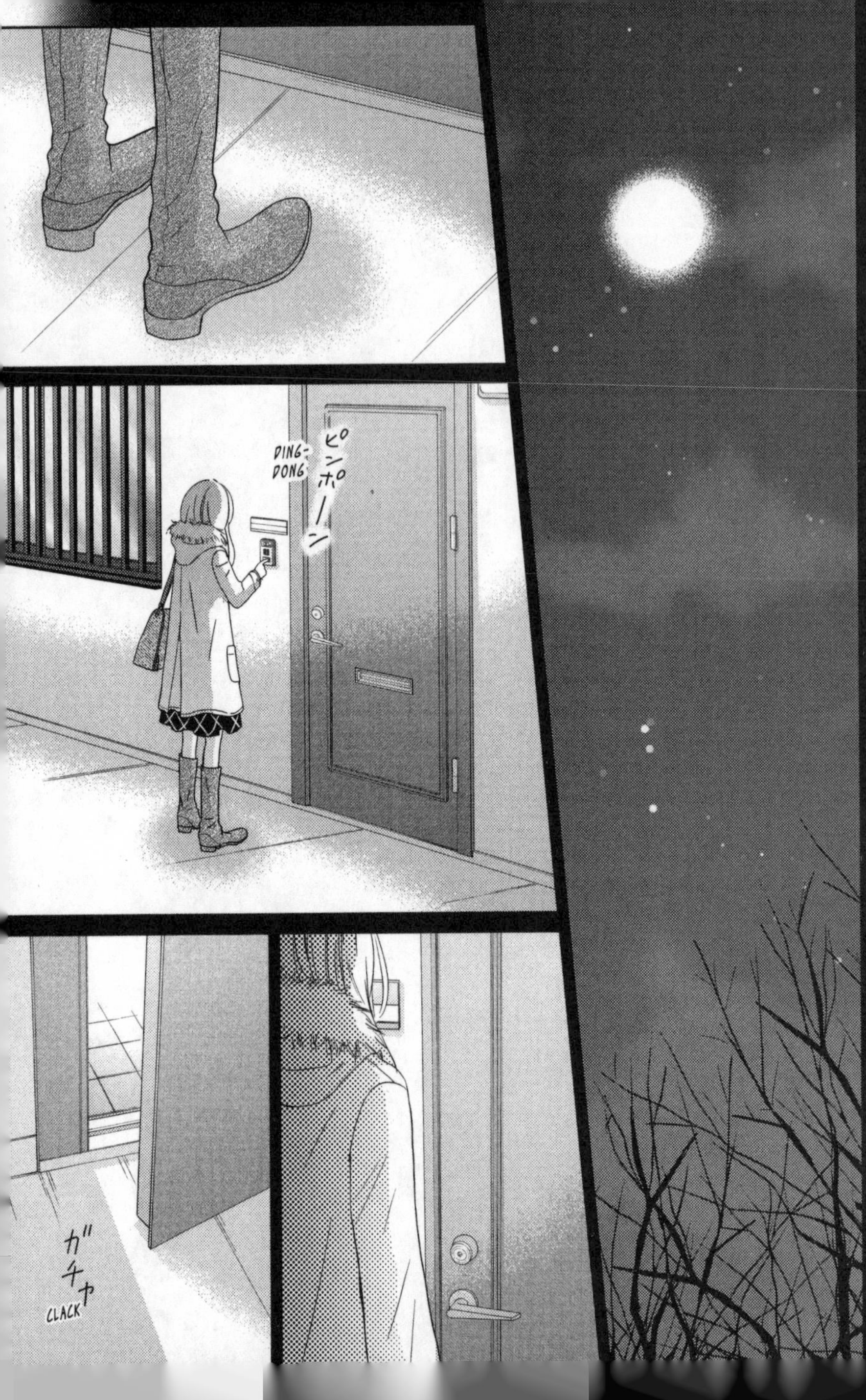
ピンポーン
DING-DONG
ガチャ
CLACK

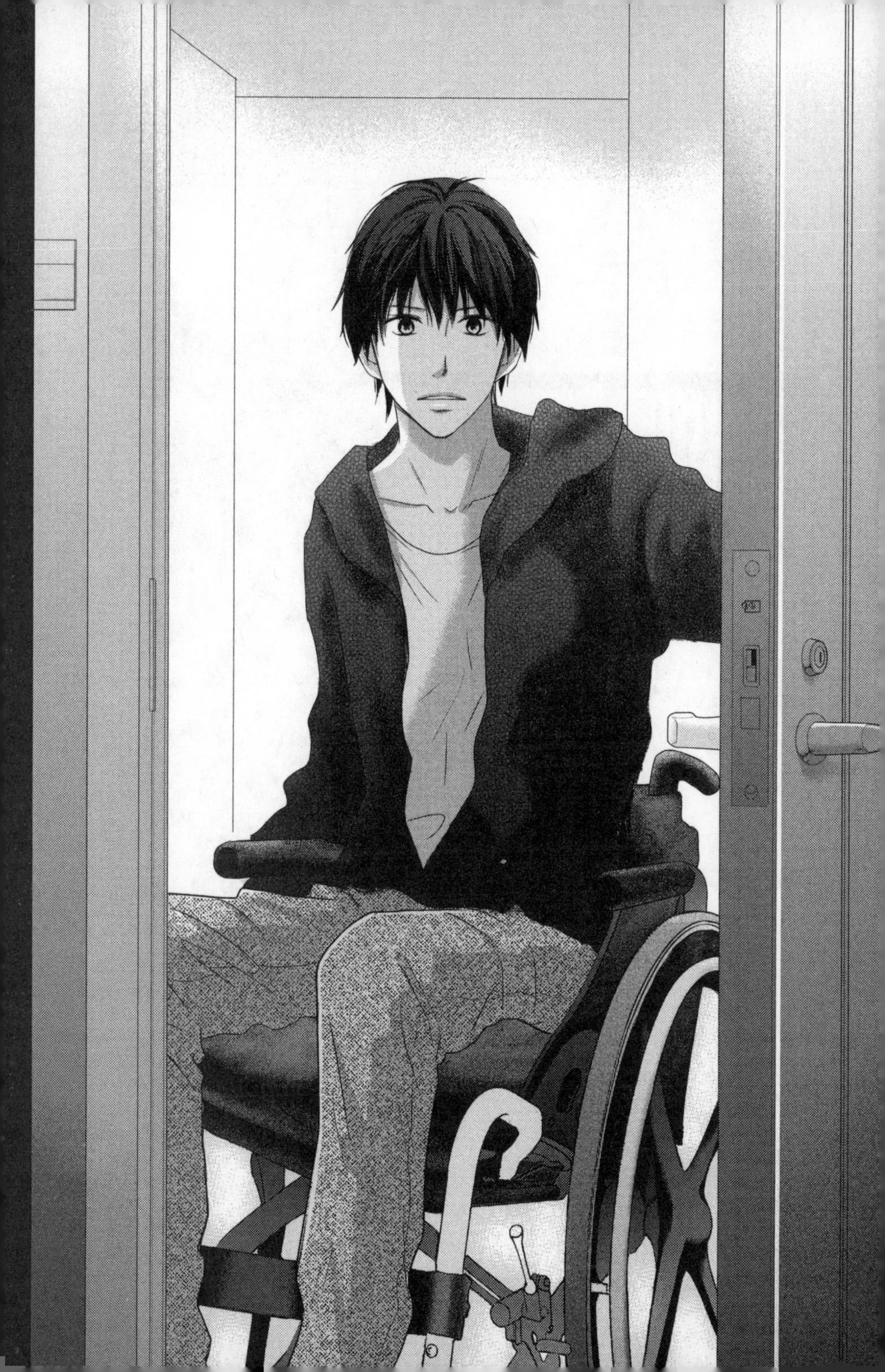

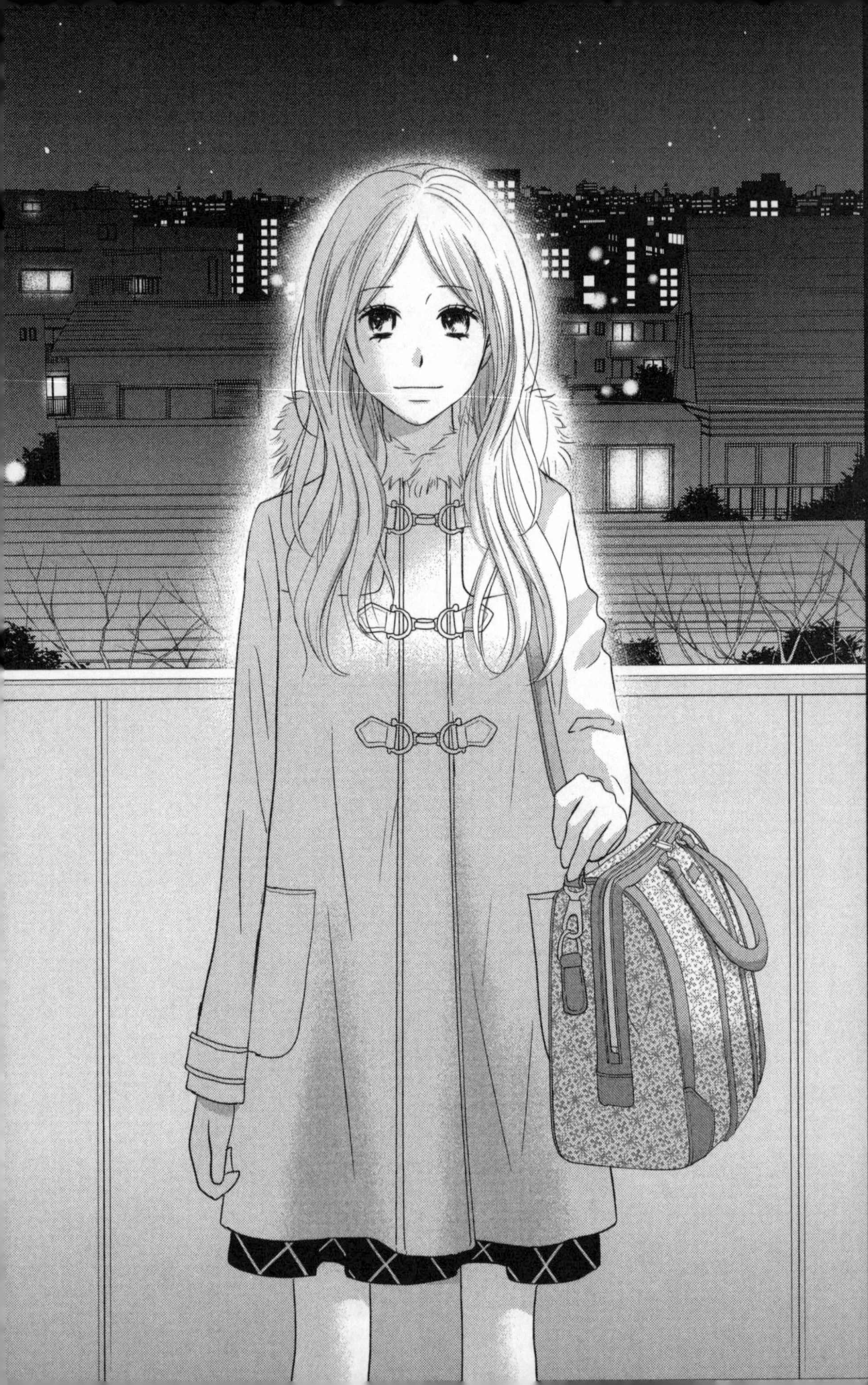

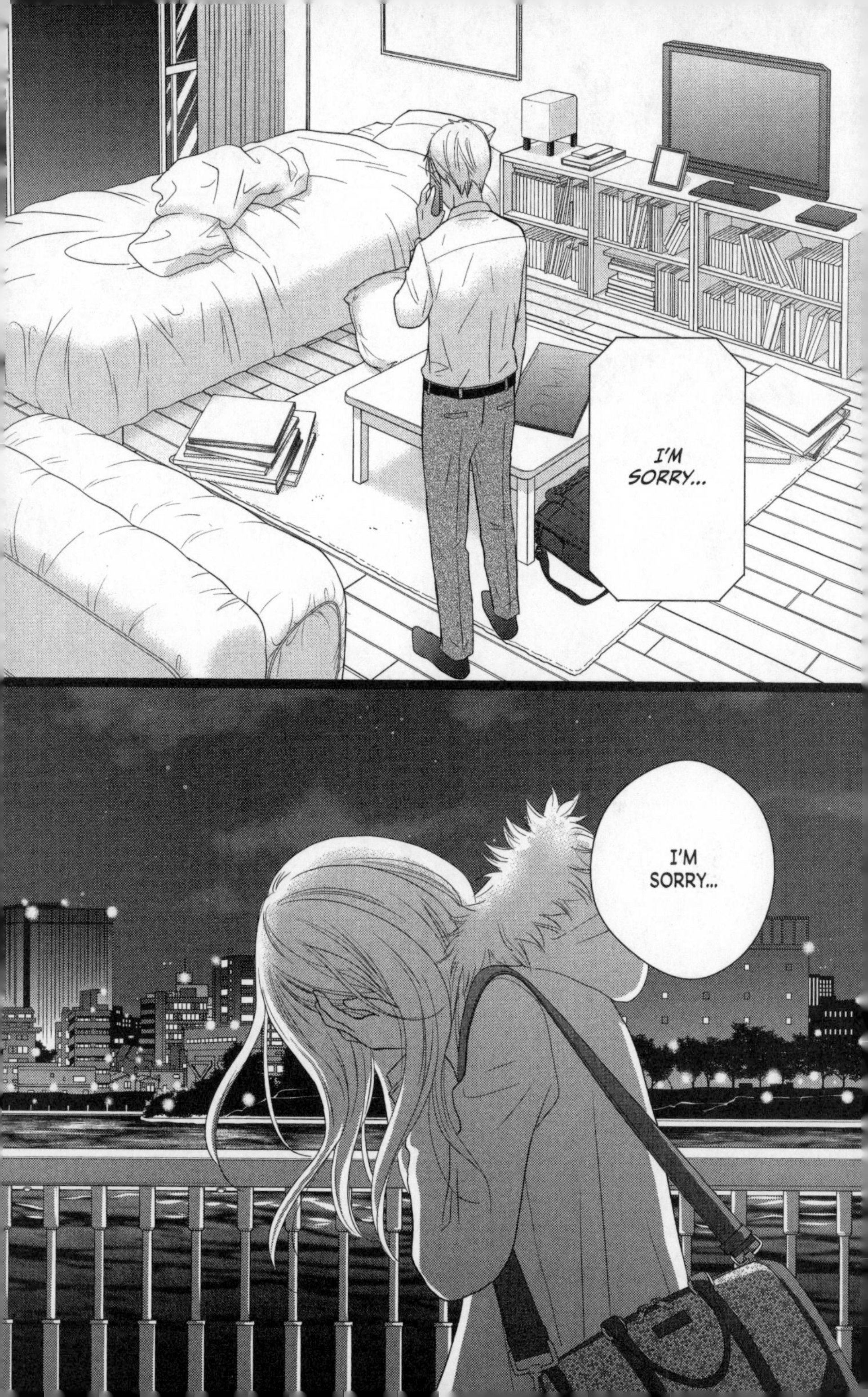
I'M SORRY...
I'M SORRY...

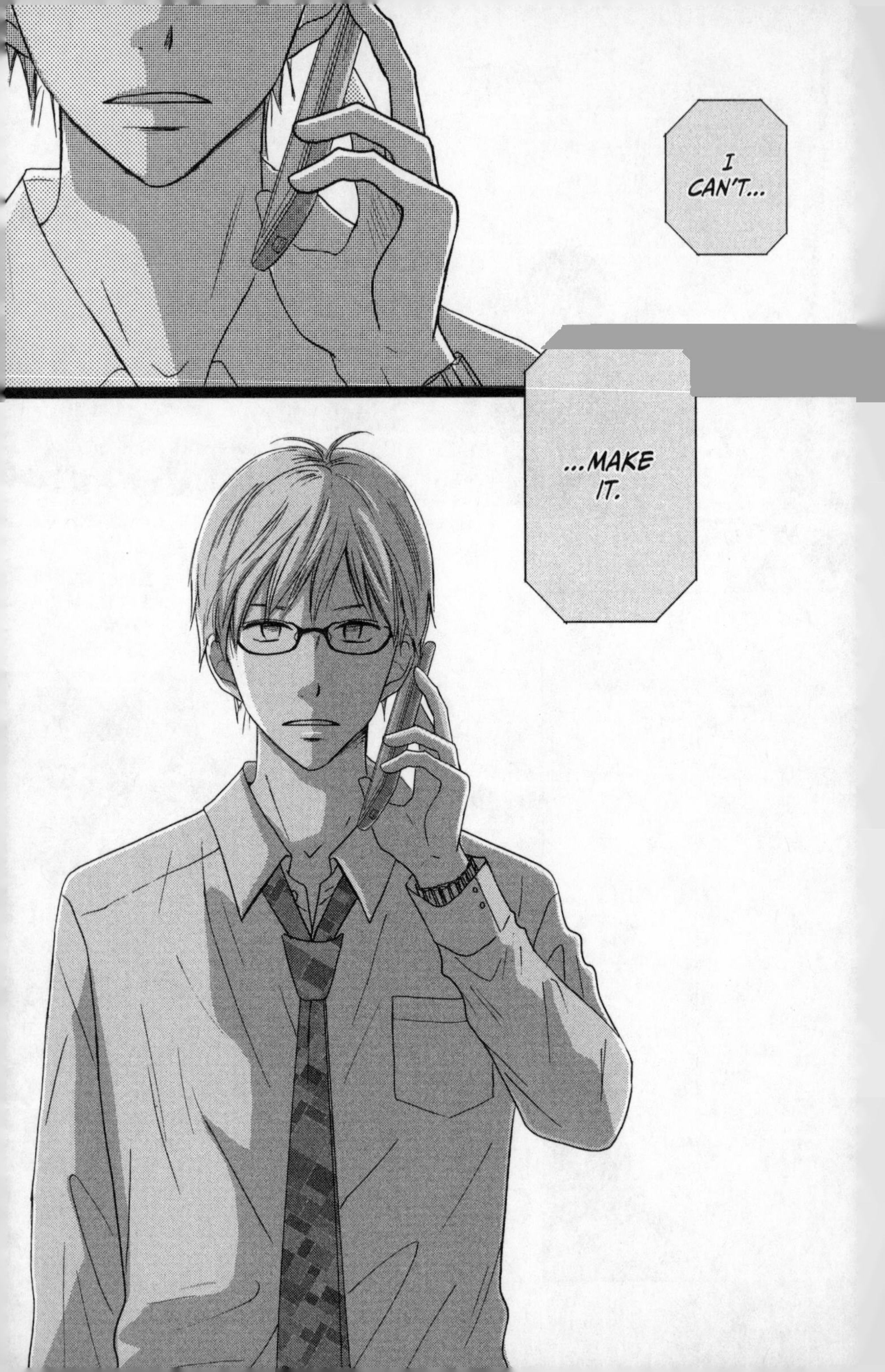
I CAN'T...
...MAKE IT.

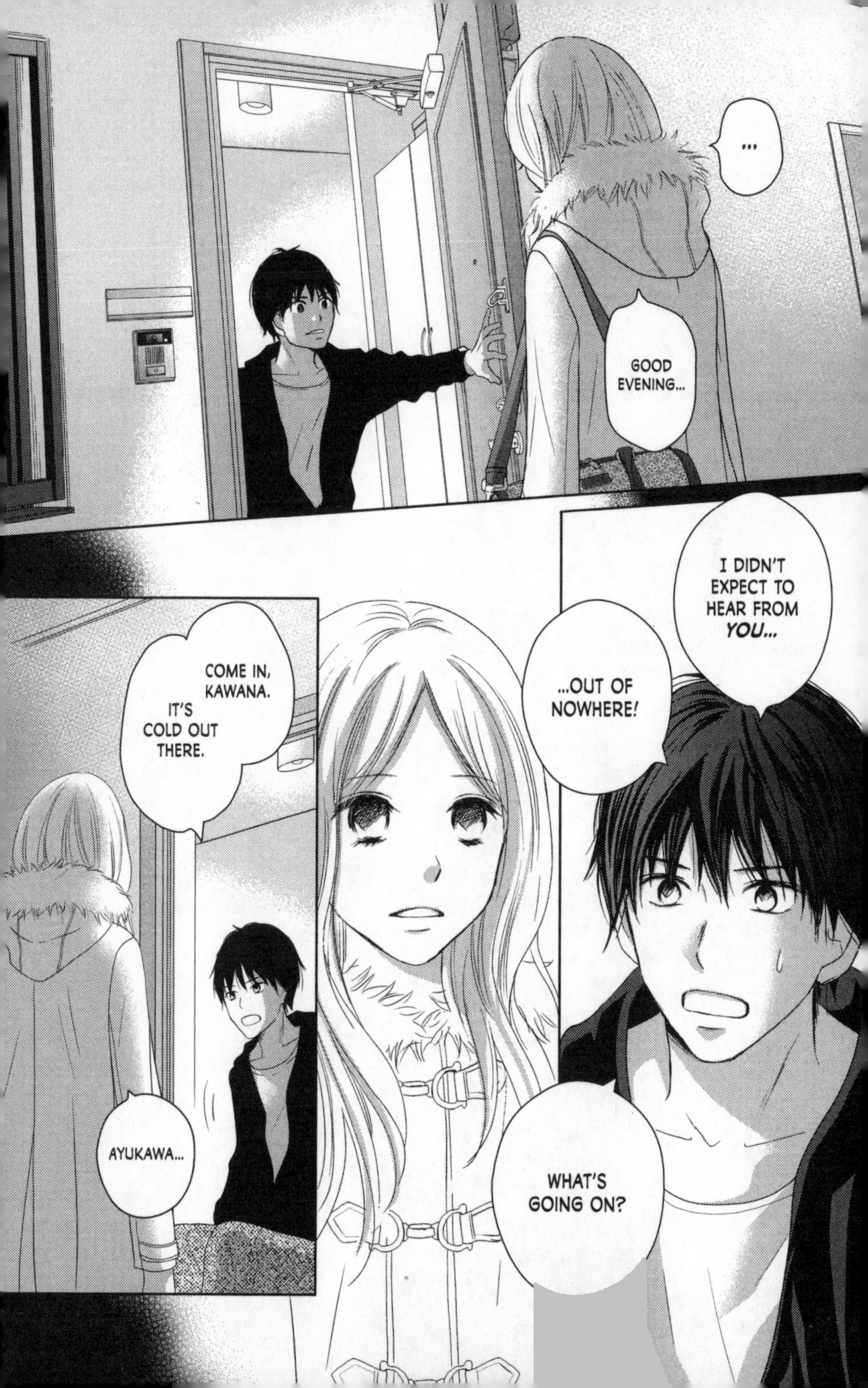
...
GOOD EVENING...
I DIDN'T EXPECT TO HEAR FROM *YOU*...
...OUT OF NOWHERE!
WHAT'S GOING ON?
COME IN, KAWANA. IT'S COLD OUT THERE.
AYUKAWA...

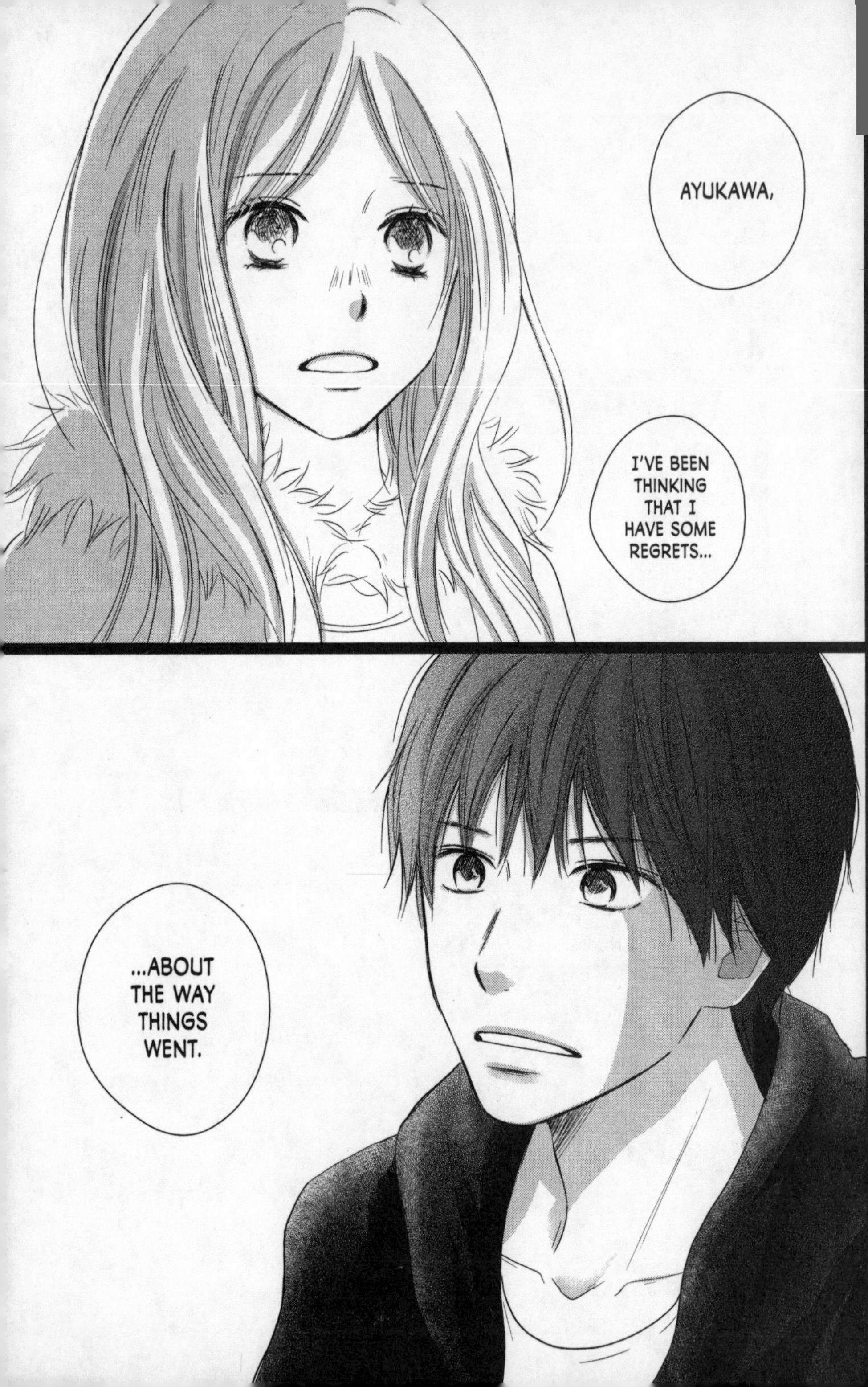

AYUKAWA,
I'VE BEEN THINKING THAT I HAVE SOME REGRETS...
...ABOUT THE WAY THINGS WENT.

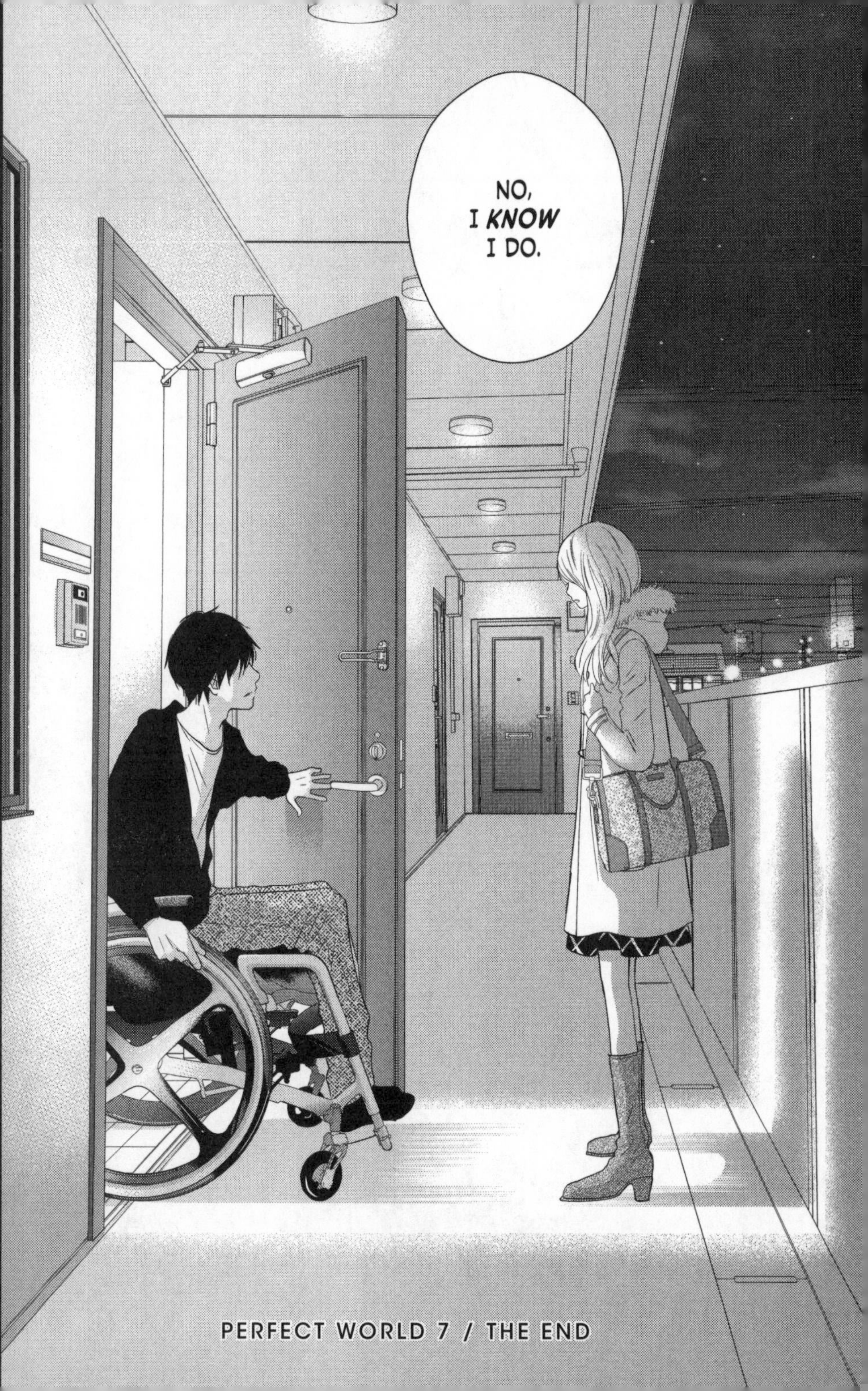
NO, I *KNOW* I DO.
PERFECT WORLD 7 / THE END

PERFECT WORLD

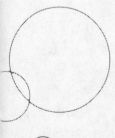

— Thank you so much for reading *Perfect World* volume seven! —

I can't tell you how much I always appreciate all your kind words of support...!

To prepare for this story arc, I got in touch with several social workers who've been providing support for people with disabilities ever since the Great East Japan Earthquake of 2011, and I got to hear all sorts of stories from them about what it was like. I actually kept up my research once the arc made it to print, too, and as it turned out, the topic of natural disaster preparedness came up quite a few times. I knew it would be a tough subject to tackle, but that only made me want to do it more!

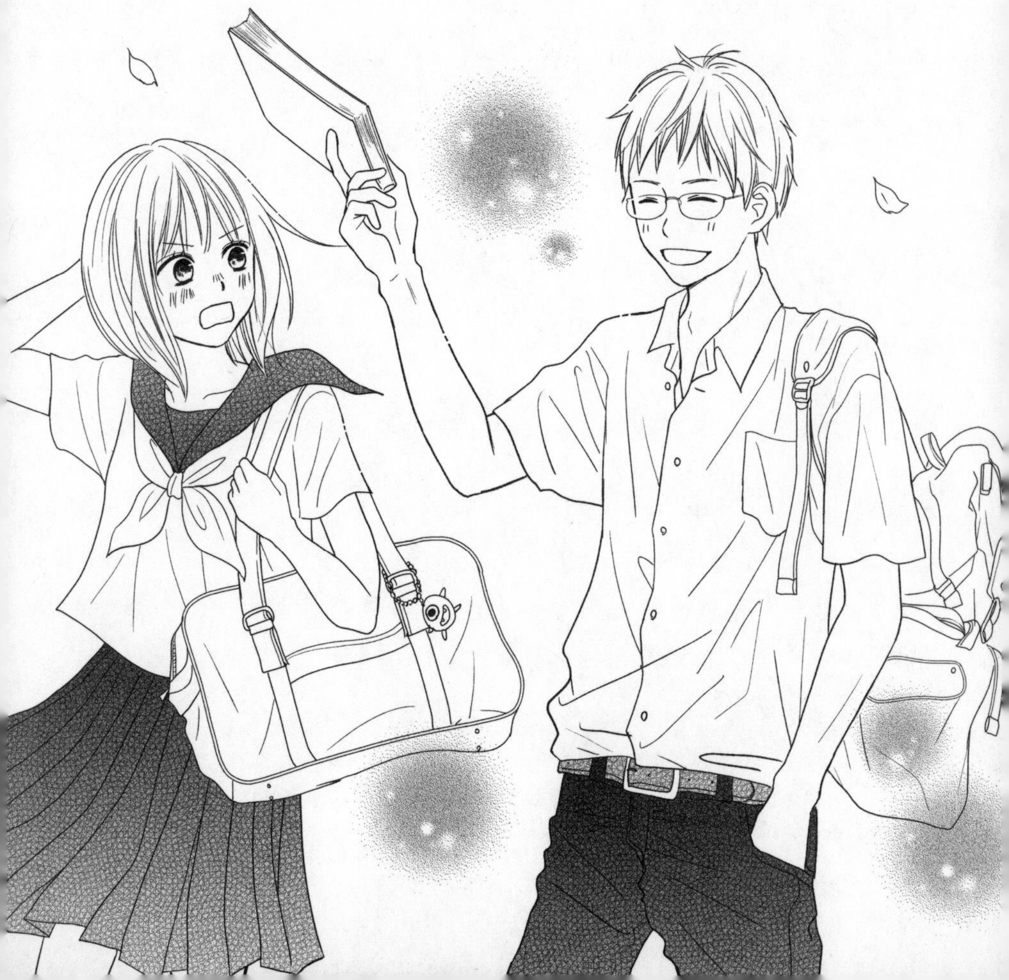

— From the bottom of my heart, thank you to all of those who helped me. —

* Kazuo Abe-sama from Abe Kensetsu Inc.
* Ouchi-sama * Yamada-sama * Kamata-sama * Yaguchi-sama

* Those at OX Kanto Vivit
* Those at AJU Independent Housing Social Services
* Those at Fureai Social Services in Nagoya

* My editor, Ito-sama * Everyone from editorial at *Kiss*
* The designers, Kusume-sama and Nagai-sama
* My assistants, T-sama, K-sama, and TN-sama

* Everyone involved in getting this sold
* My family, friends, and also my readers

I would be honored to see you
again in the next volume!

RieAruga

◄ KAMOME ►
SHIRAHAMA

Witch Hat Atelier

A magical manga
adventure for
fans of Disney
and Studio
Ghibli!

Witch Hat Atelier © Kamome Shirahama/Kodansha Ltd.

The magical adventure that took Japan by storm is finally here, from acclaimed DC and Marvel cover artist Kamome Shirahama!

In a world where everyone takes wonders like magic spells
and dragons for granted, Coco is a girl with a simple dream:
She wants to be a witch. But everybody knows magicians
are born, not made, and Coco was not born with a gift for
magic. Resigned to her un-magical life, Coco is about to
give up on her dream to become a witch...until the day
she meets Qifrey, a mysterious, traveling magician. After
secretly seeing Qifrey perform magic in a way she's never
seen before, Coco soon learns what everybody "knows"
might not be the truth, and discovers that her magical
dream may not be as far away as it may seem...

KC
KODANSHA
COMICS

Knight of the Ice ©Yayoi Ogawa/Kodansha Ltd.

SKATING THRILLS AND ICY CHILLS WITH THIS NEW TINGLY ROMANCE SERIES!

A rom-com on ice, perfect for fans of *Princess Jellyfish* and *Wotakoi*. Kokoro is the talk of the figure-skating world, winning trophies and hearts. But little do they know... he's actually a huge nerd! From the beloved creator of *You're My Pet* (*Tramps Like Us*).

Chitose is a serious young woman, working for the health magazine *SASSO*. Or at least, she would be, if she wasn't constantly getting distracted by her childhood friend, international figure skating star Kokoro Kijinami! In the public eye and on the ice, Kokoro is a gallant, flawless knight, but behind his glittery costumes and breathtaking spins lies a secret: He's actually a hopelessly romantic otaku, who can only land his quad jumps when Chitose is on hand to recite a spell from his favorite magical girl anime!

KC
KODANSHA
COMICS

A SMART, NEW ROMANTIC COMEDY FOR FANS OF *SHORTCAKE CAKE* AND *TERRACE HOUSE*!

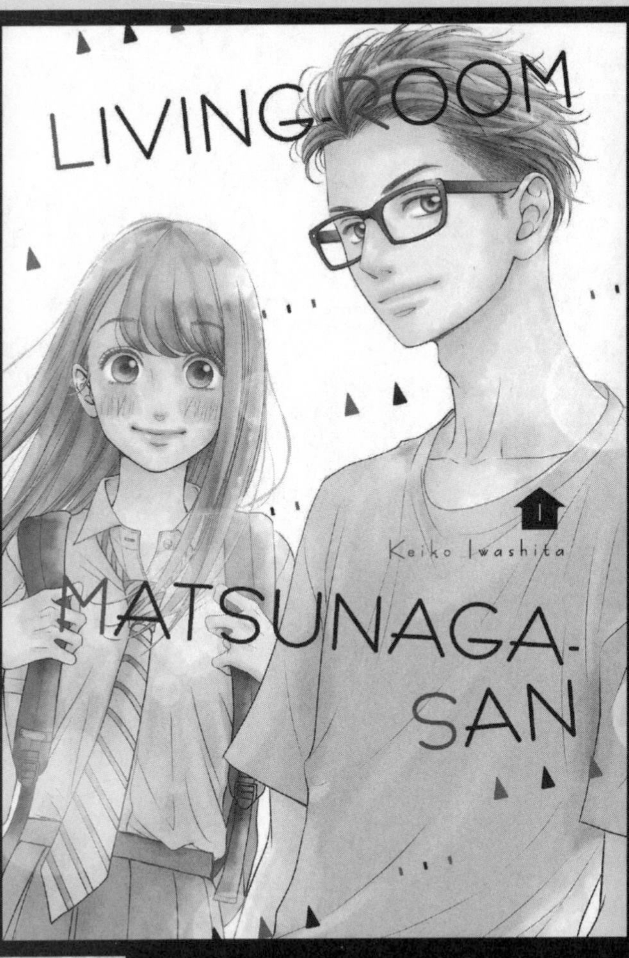
LIVING-ROOM
MATSUNAGA-SAN
1
Keiko Iwashita

A romance manga starring high school girl Meeko, who learns to live on her own in a boarding house whose living room is home to the odd (but handsome) Matsunaga-san. She begins to adjust to her new life away from her parents, but Meeko soon learns that no matter how far away from home she is, she's still a young girl at heart — especially when she finds herself falling for Matsunaga-san.

KC KODANSHA COMICS

MAGIC KNIGHT RAYEARTH
25TH ANNIVERSARY EDITION
CLAMP

A BELOVED CLASSIC MAKES ITS STUNNING RETURN IN THIS GORGEOUS, LIMITED EDITION BOX SET!

This tale of three Tokyo teenagers who cross through a magical portal and become the champions of another world is a modern manga classic. The box set includes three volumes of manga covering the entire first series of *Magic Knight Rayearth*, plus the series's super-rare full-color art book companion, all printed at a larger size than ever before on premium paper, featuring a newly-revised translation and lettering, and exquisite foil-stamped covers.

A strictly limited edition, this will be gone in a flash!

Perfect World 7 is a wor
places, and incidents are the
or are used fictitiously. Any res
persons, living or de

A Kodansha Comics
Perfect World 7 co
English translation c

Published in the United States by Kodansha Comics, an imprint of Kodansha USA Publishing, LLC, New York.

Publication rights for this English edition arranged through Kodansha Ltd., Tokyo.

First published in Japan in 2018 by Kodansha Ltd., Tokyo as *Perfect World*, volume 7.

ISBN 978-1-64651-107-5

Original cover design by Tomohiro Kusume and Maiko Mori (arcoinc)

Printed in the United States of America.

www.kodansha.us

9 8 7 6 5 4 3 2
Translation: Erin Procter
Lettering: Thea Willis
Additional lettering: Sara Linsley
Editing: Nathaniel Gallant, Jesika Brooks
Kodansha Comics edition cover design by Phil Balsman

KC
KODANSHA
COMICS

Publisher: Kiichiro Sugawara

Director of publishing services: Ben Applegate
Associate director of operations: Stephen Pakula
Publishing services managing editors: Alanna Ruse, Madison Salters
Assistant production managers: Emi Lotto, Angela Zurlo